KANT, RELIGION, AND POLITICS

This book offers a systematic examination of the place of religion within Kant's major writings. Kant is often thought to be highly reductionistic with regard to religion – as though religion simply provides the unsophisticated with colorful representations of moral lessons that reason alone could grasp. James DiCenso's rich and innovative discussion shows how Kant's theory of religion in fact emerges directly from his epistemology, ethics, and political theory, and how it serves his larger political and ethical projects of restructuring institutions and modifying political attitudes toward greater autonomy. It also illustrates the continuing relevance of Kant's ideas for addressing issues of religion and politics that remain pressing in the contemporary world, such as just laws, transparency in the public sphere, and other ethical and political concerns. The book will be valuable for a wide range of readers who are interested in Kant's thought.

JAMES J. DICENSO is Professor in the Philosophy of Religion at the University of Toronto. He is the author of two previous books, *Hermeneutics and the Disclosure of Truth* (1990) and *The Other Freud: Religion, Culture and Psychoanalysis* (1999), and has published numerous scholarly articles in international journals.

KANT, RELIGION, AND POLITICS

JAMES J. DICENSO
University of Toronto

CAMBRIDGE UNIVERSITY PRESS
Cambridge, New York, Melbourne, Madrid, Cape Town,
Singapore, São Paulo, Delhi, Tokyo, Mexico City

Cambridge University Press
The Edinburgh Building, Cambridge CB2 8RU, UK

Published in the United States of America by Cambridge University Press, New York

www.cambridge.org
Information on this title: www.cambridge.org/9781107009332

© James DiCenso 2011

This publication is in copyright. Subject to statutory exception
and to the provisions of relevant collective licensing agreements,
no reproduction of any part may take place without the written
permission of Cambridge University Press.

First published 2011

Printed in the United Kingdom at the University Press, Cambridge

A catalogue record for this publication is available from the British Library

Library of Congress Cataloguing in Publication data
DiCenso, James, 1957–
Kant, religion, and politics / James DiCenso.
 p. cm.
Includes bibliographical references and index.
ISBN 978-1-107-00933-2 (hardback)
1. Kant, Immanuel, 1724–1804. 2. Religion. 3. Political science–Philosophy.
4. Ethics. I. Title.
B2798.D458 2011
193–dc23
2011017977

ISBN 978-1-107-00933-2 Hardback

Cambridge University Press has no responsibility for the persistence or
accuracy of URLs for external or third-party internet websites referred to in
this publication, and does not guarantee that any content on such websites is,
or will remain, accurate or appropriate.

Contents

Acknowledgements		*page* vi
List of abbreviations		vii
1	Introduction: on religion, ethics, and the political in Kant	1
2	Religion, politics, enlightenment	24
3	Knowledge and experience	69
4	Illusions of metaphysics and theology	108
5	Autonomy and judgment in Kant's ethics	162
6	Ethics and politics in Kant's *Religion*	219
Bibliography		283
Index		291

Acknowledgements

The initial research for this project was supported by a University of Toronto Connaught Research Grant, for which I remain deeply grateful. I am also grateful to Hilary Gaskin of Cambridge University Press, who wisely recommended that the text be modified from its initial structure to the more streamlined form it now has, and whose overall support for the project has been invaluable. The book has also benefited from the input of a number of students, colleagues and friends. I would like to thank all the participants in my seminar on Kant's ethics and theory of religion over the past several years; their many questions and observations helped to sharpen my understanding of a number of key issues. In particular, a debt of gratitude is owed to Paul York and Babak Bakhtiarynia, each of whom also read the manuscript and offered many trenchant and helpful suggestions. William Wahl provided valuable research assistance. Stanley Fefferman was a remarkable friend and conversation partner throughout the long process of writing; his many insights often provided a badly needed stimulus to my own thinking. Finally, and above all, I would like to thank my wife Eleanor, who was the first to read the manuscript as it took shape, and whose comments helped me improve the text in countless ways. Her patience and constant support made it possible for me to complete the project.

Abbreviations

Kant's works are cited within the text by volume number and page following the German Academy Edition. The pagination in that edition is given in the margins of the English translations published by Cambridge University Press. The *Critique of Pure Reason* is cited according to the first edition of 1781 (A) or second edition of 1787 (B) pagination. (See Bibliography for further information.)

Otherwise the following abbreviations are used:

A	*Anthropology from a Pragmatic Point of View*
CB	"Conjectural Beginning of Human History"
CF	*The Conflict of the Faculties*
CJ	*Critique of the Power of Judgment*
CPrR	*Critique of Practical Reason*
E	"An Answer to the Question: What Is Enlightenment?"
GR	*Groundwork of the Metaphysics of Morals*
IH	"Idea for a Universal History with a Cosmopolitan Aim"
L	*Lectures on Logic*
LE	*Lectures on Ethics*
LM	*Lectures on Metaphysics*
LP	*Lectures on Pedagogy*
LPR	*Lectures on the Philosophical Doctrine of Religion*
MM	*The Metaphysics of Morals*
MT	"On the miscarriage of all philosophical trials in theodicy"
OP	*Opus Postumum*
OPA	*The Only Possible Argument in Support of a Demonstration of the Existence of God*
OT	"What does it mean to orient oneself in thinking?"
PP	"Toward Perpetual Peace"

PR	*Prolegomena to Any Future Metaphysics*
R	*Religion within the Boundaries of Mere Reason*
RPT	"On a recently prominent tone of superiority in philosophy"
TP	"On the common saying: That may be correct in theory, but it is of no use in practice"

CHAPTER I

Introduction: on religion, ethics, and the political in Kant

GENERAL THEMES OF THE INQUIRY

In Kant's writings, the topic of religion occupies a strategic space at the confluence of epistemology, ethics, and politics. Inquiries into the validity of religious truth claims and the possible meanings of religious writings and images form a vital part of Kant's ethical and political project. This project focuses on advancing human autonomy, both individually and in terms of political concerns with shared worldviews, laws, and rights. In its mature form, this line of inquiry begins with the *Critique of Pure Reason*, is further developed in Kant's ethical writings and the *Critique of the Power of Judgment*, and reaches fruition in *Religion within the Boundaries of Mere Reason*. This body of work constructs an intricate framework for understanding religion not only in relation to epistemological issues, but as relevant to both ethical and political considerations. It shows that religion, as both personal and cultural, is profoundly connected with the ethical and political possibilities of human beings. The structure of this investigation is wider than any of Kant's specific inquiries. It addresses both individual ethical reflection and possible ameliorations of social and political conditions that have an effect upon our ethical development.

A study of Kant's critical writings shows that his general position on the status of religious doctrines remains consistent throughout this extensive body of work. *The Critique of Pure Reason* is not simply an inquiry into the conditions of human knowledge, explicating the organizing concepts of the understanding in relation with input from sense intuitions. In fact, this epistemological model, groundbreaking as it is, also forms something of a prelude to a critique of all speculative systems of thought. Metaphysical and theological systems, operating without the benefit of empirically verifiable sensory input, are shown to be incapable of providing knowledge of any kind. These systems overstep the bounds of human understanding, and their various doctrinal claims concerning truth and reality cannot compete directly with the verifiable findings of the physical sciences, or with the publicly tested methods of social and humanistic studies. Kant systematically challenges the possibility of attaining objectified knowledge of supersensible realities, and in light of these interrogations he comes to be seen, in Moses Mendelssohn's well-known phrase, as the "all-crushing" critic of metaphysics.[1] Even in the first *Critique*, however, Kant repeatedly argues that the rational ideas formulated in metaphysics and theology can serve as regulative principles offering rules for thought. In this mode, they still offer no knowledge of reality, but they can provide conceptual and procedural guidelines, most especially for practical reasoning in establishing criteria for ethical and political amelioration. In rejecting supersensible knowledge claims, Kant also opens the way to reinterpreting the objects of speculative theology as representations of regulative principles with potential ethical-political significance.

There are substantial discussions of rational theology as a subset of general metaphysics in the first *Critique*. These analyses address traditional proofs for the existence of God, as well as theological doctrines concerning the origins of the cosmos and the possibility of an immortal soul. These inquiries into theology are not merely a by-product of Kant's epistemology; they are quite central to his endeavors to define and advance human autonomy. This is because the perpetuation of metaphysical-theological constructions insusceptible to public testing constitutes a form of intellectual heteronomy that works against our capacity to cultivate open, critical thinking across a variety of domains (e.g., knowledge, ethics, and social institutions). Heteronomy appears not only when physical coercion is used in the political sphere to control a populace, but also and more insidiously whenever claims to truth and authority are made that refuse to be subjected to sharable criteria of assessment and open public discussion. In the first *Critique*, heteronomy is engaged in terms of the thought-systems of traditional metaphysics and rational theology. Religious phenomena such as scriptures and traditions that can implement heteronomous worldviews do not receive much direct attention. However, while some of Kant's shorter writings from the same period (such as the essay "What Is Enlightenment?") show a greater concern with the direct ethical and political import of religion in its social manifestations, it is only with *Religion within the Boundaries of Mere Reason* that a more detailed analysis

---

[1] See Manfred Kuehn, *Kant: A Biography* (Cambridge University Press, 2001), p.251; I will discuss Kant's refutation of traditional metaphysical and theological arguments in some detail over the next two chapters.

of religious traditions is formulated. These later analyses engage doctrines of theology, but also institutionalized public forms such as churches and the patterns of authority governing these associations, as well as the textual resources of scriptures such as narrative, parable, and personification. As inclusive in this way, the rubric of *religion* is wider than that of theology per se, and contains the latter as a subset. In Kant's treatment, none of these religious phenomena are analyzed on their own terms (i.e., as possessing supernatural authorization unquestionable by mere reason). They are rather studied as historically formed developments intertwined with social and political life in its various manifestations. Most importantly, Kant addresses the political influence of these traditions by analyzing how they shape the identities and worldviews of their communities. These inquiries engage a set of phenomena that, in some form, is endemic to virtually all cultures throughout history. Moreover, despite enormous social and cultural changes in the past two centuries, including the rise of apparently secular societies, the massive proliferation of technologies, and the increasing influence of multi-national corporations, religion in some variety remains directly and indirectly influential in most parts of the world. Even for many who are not explicitly religious in a traditional sense, the worldviews and thought-patterns established through centuries of cultural formation often retain an influence in addressing larger issues of values and ethics.

My discussion will follow Kant's linguistic practice in employing the conceptual category of religion as cutting across the multiplicity of specific religious traditions, without seeking to efface their often profound differences in doctrine and practice. Despite these distinctive features, which are clearly indispensable for the historian of religions, the inclusive category of religion provides a conceptual framework sustaining a wider scope of analysis on a philosophical level. It also facilitates a method of interpretation and questioning with the potential to engage multiple religions in relation to ethical and political concerns, such as the furtherance of distributive and restorative forms of justice and of human rights and freedoms. In fact, the particular analyses Kant undertakes, while focusing mainly on Christian sources, are presented as a template for a general interpretive methodology that can in principle be applied more broadly (and he discusses, albeit in passing, a significant number of traditions in this regard). Kant's interpretation of religious traditions is intrinsic to a wider program, focusing on ethical and political concerns. Religion is especially important to these considerations because it is at once a public, institutionalized set of phenomena, and an inherited set of doctrines affecting the worldviews and mindsets of individuals. In other words, it is both *external* (taking the form of shared writings, institutions, and cultural traditions) and *internal* (taking the form of worldviews, beliefs, and priorities). It therefore has both political and ethical implications, and in this way occupies a strategic role in the historical interplay of heteronomy and autonomy. Kant is especially concerned with how matters of doctrine and their accompanying symbol systems play a role in shaping the attitudes and modes of thinking of a populace or community. Do they foster passivity and subservience to power and authority, or do they foster a capacity to question and reflect openly upon existing conditions in accordance with universalizable principles?

RELIGION AND THE POLITICAL

In claiming that Kant's inquiries into religion have both ethical and political significance, I am especially concerned with *the political* as describing collective ideational resources as well as institutions and organizations shaped by these ideas. Free-floating doctrines and ideologies can have an impact in the public sphere without necessarily serving as the ideational basis for specific associations or institutions, although they can also be harnessed to these organizational structures. The broader concept of the political that I am using therefore includes politics per se, but extends further to designate cultural systems of meaning by which societies and communities orient themselves in establishing their overall priorities and values. Kant discusses religious communities and churches in this regard, but the model could also include any non-governmental organization informed by specific principles or goals.

A helpful way of clarifying this sense of the political is through the French distinction between *la politique* and *le politique*, which has been summarized by the historian Stephen Englund. His discussion occurs in the context of analyzing political developments in the Napoleonic era, but they have a more general application as well. Englund notes that *la politique* "means politics, and is what comes to mind when a newscaster speaks of politicians, campaigns, lobbies, and diplomacy." In contrast with this more circumscribed domain, *le politique*, rendered as "the political," addresses non-governmental cultural forces that can directly and indirectly influence a given population. Englund summarizes the concept in a manner that is most germane to our present concerns: "*Le politique* transfers attention from the rough-and-tumble of the struggle for gain in the public arena to the larger picture, which is the forms, uses, and distribution of power in society. As such, it points to a vast range of phenomena – from social organization and economic structure to culture and intellectual production." Moreover, from among these various cultural forms categorized under *le politique*, Englund singles out one that is of special interest to the present project: "For example, a thing as seemingly removed from 'politics' as *religious faith* may yet be shown to participate in *le politique*."[2] Religion is a key feature of the political in this wider sense, because it often has a profound influence in shaping people's identities, ethical values, and priorities; it thereby informs how they understand their world and their relations to one another. Its influence is less *localized* than that of political institutions per se; it may take the form of sub-communities within larger social-political frameworks, and it may have a trans-national presence cutting across a variety of diverse nation-states and cultural entities. It may very well be this less localized status that contributes to the ongoing power of religions to influence profoundly the way politics in the narrower sense is conducted.

While a notion precisely synonymous with *le politique* may not appear in Kant's writings, the rubric conveys some overarching themes in his work developed over an extensive period. Even in his explicitly social and political works, Kant is concerned not just with the mechanisms of state apparatus, or even with inter-state and inter-societal relations on the cosmo-political level. He also addresses the more pervasive if less tangible realm of shared patterns of thinking and systems of norms characteristic of the political in the broader sense. In this respect, he recognizes that organized religions have significant ethical and political power. This multi-leveled influence of religious traditions and authorities was still prominent in the Europe of Kant's time, which also explains why, like many of his contemporaries, he devoted considerable attention to issues

---

[2] Stephen Englund, *Napoleon: A Political Life* (Cambridge, MA: Harvard University Press, 2004), pp.142–43 (I have italicized the reference to religious faith). One political theorist who develops this distinction between politics and the political is Claude Lefort; see *Democracy and Political Theory* (Minneapolis: University of Minnesota Press, 1988), pp.216–17. Likewise Pierre Rosanvallon defines "the political" as "everything that defines political life beyond the immediate field of partisan competition for political power, everyday governmental action, and the ordinary function of institutions." *Democracy Past and Future* (New York: Columbia University Press, 2006), p.35. I should also note that this broader understanding of the political, concerning the way cultural worldviews, mores, and religious systems influence the organization of collective existence differs considerably from the definition of the twentieth-century legal and political theorist Carl Schmitt. He narrowly insisted that "the specific political distinction to which political actions and motives can be reduced is that between friend and enemy." Carl Schmitt, *The Concept of the Political* (University of Chicago Press, 1996), p.26.

concerning religion.[3] However, even with the rise of apparently secular nation-states, and even where religious institutions have been officially separated from the formal operations of governance, the force of religious worldviews remains significant for large numbers of people globally. In affecting the attitudes and priorities of communities, sub-communities, and individuals, religious doctrines can indirectly inform what types of leadership, which agendas, and which policies members of a society will prioritize. Accordingly, many of these issues remain prominent in today's world, if in altered ways. Therefore, it is extremely important that Kant approaches religion not only in relation to the question of what we can or cannot legitimately know, but also as intertwined with *practical* concerns about the possibility of realizing sharable ethical principles under phenomenal conditions. A key theme of these analyses concerns the difficulties in applying ethical principles by human beings already informed by a variety of contingent social and political forces. The need for analyzing the priorities of existing conceptual and political institutions, including those associated with religious traditions, arises from this concern. His approach to religion is therefore multi-faceted, and it is both critical and constructive. As he brings clear ethical principles to bear on existing traditions, Kant also formulates interpretive paradigms for comprehending such traditions in relation to rational ethical principles. These inquiries still have much to offer in clarifying the interrelations among religion, ethics, and politics on a more encompassing theoretical level of analysis.

Is this conceptual approach to religion and the political too abstract? To be sure, Kant's work on ethical, religious, and political issues generally operates on a *meta-theoretical* level that draws from empirical examples rather sparingly. Because of this, and also because of the strategic use of binary categories in his critical analyses, Kant's thinking is sometimes associated with various strains of idealist thought. This categorization makes it easier to dismiss his work as disconnected from the various social and political realities within which we live and make decisions. However, two main points should immediately be made in this regard. First, as I will demonstrate, Kant argues that public, empirically based experience yielding sensory-intuitions is a key requisite for knowledge claims. Simultaneously, as the concomitant of this empirical element in his thinking, he develops an extensive critique of all thought-systems,

---

[3] Some historians have concluded that "the popular sobriquet for the eighteenth century – 'the age of reason' – has less justification than 'the age of religion' or 'the Christian century'." Tim Blanning, *The Pursuit of Glory: Europe 1648–1815* (London: Penguin Books, 2007), p.385. Blanning is paraphrasing Derek Beales.

philosophical, theological, and religious, whose explanatory frameworks operate within closed relations of ideas, and hence really are disconnected from experience. Second, while Kant is intensely concerned with *ideas*, *ideals*, and *principles* (which will be defined more closely in the following chapters), he consistently argues that ideas can have considerable impact on the decisions and actions of both individuals and communities. In fact, I would propose that we are always informed by ideas of one kind or another. What Kant helps us accomplish is to interrogate the status of those ideas. Have they been refined through open dialogue and principled analysis, or are they functioning dogmatically and surreptitiously to influence the assumptions and priorities of a given populace? In this way, the dogmatic conceptions constructed speculatively by metaphysicians or transmitted by the cultural authority of religions are subjected to a critical analysis that is both epistemological and ethical. This critique is a component of Kant's endeavor to formalize universalizable principles that guide autonomous ethical and political practice. Once procedures for assessing ideas and principles in terms of the criteria of universalizability and inclusivity have been formulated, Kant then concentrates on how we can apply such critically revised ideas and principles within various cultural and political domains.

Pheng Cheah, who discusses Kant's work in a contemporary global political context, also links its overarching themes with an interrogation of the political. Cheah argues that "it is the essence of the political to waver between reality and ideals, between what is and what ought to be, in the endeavor to realize the ideal and to idealize reality."[4] In other words, the political is constituted as much by conceptual formations, such as belief systems, inherited norms, and ideologies, as it is by the institutions and practices of nation-states. Cheah then builds on this multiform understanding of the political, showing that the impact of ideas is essential to all social-political transformation: "Insofar as freedom must be regarded as an ideal that is capable of being realized, the distinction between ideal and real can and must be crossed. Conversely, one must regard the existing world as something that can be transformed in accordance with a rational and universal image."[5] There are a number of issues encapsulated in these very Kantian statements. First, the dynamic relation between ideas and existing conditions indicates that human reality is already constituted by

---

[4] Pheng Cheah, *Spectral Nationality: Passages of Freedom from Kant to Postcolonial Literatures of Liberation* (New York: Columbia University Press, 2003), p.24.
[5] Ibid., p.36.

various ideational systems, as transmitted through political authorities, religious institutions, cultural traditions, and other official and unofficial forms of media. These can operate as the structuring background for judgments and decisions made by individuals, often outside the range of conscious awareness, critical reflection, and open discussion. Second, because we are phenomenal beings strongly affected by sense experience as well as socialized beings informed by culturally transmitted languages, customs, and mores, the engagement between more formalized regulative ideas such as freedom, truth, justice, or the *realm of ends* and existing empirical conditions needs to be mediated. One consequence of the social and phenomenal constitution of human beings is that ideas applied *in situ* always require the principled judgment of autonomous individuals, a point Kant frequently stresses when formulating his ethical theory. Ideas such as social justice and equality can provide general regulative guidelines for making judgments in varying circumstances, but not fixed blueprints for ethical-political transformation. Actual political realities can never conform to any closed order of ideas; however, the latter can through autonomous human efforts have indirect ameliorative effects upon things as they are. To be sure, any such transformative process will also remain incomplete and open to variation and correction.

Cheah also writes of "culture *qua* incarnation of human ideals," and this is an important way to understand the cultural and political influence of religion. He argues that cultural activity "supplies the ontological paradigm of the political because it is purposive activity through which we transcend our finitude and become free." This active understanding of culture, which includes elements of religion as a subset, indicates that it is a sphere of objectification where human freedom can be expressed or suppressed; i.e., where our potential for autonomy is played out. The fact that cultural production is not merely a reprieve from political realities, but can have some ameliorative impact, indicates what Cheah calls "the axiomatic sense of culture's cobelonging with politics."[6] Culture, thus defined, overlaps with the definition of the political articulated by Stephen Englund in the tradition of Lefort and Rosanvallon. It indicates a broad area of conceptual activity including not only religion but artistic, humanistic, and scientific endeavors expressing ideas and values that can restructure given social-political conditions (or that might intentionally and unintentionally have the opposite effect of encrusting prevailing assumptions). Subsequently, Cheah argues that the notion of

[6] *Ibid.*, p.7.

culture is essential to Kant's humanistic and historical project: "Culture (*Kultur*), as an objective realm broadly defined to include legal and political institutions and the arts and sciences, is the historical medium for the development of our rational capacities."[7] It is noteworthy that theorists have invoked notions like culture and the political to inquire into ethical concerns irreducible to either the problem-solving activity of individuals or the organized politics of nation-states. Insofar as cultural expressions of free-floating and institutionally harnessed sets of ideas affect the way we perceive and relate to others, they impact upon the ethical sphere. There is a dynamic or two-way interface between internal attitudes and external conditions, or between individual and collective ethical orientations.

To indicate how ethical principles are affected by cultural and political forces, and how political decisions, practices, and modes of organization often have substantial ethical implications, I will frequently have recourse to the hybrid expression *ethical-political*. This phrase is not explicitly used by Kant, although it echoes his references to the *ethico-civil* society, juxtaposed with the *juridico-civil* society, in *Religion*. Of course, it is an axiom of Kantian ethical and legal theory that ethics concerns the internal sphere of will and intentionality, and must be voluntary, whereas law and politics concern the external sphere of statutory codes that might be coercively enforced (see, for example, MM, 6:312). However, while this set of distinctions serves certain important functions, for example in distinguishing ethical decisions from observable consequences, Kant is also concerned with the public and political manifestation of ethical principles, as appears for example in his notion of the realm of ends. Ethical principles and maxims require both judgments and actions, if they are to modify shared conditions within socially constructed worlds. As others have noted, this cannot be reduced to a mere "application" of the categorical imperative, but includes a critical engagement with the institutions and traditions that shape our priorities.[8] An understanding of the ethical-political along these dynamic or interactive lines helps clarify how Kant negotiates an innovative approach to questions of religion. Even as he develops formidable epistemological critiques of metaphysical, theological, and religious systems disconnected from testable public and empirical realities, he also argues that many of the ideas and ideals

---

[7] *Ibid.*, p.75.
[8] See Arthur Ripstein, *Force and Freedom: Kant's Legal and Political Philosophy* (Cambridge, MA: Harvard University Press, 2009), pp.6ff.

conveyed by these traditions, *if ethically interpreted and applied*, can have a transformative effect within social and political realities.

It is also very important that this concern with religious representations of ethical mores reveals a variegated understanding of discursive and symbolic resources. While for Kant the register of literal description is privileged with respect to epistemological issues, he also recognizes the possible constructive uses of non-literal narratives and images in other types of inquiry. For example, as a general rule for interpreting religious phenomena Kant discerns potential non-literal ranges of meaning in concepts and figures where a literal reading is discredited by epistemological or ethical principles. In this way, more complex linguistic resources such as symbol, metaphor, and analogy are grasped as relevant to expressing ethical aims in ways that are more intuitively accessible to human beings. Religions therefore emerge as focal areas of conceptual and cultural production with the potential to embody ethical ideas in more widely accessible representational forms. To be sure, the ethical principles Kant advocates do not always correspond to the principles overtly expressed by religious traditions; his analysis of these is therefore be critical as well as constructive. Although Kant never relinquishes the strict critical limits placed on knowledge claims central to the first *Critique*, he consistently allows that religious writings and traditions can assist in mediating abstract ethical ideas within specific social and political configurations. However, to serve this mediating function the parochial and exclusive elements in religions must be critically isolated. Religious sources are approached in a manner informed by inclusive and egalitarian ethical principles in accordance with the formulae of the categorical imperative. In other words, Kant's criticism of cultural traditions and institutions, including both religious and political ones, is guided by clearly defined principles.

In accordance with his ethical interpretation of traditions, Kant's approach to religion and theology emphasizes *human autonomy*. Since autonomy means the rational capacity to generate and follow laws that apply equally to all, it is simultaneously an ethical and a political concept. The question of cultivating one's own autonomy cannot be addressed without considering the autonomy of all other persons, and how these autonomous beings can be harmonized in a realm of ends. Hence there is an affinity between autonomy and ideas of reason, insofar as these assist us in attaining more encompassing, universalizable perspectives that are inclusive of the views and rights of others, as I will explicate in the following chapters. One of Kant's interpretive methods is to assess religious and theological concepts with reference to their capacity to express such inclusive ideas of reason as freedom, equality, and justice. At the same time, this representational function must be sharply differentiated from the *heteronomous* tendencies of religions manifested throughout human history. This is especially the case when heteronomous religious and political structures claiming unquestionable authority are not only imposed upon a populace, but when they also convey non-universalizable parochial principles. These then serve as the bastion of privilege and corruption in their various manifestations, because they support laws and customs that favor some individuals or groups to the exclusion of others. These discriminatory practices blatantly contradict the principles of freedom, justice, and equality intrinsic to moral laws. This is why the critical philosophy is as much oriented toward critiquing repressive systems of governance as in critiquing dogmatic metaphysical systems with their unfounded claims about the order and meaning of reality.

Kant uses ideas of reason expressed in metaphysical and religious concepts to interrogate existing social-historical forms of religion and the often parochial ethical-political sensibilities they sustain. In this way his work explicates a *double meaning* to religion. On the one side, religion indicates specific, often exclusive historically conditioned traditions that can be welded to narrow-minded customs and inequitable authority structures. On the other side, religions can be vehicles for representing inclusive ethical principles (truth, justice) compatible with the categorical imperative. Kant increasingly categorizes the operative distinction as a contrast between *historical or statutory religion* on the one side, and *ethical or rational religion* on the other. Importantly, these two modalities of religion are not necessarily incommensurable; in other words, historical religions can be the medium of moral religion. The crucial issue is that Kant's critical methodology distinguishes autonomous from heteronomous features that often coexist within the very same set of institutions, teachings, or practices. This process of rethinking the meaning and function of religion exemplifies the strategy of drawing upon culture to transform culture as discussed, for example, by Cheah. It is evident throughout Kant's critical philosophy, and it exhibits an ethical-political dimension from the very start.

To be sure, it is sometimes difficult to discern the broader thematic continuity in Kant's writings, starting with the enormously challenging and often abstruse inquiries into the transcendental conditions of cognition in the first *Critique*, through the development of an *a priori* approach to ethics, and finally to a concern with an open inquiry into religion and politics in a cosmopolitan framework. As I will illustrate, there is a series of links between the critical philosophy's concerns to determine the scope and limits of human knowledge, the critique of speculative thought-forms such as metaphysics and theology that transgress those limits, and an ethically informed inquiry into public institutions, including religious ones. The issue of autonomy, as at once epistemological, ethical, and political, is one of the main threads connecting these various domains of inquiry.

Although there are important shifts in emphasis, from the predominantly epistemological focus of the first *Critique* to the more historical and cultural inquiries of *Religion*, there remains considerable continuity in interpretive approach to these inquiries. This is why even Kant's critical analyses of the rationalist metaphysics and theology of his day, which might appear to be of merely historical interest, continue to be important for contemporary ethical and political investigations. In assessing these conceptual traditions, Kant analyzes heteronomous modes of thought which still subtend many ways of thinking about ethical and political issues on the global public stage. In general, this type of thinking tries to legitimize structures of power and authority in such a way that they are placed beyond the reach of open discussion and critique. The relation between heteronomy in religion, culture, and politics is directly evident in Kant's analyses of historical religions, where he addresses their potential either to inhibit or to foster ethical and political progress concerning the rights and freedoms of all. These analyses are guided by the distinction between heteronomy (or anthropomorphic servile faith that caters to fear and selfishness), and autonomy (or moral religion that assists us in cultivating ethical principles). It is important to note that the patterns of relating to authority established in religious traditions often carry over into other spheres of political life. Hence the initial critique of rationalist metaphysics and theology takes on added significance insofar as it also provides the model for approaching the discourses and symbol systems of historical religions with profound ethical-political influence.

STRUCTURE OF THE INQUIRY

I begin with an overview of Kant's broader epistemological and political concerns in chapter 2. This discusses the critical philosophy in relation to the influence of Rousseau and the ethical and political issues he addresses, such as the possibility of communities living together under just laws. I then demonstrate that Kant's epistemological inquiries are intertwined with issues of human autonomy and with establishing principles of freedom, justice, and equality. Here my intention is to show that the problems of how we obtain knowledge, and what kinds of knowledge claims may be legitimated, are already presented as a component of a wider ethical-political project that includes an analysis of religion. Kant establishes a methodology for disciplining our use of reason in a way that counteracts immature tendencies associated with unbridled enthusiasm and superstition that cater to our fantasies and fears. This disciplining conjoins autonomy with publicly verifiable criteria for knowledge, and these features directly carry over into ethical and political concerns. In other words, the same criteria of openness, public accountability, and verifiability are employed with regard to political institutions, explicitly including religious ones, and the type of authority they claim over members of a community. In explicating this approach to institutions as either fostering autonomy or as imposing forms of exclusion and domination, I also outline some of the key overarching elements of this wider ethical-political project, drawing on "What Is Enlightenment?," the third *Critique*, and other writings. It is extremely important that Kant's ethical-political analyses are clearly responding to the inherited privilege and inequality characterizing the *ancien régime*-type institutions that dominated the Europe of his time. Therefore, I also discuss his seminal reflections on the French Revolution and his historical model prioritizing the progressive reform of existing institutions based on applying universalizable principles.

Having established the general methods and broader goals of my inquiry, I then examine the arguments of the first *Critique* more closely, with occasional reference to other writings, in chapters 3 and 4. While this undertaking slows the pace and increases the difficulty of the exposition, it is essential for several reasons. A core theme is how Kant's epistemology conjoins a focus on empirical intuitions as necessary to all knowledge claims, with human autonomy as actively structuring these intuitions through the understanding. This model establishes the empirical and publicly verifiable criteria for assessing all views of reality; it thereby rules out supersensible claims based on mere speculation, or the rote transmission of authority, as valid forms of knowledge. Kant's critique of the assumptions of dogmatic metaphysics and theology emerges directly from this epistemological model. However, I also illustrate that this critique is simply a first step in a wider project of rethinking the significance of the ideas of reason reflected in various metaphysical and theological concepts. It establishes that from the beginning Kant is interested in non-literal (i.e., ethical and political rather than ontological) interpretations of metaphysical and theological concepts such as God and the highest good.

Hence, while covering some familiar territory in the theory of knowledge, I cast it in a new light by framing it as a prelude to an ethical and political inquiry in which the theme of religion figures prominently.

A clear line of demarcation is established in the first *Critique*: between traditional metaphysics and theology as making explanatory claims about reality based solely on the relations of ideas, thereby engendering illusory heteronomous constructs, and an ethical reinterpretation of these ideas. This distinction clears away misconceptions that might arise from Kant's idiosyncratic redeployment of many traditional terms. It is essential that Kant first refutes what he takes to be erroneous patterns of thinking and arguing. These erroneous modes of thought create literal, hypostasized conceptions that turn *rules of thought* into specious arguments for *supersensible entities*. In doing so, they help instate heteronomous modes of conceiving the order of reality, which can then serve (and have served) to subtend heteronomous modes of social and political organization. Once these illusions have been critically winnowed, a path is opened for non-literal reinterpretations, beginning with Kant's efforts to link the concepts of soul, cosmos, and God to ethical concerns in the postulates of practical reason, but attaining its fullest development only in *Religion*'s more detailed inquiries into historical traditions. The main mediating link between the first *Critique* and *Religion* is the practical, regulative interpretation of ideas and ideals, whether appearing more abstractly in metaphysics and theology, or in the more concrete representational forms of religions.

Building directly on the ethical reinterpretation of metaphysical concepts, chapter 5 turns to a more sustained explication of Kantian ethics. I focus mainly on the *Groundwork of the Metaphysics of Morals* and the *Critique of Practical Reason* in order to clarify the autonomous ethical model arising out of this departure from traditional concerns with supersensible knowledge. Here I also establish the basis for the universalizable ethical ideas subtending Kant's inquiries into religion as a cultural and political phenomenon. A central theme of this chapter is that Kant undertakes a *two-stroke* approach to ethical reasoning.

The first step involves *abstracting* ethical principles from the contingent physical, biographical, and political influences that inevitably impinge upon our thinking and willing. This procedure generates a formal model of lawfulness that unfolds into the fully universalizable principles of the categorical imperative. In order to develop the political implications of the critical philosophy, Kant formulates an ethical model that interacts with historical and political sources, but is not dependent on them. The critical separation of rational principles from heteronomous and parochial sources is therefore the crucial first component of an ultimately dynamic ethical-political model. The need to counteract heteronomy is one of the strategic motivations for Kant's efforts to formulate an *a priori* ethics generating formal procedures for assessing maxims. As lawful, these *a priori* principles of morality are characterized by consistency, inclusivity, and egalitarianism; they are encapsulated in the various formulae of the categorical imperative that proceed from a greater degree of abstraction to the more intuitive formulations of humans as *ends in themselves* and the *realm of ends*. These imperatives give expression to regulative practical procedures, governed by principles of autonomy and universalizability, designed to counteract self-centeredness, injustice, and favoritism. This first step is often taken in isolation by commentators, whereby it is misinterpreted as a rigid ethical model disconnected from the changeable realms of history and politics.

However, the second step, equally crucial to Kantian ethics but less often noted, requires the *application* of these regulative principles through autonomous acts of judgment within specific interpersonal and political situations. In other words, arriving at the formal criteria of the categorical imperative is simply the first phase, and in some ways the simpler phase, of a dynamic ethical model ultimately oriented toward improving both our individual lives and the shared political worlds we inhabit. In this way, my analysis counteracts many persistent stereotypes about Kantian ethics as individualistic and as disconnected from social and political engagement. Kant recognizes that the task of applied ethics is exceedingly challenging. It is one thing to reason out a formal rubric for ethical judgment, and quite another to live in accordance with the relevant ideals and principles. Therefore, his major ethical writings frequently refer to the insular or unethical principles and maxims discernible within actual human behavior. We are highly fallible beings, subject to physical inclinations, to egotistical motivations, and to parochial forms of social conditioning. Moreover, our own maxims or governing principles are often obscure to us, and we are readily capable of self-deception when it suits our immediate interests. In response to these mutually reinforcing chronic problems, Kant inquires into how pedagogical resources might assist us in applying formal principles under varying phenomenal conditions. This is one of the key instances where he draws from the resources of culture to address the corrupt maxims and institutions operative in our daily lives. Autonomous ethical principles transmitted by cultural phenomena such as religions, when critically liberated from their accompanying heteronomous and parochial attitudes by the application of the criteria of universalizability, become a resource in the service of universalizable ethics. In this way, formal ethical principles provide the methodological touchstone by which ideas conveyed within the frameworks of traditional forms of metaphysics and religion might be reconceptualized. What is essential is that these traditions, in their various forms, are intertwined with the social and political realities that shape our lives; explicating them with reference to ethical principles is therefore a strategic point of mediation between the ideational and the political. An initial attempt at this rethinking occurs in the formulation of the *postulates of practical reason*. Kant draws upon conceptions that were shown to be epistemologically unsound in the first *Critique*, such as soul, cosmos, and God, and reinterprets them as practically significant. While Kant is adamant in maintaining a boundary against specious supersensible knowledge claims, he readily appropriates religious ideas to address issues of motivation, focus, and the actualization of principles in our lives. This analysis forms a prelude to the much deeper and more detailed inquiries into the ethical and political function of collective representations in *Religion*.

Throughout these analyses, the theme of autonomous versus heteronomous ethical and political models is crucial. Autonomy means that we are in principle able to think through practical laws according to the rational criteria of universality and inclusivity. It does *not* mean that we are disembodied, apolitical beings who are readily able to think and act according to ideal laws of freedom. Autonomy opposes coercion, but it is equally opposed to what Kant, following the social contract tradition, terms "lawless freedom." This latter term designates merely an undisciplined acting out of our immediate, narrowly conceived, and self-centered wishes and desires. It is therefore coextensive with human relations based on selfishness, antagonism, and the rule of the stronger. As Kant specifies, this type of lawless freedom can easily continue to exist within organized states; indeed, parochial political laws may be designed to reinforce the domination of the stronger (such as the super-rich or mega-corporations). Autonomy is therefore an ongoing task, connected not only with our individual ability to freely choose and act in accordance with just laws and principles, but also with the ethical transformation of the institutions governing existing societies. Moreover, in regard to this task it is most important that the categorical imperative formulae are understood as *regulative*. That is, they are not rigid blueprints for thought or action, but rather general rules for thinking in terms of universal principles such as inclusivity, truth, and justice. Practically, they assist us in cultivating autonomy in our applied ethical reflection under phenomenal conditions. As rules, the principles of the categorical imperative require judgment capable of taking into consideration opposing values and priorities and of addressing contexts where competing norms and goals often come into conflict. The categorical imperative offers guidelines for clarifying and assessing our various individual and collective maxims. This means that even the most abstract formulation based on the principle of universality is already oriented toward application under phenomenal conditions; it helps us take stock of the priorities already operative in our lives. Moreover, the principle of universalizability informing the categorical imperative formulae already includes other-directedness and social concerns, so that formulations explicitly directed toward these ends (others as ends in themselves, the realm of ends) logically unfold from the initial more abstract formulation. Hence *Kant's ethics is already politically oriented*, although this dimension is only gradually explicated and developed.

Finally, chapter 6 follows the arguments of *Religion within the Boundaries of Mere Reason* with regard to the intertwined issues of ethical practice and the reform of politically influential institutions. The primary aim of this analysis is to elucidate the place of *Religion* within the critical philosophy, especially in relation to the first *Critique* and the ethical writings. I show that questions concerning the meaning and function of religion are deeply intermeshed with ethical-political considerations. Above all, I argue that the interpretations of religious doctrines and images presented in *Religion* are fully consonant with Kant's critical epistemology and ethics of autonomy. His analysis of religion follows directly from concerns with mediation and application raised in the ethical writings. In the Preface to the second edition of *Religion*, Kant claims that specialized knowledge of his critical writings is *not* necessary for understanding the book. "Only common morality is needed to understand the essentials of this text," he states, "without venturing into the critique of practical reason, still less into that of theoretical reason" (R, 6:14). To a certain degree, this may indeed be the case, although even the assumption of "common morality" is no doubt weightier and less certain than Kant here implies. However, as I will illustrate, while *Religion* can be read independently, it takes on enhanced significance within the context of the critical corpus. It develops a series of issues and problems arising in the three *Critiques* and other writings on history and politics. Additionally, there are key concepts and terms appearing in *Religion* that can only be understood in light of the meanings articulated in the other critical writings.

The first guideline to understanding Kant's approach to religious discourse concerns the problem of application, which is both ethical and political. Having formulated the variations of the categorical imperative in such a way as to increasingly direct ethical reflection toward human interrelations and institutions, Kant remained preoccupied with the possibility of bringing ethical laws into fruition in the world. This issue necessarily involves addressing the historical and cultural forces that operate to shape people's maxims and priorities in any given social or political configuration. Among these wider political influences, religion often figures prominently. Hence one of the core endeavors of Kant's analyses of scriptures and institutions is to assess and modify these influential traditions in relation to their promotion of either autonomy or heteronomy. He will present these as two modalities of religious practice manifesting in all traditions: one autonomous, authentic, and ethical; the other heteronomous, counterfeit, and unethical.

Second, Kant is well aware that different registers of language might be valuable in this process of application within cultural contexts. As I will show, Kant never makes theological or supersensible knowledge claims of any kind. He interprets religious language, as found in scriptural and other sources, as a phenomenal, culturally influential resource for assisting our autonomous ethical practice. He consistently reiterates that he is drawing upon inherited representations and symbols as a way to facilitate ethical reflection among fallible, embodied, socially conditioned persons. Religious representations such as God as the *one who knows the heart* are analyzed as a means of making ethical principles more imaginatively and intuitively accessible; they manifest ethical ideals in the public sphere. They do not replace autonomous ethical reflection, but they can facilitate this reflective process by helping us grasp and modify our own governing maxims in relation to representationally configured universalizable principles. In these endeavors, Kant focuses almost exclusively on biblical sources and on the Christian tradition. However, he does make passing reference to several traditions, and, most importantly, he explicitly claims that his general interpretive methods built around ethical principles can be applied, *mutatis mutandis*, to all traditions. Therefore, my analysis presents *Religion* as a major work responding to the problem of applied ethical judgment on individual and collective levels. Among other themes, I address how the concept of radical evil extrapolates upon the analyses of corrupt maxims in the ethical writings, how religious discourse is misconstrued if reduced to a merely literal level of meaning, how religion connects with the problem of applying ethical principles in social and political contexts, and how the conflict between autonomy and heteronomy plays out within Kant's interpretation of religion. Throughout these analyses, I illustrate that Kant's concerns are both ethical, directed at the inner dispositions and maxims governing individual choices, and political, directed at the publicly transmitted institutions, worldviews, and belief systems that can impact upon our choices and judgments.

INTERPRETING KANT

This analysis engages Kant as a critic of rationalist metaphysical thought, as a thinker who inherits metaphysical and theological categories from the European tradition, and finally as one who reinterprets the significance of inherited concepts within a new paradigm. The critical philosophy still employs much of the language and conceptual structures of the traditional metaphysics (especially Leibnizian and Wolffian) that influenced Kant's pre-critical writings, even as he questions such metaphysical systems. In a parallel if less obvious way, Kant is also steeped in the biblical and Christian traditions, and the discursive frames of those traditions often influence his work even as he actively reinterprets them. The presence of a variety of terms and concepts inherited from these traditions is understandable; these form the historical and cultural contexts out of which the critical philosophy emerges, and to which it responds. In doing so, Kant establishes new models of thought, and advances ideas of autonomy concerning human subjectivity, ethics, and politics that have lasting import. At the same time, the inevitable shaping of these inquiries by massively influential traditions leads to the problem that he is often interpreted as being less inventive in his metaphysical and religious views than is actually the case, given a close reading of his work. This recognition is especially important with regard to his analyses of theology and religion.

I am presenting Kant as a thinker solidly in the tradition of European Enlightenment, i.e., as someone advocating the free and open use of our rational faculties to try to better understand ourselves and to improve the social-political worlds in which we live. Unfortunately, it has become commonplace to criticize the rationalism and universalism of the Enlightenment, including Kantian thought, and to decry its abstract quality and its disconnection from psychological, historical and cultural forces. Jonathan Glover expresses this view in stating: "Now we tend to see the Enlightenment view of human psychology as thin and mechanical, and Enlightenment hopes of social progress through the spread of humanitarianism and the scientific outlook as naïve."[9] Glover's general point is well taken, and I do not believe that Kant's work or that of any other thinker holds all the answers to our present ethical and social dilemmas. There is no question that the lessons of modern history – with which Glover's work powerfully confronts us – make it impossible to reasonably maintain naïve Enlightenment views of the ultimate victory of reason and the myth of progress it engendered. Yet, dispelling naïve or over-ambitious rationalist models does not warrant a swing to the opposite, more dangerous extreme of irrationalism in its many forms (including religious and political forms, often working in tandem). It is therefore noteworthy that Amartya Sen also cites Glover's critique of Enlightenment rationalism, but argues that this should not be used as a pretext for dismissing the indispensable role of open reasoning in ethical and political analysis. He asks: "Is it really right to place the propensity towards premature certainties and the unquestioned beliefs of gruesome political leaders on the Enlightenment tradition, given the pre-eminent importance Enlightenment authors attached to the role of reasoning in making choices, particularly against reliance on blind belief?"[10] Like Sen, I hold that many of the horrors of modern history are attributable not to *too much* reason, but to a *failure of reason* and a readiness by many to be seduced and coerced by irrational ideologies catering to base emotions. When this irrationalism is conjoined with the destructive power of technology (based on strictly instrumental applications of reason), the results can be catastrophic. But the dominance of mere instrumental or mechanical reasoning and its technological projects is the antithesis of what Kant is advocating with his focus on ethical and political amelioration based on universalizable principles.

The task of learning to think more clearly about ethical and political questions is not simply a matter of logical refinement, but of taking empirical occurrences and new insights into account. Hence, a contemporary thinker concerned to expand the parameters of rational inquiry cannot remain blissfully unaware of the two centuries after Kant, or of the ensuing history of ideas, including Marxist, psychoanalytic, feminist, postcolonial, and transnational theories. While the present work will not directly engage any of these intellectual domains, some of them

---

[9] Jonathan Glover, *Humanity: A Moral History of the Twentieth Century* (London: Pimlico, 2001), p. 7.
[10] Amartya Sen, *The Idea of Justice* (Cambridge, MA: Harvard University Press, 2009), p.35. A few pages later, Sen adds: "the remedy for bad reasoning lies in better reasoning, and it is indeed the job of reasoned scrutiny to move from the former to the latter" (p.49).

remain in the background, stimulating the questions, critiques, and counterviews that a responsible contemporary inquiry must consider. Nevertheless, I have come to the considered conclusion that Kant's work is not simply superseded by subsequent modes of thinking; rather, these inquiries might help us draw out its insights and implications, as well as pinpoint certain problems and limitations. I argue that the standards of reason, and especially the principles of practical reason, provide invaluable resources for engaging ongoing questions of ethics and cultural coexistence. Kant's increasing emphasis on practical reason in the latter portion of his intellectual life is highly significant to these broader concerns. Despite historically and culturally derived limitations evident in some sections of Kant's work, it exhibits a broader and more dynamic understanding of the interaction of reason and culture than is usually recognized. As I have noted, in contradistinction to predominant caricatures, Kant emphasizes the need to bring the reflective activities of pure practical reason into dynamic conjunction with existing social, political, and religious resources. This approach to religion offers a critical engagement with the parochial elements of inherited traditions while, if approached carefully, avoiding the pitfalls of a disembodied rationalism that cannot respond to the complexities of lived human experience.

I want to conclude this introductory chapter with some remarks about the configuration of the text. Every chapter makes extensive use of quotations to support and clarify my interpretations, which no doubt slows down the discussion. This close attention to the texts is absolutely necessary, because quite often general summaries of Kant's arguments tend to perpetuate long-standing stereotypes that do not always hold up to rigorous analysis. Substantiating each step of the inquiry and exposition with supporting quotations is an important way to document my interpretive claims, as well as to help readers consult the texts themselves to determine if my analyses are accurate. Although I use the generally reliable translations in the Cambridge Edition of Kant's work in English, key terms and phrases in German are frequently given in brackets. On some occasions, this is done to indicate alternative meanings elided in translation, or to stress the recurrence of key terms, some of which are translated in multiple ways; quite often, however, I do this simply to add emphasis to a key point. In a few cases, which are always noted, I have modified the translations. This happens especially in working with *Religion*, where the choice of English terms sometimes obscures a significant line of thought or recurring theme.

As an elementary hermeneutical principle, it is extremely important when endeavoring to understand any text closely not to tear specific statements *out of their wider context*. This is especially important with regard to a thinker as complex as Kant, where quite often the arguments are built up in stages, including an engagement with opposing perspectives. In other cases, Kant is assessing traditional modes of discourse according to the criteria of the critical philosophy, and not necessarily subscribing to the mode of discourse he is describing. Therefore, I have tried to locate specific points as much as possible within the broader textual frameworks where they are embedded, so as to avoid misrepresenting their meaning. Specific phrases must be understood within the sentences and paragraphs within which they occur, specific paragraphs within the wider structure of the text, and specific writings with reference to the encompassing corpus of the critical philosophy. I have found this interpretive methodology to be especially important with respect to *Religion*, which, as I have noted, makes consistent sense within the context of *preceding* writings such as the three *Critiques*, as well as subsequent writings such as *The Conflict of the Faculties* and *The Metaphysics of Morals*. This continuity with the critical philosophy is obscured only when Kant's presentation of religious ideas, as drawn from traditional sources, is forcibly dislodged from the interpretive frameworks and procedures he establishes.

The status of the very important *Critique of the Power of Judgment* is somewhat atypical in regard to this project. I do not devote a specific chapter to the third *Critique*; yet, I draw upon it repeatedly. Because only some of its densely interwoven themes are directly relevant to my analysis, I use the third *Critique* selectively and strategically. It is especially relevant in contributing to Kant's views on the imagination and representation, as well as to interrelations among his theories of ethics, politics, and religion. Later works such as *The Conflict of the Faculties* and *The Metaphysics of Morals* are also utilized in a selective and strategic manner, if less substantially.

Throughout my account I have drawn on many scholars to help clarify my arguments, and I am deeply indebted to their work in Kant's epistemology, ethics, political theory, and theory of religion. However, my analyses and conclusions often differ from those formulated by other scholars. This is especially so in regard to some recent endeavors to interpret Kant as being far closer to traditional heteronomous theology than a serious reading of his texts can possibly support. Nevertheless, except in a few important instances, I have not attempted to argue with other scholars. Rather than engage in polemics, for the most part I have sought to establish my conclusions as clearly as possible by going directly to Kant's texts, and to make my case positively rather than negatively. I will leave it to readers to determine if this has been convincing and enlightening. Finally, I should note that while I have tried to be as thorough as possible in my analysis of *Religion* in chapter 6, my exposition has been shaped by a thematic focus on the interplay of ethics, politics, and traditions, as well as by the limits of space. However, I have found *Religion* to be a veritable goldmine of valuable insights into the ethical and political import of religious traditions. Since its complete scope cannot be addressed within this volume, it is my intention to provide a full-scale commentary and analysis of this work in the near future.

CHAPTER 2

Religion, politics, enlightenment

INJUSTICE, HUMAN RIGHTS, AND THE POLITICAL

Before discussing the first *Critique* more closely over the following two chapters, I want to outline how Kant defined his long-term intellectual goals in broader ethical and political terms. This includes a discussion of the types of political and economic conditions he opposed, how his inquiries into the seemingly abstruse domains of metaphysics and theology formed a crucial component of a sustained inquiry into human autonomy, and how he developed his approach to individual and collective reform.

One of Kant's most renowned *Reflections*, entitled "Remarks on the Observations of the Beautiful and Sublime," discusses a major transformation occurring in his self-understanding as a scholar. He describes turning away from being an investigator (*Forscher*) driven by the "thirst for knowledge," characterized by a sense of superiority in which one expresses "contempt for the rabble." This shift in focus concerns a preoccupation with broader issues of human rights that link ethical and political concerns. Reflecting on this change in his thinking, Kant continues: "*Rousseau* brought me around. This blinding superiority disappeared, I learned to honour human beings, and I would find myself far more useless than the common laborer if I did not believe that this consideration could impart to all others a value in establishing the rights of humanity."[1] In her work on Kant's ethics and politics, Susan Meld Shell also quotes this passage, and summarizes this shift in orientation as follows: "after Rousseau, 'what really matters' is the rights of man. No longer does Kant believe that the honour of mankind lies in intelligence and learning,

---

[1] Immanuel Kant, *Bemerkungen*, xx, 44; translated in *Notes and Fragments*, ed. Paul Guyer, trans. Curtis Bowman, Paul Guyer, and Frederick Rauscher (Cambridge University Press, 2005), p.7.

the province of a few 'noble souls'."[2] The theme of relinquishing a privileged approach to philosophy reinforces the political implications of this reorientation from an overriding concern with knowledge for its own sake, to broader ethical and cosmopolitan inquiries. This point has also been elaborated by Sankar Muthu to illustrate the political significance of Kant's approach to human rights:

> One of the key legacies of Kant's intensive engagement with Rousseau's thought is the attempt to explain how all humans are equally of absolute worth, for, following Rousseau, the oppressive social practices and beliefs that seem to reign in modern societies puts this equality at risk. People do not value themselves as intrinsically worthy beings, who are both capable of respecting others and who can demand such moral respect from others, because the social dynamics of modern life appear to reduce their value to one of exchange.[3]

Muthu's point, in addition to making more explicit the political concerns driving Kant's critical work, also highlights their abiding relevance. Although the particulars of social oppression and injustice vary considerably over time and among different social and political configurations, the problem of furthering conditions that promote human dignity and equality clearly remains a pressing task.

In his monumental biography, Manfred Kuehn quotes the same Reflection, and dates it as immediately following the publication of the *Observations* in 1764; that is, just before the intense period of intellectual activity that generated the first *Critique*.[4] Hence, it should not be surprising if we find clear indications of these preoccupations with virtue and human rights throughout that work. Moreover, recognizing these encompassing ethical-political goals avoids a narrow technical interpretation of the critical philosophy. As Richard Velkley notes with regard to the critical project, "Rousseau brings to Kant's attention that an instrumental conception of the role of reason in such a project is ultimately self-defeating."[5] This is crucial, since Kant's work is sometimes reduced to an advocacy for this form of instrumental reason, especially when it is collapsed into a generic understanding of "the Enlightenment project" with its putative vision of technical progress. This interpretation loses sight of a wider

---

[2] Susan Meld Shell, *The Rights of Reason: A Study of Kant's Philosophy and Politics* (University of Toronto Press, 1980), p.21.
[3] Sankar Muthu, *Enlightenment against Empire* (Princeton University Press, 2003), p.139.
[4] Kuehn notes that although "he was never a slavish follower of Rousseau, Kant's 'Remarks' show how Kant thought that Rousseau's method was important for the doctrine of virtue." Manfred Kuehn, *Kant: A Biography* (Cambridge University Press, 2001), pp.131–32.
[5] Richard Velkley, *Freedom and the End of Reason: On the Moral Foundation of Kant's Critical Philosophy* (University of Chicago Press, 1989), p.12.

human and practical (i.e., ethical-political) program. Kant's emphasis on evenly distributed questioning and reflection, conjoined with a focus on communication and public accountability, attests to ethical and political concerns that cannot be reduced to, and are not always compatible with, an instrumental use of reason.

To further clarify the links between the inquiries of the first *Critique* and the Rousseau-inspired emphasis on human rights and freedoms within a political context, we can take our bearings by recalling Rousseau's famous opening words from Chapter 1 of *The Social Contract*: "*Man is born free, and everywhere he is in chains*. He who believes himself the master of others does not escape being more of a slave than they."[6] In a succinct declaration, Rousseau articulates core issues of inequality, domination, and heteronomy in human relations, indicating that unjust relations *abrogate the autonomy of all*. Moreover, he voices a critical concern also running through Kant's mature work: how rational beings construct and inhabit social-political worlds that suppress their own potential for autonomy. These problems are interwoven with institutions that favor some individuals and groups over others, that suppress truth, and that establish and uphold unjust laws. Hence autonomy, as the rational and public institution of inclusive egalitarian laws, is interconnected with justice; when one is suppressed so is the other. The problem is as old as human history, takes many forms, and afflicts us to this day.

The lineaments of institutionalized injustice are evident in the absolute states of early modern Europe. As Charles Taylor summarizes, these emerged as "the most prominent answer in seventeenth-century Europe to the disorder of religious war." He further notes that this model of the state "was less radically different from the pre-modern ideas. It was, for one thing, still hierarchical: it saw society made up of tiered ranks or orders, largely derived from the earlier mediaeval dispensation."[7] Kant is writing in a context where the type of modern nation-state has been established, but where traditional, inherited forms of inequality and privilege still predominate. As the historian William Doyle summarizes, in the *ancien régime* France of Rousseau's and Kant's time, "*privilege* was the hallmark of a country without uniform laws or institutions."[8] "Privilege" is a key term expressing unfair treatment of some and favored treatment

---

[6] Jean-Jacques Rousseau, *The Social Contract*, in *The Basic Political Writings*, trans. Donald A. Cress (Indianapolis: Hackett, 1987), Book I, Chapter I, p.141; italics added.
[7] Charles Taylor, *A Secular Age* (Cambridge, MA: Harvard University Press, 2007), p.127.
[8] William Doyle, *The Oxford History of the French Revolution* (Oxford University Press, 2002), p.27.

of others; it therefore indicates the antithesis of universalizable laws of justice. Favoritism and privilege took many forms, but as Doyle explains, "nobles were entitled to more privileges than most." He outlines some of the most egregious of these:

> [T]hey were entitled to trial in special courts ... they were not subjected to the *corvée* [forced labor for road construction and maintenance], billeting of troops, or conscription into the militia. Above all they enjoyed substantial fiscal advantages. They escaped much of the weight of the *gabelle*, the hated, extortionate, salt monopoly; they paid no mutation duties on transferring feudal property (*franc-fief*); and nobility conferred exemption from the basic direct tax, the *taille*.[9]

Such examples of class-based inequality, where laws and customs ensure that the wealthy gain while the poor are penalized to the point of destitution, could easily be multiplied at length.

Lack of justice and equal rights were manifested in a wide variety of forms beyond those based on rank or class. For example, in France Protestants had since 1685 "enjoyed no toleration," and Louis XVI had even sworn "to extirpate heresy."[10] This religious intolerance is in certain ways endemic to the very fabric of absolutist monarchy. The monarch, as François Furet relates, "was not subject to the laws, since he was their originator." This absolutist model of sovereignty had its grounding in the religious worldview instilled in the populace at all levels: "that lifelong possession of the highest authority in the land was accountable to God alone, the true source of all human law."[11] Since the monarch's authority ultimately derived from the established church, it is not surprising that favoritism would be directed toward that institution, conjoined with discrimination against other sects and faiths. Moreover, as Furet further argues, the status of being above earthly laws meant that "despotism was monarchy's temptation."[12] This collaboration of church and state in sustaining absolutism reveals the larger scope of the political, in which worldviews, belief systems, and inherited mores have a profound impact on the legal and economic ordering of social realities.

To be sure, Kant did not have to look to *ancien régime* France for such dreadful examples of inequality and oppression. In the Prussian state in

---

[9] *Ibid.* [10] *Ibid.*, p.7.
[11] François Furet, *Revolutionary France: 1770–1880* (Oxford: Blackwell, 1988), pp.3–4. Charles Taylor also notes the affinity between the command structure of absolute monarchy and "the post-Tridentine Catholic Church." He remarks: "the fatal enmeshing of the Church in the *ancien régime* becomes denser with this affinity." Taylor, *A Secular Age*, p.128.
[12] Furet, *Revolutionary France: 1770–1880*, p.4.

which he resided, similar patterns of class-based injustice supported by a consortium of church and state were widely evident. In Eastern Prussia for example, in the seventeenth century and later "a formerly free peasantry ... [was] reduced to a particular form of serfdom, inherited servitude (*Erbuntertänigkeit*)." This state of affairs allowed "the manorial lords, the Junkers," to obtain "powers and law enforcement well beyond those of the manorial police. The result was the transformation of the manor into a self-enclosed political entity, its lord into a sovereign in his own right." This privileged position of being literally a law unto oneself was once more reinforced and sustained by religious belief: "For Lutherans, it was self-evident that this authority had no less claim on their obedience than the territorial lord. The proximity of throne and altar at the apex of the state found its parallel at a lower level in the relationship between the manorial lord and 'his' parson."[13] To cite another example from Kant's lifetime, under Frederick II (1740–86) "the Junkers were granted sweeping privileges: the middle classes were no longer able to purchase noble estates, and the government granted credit to economically struggling manors."[14] Many such instances could be presented of the monarchical and ecclesiastical authorization of blatant privilege, but these should suffice to establish the point.[15] Most importantly, in both the French and Prussian cases (and in the many other such examples that could be proffered), the institutionalized support for privilege not only violated and prevented the rule of law, but was additionally based upon unjust parochial laws and

---

[13] Heinrich August Winkler, *Germany: The Long Road West*, vol. 1, *1789–1933* (Oxford University Press, 2006), p.24.

[14] *Ibid.*, p.25. Frederick II is also known as Frederick the Great, considered in his day as a paragon of "enlightened absolutism." Frederick had a rather mixed position with regard to human rights and freedoms, however. As Winkler notes, Frederick "opened his country to western ideas and prompted a kind of cultural revolution. At the same time, he restored privileges to the aristocracy, whom he could not otherwise integrate into his military machine. In so doing, he again pushed Prussian society ... in the direction of an autocracy supporting itself upon nobility and serfdom" (p.28). To be sure, there were greater freedoms of expression under Frederick II than there would be under his nephew and successor, Frederick William II, who has been described as "a religious fanatic." Allen W. Wood, "General Introduction," in Immanuel Kant, *Religion and Rational Theology*, ed. and trans. Allen Wood and George di Giovanni (Cambridge University Press, 1998), p.xv. This is the monarch infamous in Kantian circles for having, along with his Minister of Education and Religious Affairs, Johann Christoph Wöllner, promulgated an edict "pledging the removal from their offices, both ecclesiastical and professorial" of those propagating Enlightenment thought (p.xvii). A second edict was directed toward "suppressing irreligious writings" and establishing a commission to censor all books dealing with moral and religious topics (p.xix). This latter law was used by the authorities to suppress Kant's *Religion*.

[15] For a more general account of the special burdens placed on peasants and other poorest members of European societies, see Tim Blanning, *The Pursuit of Glory: Europe 1648–1815* (London: Penguin Books, 2007), pp.157ff.

conventions. With regard to the French case, we might note the assessment of Emmanuel Joseph Sieyès, a contemporary of the revolutionary era and author of the influential *Essai sur les privilèges* and *Qu'est-ce que le Tiers État?* Furet summarizes the analysis developed in these works: "What is it, what else can it be, this privilege, if not the ultimate corruption of the concept of law, since it forms categories of individuals who are strangers to what makes the community?" Furet then relates Sieyès' argument that this abrogation of "democratic universalism" gives rise to a sense not only of entitlement, but also of being "outside citizenship," of "belonging to another race, the passion for domination, exaggerated self-esteem, etc."[16] In light of these historical and political realities, we might note that Kant's continuous preoccupation with universalizable moral laws and principles, having both ethical and political significance, offers a critical antidote to such institutionalized injustice of positive or statutory laws based on artificially dividing a populace into discrete sectors.

Kant's egalitarian views are based on principles of reason combined with those of public accountability and freedom of speech. In this respect, he develops a political model espousing many of the ideals central to modern democracies; indeed, even the most advanced democracies of the present still fall short of these ideals. However, while Kant is a strong advocate for republican political systems that institute just laws, he does not formally espouse a democratic model. To understand this, we should bear in mind that in Kant's era democracy per se was hardly anywhere in evidence. Even in the United States, only an incipient movement toward inclusive representative democracy had taken shape. In Sean Wilentz's summary:

> [I]mportant elements of democracy existed in the infant American republic of the 1780s, but the republic was not democratic. Nor, in the minds of those who governed it, was it supposed to be. A republic – the *res publica*, or "public thing" – was meant to secure the common good through the ministrations of the most worthy, enlightened men. A democracy … "the rule of the people" – dangerously handed power to the impassioned, unenlightened masses.[17]

Wilentz further notes that even after several decades, when judged by the standards of inclusive democracy "the American democracy of the mid-nineteenth century was hardly a democracy at all: women of all classes and colors lacked political and civil rights; most blacks were enslaved … the remnant of a ravaged Indian population in the eastern states had been

---

[16] Furet, *Revolutionary France: 1770–1880*, p.47.
[17] Sean Wilentz, *The Rise of American Democracy: Jefferson to Lincoln* (New York: W. W. Norton, 2005), p.xvii.

forced to move west, without citizenship."[18] In the course of this discussion, Wilentz also conveys a sense of what democracy can ideally represent in remarking that "democracy appears when some large numbers of previously excluded, ordinary persons – what the eighteenth century called the 'many' – secure the power not simply to select their governors but to oversee the institutions of government, as officeholders and as citizens free to assemble and criticize those in office."[19] This model of democracy realizes many of the core principles of Kant's vision of a just society: the inclusiveness of laws equally applicable to all, and the need for public awareness and debate concerning all laws and political undertakings (e.g., military expeditions, tax exemptions, etc.).

Kant's republican model articulates some of the fundamental principles of modern democracy, without focusing simply on representative government. His mature thinking formulates ethical-political principles designed to counteract injustice and establish mutual freedom and equality in an open public sphere. For example, in "Theory and Practice" he describes the "principles of a civil condition" as excluding a "paternalistic government" in which subjects are treated "like minor children" (TP, 8:291; and cf. E, 8:35). A just constitution is also described as one in which citizens have equal rights; despite the unequal talents and circumstances that can lead to unequal material resources "they are nevertheless all equal to one another as subjects." This point shows that Kant focuses on laws and institutions providing equal rights and opportunities for all, rather than on artificially imposed material uniformity. His vision conjoins just, egalitarian institutions with recognition of earned merit based on individual ability. Most importantly, in stark contrast with all *ancien régime* societies, the principle of egalitarianism rules out "a *hereditary* prerogative (privileges [reserved] for a certain rank)" (TP, 8:292). These inherited privileges based on class or other factors are both wrong and counterproductive, because they have nothing to do with ability and effort; they block the endeavors of many to realize their potential while granting to others unmerited advantages. Finally, Kant summarizes the overarching principles supporting these arguments in presenting the idea of "an *original contract*" which need not "be presupposed as a *fact*" but rather is "*only an idea* of reason, which, however, has its undoubted practical reality" in binding legislators (TP, 8:297). The fundamental binding principle derived from this social contract is as follows: "if a public law is so constituted that a whole people *could not possibly* give its consent to it

---

[18] Ibid., p.xviii. [19] Ibid., p.xix.

(as, e.g., that a certain class of *subjects* should have the hereditary privilege of *ruling rank*), it is unjust [*nicht gerecht*]" (TP, 8:297). In the ensuing chapters, I will explicate such universalizable ideas and principles as crucial to political coexistence.

However, in arguing that the critical philosophy formulates ethical-political principles counteracting favoritism and injustice, I am not claiming that Kant was able to apply these inclusive egalitarian principles to every case infallibly. It is well documented that Kant internalized many presuppositions of his era concerning women, non-Western cultures, and non-Christian religions, and comments reflecting these parochial assumptions are scattered through his work (although they are actually quite rare in his major published writings).[20] Rather, my point is that Kant's work provides systematically derived principles of justice and equality that can

---

[20] Allen Wood lists several of Kant's statements that are deficient in applying egalitarian principles. For example, Wood notes Kant's support of the death penalty, and acknowledges that "Kant's views about sex are repugnant to nearly everyone today (as they were to many in his own time)." Allen W. Wood, *Kant's Ethical Thought* (New Haven: Yale University Press, 1999), p.2. Additionally, Wood summarizes Kant's problematic views on "race and gender," such as his ordering of "races" based on skin color, and his belief that "women ... are not suited by temperament or intellectual endowment to be treated as full adults in the public sphere" (p.3). However, Wood also emphasizes that these comments do not convey the quality of Kant's ethical thinking. In the wider range of his writings, Kant does pay attention to personal, social, and historical factors affecting ethical decision-making, and he offers resources for more progressive ethical positions. Wood helps us grasp the abiding significance of Kant's ethical thought that transcends the opinions he sometimes advocated: "respecting the unity of Kant's thought is not only compatible with but even requires distinguishing the teachings that are central to it from those that are peripheral, and separating the conclusions that actually flow from the principles from the conclusions he may have drawn but do not follow" (p.4). Along similar lines, Robert Louden notes that "an unresolved tension exists between the core message of universality in [Kant's] ethics and his frequent assertions that many different groups (who when taken together constitute a large majority of the human race) are in a pre-moral state of development." Robert B. Louden, *Kant's Impure Ethics* (Oxford University Press, 2000), p.15. What I want to emphasize is precisely this *tension*; the principles Kant articulates are indeed based on inclusive universalizability, although our capacity to bring increasingly diverse groups within the sphere of this universalizability requires knowledge and judgment, qualities which are partly culture-dependent and which at best develop only incrementally. When Louden summarizes Kant as viewing most humans as being in a "pre-moral" condition, there is nothing innate about these views. All human beings are capable of moral development, but cultural and historical factors also play an important role (as Louden also notes; p.20). By contrast, Muthu notes a progression in Kant's discussions of race. After citing some stereotypical views of non-European peoples Kant internalized from sources such as travel writings, Muthu remarks: "In Kant's later years, when he developed his theory of humanity as cultural agency and his anti-imperialist political thought, the hierarchical and biological concept of race disappears in his published writings." Muthu, *Enlightenment against Empire*, p.182. In some areas, for example in attacking colonialism, Kant *did* apply his egalitarian principles rigorously, and was in this respect well ahead of his time. Louden also cites several passages where Kant indicates that his model of "rational beings" is inclusive of women, as it obviously must be (see *Kant's Impure Ethics*, p.84 and "What Is Enlightenment?" E, 8:35).

continue to counteract these parochial views through the ongoing efforts of succeeding generations. Kant himself, far from being a naïve idealist, also acknowledges the many subjective and political factors that impede us in recognizing and applying ethical principles. This is why cultivating our capacity for autonomous judgment is conjoined with an analysis of public institutions that either foster or impede progress in enlightenment.

EPISTEMOLOGY AND THE POLITICAL

The ideas of Rousseau assist Kant in addressing ethical and political concerns with institutionalized injustice. However, this preoccupation does not mean that epistemological issues are inconsequential to his critical writings. It rather helps us understand how Kant comes to cast questions of knowledge in a more profound light, and how this recasting provides the basis for ethical-political inquiries. Working within the realm of concepts on a high level of abstraction may seem far removed from any immediate impact upon the social-political conditions within which we live our lives. However, the operative approach governing Kant's work, as noted earlier, is that ideas do have an impact, if often indirect, upon the institutions and practices that shape any given political sphere. Recently, Jonathan Israel has made a similar point with regard to the revolutionary influence of Enlightenment thought. Arguing against the view that ideas do not change political conditions, he notes that "virtually all eighteenth and nineteenth century commentators" insist that "'philosophy' was incontestably the prime cause of the changes in social attitudes."[21] This position was taken by many who were close to the developments of the Enlightenment era, and it was held, Israel notes, by both proponents and opponents of Enlightenment (the result was that opponents of the Enlightenment came to consider radical ideas dangerous). Most importantly, Israel further points out with regard to "the misery, exploitation, and economic hardship suffered by the most downtrodden" that the unjust political systems creating these conditions are always *ideationally and ideologically supported*. The material conditions of the disenfranchised strata of societies "are organized and systematized on the basis of doctrines in which they trust implicitly and which theorize, buttress, and legitimize the political, religious, and economic instruments of their own exploitation."[22] This is a crucial point, for it indicates that a society's

---

[21] Jonathan Israel, *Enlightenment Contested: Philosophy, Modernity, and the Emancipation of Man 1670–1752* (Oxford University Press, 2006), p.21.
[22] Ibid., p.22.

capacity to foster the internalization of self-legitimizing norms and worldviews, even among those who are most disadvantaged by them, is an essential element in maintaining an inequitable status quo. Israel argues that in order to understand transformative periods such as the Enlightenment, we must take a nuanced view that incorporates "a two-way traffic, or dialectic of ideas and social reality."[23] This understanding of the ideational dimensions of history and politics is crucial to understanding Kant's position as well. Looking back, we can grasp the significance of his work as a contribution to the broader changes in thinking accompanying gradual social and political transformation. Additionally, we will see that it continues to offer a model for engaging inherited thought-systems that subtend institutionalized injustice.

A well-known statement from the *Prolegomena to Any Future Metaphysics* of 1783 elaborates the link between the epistemological and ethical-political aspects of the critical philosophy. Kant mentions that "the remembrance of *David Hume* was the very thing that many years ago first interrupted my dogmatic slumber and gave a completely different direction to my researches in the field of speculative philosophy" (PR, 4:260). This emphasizes the critical philosophy's concern with mapping out the scope of human knowledge as a radical departure from the conceptual patterns of traditional theology and metaphysics. Following from this awakening, one of the main projects of the first *Critique* is to adjudicate ungrounded speculations. This endeavor builds on a key principle of Humean skepticism: not to accept truth claims simply on the basis of inherited custom or authority.[24] Hume's influence, assisting Kant in questioning the received truths of metaphysics, combines with that of Rousseau, initiating a fresh approach to the interconnection of epistemology and politics. However, in a related passage, Kant also distances himself from Humean skepticism in a key respect. He notes that "the acute man," that is, Hume, was "looking only to the *negative* benefit that curbing the excessive claims of speculative reason would have." Of primary concern is that Hume "lost sight of the positive harm that results if reason is deprived of the most important vistas [*wichtigsten Aussichten*], from which alone it can stake out for the will [*dem Willen*] the highest goal of all the will's endeavors" (PR, 4:258). This emphasizes the need for more encompassing ranges of vision, extending beyond the skeptical

---

[23] Ibid., p.23.
[24] See Hume, *A Treatise of Human Nature*, ed. L. A. Selby-Bigge (Oxford University Press, 1965), pp.104–05.

demolition of unfounded metaphysical claims and their popular counterparts. These wider vistas are intimately connected with guiding our wills toward higher ends, an issue which takes us directly into ethical-political concerns under the rubric of practical reason. These concerns are also reflected in a key conceptual tool Kant utilizes in seeking to widen the aperture of our ethical and political vision: regulative principles (discussed in chapters 3 and 4). The core of the Kantian problem is to follow through on Hume's empiricist and skeptical contributions, to purge dogmatic metaphysics of its illusions, while at the same time reconceptualizing the wider questions of meaning and purpose, or ends, traditionally associated with metaphysics and theology.

From the opening pages of the *Critique of Pure Reason* there are clear indications of the wider program of ethical-political inquiry that are elaborated in subsequent writings. The first *Critique* is often approached solely in terms of its inquiries into the conditions of knowledge, which is understandable given the complexity and importance of these themes. However, Kant also elaborates a series of interconnections among issues of ethics, politics, and religion for which the problems of epistemology form the essential entry point. Onora O'Neill has stressed that "the first *Critique* is not only deeply antirationalist [in critiquing rationalist metaphysics] but profoundly political."[25] In similar terms, Otfried Höffe emphasizes that the repeated references in the first *Critique* to concepts such as "the Platonic republic (B372–74), civil legislation (B358, 372ff.), a constitution providing for the greatest human freedom (B373), and perpetual peace (B780)" invite what he describes as "a cosmo-political reading" (i.e., a political inquiry on an international level). While noting the presence of these political concerns, Höffe also concludes that "the references are, however, too cursory and accidental to justify a proper political reading."[26] This may be so; certainly the first *Critique* offers no fully developed theory of the state or international (cosmopolitan) relations, or of the relation between the positive laws of states and natural laws (or universal laws of virtue), the realm of ends, and other such focal points of Kantian ethical-political inquiry. These matters are addressed in subsequent works such as "Theory and Practice," "Perpetual Peace," *The Metaphysics of Morals*, and *Religion*. Nevertheless, there are indications of encompassing ethical and political concerns informing Kant's epistemological inquiries, thereby

---

[25] Onora O'Neill, *Constructions of Reason: Explorations of Kant's Practical Philosophy* (Cambridge University Press, 1989), p.4.
[26] Otfried Höffe, *Kant's Cosmopolitan Theory of Law and Peace* (Cambridge University Press, 2006), p.205.

Epistemology and the political 35

adding another level of significance to them. In other words, the passages noted by Höffe are not so much "accidental" as they are indications of a more far-reaching critical project in which epistemology, ethics, and political concerns intersect. The first *Critique* establishes the conditions for all of Kant's ensuing practical thinking.

Obviously, Kant's detailed treatments of epistemology, ethical theory, and other investigations stand on their own as major contributions to their relevant fields. Nevertheless, even the explicitly epistemological concerns of the first *Critique* are an essential element in an overall project that is to a large extent ethically and politically oriented. This interconnection was articulated in Theodor Adorno's lectures on the *Critique of Pure Reason*, which summarize Kant's epistemological model as holding that "human beings are the subjects of their world and not just the objects." Developing the implications of this approach, Adorno notes: "Kant's critique of reason would not be conceivable in the absence of this idea of the social and political emancipation of the human subject that has ceased to act out a submissive role towards the world and instead has discovered in the freedom and autonomy of the subject the principle which alone enables the world to be known."[27] I will further explicate our active role in attaining knowledge of the world in the following chapters. Here it suffices to say that Kant integrates issues of how we *know* with a vision of how we *should be*, thereby showing how autonomous knowledge provides a basis for autonomous laws and judgments.

However, it is incorrect to assume that Kant replaces externally based heteronomy with a rational subject individually able to establish new bases for knowledge and truth. Rather, *any* predetermined basis of knowledge is relinquished for a more interactive model of truth and ethics. Willi Goetschel has argued that in the conceptual revolution initiated by Kant, "Critique no longer means a simple, topical application of given standards. Critique opens up, becoming a self-reflective process in which reason no longer determines truth."[28] In making the apparently odd claim that reason no longer determines truth, Goetschel is in agreement with O'Neill's declaration that the first *Critique* is anti-rationalist. This may be a somewhat hyperbolic way of saying that, according to Kant, strictly rationalist models of reality are inadequate. Goetschel therefore clarifies the point in noting that "Kant defines reason as nothing other than

---

[27] Theodor Adorno, *Kant's Critique of Pure Reason* (Stanford University Press, 2001), p.135.
[28] Willi Goetschel, *Constituting Critique: Kant's Writing as Critical Praxis* (Durham, NC: Duke University Press, 1994), p.4.

universal reason, envisioned as the chorus of voices of 'everybody'. *His epistemological model is thus intrinsically political*."[29] The very universality of reason requires a set of open, public forums to adjudicate all information relevant to a case: this is the antithesis of any form of rationalism that hypostasizes reason. Accordingly, Goetschel remarks on Kant's *principle of publicity*, which I expand on below, and concludes: "this principle assumes autonomous use of reason only to be possible as public use, that is, free from external authority."[30] With these incisive comments, we further see how the theory of knowledge in the first *Critique* provides the essential elements for articulating the interconnections among autonomy, publicity, and the political. The movement from fixed truths linked with an ontological order and traditional authorities, to a reflective model that is interactive and politically transformative, is central to this project. These points will take time to work out; here I provide only an overview of the interpretive framework, focusing on a critique of heteronomy on multiple levels, within which a closer reading of the first *Critique* takes shape.

Many passages confirm a program extending beyond epistemological concerns to ethical and political issues. These supplement the references given by Höffe, but are equally significant for their strategic placement within the text. For example, in the Preface to the first edition (1781), Kant outlines his overarching preoccupation with the problems of classical metaphysics, in which "reason sees itself necessitated to take refuge in principles that overstep all possible experience" (Aviii). Analyzing the conceptual problems endemic to metaphysics, Kant has recourse to a series of graphically political metaphors to characterize the status of the former "queen of the sciences," which has now become "despised on all sides."[31] During the period when metaphysics was unchallenged, "under the administration of the **dogmatists**, her rule was **despotic**. Yet because her legislation still retained traces of ancient barbarism, this rule gradually degenerated through internal wars into complete **anarchy**; and the skeptics, a kind of nomads who abhor all permanent cultivation of the soil, shattered civil unity from time to time" (Aix).[32] This is a remarkable

---

[29] *Ibid.*, p.5; italics added.   [30] *Ibid.*, p.6.
[31] O'Neill also notes political metaphors operative throughout the first *Critique*. She emphasizes that "the three political metaphors on which he rests most are those of tribunal, debate, and community." *Constructions of Reason*, p.17.
[32] In this regard, see David Hume, *Dialogues Concerning Natural Religion*, in *Dialogues and Natural History of Religion*, ed. J. C. A. Gaskin (Oxford University Press, 1993), p.89. Therein, the character of Philo, who represents the skeptical position, reflects as follows: "how complete must be *his* victory, who remains always, with all mankind, on the offensive, and has himself no fixed

portrayal of the modern history of ideas in political terms: a despotic ruler, overstepping the bounds of its authority and now enfeebled, has engendered a destabilized situation. In Kant's account, anarchy rules as skeptics undertake a kind of guerrilla warfare against the previously settled territories of the metaphysicians. However, while skepticism is valuable for questioning existing patterns of thought, it lacks the conceptual resources to establish new guiding principles.

Later in the *Critique*, Kant supplements this account with an alternate set of images. He offers an overall assessment of metaphysics as follows: "although we had in mind a tower that would reach the heavens, the supply of materials sufficed only for a dwelling that was just roomy enough for our business on the plane of experience and high enough to survey it" (A707/B735).[33] This oblique reference to the biblical narrative of the Tower of Babel, which sought to reach the heavens but instead crumbled to the ground, is followed by a further remark that such a "bold undertaking," representing the ambitions of speculative metaphysics, "had to fail from lack of material, not to mention the confusion of languages that unavoidably divided the workers over the plan and dispersed them throughout the world, leaving each to build on his own according to his own design" (A707/B735). As O'Neill trenchantly notes, the analogy employs images of dispersal and fragmentation that evoke the post-metaphysical nomads, or skeptical empiricists. Hence the task Kant sets himself is not only to eschew grandiose metaphysical claims, but moreover to "avoid the fate of the 'nomads' – isolation, dispersal, noncommunication." Most importantly, O'Neill adds that this fate, in which each works on their own in dispersed isolation, engenders "nonlawlike, hence unsharable, principles."[34]

In response to the challenges of skepticism, the metaphysicians fall back "into the same old worm-eaten **dogmatism**" (Ax). This dogmatism is a defensive measure; the former despot cannot venture forth with new initiatives, but retreats behind the fortified walls of authority and custom, i.e., heteronomous thought-forms and modes of imposing them on others. The failure of progressive mediation between these incommensurable parties produces a situation in which "what rules is tedium and complete **indifferentism**, the mother of chaos and night in the sciences" (Ax).

---

station or abiding city, which he is ever, on any occasion, obliged to defend?" At the very end of the *Critique*, Kant mentions Hume explicitly as a representative of the skeptical school, while citing Christian Wolff as an example of the dogmatic school (A855/B883).

[33] This passage is also discussed by Onora O'Neill, "Vindicating Reason," in Paul Guyer, ed., *The Cambridge Companion to Kant* (Cambridge University Press, 1992), p.290.

[34] Ibid., p.297.

This aptly characterizes the disillusionment following from the ultimate failure of any despotic rule. However, Kant quickly introduces a note of hope into this distressing scenario. He emphasizes that the benighted anarchy in the humanistic sciences might also signal "the origin, or at least the prelude, of their *incipient transformation and enlightenment*" (Ax, italics added). Because well-worn patterns of thought have failed to engage the intellectual challenges proffered by the nomads, and because these challengers can themselves offer only negative lines of argument, what is required is an entirely fresh approach to knowledge and truth. Furthering this potential process of enlightenment is the main task of the *Critique* and subsequent writings. It consists not only in inventing a new epistemological model, but also in reinterpreting the major concepts and even images of the metaphysicians and theologians, imbuing them anew with humanly relevant significance.

O'Neill portrays the path blazed by Kantian thought as being informed by both metaphysicians and skeptics, but following neither. She argues with respect to dogmatic metaphysics that "it is unreasonable to posit capacities, insights, and transcendent authorities we lack: This is the unreason of transcendental realists, including Platonists and traditional theists." Reciprocally, she notes of the nomadic camp that "it is unreasonable to assume that thinking and acting can be wholly arbitrary and nonlawlike, as skeptics and postmodernists claim to." Finally, she makes a parallel argument with regard to those who forsake grand encompassing visions only to dwell within the particular confines of local frameworks of knowledge: "It is unreasonable to assume that the fundamental principles of thought and action need reflect only some local authority, as the acolytes of *Schwärmerei* or communitarianism do."[35] O'Neill rejects these various forms of unreason and resists collapsing Kant's insights into these familiar models; this initiative also sets the tone for the present project.

Because the critical philosophy eschews the grandiose ventures of metaphysics, Kant warns his readers that his undertaking will not cater to the "dogmatically enthusiastic lust for knowledge [*dogmatisch schwärmende Wißbegierde*]." This desire, he continues, "could not be satisfied except through magical powers in which I am not an expert" (Axiii). This crucial disavowal should serve as a guide for our subsequent discussions

---

[35] Ibid., p.298. This argument is developed at length in a subsequent publication, where O'Neill advocates "inclusive practical reasoning." As she argues with regard to the communitarian attempt to ground norms in the inherited traditions of local communities: "they cannot premise all their reasoning on categories, beliefs, desires or norms that are confined to such restricted groups of 'insiders'." Onora O'Neill, *Towards Justice and Virtue* (Cambridge University Press, 1996), p.54.

of Kant's work, for there may be moments when we are tempted to mistrust this statement and attribute a more traditional metaphysical or theological approach to his arguments. Moreover, Kant insists that philosophy's efforts "to abolish the semblance [*Blendwerk*] arising from misinterpretation" will necessitate that "many prized and beloved delusions [*Wahn*] have to be destroyed in the process" (Axiii). He is preparing us for the loss of comforting illusions accompanying the turn from traditional metaphysics toward the process of enlightenment.

EXCURSUS ON "ENTHUSIASM"

Two key critical terms appearing throughout Kant's engagement with metaphysics and religion are *enthusiasm* and *delusion*. The second term may be self-evident in reflecting disordered representations of reality, and will in any case be discussed in subsequent chapters. However, because of its strategic significance, I should note that the seemingly innocuous "enthusiasm" (*Schwärmerei*) is a key word in early modern critiques of both knowledge claims and power structures founded on irrational needs. It conveys the sense of narrowly focused passions and allegiances insusceptible to the mitigating influences of reason and argument. Kant follows an established tradition of critical thinking about the dangers of enthusiasm appearing in various modern thinkers. For example, in his *Theological-Political Treatise*, Spinoza argued against the manipulation of religious emotions for despotic political ends. He refers to the common practice in which individuals "parade their own ideas as God's word, their chief aim being to compel others to think as they do, while using religions as a pretext." Alas, even a cursory examination of contemporary political culture informs us that such practices have not been relinquished with the passing of the centuries. In any case, Spinoza addresses how unbridled enthusiasm and the accompanying disdain for reason make us more readily prey to these manipulations. "Indeed," he continues with regard to the political exploitation of religious sensibilities, "religion is manifested not in charity but in spreading contention among men and in fostering the bitterest hatred, under the false guise of zeal in God's cause and a burning enthusiasm. To these evils is added superstition, which teaches men to despise reason and Nature, and to admire and venerate only that which is opposed to both."[36] Here, the feverish passions of enthusiasm are welded

---

[36] Baruch Spinoza, *Theological-Political Treatise*, trans. Samuel Shirley (Indianapolis: Hackett, 2001), p.86.

to the anti-rational sentiments of superstition, producing a heady brew in which people are more than usually subject to ideological manipulation.

A lucid exposition of the phenomenon also appears in John Locke's chapter on enthusiasm in the *Essay Concerning Human Understanding*. Locke defines enthusiasm as "a third Ground of Assent," other than those of reason or faith, which seeks to impose revelatory truth without any reliance on or scrutiny by reason. "I mean *Enthusiasm*," he states, "which, laying by Reason, would set up Revelation without it. Whereby in effect it takes away both Reason and Revelation, and substitutes in the room of them the ungrounded Fancies of a Man's own Brain."[37] As with Spinoza, enthusiasm is associated with fantasy and delusion, making dogmatic claims insusceptible to the scrutiny of public examination. Locke adds a further point that parallels Spinoza's arguments linking enthusiasm and despotic modes of political organization. Those who exhibit "bias and corruption" in their judgments have concomitant tendencies to assume "an Authority of Dictating to others, and a forwardness to prescribe their Opinions." Locke then establishes the crucial link between the undisciplined pseudo-truths of enthusiasm and the tyrannical zeal to impose these fallacies on others. "For how almost can it be otherwise, but that he should be ready to impose on others Belief, who has already imposed on his own? Who can reasonably expect Arguments and Conviction from him, in dealing with others, whose Understanding is not accustomed to them in his dealing with himself?" Continuing in this vein, Locke portrays the enthusiast as one who "does Violence to his own Faculties," and who "Tyrannizes over his own Mind," thereby establishing a pattern in which the same tyrannical approach is taken with regard to others.[38] This argument indicates how an irrational cast of mind with regard to one's own beliefs and assertions can pave the way for political despotism. An enthusiast in a position of authority might very well follow the pattern Locke indicates, and impose ideologies on others. Reciprocally, the uncritical enthusiastic cast of mind makes the multitude more susceptible to the dogmatic zeal of these tyrants, as emphasized in Spinoza's analysis of the political misuse of religion.

The notion of enthusiasm also plays an important role in Hume's thought, and he adds significant nuances to the concept that characterize its political as well as religious implications. In his famous essay on the

---

[37] John Locke, *An Essay Concerning Human Understanding*, ed. Peter H. Nidditch (Oxford University Press, 1975), p.698; italics original.
[38] *Ibid.*

topic, Hume explicates "the pernicious effects of *superstition* and *enthusiasm*, the corruptions of true religion." He further specifies that "these two species of false religion, though both pernicious, are of a very different, and even contrary nature."[39] Knud Haakonssen notes of these two corrupting tendencies that "both were developments of conflicting theological doctrines that appealed to two different types of personalities. Both had come to be associated with opposing political interests."[40] Hence, under the rubric of superstition, Hume categorized "weakness, fear, melancholy, together with ignorance." These are characteristics that in religious life emphasize appeasing invisible powers by methods that consist in "ceremonies, observances, mortifications, sacrifices, presents, or in any practice, however absurd or frivolous, which either folly or knavery recommends to blind and terrified credulity."[41] This psychological orientation in religion is associated with political predilections for fixed authoritarian structures, such as "priestly power," which, continues Hume, "may justly be regarded as an invention of a timorous and abject superstition."[42] Haakonssen further summarizes the relation between this mode of religious orientation and a passive relation to political authorities: "In society and politics, the superstitious person is disposed to accept established forms and powers as inherent in the nature of things and to see society as a hierarchical structure with a monarch as the unitary authority and sovereignty as a divine right."[43]

In contrast with the superstitious predilection for hierarchically established systems of collective order, the enthusiasts are subject to more varying, individual episodes of zealous passion. Hume describes the type of religious personality prone to "raptures, transports, and surprising flights of fancy." This form of elevation tends to engender "presumption and

---

[39] David Hume, "Of Superstition and Enthusiasm," in *Essays: Moral, Political, and Literary*, ed. Eugene F. Miller (Indianapolis: Liberty Classics, 1987), p.73. Concerning these two general types, Gaskin adds another important association: "These corruptions were superstition, usually associated with the Church of Rome, and enthusiasm, usually associated with the newly converted and with extreme Protestant sects." J. C. A. Gaskin, "Hume on Religion," in David Fate Norton, ed., *The Cambridge Companion to Hume* (Cambridge University Press, 1993), p.315.

[40] Knud Haakonssen, "The Structure of Hume's Political Theory," in Norton, ed., *The Cambridge Companion to Hume*, p.182.

[41] Hume, "Of Superstition and Enthusiasm," p.74.

[42] Ibid., p.75.

[43] Haakonssen, "Structure of Hume's Political Theory," p.183. Rousseau makes similar reference to the use of religion to sanctify political authority: "This is what has always forced the fathers of nations to have recourse to the intervention of heaven and to credit gods with their own wisdom, so that the peoples, subjected to the laws of the state as to those of nature and recognizing the same power in the formation of man and of the city, might obey with liberty and bear with docility the yoke of public felicity." Rousseau, *Social Contract*, Book II, Chapter VII, p.164.

confidence," and because the source of these raptures is experienced as "altogether unaccountable, and seeming quite beyond the reach of our ordinary faculties," they are "attributed to the immediate inspiration of that Divine Being, who is the object of devotion."[44] Enthusiasts therefore presume to attribute their idiosyncratic states of rapture to a divine source, so that any resulting claims they might make are given unconditional ideological rationalization. Hume is quite even-handed, but equally severe in assessing both superstition and enthusiasm: each expresses an excess of feeling leading to the dominance of passions over principles, evidence, and balanced judgment. Hume's linking of enthusiasm with illumination is particularly significant, because Kant, too, employs these terms as bywords for dangerous religious attitudes that grant excessive authority to undisciplined inspirations. Hume observes that enthusiasm, being of a "presumptuous boldness of character," comes to "beget the most extreme resolutions; especially after it rises to that height as to inspire the deluded fanatic with the opinion of divine illuminations, and with contempt for the common rules of reason, morality, and prudence."[45] As with Locke, though stating it more forcefully, Hume is concerned with the abandonment of reasonable discourse and public accountability ensuing from enthusiasm and illumination. Being more taken by spontaneous passions, enthusiasts do not fit easily into established formats of religious and political orders. Rather, "they often incline to forceful remodeling of authority and generally see self-government as the only proper government, at least in principle."[46] They may therefore seek to incite ethical and political change, but this is not based on reasonable, publicly debatable principles and laws.

This understanding of enthusiasm, designating an impassioned state of mind that rejects established ecclesiastical and political structures, appears, for example, in Kant's discussions of the French Revolution, an event of virtually unique significance for his historical and political thinking. Howard Caygill summarizes: "As the irruption of idea into affect and action, enthusiasm is capable of inspiring events which break the continuum of history; the main example of this for Kant was the contemporary French revolution inspired by the idea of the republic, an event which was both the outcome of enthusiasm and the source of enthusiastic feelings in its spectators."[47] This example is also telling, because as we shall see

---

[44] Hume, "Of Superstition and Enthusiasm," p.74.
[45] *Ibid.*, p.77.
[46] Haakonssen, "Structure of Hume's Political Theory," p.183.
[47] Howard Caygill, *A Kant Dictionary* (Oxford: Blackwell, 1995), p.176.

it indicates why, despite his progressive views, Kant exhibits considerable ambivalence with regard to revolutionary activity. While he embraced the French Revolution as indicating humanity's potential for significant political change based on ideas and principles, at the same time he was repelled by the overwhelming of principle by the violence and disorder engendered by enthusiastic zeal (among other causes; see the last section of this chapter for further discussion).

Although he never cites them directly on the topic of enthusiasm, Kant's analyses seem to build upon those of his predecessors. He follows Spinoza in extracting from Scripture a rational, morally oriented kernel of truth from the overlaying enthusiastic and superstitious elements. Likewise, while Kant does not offer quite so detailed an account of enthusiasm as Locke, he similarly portrays traditional metaphysics as despotic as well as dogmatic. This, however, is not to say that these two thinkers are in full agreement on their interpretation of religion. Locke, for example, more readily accepts the authority of what he understands to be the genuine revelation of the Bible. By contrast, Kant understands any claim to revelation as a historical phenomenon, and he evaluates this as decidedly secondary to the interpretive guidelines formulated through practical reason. With regard to Hume, Kant similarly employs the concept of enthusiasm to designate irrational orientations toward "individual illuminations." In *Religion*, for example, in discussing various forms of dogmatic faith, he refers to "supposed inner experience (effects of grace), *enthusiasm*," as well as "alleged outer experiences (miracles), *superstition*" (R, 6:53). Additionally, Kant formulates an even-handed assessment of prototypical Catholic and Protestant modes of religiosity, each of which is seen to depart in different ways from moral religion as he defined it. These arguments, which I will develop at greater length, parallel those of Hume in linking enthusiasm with an inner and hence more individualized form of emotional transport, while superstition focuses on putative outer experiences.

Kant develops these issues in detail over a variety of publications, including a direct analysis of the historical and political aspects of the problem in *Religion*. We can note for the moment that, in relation to political analysis, another counterpart to enthusiasm is fanaticism (*Fanatismus*), in which the tendency to unbridled zeal is channeled into uncritical advocacy for specific religious and political ideologies. Ultimately, Kant explicates the procedures by which such deleterious irrational tendencies might be mitigated and dispelled, advocating an enlightened autonomy for all under just laws.

INTERSECTIONS OF METAPHYSICS, RELIGION, AND THE POLITICAL

Let us return to Kant's preliminary sketch of the woeful state of metaphysics in the late eighteenth century. A highly significant note explicates the significance of the critical philosophy not only for interrogating speculative metaphysics per se, but also for undertaking cognate inquiries on cultural and historical levels. In this way, the political metaphors characterizing the failures of metaphysics slide over into a more direct form of political analysis. Kant is unequivocal in asserting that "Our age is the age of criticism, to which everything must submit." He immediately explains what this might mean, with specific reference to the issue of religion, by calling for "public examination" of all socially sanctioned authorities. Concerning this need for unrestricted, open public inquiry and examination, Kant continues:

> **Religion** through its **holiness** and **legislation** through its **majesty** commonly seek to exempt themselves from it. But in this way they excite a just suspicion against themselves, and cannot lay claim to that unfeigned respect that reason grants only to that which has been able to withstand its free and public examination. (Axin.)

This powerful call for unrestricted inquiry addresses two key domains that often claim privileged status: religious tradition and political authority. Its occurrence at the opening of the first *Critique* unambiguously links that work to a wider ethical-political program. Even the somewhat recondite inquiries into pre-critical idealism, metaphysics, and rational theology are part of a project advocating open public discourse and furthering human autonomy. This is not merely a negative form of criticism, but also involves the constructive task of *rethinking* the significance of religious concepts.

Significantly, these concerns with open inquiry are reiterated toward the close of the first *Critique*. This reappearance serves to bookend the epistemological investigations that form the bulk of the work, so as to contextualize its analyses within an explicit politically oriented inquiry where the topic of religion is a major concern. In the section on "the discipline of pure reason with regard to its polemical use," Kant stipulates that "reason must subject itself to critique in all its undertakings, and cannot restrict the freedom of critique through any prohibition without damaging itself and drawing upon itself a disadvantageous suspicion." This clarifies that Kant is not assuming a self-contained reason (such as

Intersections of metaphysics, religion, and the political 45

the hypostasized reason he discerns in traditional metaphysics), sheltered from scrutiny and critique. The freedom for critical inquiry is not just applied externally to others; it also has a reflexive function in checking the uses of reason by those claiming to speak on its behalf:

> Now there is nothing so important because of its utility, nothing so holy, that it may be exempted from this searching review and inspection, which *knows no respect for persons*. *The very existence [Existenz] of reason depends upon this freedom, which has no dictatorial authority*, but whose claim is never anything more than the agreement of free citizens, each of whom must be able to express his reservations, indeed even his *veto*, without holding back. (A738/B766; italics added)

This politically charged comment contains several germinal ideas that are explicated over many ensuing publications. Stating that reason knows no respect for persons means that nobody is protected by status or privilege from rational judgment based on principles. The comprehensiveness of critical questioning is pointedly addressed to domains of the social and political that, by virtue of either *utility* (including economic and military policies) or *holiness* (religion) might seek exemption from public scrutiny. It is equally crucial that freedom in the public realm is the lifeblood of reason itself.[48] In elaborating this point, Kant characterizes the role of reason as a "judicial" one serving as "the supreme court of justice for all disputes" (A739–40/B767–68).[49] This model of a judicial process fosters open dialogue among disagreeing stances, seeking rational mediation.

On this basis, commentators as diverse as O'Neill, Goetschel, and Cheah understand the public and cultural realms as being, for Kant, the locus for the development of our rational faculties. Surely this opens up a major set of issues! Indeed, throughout the three *Critiques*, throughout *Religion* and other writings on history and the political, Kant articulates an open-ended critical interplay among reason, communication, and public freedom in relation to socio-political institutions. This is expressed in

---

[48] With reference to this passage, Höffe notes that "the democracy signaled by the 'agreement of free citizens' may on no account be understood empirically, as though a majority ruling were relevant to reason and metaphysics." Höffe, *Kant's Cosmopolitan Theory of Law and Peace*, p.217. It is important, as Höffe stresses, to avoid conflating open public discourse with an immediate tyranny of the majority: Kant takes a long-term view, wherein the gradual exposure of methods and knowledge claims to open assessment will give resolution to the scope and findings of reason. Further, in the context of this discussion, Höffe notes Kant's reservations concerning "direct democracy," especially the risk of this turning into "a dictatorship, the very opposite of a republic" (*ibid.*).

[49] O'Neill remarks that "the tribunal provides an appropriate image for a critique or judging of reason. If Kant depicts the authority of reason as a tribunal that judges and deliberates, then presumably he thinks that reason too does not consist of algorithms for thinking or acting, which can be formulated as abstract rules." O'Neill, *Constructions of Reason*, p.18.

more concrete terms, for example, in *Anthropology from a Pragmatic Point of View* (1798), where Kant argues that the *principle of publicity* requires that we maintain "*freedom of the press.*" He also restates the interconnection between open, publicly sustained communicative media and the cultivation of more reasonable viewpoints. "For if this freedom is denied," he stresses, "we are deprived at the same time of a great means of testing the correctness of our own judgments, and we are exposed to error" (A, 7:128–29). It is crucial that this principle of publicity, supporting freedom of the press and freedom of expression, is correlated with the program of combating error. This means that publicity is intertwined with the pursuit of *truth*; this is not surprising, given that truth and truthfulness are cornerstones of Kant's ethical and political thinking. Moreover, in such comments, the overriding concern is whether the political and civil structures of a society can nourish reason, truth, and freedom, or whether these are suppressed. These analyses pertain directly to religious ideas and institutions, and Kant applies the criteria of freedom and truth to religion in his later analyses.

No less significantly, Kant also rejects a dictatorial authority on the part of reason, and this further reinforces his advocacy for a communicative and public model for rationally adjudicating truth claims (see A823/B851 and A829/B857). Kant differentiates the critical philosophy from the self-enclosed metaphysics attacked at the beginning of the book. He also discerns a form of closed thinking in the antithetical, but equally sweeping assertions of the skeptics. The critical mode of thinking, emphasizing the interplay of freedom and reason in the public domain and not simply assuming reason as the *a priori* endowment of isolated individuals (and even less the prerogative of a few privileged individuals), is an essential theme running through his work. The presence of these statements at the opening and penultimate sections of the first *Critique* provides a vital interpretive framework for grasping how inquiries into knowledge, metaphysics, and ethics conjoin within a social and political vision of a potentially autonomous humanity.

I have noted that Kant's approach to these matters is often characterized by the use of broadly judicial terms and imagery. At another point, he states that "one can regard the critique of pure reason as the true court of justice for all controversies of pure reason." The task of this court is to determine "what is lawful [*die Rechtsame*] in reason in general." Expanding on the metaphor of warring factions, he argues that without this process of adjudication, "reason is as it were in a state of nature, and it cannot make its assertions and claims valid or secure them except through war." By contrast with this pre-political state of nature, critique provides the necessary rules for determining the scope and ends of reason, and hence "grants us the peace of a state of law" (A751/B779). Following this passage, Kant makes a series of related points that are of crucial import. In opposition to the figurative state of nature in which each is pitted against all others engendering "a state of injustice and violence," he proposes that the state of law "limits our freedom in such a way that it can be consistent with the freedom of everyone else and thereby with the common good." This theme of mutual freedom under just laws is central: it is the strongest alternative to the Hobbesian argument that the anarchy of the state of nature can only be counteracted by the imposition of absolute sovereignty. Kant adds that public communication of one's views is "an original right of human reason, which recognizes no other judge than universal reason itself, in which everyone has a voice" (A752/B780). These judicial and legislative terms also link epistemology with a political level of inquiry. Most essential is the description of "universal human reason" as including the voice of all, thereby linking universalizability with inclusiveness and open communication. I am proposing that these inquiries into the scope and limits of human knowledge, and into the traditions of thought that transgress those limitations, are undertaken not only with the aim of establishing a self-reflective and empirically informed epistemological model; these epistemological inquiries also have ethical and political significance in establishing a framework for open, truthful, and autonomous human interrelations, inclusive of all.

Insofar as the social and political domains are, in any instance, constituted not only by free-floating structures of power and knowledge but also by individuals who internalize and act on these, then epistemological and political concerns are necessarily interconnected. We might pose the Kantian problem as follows: how can we establish a more adequate paradigm for either ethical or political theory, or for any form of practice based thereon, without clearing away the unfettered speculations of the metaphysicians and theologians, as well as the accompanying reliance on unquestioned tradition and authority as the necessary bulwarks of order and virtue? In essence, there can be no well-informed public discourse unless the mantle of sacrosanct authority assumed by those perpetuating historically transmitted dogmas is stripped away, unless authority based on the inherited worldviews of both ecclesial and state powers is publicly questioned and fairly adjudicated, and unless transparent methodologies for the free use of reason by all are established. This critical endeavor is the *sine qua non* for a Kantian approach to both ethics and politics, and it forms the heart of his contribution to the task of enlightenment.

ENLIGHTENMENT, FREEDOM, AND PUBLICITY

The emphasis on open public inquiry in the first *Critique* is also evident throughout Kant's shorter writings on social and political issues. We saw that in response to the deadlock between traditional metaphysics and skepticism, Kant advocated a new path of inquiry associated with the critical philosophy and the *task of enlightenment*. Since neither traditional metaphysics nor the skeptical philosophy of his time can generate this enlightenment, a new way of thinking must arise.

From among Kant's shorter works, one of the most important articulations of this approach is the essay of 1784, "An Answer to the Question: What Is Enlightenment?" published precisely between the first and second editions of the *Critique of Pure Reason*. This is often classified as an occasional piece written in response to rising public debate in late eighteenth-century Germany about the nature of *Aufklärung*, and examined in relation to the contemporary views of Mendelssohn, Reinhold, Fichte, and others.[50] To be sure, Kant's reflections appear toward the end of an era of dramatically heightened questioning and exploration, without which it could not have occurred. In this respect, Jonathan Israel details how "after 1650, a general process of rationalization and secularization set in which rapidly overthrew theology's age-old hegemony in the world of study, slowly but surely eradicated magic and belief in the supernatural from Europe's intellectual culture, and led a few openly to challenge everything from the past."[51] These historical developments provided the basis for Kant's work, and it is important to retain a sense of this larger variegated program of enlightenment. Nevertheless, Kant's approach to the issue of enlightenment is interconnected with themes that are vital to the critical philosophy as a whole. Therefore I will emphasize the internal consistency of Kant's arguments rather than their classification within a generic "enlightenment project."[52]

---

[50] For representative essays by other Enlightenment-era thinkers, see James Schmidt, ed., *What Is Enlightenment? Eighteenth-Century Answers and Twentieth-Century Questions* (Berkeley: University of California Press, 1996).

[51] Jonathan Israel, *Radical Enlightenment: Philosophy and the Making of Modernity, 1650–1750* (Oxford University Press, 2001), p.4. This monumental exposition of the radical Enlightenment is continued in *Enlightenment Contested*.

[52] Sankar Muthu dismantles the stereotype of monolithic Enlightenment thinking, arguing that "'the Enlightenment' *as such* and the notion of an overarching 'Enlightenment project' simply

Kant's "Enlightenment" essay amplifies the social and political concerns subtending the critical philosophy, clarifies interconnections among reason, religion, and the political, and shows the abiding relevance of these concerns. He interrogates the parochial ideas and institutions undergirding unjust societies, seeking to dislodge these with more universalizable and hence fairer principles. The essay opens with the famous call for an autonomous exercise of our rational faculties: "*Minority* [*Unmündigkeit*] is inability to make use of one's own understanding without direction from another. This minority is *self-incurred* when its cause lies not in lack of understanding but in lack of resolution and courage to use it without direction from another. *Sapere aude!* [from Horace's *Epodes* 1.2, 40: 'dare to be wise'] Have courage to make use of your *own* understanding! is thus the motto of enlightenment" (E, 8:35). This exhortation stresses the free use of our critical faculties in open public discourse, and the need to overcome tendencies to abrogate this freedom in deferment to hegemonic power. The problem of assuming the status of *minors*, in which we fail to exercise our potential capacities for rationality and autonomy, is also shown to be simultaneously personal and political in nature. The call to courage indicates a response to the fear of autonomy instilled in large segments of the population.

It is simply incorrect to accuse Kant of blaming the masses for their failure to engage in the task of enlightenment and to liberate themselves from the shackles of superstition and servitude. For example, a recent commentator follows the views of J. G. Hamann in declaring that "Kant is saying that those in need of enlightenment are immature, deprived of the right to speak for themselves, through their own fault."[53] To the contrary, the fact that Kant immediately turns to an inquiry into the role of political and ecclesial authorities in perpetuating immaturity indicates that the problem is far more complex than simply a failure of courage on the part of the benighted masses. If people allow themselves to remain "minors for life" then "it becomes easy for others to set themselves up as their guardians [*Vormündern*]" (E, 8:35). He explicitly indicates the culpability of those seeking dominance by maintaining some elements of a

---

do not exist" (*Enlightenment against Empire*, p.264). This does not mean that there is no continuity among various thinkers of this epoch: it simply warns us not to collapse their unique views into an overriding rubric. In a related vein, Goetschel notes that enlightenment describes an ongoing task: "the word enlightenment [*Aufklärung*] thus shows itself to be a term of *process*" (*Constituting Critique*, p.150).

[53] Garrett Green, "Modern Culture Comes of Age: Hamann versus Kant on the Root Metaphor of Enlightenment," in Schmidt, ed., *What Is Enlightenment?*, p.293.

population, including women, in a subservient position: "That by far the greatest part of humankind (including the entire fair sex) should hold the step toward majority to be not only troublesome but also highly dangerous will soon be seen to by those guardians who have kindly taken it upon themselves to supervise them" (E, 8:35). Hence the guardians of a people, i.e., those with political authority, have a vested interest in instilling diffidence and self-doubt; they utilize psychological and doctrinal as well as physical means to keep others in a condition of minority. It is noteworthy that, along with his focus on individual responsibility, Kant is sensitive to the oppression of women and other disempowered groups at the hands of these so-called guardians.

Moreover, Kant endeavors to reform the operative principles of political authorities: if they are "themselves incapable of any enlightenment," then the public may be "suitably stirred up" (E, 8:36). Those self-appointed guardians are by no means a vanguard of enlightenment; their authoritarianism may provoke an enlightened reaction among members of a community. There may also be an implicit reference to the guardians in Plato's *Republic* here, especially since the first *Critique* discusses this text with reference to an ethical society. Kant is consistent in questioning authoritarian structures inhibiting human potential, illustrating how psychological states of dependency and immaturity are intertwined with cultural and political institutions. In this respect, Sankar Muthu notes that "Kant's hatred of paternalism" has implications for addressing the relations *among cultures* as much as authorities with members of a given society. "Kant was just as troubled by the paternalism that European imperial powers exhibited toward non-European peoples as he was by the paternalism of political and ecclesial authorities that disciplined and infantilized individuals within European nations."[54] This interpretation is substantiated by a sustained analysis in which Kant is discussed as the main figure, along with Diderot and Herder, representing a trend in Enlightenment thinking that opposed European imperialism.[55] Similarly, Pheng Cheah responds to various postcolonial criticisms of enlightenment rationality.

[54] Muthu, *Enlightenment against Empire*, pp.172 and 180.
[55] Kant directly attacks imperialism and colonialism in several places. In *The Metaphysics of Morals*, he writes of the settlement of Europeans in lands inhabited by indigenous peoples, and argues that "this settlement may not take place by force but only by contract, and indeed by a contract that does not take advantage of the ignorance of these inhabitants with respect to ceding their lands." Moreover, noting the specious rationalizations that seek to justify the use of force for the alleged purpose of "civilizing" these indigenous peoples, Kant insists that "all these supposedly good intentions cannot wash away the stain of injustice in the means used for them" (MM, 6:353; Kant also critiques colonialist attitudes in *Perpetual Peace*; see PP, 8:358–59).

In contrast to the instrumental rationality often associated with "the enlightenment," Cheah emphasizes enlightenment as "the attitude of self-questioning that allows one to escape self-incurred tutelage (à la Kant)."[56] This concurs with Kant's Rousseau-inspired turn to an ethical-political approach to knowledge. The main point is that, far from casting blame on downtrodden peoples, Kant calls for an enlightening of public institutions so as to foster a milieu of openness and questioning conducive to the individual exercise of autonomy.

Confining ourselves to the issue of intra-societal relations, there are certainly psychological as well as explicitly political factors at work in suppressing the pursuit of freedom and truth characterizing enlightenment. Kant is not inattentive to human needs for consolation and guidance in the face of life's difficulties; these needs are a major source sustaining heteronomous religious worldviews as well as paternalism and authoritarianism. To ignore Kant's consistent focus on the mutually sustaining interplay between subjective needs and authoritarian structures is to grossly misrepresent his argument. Neither one-sided approach to heteronomy can be warranted: that which places responsibility solely on the failures of individuals in isolation from the effects of social-political institutions, or the antithetical approach viewing social and political forces deterministically and absolving individuals of responsibility. Hence an enlightened reason is inimical to predetermined and formulaic uses of reason: "Precepts and formulas, those *mechanical instruments* of a rational use, or rather misuse, of his [a minor's] natural endowments, are the ball and chain of an everlasting minority" (E, 8:36; italics added). The minor is not simply one who has failed to develop his or her rational faculties. Instead, there is a constrained employment of reason that restricts the scope of inquiry and the pursuit of truth according to the well-worn pathways of established traditions and ideologies. It is significant that Kant characterizes this deficient use of reason as *mechanical*, further indicating his resistance to strictly instrumental applications of reason and to the dehumanizing worldviews sustained thereby. Reason itself can be made subservient to fixed authority structures as a way to inhibit the liberating imperative of enlightenment. This is the most insidious use of the vehicle of our freedom against freedom, and it directly connects with Kant's critiques of speculative metaphysics and theology. It is this misuse against

---

[56] Pheng Cheah, *Spectral Nationality: Passages of Freedom from Kant to Postcolonial Literatures of Liberation* (New York: Columbia University Press, 2003), pp.267–68.

which much of the critical philosophy is directed, and which exemplifies the interpenetration of epistemological and political concerns.

Having advocated autonomous reason resisting control from external authorities and rote formulae, Kant turns to the deeper political implications of his argument. "But that a public should enlighten itself [*selbst aufkläre*] is more possible; indeed this is almost inevitable, if only it is left its freedom" (E, 8:36). Our rational endowments do not assure freedom; the need to establish political conditions that enable this capacity to be cultivated and exercised publicly remains paramount. Kant proposes that "for this enlightenment ... nothing is required but *freedom*," and calls this "the least harmful of anything that could be called freedom." Most importantly, this enlightened freedom is contrasted with the "lawless freedom" of the hypothetical state of nature. The public use of reason emphasizes the mutually supportive interplay between reason and the political: "The *public* use [*der öffentliche Gebrauch*] of one's reason must always be free, and it alone can bring about enlightenment among human beings" (E, 8:37). As noted, the first *Critique* formulates a public and testable approach to knowledge and truth, which is summarized toward the end of the work: "All knowing (if it concerns an object of reason alone) can be communicated" (A829/B857). The open exercise of reason requiring freedom of expression is profoundly interconnected with public conditions.[57] Hence Kant's proclamation on the part of enlightenment has a wide and variegated audience. He is addressing average people who are encouraged to cultivate their faculties for open inquiry, as well as public authorities who establish the political circumstances whereby enlightenment is either fostered or suppressed.

A thematically related essay published two years after the essay on enlightenment ("What does it mean to orient oneself in thinking?" of 1786), clarifies the interdependency of reason, speech, and public institutions. Here Kant outlines three interrelated aspects of the *freedom to think*:

The freedom to think is opposed **first** of all to *civil compulsion*. Of course it is said that the freedom to *speak* or to *write* could be taken from us by a superior power, but the freedom to *think* cannot be. Yet how much and how correctly would we *think* if we did not think as it were in community with others to whom we *communicate* our thoughts, and who communicate theirs with us! Thus one

---

[57] Onora O'Neill notes that focusing on Kant's "defense of freedom of opinion ... fails to face the central puzzle of the text, which is that Kant equates enlightenment not with reason but with an oddly characterized practice of *reasoning publicly*" ("Vindicating Reason," p.298; italics added).

can very well say that this external power which wrenches away people's freedom publicly to *communicate* their thoughts also takes from them the freedom to *think* – that single gem remaining to us in the midst of all the burdens of civil life, through which alone we can devise means of overcoming all the evils of our condition. (OT, 8:144)

This comment adds crucial nuances concerning the inter-dependency of thought and speech. Rather than proclaiming an abstracted faculty of reason uncontaminated by the political, and far from chastising the poor masses for their failure to have the courage to be free, Kant shows that external constraints can adversely affect even our inner capacities and modes of thinking. Most importantly, the concluding point indicates how freedom of thought is connected with the task of ameliorating the evils of existing political conditions.

Kant then argues that "**Second**, freedom to think is also taken in a sense in which it is opposed to *compulsion over conscience [Gewissenszwang]*." Here the intrusion of the political into the psychological explicitly pertains to our capacity for ethical reflection. Moreover, this type of compulsion need not be enforced by external coercion, such as publication bans or the physical force exercised by civil authorities. This analysis explicates constraint as operating through the promulgation of ideas and worldviews, hence as functioning internally as well as externally. Constraint can be implemented not only by government officials but by pedagogues and pundits of various kinds:

[E]ven without having external power some citizens set themselves up as having the custody of others in religious affairs, and instead of arguing they know how to ban every examination of reason by their early influence on people's minds [*auf die Gemüter*], through prescribed formulas of belief accompanied by the anxious fear of *the dangers of one's own investigation*. (OT, 8:145)[58]

Coercion is exercised, particularly though not exclusively in matters of religion, by early indoctrination, cultivating rote formulaic belief, inducing fearfulness concerning autonomous inquiry, and propagating

---

[58] The term *Gemüt* is used throughout Kant's writings, and is not fully rendered by "mind." *Gemüt* can mean mind, but also has associations with nature, disposition, and even feeling. Caygill stresses that "*Gemüt* is a key term in Kant's philosophy … It does not mean 'mind' or 'soul' in the Cartesian sense of a thinking substance, but denotes instead *a corporeal awareness of sensation and self-affection*." Caygill, *Kant Dictionary*, p.210; italics added. This special significance of a mental receptivity connected with sensory experience is crucial. Caygill therefore stresses that "*Gemüt* does not designate a substance (whether material or ideal) but is the position or place of the *Gemütskräfte* (the *Gemüt*'s powers) of sensibility, imagination, understanding and reason" (*ibid.*).

predominant assumptions through cultural media. These are themes that reappear in greater detail in *Religion*, where pejorative references to authorities influencing people's minds (*die Gemüter*) appear repeatedly. At this point, Kant touches on the ideological qualities attached to all forms of indoctrination, and reiterates his concern with formulaic thinking, indicating that this is anything but a marginal theme. He describes how ingrained patterns of thinking become operative within our personalities, having been internalized from the worldviews of parents, guardians, and other cultural authorities. These entrenched norms inhibit our capacity to raise doubts or provide counterviews (this is why the theme of *courage* is prominent). The individual and political cannot be fully separated: freedom and enlightenment are simultaneously a matter of public institutions and private attitudes.

Finally, in contrast to what opposes freedom, Kant turns to a more positive definition: "**Third**, freedom in thinking signifies the subjection of reason to no laws except *those which it gives itself*; and its opposite is the maxim of a **lawless use** of reason [*gesetzlosen Gebrauchs der Vernunft*]" (OT, 8:145). This presents autonomy as the auto-generation, through reason, of universalizable laws. It is instructive that this autonomous reason is sharply differentiated from *lawless reason*, which evokes the *lawless freedom* of the state of nature. In an oblique reference to speculative metaphysics and theology, Kant mockingly associates lawless reason with the putative "genius" who claims a privileged vision of reality. This misuse of reason overlooks that the concepts of the understanding must be applied to sense-based intuitions in order to generate knowledge. Picking up the theme of self-appointed guardians, Kant warns that "if reason will not subject itself to the laws it gives itself, *it has to bow under the yoke of laws given by another*; for without any law, nothing – not even nonsense – can play its game for long" (OT, 8:145; italics added). He follows this comment by referring again to the "bold flights" of genius as giving rise to enthusiasm (*Schwärmerei*) and illumination (*Erleuchtung*) which declare that "reason's superior lawgiving is invalid." By repudiating reason, which "alone can command validly for everyone, a confusion of language [*Sprachverwirrung*] must soon arise among them" in which "each one now follows his own inspiration [*Eingebung*]" (OT, 8:145). This echoes the Tower of Babel imagery in the *Critique*'s account of lawless nomads. Kant also brings enthusiasm into a dynamic relation with superstition, noting that the chaos of varying illuminations soon gives way to "the complete subjection of reason to facts, i.e. **superstition** [*Aberglaube*], because this at least has the *form of law* [*gesetzliche Form*] and so allows tranquility to be restored" (OT, 8:145).[59] Superstition represents heteronomous order intervening when reason fails to give itself laws. It allies itself with the parochial norms and laws of given societies (i.e., to "facts") to maintain order – to the detriment of any progressive change. This critical distinction between autonomous laws of reason and the yoke of externally based laws is essential to understanding the task of enlightenment.

The enlightenment essay, like the *Critique*, emphasizes religion as a public phenomenon with extraordinary political import, providing a crucial test case for freedom of thought and communication in the pursuit of truth. In a typically balanced if cautious manner, Kant allows that religious specialists might not be completely unrestricted in making official proclamations within the confines of their specific communities: "a clergyman is bound to deliver his discourse to the pupils in his catechism class and to his congregation in accordance with the creed of the church he serves, for he was employed by it on that condition." A few lines later Kant concludes that "an appointed teacher's use of reason before his congregation is merely a *private use*," since a congregation is still only a "domestic gathering." Following this portrayal of official duties as occurring within a private context, he immediately turns to the status of clergy as rational beings with definite public responsibilities. He sharply differentiates between the freedom that should accompany public duties and agreements made privately: "as a scholar he has complete freedom and is even called upon to communicate to the public all his carefully examined and well-intentioned thoughts about what is erroneous in that creed and his suggestions for a better arrangement of the religious and ecclesiastical body" (E, 8:38). In this way, the freedom of public intellectuals and religious practitioners is a means whereby the doctrines of traditions might be critically ameliorated.

Anticipating the hermeneutical endeavors of *Religion*, Kant indicates that there may be interpretive strategies for applying autonomous reason as the criterion for understanding the inherited representations (i.e., symbols, narratives) of traditions. Clergy "can nevertheless undertake to deliver [the precepts of a religious community] because it is still not altogether impossible that truth may lie concealed in them, and in any case there is at least nothing contradictory to inner religion [*der innern Religion*] present in them" (E, 8:38). At this point, I will simply highlight

---

[59] In Hume's *Dialogues Concerning Natural Religion*, Philo similarly observes that "fits of excessive enthusiastic joy, by exhausting the spirits, always prepare the way for equal fits of superstitious terror and dejection." *Dialogues and Natural History of Religion*, p.128.

this notion of inner religion and its association with potential truths, specifically ethical truths, contained within traditions. I should also reiterate that this interpretive approach plays a *critical* function in relation to established heteronomous religion. In this way, the existing resources of traditions are drawn into the critical project of cultivating more enlightened societies. However, Kant does not only advance hermeneutical strategies. He unequivocally advocates open public inquiry in matters of religion: "a clergyman in the *public use* of his reason … enjoys an unrestricted freedom to make use of his own reason and to speak in his own person." If this autonomous use of reason is not permitted, an inherent contradiction arises between the proclaimed authority of an established religion and its refusal to allow public discussion. This ultimately undermines that religious community's claims to speak in the name of truth: "For that the guardians of the people (in spiritual matters) should themselves be minors is an absurdity [*Ungereimtheit*] that amounts to the perpetuation of absurdities" (E, 8:38). These arguments are not merely critical of authoritarian structures in politics and religion. They also draw upon ethical criteria in assessing statutory laws with reference to consistency, inclusivity, and justness.

Discussing a hypothetical scenario that tests the validity of statutory obligations, Kant asks: "should not a society of clergymen … be authorized to bind itself to an unalterable creed [*unveränderliches Symbol*], in order to carry on an unceasing guardianship [*Obervormundschaft*] over each of its members and by means of them over the people, and even to perpetuate this?" (E, 8:38). Unhesitatingly, he concludes that such an agreement "is quite impossible" because it would work "to keep all further enlightenment from the human race forever." It would therefore be "null and void, even if it were ratified by the supreme power" (E, 8:39). *No putative supreme authority has the legitimate right to impose repressive and unjust laws.* In the course of this analysis, Kant also makes a parenthetical remark that is pregnant with additional significance: "One age cannot bind itself and conspire to put the following one into such a condition that it would be impossible for it to enlarge its cognitions [*Erkenntnisse zu erweitern*] (especially in such urgent matters) and to purify them of errors, and generally to make further progress in enlightenment" (E, 8:39). This is a crucial point, with profound ethical implications concerning our responsibility for future generations. Moreover, this matter of *enlarging cognitions* encapsulates the intertwining of epistemological, ethical, and political concerns with truth addressed here. Attempts to coerce a populace into conformity by imposing ecclesiastical dogmas would constitute nothing less than "a crime against human nature, whose original vocation [*ursprüngliche Bestimmung*] lies precisely in such progress" (E, 8:39). Imposed dogmas block open public inquiry, thereby inhibiting future progress in enlightenment, i.e., in our capacity to think and choose guided by reason and the pursuit of truth. Here Kant employs a regulative or guiding principle of an original vocation for progress in enlightenment. Regulative principles, as I will later clarify in greater detail, provide critical guides for analyzing social and political conditions and their impact on this progress.

At the end of this discussion of religion, Kant reiterates the deep historical connections between religious and political authorities: "I have put the main point of enlightenment, of people's emergence from their self-incurred minority, chiefly in *matters of religion* because our rulers have no interest in playing guardian over their subjects with respect to the arts and sciences and also because that minority, being the most harmful, is also the most disgraceful of all" (E, 8:41).[60] The case of religion is paradigmatic for instituting open, principled discourse in the public sphere. I want to propose that this is a guiding thread for his more detailed inquiries into the interconnections among knowledge, religion, and the political. While Kant specifically discusses the situation of Christian clergy in his own time and place, his comments have a wide-ranging application, *mutatis mutandis*, to all religious traditions and all societies. Kant's inquiry into progress in enlightenment is informed by an underlying confidence in our inherent ability to liberate ourselves from oppressive and stultifying heteronomy, whether epistemological, spiritual, or directly political. "People gradually work their way out of barbarism [*Rohigkeit*] of their own accord if only one does not intentionally contrive to keep them in it" (E, 8:41). The reference to barbarism describes an unenlightened status characterized by passive acquiescence in unjust statutory laws supported by specious rationalizations. Such a condition can be imposed on a populace by political despotism, using ideological as well as physical forms of coercion. In developing this point, Kant conveys the regulative idea of ethical-political progress

---

[60] Subsequent history showed that totalitarian regimes, such as those of Nazi Germany, the Soviet Union, and Communist China, in addition to suppressing or controlling religion, sought to control aesthetics. These facts of history show, if anything, that the correlation between the political and various cultural forms of representation (including religion and aesthetics as well as mass media) is even more important than Kant could see from his historical vantage point. See Jean-Luc Nancy, *The Ground of the Image* (New York: Fordham University Press, 2005), pp.38ff., for a trenchant critique of "Nazi representation."

toward truth and justice in more figurative terms. He notes that in the Prussia of his time a significant degree of civil liberty is *not* in evidence, but expresses hope that within this casing of social control a freedom of spirit may be growing:

> Thus when nature has unwrapped, from under this hard shell, the seed for which she cares most tenderly, namely the propensity and calling to *think* freely [*den Hang und Beruf zum Freien Denken*], the latter gradually works back upon the mentality [*Sinnesart*] of the people (which thereby gradually becomes capable of *freedom* in acting) and eventually even upon the principles of *government*, which finds it profitable to itself to treat the human being, *who is now more than a machine*, in keeping with his dignity. (E, 8:41–42)

There is a propensity for autonomous use of reason in all human beings, and this potential to regulate ourselves by principles, rather than be controlled by others, is a key element in human dignity. Autonomy can potentially germinate even under somewhat oppressive external conditions; however, the germ of freedom will properly emerge only within social and political conditions that do not actively inhibit its development. Additionally, the unfolding of freedom in thinking enables freedom of action (meaning the freedom to act *ethically*, according to autonomously generated moral laws rather than the dictates of externally imposed authority). Finally, the inner mentality of a people is inherently connected with their activities in relation with others, so that an inner moral orientation cannot ultimately be segregated from participation in the public realm.

The critique of heteronomous authority is correlated with advocacy for forms of government and civil society that more adequately foster autonomy. The underlying principle of such polities is encapsulated in an oft-repeated formulation: "The touchstone of whatever can be decided upon as law for a people lies in the question: whether a people could impose such a law upon itself" (E, 8:39; cf. TP, 8:297). This articulates an open circuit between our autonomous capacity for law-giving and political forms that either block or cultivate that autonomy. Politically instituting mutual autonomy is essential to emerging from the status of *machines*. What characterizes a machine is subjection to external control (heteronomy); in more contemporary terms we would say that it is programmed. If reduced to the malleable status of machines, people are not treated with respect and dignity, or as ends in themselves; they are devalued and dehumanized. This subjugation can be ideational and cultural as much as physical: hence the theme of rote or mechanical thinking instilled in a populace by authorities reappears with even greater significance. If Kant is a major spokesperson for *enlightenment*, what he is advocating is a rethinking of civic and cultural institutions in a way that establishes principles of public questioning, open dialogue, and rationally self-instituted laws by and for all.

This model of Enlightenment is most certainly *not* reducible to the dominance of instrumental reason and its now omnipresent offspring, technology, as many critics have claimed. James Schmidt has responded to the reduction of enlightenment to a disconnected model of reason based on the metaphor of vision often used to describe instrumental reason. By contrast with this stereotype, Schmidt highlights the significance of themes of *speech* and *communication* in Kant's enlightenment essay. He notes that Kant "did not invoke those images of light that have cast such a shadow over recent criticisms of the Enlightenment. He instead talked about speech. For him, enlightenment demanded not a world in which everything stood naked to the light but rather a world in which it was possible to speak without fear."[61] Schmidt invokes the image of Jeremy Bentham's all-seeing Panopticon overseers (as discussed in Michel Foucault's *Discipline and Punish*).[62] He affirms that Kant's emphasis on open public discourse, which is by definition multi-faceted, contentious, and open-ended, actually stands in sharp contrast with the Panopticon.[63] Addressing the way Bentham's image encapsulates a hyper-rationalist dream of a "world without shadows," Schmidt notes that "there might be something pathological in that dream: for to want to see everything is to aspire to the standpoint of God or to that of the guardian in the Panopticon's tower."[64] This is crucial for understanding the critical philosophy. As I have indicated, one of Kant's main concerns in the critique of metaphysics is undermining the "god's-eye view" of the dogmatists, which extends beyond any possible experience and beyond the limits reason sets for itself. Kant wants to bring reason back to earth and into the company of humans and their finite conditions, while at the same time providing a vision that infuses our collective imagination and our interpersonal relations with a dynamic capacity for amelioration.

This public, dialogical model is crucial in separating Kant's thinking from traditional dogmatic metaphysics with its speculative claims to knowledge, from locally and parochially focused communitarians bound to an exclusive tradition, and from those who prioritize an instrumental

---

[61] James Schmidt, "Introduction: What Is Enlightenment? A Question, Its Context, and Some Consequences" in Schmidt, ed., *What Is Enlightenment?*, p.29.
[62] Michel Foucault, *Discipline and Punish: The Birth of the Prison* (New York: Vintage Books, 1979), pp.195ff.
[63] Schmidt, "Introduction: What Is Enlightenment?," p. 28.
[64] Ibid., pp.30–31.

use of rationality in the advance of technology as an end in itself without reference to human well-being. This ethical and political line of thinking is also explicitly formulated in the *Critique of the Power of Judgment*. Kant proposes "the following maxims of the common human understanding … 1. To think for oneself; 2. To think in the position of everyone else; 3. Always to think in accord with oneself" (CJ, 5:294). These are some of the key regulative guidelines for broadening the vistas of our ethical and political sensibilities. He then explicates these maxims in a way that provides a template for our subsequent analyses:

> The first is the maxim of the **unprejudiced** way of thinking [*vorurteilfreien*], the second of the **broad-minded** way [*die erweiterten*], the third that of the **consistent** way [*die consequenten Denkungsart*]. The first is the maxim of a reason that is never **passive**. The tendency toward the latter, hence toward heteronomy of reason [*zur Heteronomie der Vernunft*], is called **prejudice**; and the greatest prejudice of all is that of representing reason as if it were not subject to the rules of nature on which the understanding grounds it by means of its own essential law: i.e., **superstition**. Liberation from superstition is called **enlightenment**, since, although this designation is also applied to liberation from prejudices in general, it is superstition above all (*in sensu eminenti*) that deserves to be called a prejudice, since the blindness to which superstition leads, which indeed it even demands as an obligation, is what makes most evident the need to be led by others, hence the condition of a passive reason. (CJ, 5:294–95)

This crucial passage indicates how progress in enlightenment is antithetical to the imposition of supposedly universal viewpoints and norms attained through a dissociated use of reason. Kant opposes the passive attitude of being controlled by others; yet he recognizes that overcoming parochialism and prejudice requires that we engage with the views and situations of others as much as possible.

"The greatest prejudice of all" is superstition, because this is the antithesis of autonomous inquiry. As we have seen, superstition is linked with a despotic ethical-political orientation: it entails the need to be led by others, and hence the passive internalization of parochial norms. Throughout his work, Kant advocates comparative experience and open reflection as central to breaking free of the parochial attitudes he calls "**narrow-minded**." Hence, concerning the second maxim of a broad-minded, inclusive mode of reflection, he further states that:

> [T]he issue here is not the faculty of cognition, but the **way of thinking** needed to make a purposive use of it … which reveals a man of a **broad-minded way of thinking** [*erweiterter Denkungsart*] if he sets himself apart from the subjective private conditions of the judgment, within which so many others are as

if bracketed, and reflects on his own judgment from a **universal standpoint** [*allgemeinen Standpunkt*] (which he can only determine by putting himself into the standpoint of others [*in den Standpunkt anderen versetz*]). (CJ, 5:295)

This articulates a key distinction between knowledge generated by the categories of understanding in relation to sense-impressions (i.e., cognition), and the ways of thinking that inform our ethical and political modes of relating with others. Moreover, Kant insists that cultivating inclusive egalitarian universal perspectives – which is always a work in progress – requires engaging a multiplicity of individual and cultural viewpoints. Therefore universalization is an interactive process requiring a principled assessment of one's own perspectives and priorities in relation with others. This dynamic approach is sharply contrasted with two seemingly antithetical forms of rigid subjective judgment that close off access to other perspectives: either the communitarian one that immerses itself in a specific culturally determined worldview, or that of the abstract universal that does not engage the multiple standpoints of others. Kant's model differs from either of these because he recognizes that we cannot progress along a path of universalization without engaging with others. As I will illustrate in the following chapters, universality is the antithesis of heteronomously imposing a particular standpoint upon others (i.e., it is not imperialist).[65] It requires reflection and judgment based on the widest possible experience, guided by regulative principles.

In advocating a process of emerging from a condition of minority by learning to think for ourselves, Kant engages the problem of *prejudice* associated with insular modes of thinking and relating. However, contrary to the judgment of Hans-Georg Gadamer, Kant is by no means abandoning historical and cultural richness in favor of a disassociated model of reason.[66] Kant acknowledges that we always begin, as embodied

---

[65] Stephen Bronner emphasizes that although a debased form of "universalism can be found in western imperialist propaganda … such universalism is not universal at all: it lacks reciprocity, an open discourse, and a concern with protecting the individual from the arbitrary exercise of power." He therefore argues that reciprocity "is what differentiates Enlightenment universalism from its imitators, provides it with a self-critical quality, and enables it to contest Euro-centrism and the prevalent belief in a 'clash of civilizations'." Stephen Eric Bronner, *Reclaiming the Enlightenment: Toward a Politics of Radical Engagement* (New York: Columbia University Press, 2004), p.xii.

[66] In Gadamer's words: "there is one prejudice of the Enlightenment that defines its essence: the fundamental prejudice of the Enlightenment is the prejudice against prejudice itself, which denies tradition its power." Hans-Georg Gadamer, *Truth and Method*, trans. Joel Weinsheimer and Donald G. Marshall (New York: Crossroad, 1992), p.270. While Gadamer rightly seeks to cultivate a historical understanding of reason in relation to traditions, he misrepresents the Enlightenment and especially the Kantian project of bringing critical principles and laws to bear upon these traditions in an effort at rectifying their contemporary influence.

historical subjects, with certain forms of social conditioning such as pre-judgments derived from religious and political sources. The task of Enlightenment does not simply dismiss these existing conditions; it takes the more circumscribed worldviews of given religious-political configurations as the necessary starting points for critical reflection in the pursuit of truth and justice. This is an argument with significant implications for engaging not only a multiplicity of individual views, but also the diversity of cultures and religions. The role of principles and laws in making judgments is essential to Kant's overall arguments. Freedom, equal rights, and respect for others based on the principle of human dignity are the cornerstones of the Kantian ethical-political model. Here the "Orientation" essay is again relevant. While discussing the importance of using freedom lawfully, Kant concludes with a footnote that links these concerns to the Enlightenment essay: "*Thinking for oneself* means seeking the supreme touchstone of truth in oneself (i.e. in one's own reason); and the maxim of always thinking for oneself is **enlightenment**" (OT, 8:146). To clarify that he is not simply invoking an individualistic model of reason, Kant adds: "To make use of one's own reason means no more than to ask oneself, whenever one is supposed to assume something, whether one could find it feasible to make the ground or the rule on which one assumes it into a universal principle for the use of reason" (OT, 8:146). This invocation of the categorical imperative as a guideline for judgment is crucial to harmonizing one's autonomy with that of all others.

KANT AND THE FRENCH REVOLUTION

The categorical imperative as a reflective process governed by other-directedness expresses autonomously generated ethical-political laws, and can counteract self-serving or solipsistic attitudes (as I elucidate in chapter 5). Hence, while Kant consistently advocates social-political transformation, this exemplifies justice only when guided by moral laws. This view is evident in Kant's qualified advocacy for the French Revolution, as demonstrating the human capacity to change the world according to ideas and principles.[67] Given the influence of Rousseau's concerns with human rights and just political institutions, it is not surprising that Kant would support efforts at progressively transforming a major European society. Hence, in the third *Critique* (1790) he refers to "a recently undertaken

---

[67] This is nicely stated by Furet: "the Revolution had not only formed traditions and loyalties; it had offered to succeeding generations that unheard of example of a *recreation of society through the actions of men*." Furet, *Revolutionary France: 1770–1880*, p.309; italics added.

fundamental transformation of a great people into a state" as fostering an "organization" in which "each member should certainly be not merely a means, but at the same time also an end" (CJ, 5:375n.). This describes the French Revolution as a movement toward a just society modeled after the principles of equality and mutual freedom characterizing a realm of ends.

At the same time, Kant's support for the Revolution became qualified as the events unfolding in France increasingly gave way to enthusiasm and lawless violence. Some of these concerns were directly expressed in the late *Metaphysics of Morals* (1797), where a long footnote addressed the pivotal issue of regicide. He specifies that "of all the atrocities in overthrowing a state by rebellion, the *assassination* of the monarch is not itself the worst," since this could occur from a fear of retribution. Rather, referring to the case of Louis XVI, Kant argues that "it is the formal *execution* of a monarch that strikes horror in a soul filled with the idea of human rights." This is because execution is undertaken officially and legally (within the laws of the revolutionary state), and therefore institutionalizes "complete overturning of all concepts of right" (MM, 6:321n.). A few lines later, Kant summarizes his views:

> The reason for horror at the thought of the formal execution of a monarch *by his people* is therefore this: that while his *murder* is regarded as only an *exception* to the rule that the people makes its maxim, his *execution* must be regarded as a complete *overturning* of the principles of the relation between a sovereign and his people. (MM, 6:322n.)

While Kant's position is complex, insofar as he makes allowances for the removal of unjust authority, his position on the rule of law is explicit. The execution of Louis XVI is condemned because it violates just principles of law. Since taking the life of another human being is wrong, legally sanctioning regicide is tantamount to introducing corruption into the laws of the state.

Let us expand on these issues to better contextualize Kant's assessment. In opposing the tyranny of absolute monarchy (some manifestations of which were sketched earlier in this chapter), the revolutionaries established forms of counter-hegemony of their own. François Furet argues concerning the Revolution that: "Its political repertoire had never given the slightest opening to legal expressions of disagreement, let alone conflict: the people had appropriated the absolutist heritage and taken the place of the king."[68] This point is important not only in explaining the

[68] *Ibid.*, p.140.

relapse into authoritarianism among many of the revolutionaries, but also because it shows the importance of political principles in shaping actions and institutions. In the aftermath of the initial revolution, French society struggled to establish a regime that recognized and instituted the Rights of Man and the Citizen of 1789. However, this was acted out in terms of various imperfect and conflict-ridden efforts to consolidate individual rights and the emancipation of the individual with "the social bond," in such a way as to express "the general will" (as formulated by Rousseau).[69] Again, for a number of reasons, such as the fact that the social and political structures realizing individual freedoms in relation to the freedoms of all had not been established, and because there was little or no preparation for this model in the history of European society, the rights of individuals rapidly took the form of a despotism of the masses. Furet relates:

> The Revolution had illustrated the risks which lay in conceiving of it [i.e., society] as endowed with a sovereignty based on the agreement of contracting individuals. In fact the Revolution had in the end produced an atomized society of isolated individuals, united on the political level by a general will which was deemed to represent what they had in common; but in reality very quickly subjected to an administrative dictatorship which alone could avert the anarchy that was inseparable from that radical individualism.[70]

In this definitive example, a society seeking to establish individual freedoms without the effective functioning of a constitution establishing the separation of powers and the universal rule of law teetered between anarchy and despotism.

However, we must add to this picture the additional fact that the forces of revolution and emancipation did not simply impose their ideas in an

---

[69] See *ibid.*, pp.73–75. Note in particular Article IV of the Declaration of the Rights of Man: "Liberty consists in being able to do anything as long as it harms no one else" (quoted *ibid.*, p.74), which bears some resemblance to Kant's emphasis on mutual freedom under laws applying equally to all. In contrast to Marx's critique, this declaration does not regard the individual "as an isolated monad," but rather articulates the rights of each in relation to the rights of all others. See Karl Marx, "On the Jewish Question," in Robert C. Tucker, ed., *The Marx-Engels Reader* (New York: W. W. Norton, 1972), p.40. With regard to the relation of Christianity to the declaration, many Christians, including priests, embraced the ideals of the Revolution, and some even considered "the Gospel the perfect foundation for the rebirth of France." Arno J. Mayer, *The Furies: Violence and Terror in the French and Russian Revolutions* (Princeton University Press, 2000), p.418. However, at the highest levels of religious authority opposition was pronounced. As an example, Mayer cites Pope Pius VI's encyclical *Adeo nota* of April 23, 1791, which condemned the Declaration of the Rights of Man for "'denying the rights of God over man', leaving him 'amputated' from his Maker and at the mercy of 'a febrile liberty and equality which threatens to strangle reason'." The encyclical continues: "all 'freedom of thought and action … is a chimerical right contrary to the commands of the Creator'." Quoted in Mayer, *The Furies*, p.432.
[70] Furet, *Revolutionary France: 1770–1880*, p.292.

unobstructed social arena. They had to contend with powerful counter-revolutionary opposition in the form of supporters of the monarchy, nobility, and church who worked relentlessly to maintain or reinstate their vested interests. Hence Arno Mayer, reflecting on both the French and Russian revolutions and the "Furies" of violence they unleashed, does not merely note imperfections on the ideological level of revolutionary theory. Rather, he stresses the complex political conditions that helped engender violence and tyranny: "The Furies of revolution are fueled primarily by the inevitable and unexceptional resistance of the forces and ideas opposed to it, at home and abroad."[71] In the French case this opposition took many forms, and it operated at both the level of ideas and of force. The counter-revolutionary militias of the Vendée during 1793, for example, fought under the name of the "Catholic and Royal Army,"[72] indicating the support of traditional religious authority for the expelled monarchy. Additionally, as Mayer notes, the forces of counter-revolution outside France maintained a continual military pressure that contributed to the ongoing destabilization of the revolutionary regimes.[73] In the long term, this conflict was played out under the dictatorships of Robespierre and the Directory, followed by the Napoleonic era and the institution of Imperialism, and finally the temporary victory of the counter-revolutionary forces with the restoration of monarchy enforced by the victorious European powers in 1814 and 1815.[74] It would be a tortuous and broken path to the institution of democratic Republicanism in France. Well after his death, some of the republican ideas Kant advocated would finally be conjoined with democratic principles and institutions.[75]

---

[71] Mayer, *The Furies*, p.4. This argument, developed and illustrated at length in each case, adds an important dimension concerning the baneful impact of counter-revolutionary activities upon the course of revolutions generally minimized in Furet's analyses. Mayer's analysis of the French Revolution correlates with that of David Andress, *The Terror: Civil War in the French Revolution* (London: Little, Brown, 2005).

[72] Mayer, *The Furies*, p.328.

[73] Also see Blanning, *The Pursuit of Glory*, Chapter 13: "The Wars of the French Revolution and Napoleon: 1787–1815," for a concise and even-handed overview.

[74] Various aspects of this series of events are presented by Furet and Mayer. In addition to these sources, see Doyle, *The Oxford History of the French Revolution*; Steven Englund, *Napoleon: A Political Life* (Cambridge, MA: Harvard University Press, 2004), and Philip Mansel, *Paris between Empires: Monarchy and Revolution 1814–1852* (London: Phoenix Press, 2001).

[75] Furet's summary is most instructive. Describing the struggles against despotic monarchism in the early and mid nineteenth century, he notes that "the republican idea was indivisible from that of revolution and sovereignty. The very word 'republic' was sufficient indication that the *res publica* could not be true to its name unless it were the property of all, defined by all, agreed by all and, as far as possible, constantly reaffirmed by all." Furet, *Revolutionary France*, p.341.

This history of conflict and bloodshed may help us understand some of the reasons why Kant withdrew unequivocal support for the French Revolution, and why he came to adopt an overarching ethical-political model advocating gradual reform based on principles of respect for others under just and inclusive laws. He insists that the intellectual, ethical, and political autonomy fostered by enlightenment must be correlated with laws equally applicable to all. Lawless freedom is indicative of the state of nature; if unregulated by egalitarian principles, it is far more likely to degenerate into violence and anarchy.[76] Moreover, Kant's prioritizing of gradual critical reform over the dramatic upheavals of revolution has a broad focus in keeping with the more inclusive definition of the political that I have been using. He continues to address the reform of existing laws and institutions directly, but he complements this with emphasis on the role of *guiding ideas* and *inner dispositions* in any such possible reform. With regard to the French Revolution per se, this focus on the critical and transformative significance of *ideas* is further indicated in *The Conflict of the Faculties* (1798). Here Kant develops an alternative, reflective approach to the Revolution's relation to ethical-political progress. He considers the possibility of "some experience in the human race which, as an event [*als Begebenheit*], points to the disposition [*Beschaffenheit*] and capacity [*Vermögen*] of the human race to be the cause [*Ursache*] of its own advance toward the better" (CF, 7:84). He then writes of "an occurrence in our time which demonstrates this moral tendency of the human race" (CF, 7:85). This analysis shifts focus from the event itself to the attitudes of those who witness and respond to it. It emphasizes "the mode of thinking [*Denkungsart*] of the spectators which reveals itself *publicly* in this game of great revolutions, and manifests such a universal yet disinterested sympathy for the players on one side against those on the other." Kant highlights the awakening of a sympathetic support for freedom and equality versus tyranny and privilege. Furthermore, this sympathetic mode of thinking indicates "a moral character in humanity, at least in its predisposition [*Anlage*]." These predispositions do not develop automatically; they require individual and collective efforts to be brought to realization. Sympathy for the revolutionary endeavor to secure rights and freedoms for the general populace is disinterested, not only because the spectators (such as Kant himself) do not personally gain by the events,

---

[76] In this respect, nonviolent "velvet revolutions" such as those that have occurred in Eastern Europe since 1989 are closer to the model of reform Kant supported. See Timothy Garton Ash, "Velvet Revolution: The Prospects," *New York Review of Books*, 56, 19, December 3, 2009.

but also because their support "could become very disadvantageous for them if discovered." Moreover, it is important that Kant stresses that this "hope for progress toward the better" is in certain respects "already itself progress" (CF, 7:85). This is because it indicates a moral advance in collective attitudes and modes of thought which are essential to genuine and lasting ethical-political amelioration.

As he continues to discuss "the revolution of a gifted people which we have seen unfolding in our day," Kant notes that it "may succeed or miscarry; it may be filled with misery and atrocities to the point that a right thinking human being, were he boldly to hope to execute it successfully the second time, would never resolve to make the experiment at such a cost" (CF, 7:85). Distinct from the specific details and outcome of the Revolution, however, was its capacity to elicit a disinterested support for the progressive transformation of humanity. Kant defines these advances as follows:

[F]irst, that of the *right*, that a nation must not be hindered in providing itself with a civil constitution, which appears good to the people themselves; and second, that of the *end* (which is, at the same time, a duty), that that same national constitution alone be *just* and morally good in itself, created in such a way as to avoid, by its very nature, principles permitting offensive war. (CF, 7:85)

Here offensive war clearly refers to aggressive interventions among nation-states. However, the state of war also characterizes the figurative state of nature, i.e., as the antithesis of lawfulness. The first *Critique* describes this pre-social condition of humanity as akin to a state of war. For example, in outlining his response to lingering features of this state of lawlessness in our social relations, Kant notes that, "just as Hobbes asserted, the state of nature is a state of injustice and violence, one must necessarily leave it in order to submit himself to the lawful coercion which alone limits our freedom in such a way that it can be consistent with the freedom of everyone else and thereby with the common good" (A752/B780). For Kant, leaving the state of nature involves joining together under just, autonomously instituted laws, rather than submitting to the tyranny of an absolute sovereign.

The vision of history expressed in these writings is enormously complex. Kant's recognition of regression and progression in revolutionary events, and his focus on the ongoing responses of non-participants, removes his historical thinking from linear and deterministic models. We can learn from and build upon the products of historical activity, but this requires autonomous judgment guided by principles and applied under variable conditions. There is no sign in Kant's work of any doctrine concerning inevitability to the course of human history. It is contingent and multi-faceted, and can take the form of reversals and unmitigated catastrophes as much as it might yield ethical-political progression.[77]

[77] With reference to Kant's philosophy, Yirmiahu Yovel argues: "If there is, today, an advance in critical consciousness, it lies in the recognition that theoretical reflection and orientation of our experience is not necessarily dependent on unique theories, that capture the truth, as it were, *sub specie aeternitatis*; they are rather culture-bound and open to alteration and revisions. This will mean that 'reason' is self-transcending; its actual shapes are open to restructuring, in relation to the changing cultural experience; or to use Kant's own language, a 'regulative' idea of philosophy must here take the place of the speculative quest for a final system." Yirmiahu Yovel, *Kant and the Philosophy of History* (Princeton University Press, 1980), p.287. However, having noted the difference between regulative thinking and the speculative thinking of Hegel, Yovel remains dissatisfied with Kant's putative split between reason and nature: "This duality is the most fundamental principle of the critical system. Without it, the Copernican revolution will make no sense, and there will be no transcendental science and no necessary and universal foundations for knowledge and ethics" (p.299). However, Kant employs dualistic paradigms as a strategic tool for critical thinking: he resists the ontologization of a noumenal dimension of truth and value just as he resists the collapse of ethics into the contingent particulars of given political regimes. Kant opens up our capacity to think according to ideas and principles, which each of us must undertake individually and within communities. Yovel's interpretation is also shaped by a retrospective application of Hegelian concerns to Kant's thinking. In this regard, he proposes that "Hegel's *Aufhebung* of the Kantian dualism enables him to view rationality as embedded in the lower forms of culture, politics, religion, etc. and as explicating itself from them, and so he can accomplish more coherently what Kant failed to do: he can unite empirical and rational history in a single dynamic whole" (pp.304–05). To be sure, Yovel is satisfied with neither model in its classical form. He asks: "Is the Hegelian absolute Spirit the only alternative to Kant's dualism? Can we not conceive of history as an intelligible process while renouncing both?" (p.306). In response to this dilemma I would propose that the two models are incommensurable: Kant does not need to "unite" empirical and rational history into a systematic whole. Reason is a capacity to bring conceptual criteria to bear upon the givens of historical existence, with the end of making our future histories somewhat less riddled with violence and injustice: the two need not be reconciled in any grand metaphysical sense.

CHAPTER 3

Knowledge and experience

UNDERSTANDING AND EXPERIENCE

We have seen that the tasks of fostering open public discourse and furthering autonomy are central to Kant's critical philosophy from its initial formulations. The multi-sided interface of epistemology, ethics, and politics we have discerned in Kant's work provides the framework for a more detailed explication of the first *Critique*. For the purposes of this project, questions of knowledge and the status of supersensible ideas are approached mainly in relation to an inquiry into religion and its ethical-political significance. Hence my treatment is selective and governed by specific aims. I will minimize many of the technical issues in Kant's epistemological model as I mainly aim at setting the groundwork for his project of rethinking metaphysics and religion.

In the Preface to the *Critique of Pure Reason*, Kant characterizes classical metaphysics as a mode of thinking where reason takes refuge in principles overstepping all possible human experience. Those opening comments establish links between a disavowal of publicly accessible experience and tendencies toward *dogmatism* and *despotism*. Self-enclosed systems resisting empirical and public criteria of adjudication inevitably lapse into dogmatic rigidity. However, in the introduction to the "B" edition, Kant also anticipates the accompanying *counter-perspective* he elaborates; a tendency toward metaphysical speculation in some form is inherent to reason. In this vein, he asks: "**How is metaphysics as a natural predisposition** [*Naturanlage*] **possible?** i.e., how do the questions that pure reason raises, and which it is driven by its own need to answer as well as it can, arise from the nature of universal human reason?" (B22). These questions guide Kant's evaluation of the illegitimate uses of reason, and are tied to overturning the influence of heteronomous systems of knowledge.

Following this introductory section, the first *Critique* turns to the Transcendental Aesthetic, explicating the role of sense experience in knowledge. As Paul Guyer explains, here the term *aesthetic* indicates "a fully scientific investigation of the contribution of the senses to knowledge in general and the *a priori* forms of that contribution."[1] Consequently, Kant elaborates a theory of knowledge that engages the *publicly accessible empirical world* from which sensible intuitions arise, while equally emphasizing the *a priori* cognitive faculties ordering these intuitions. Knowledge requires sensible intuitions, and this criterion completely excludes knowledge claims constructed on purely intellectual intuitions. Kant insists on this principle from the first paragraph of the Transcendental Aesthetic, expressing the point in a way that links his epistemology to the empiricist tradition: "All thought, whether straightaway (*directe*) or through a detour (*indirecte*), must, by means of certain marks, ultimately be related to intuition, thus, in our case [i.e., the case of human beings], *to sensibility, since there is no other way in which objects can be given to us*" (B33; italics added).[2] Although Kant's epistemology becomes highly complex, the sensible reference point for valid knowledge claims about reality remains indispensable throughout. This theme is reiterated in the *Prolegomena to Any Future Metaphysics* of 1783, in response to early critics who conflated transcendental idealism with the idealism of Bishop Berkeley. The latter is portrayed by Kant as holding that "cognition through the senses and experience is nothing but sheer illusion," and as attempting to locate "truth only in the ideas of pure understanding and reason." By contrast, Kant emphasizes that "the principle that governs my idealism throughout is, on the contrary: 'All cognition of things out of mere pure understanding or pure reason is nothing but sheer illusion, and there is truth only in experience' [*und nur in der Erfahrung ist Wahrheit*]" (PR, 4:374). In other words, external and publicly accessible information is required for objective knowledge. In light of this, Arthur Collins argues against attributing to Kant "a solipsistic outlook" that has its starting point, as in Cartesian philosophy, in the abstracted *cogito* or thinking subject. Consciousness is predicated on "things outside our minds," which must consist of "public, enduring, non-mental things."[3] In fact, emphasizing sensible intuition and

---

[1] Paul Guyer, *Kant* (London: Routledge, 2006), p.53 (citing A21/B35–36).
[2] *Direct* knowledge indicates sensible experience of a single object, while *indirect* knowledge is mediated by concepts applicable to several things.
[3] Arthur Collins, *Possible Experience* (Berkeley: University of California Press, 1999), p.7. Similarly, Frederick Beiser traces Kant's opposition to solipsism to his pre-critical writings, where a critique of Leibniz is centered on the notion of pre-established harmony and its "solipsistic implications." Frederick C. Beiser, *German Idealism: The Struggle against Subjectivism 1781–1801* (Cambridge, MA: Harvard University Press, 2002), p.33.

public experience already links the first *Critique* to socially and politically relevant concerns.

This experiential cornerstone of Kant's epistemology has direct implications for his critical analyses of metaphysics, theology, and religion. The point is articulated by Guyer:

> The "Transcendental Aesthetic" not only lays the first stone in Kant's constructive theory of knowledge; it also lays the foundation for both his critique and his reconstruction of traditional metaphysics. It argues that all genuine knowledge requires a sensory component, and thus that metaphysical claims to transcend the possibility of sensory confirmation can never amount to knowledge.[4]

These critical issues are developed in the later portions of the *Critique* dealing with dialectical illusion in metaphysical speculation. Kant's refutation of idealist thought and traditional theological arguments extends beyond a mere empirically based critique, although the focus on sense experience as essential to knowledge is a necessary first step in his analysis. However, it is important that Kant's critical inquiries cannot be contained entirely within the purview of scientific inquiry.[5] While natural science provides an indispensable standard for experimentally based knowledge pertaining to the laws of nature, Kant is primarily concerned with the wider vistas opened by inquiries into ethics, politics, and religion. He therefore employs evaluative criteria based on principles rather than facts alone, in order to inquire into the inherited worldviews that have profound effects in shaping both our minds and the institutional conditions of political existence. Even with regard to questions of sensory experience, Kant's epistemological model is more sophisticated than that of empiricism, because our conceptual faculties have an active role in shaping the empirical intuitions underpinning knowledge. Hence transcendental idealism recognizes our cognitive capacities as requisite for experience and knowledge to take structured forms. In fact, the *a priori*

---

[4] Guyer, *Kant*, p.53.
[5] The concern arises that Kant has harnessed his epistemology to the natural science of his day, making assumptions based on outmoded paradigms. In this regard, Michael Friedman cites Kant's use of some "fundamental principles of Newtonian mechanics (such as the law of inertia and the equality of action and reaction) to illustrate the presence of synthetic *a priori* judgments within 'pure natural science'." Michael Friedman, "Philosophy of Natural Science," in Paul Guyer, ed., *The Cambridge Companion to Kant and Modern Philosophy* (Cambridge University Press, 2006), p.304, citing B17–21. In response to the charge that this use of Newtonian concepts welds Kant's epistemology to that model, Friedman argues that "Kant is only truly committed to much more general synthetic *a priori* principles – such as the spatial character of experience in general … but not to the more specific principles of Euclidean geometry and Newtonian physics to which he happens to appeal" (p.331).

features of Kant's epistemology also have important critical features; they enhance his explanation of how traditional metaphysics and theology construct illusory thought realms based on these same cognitive faculties, taken in abstraction from experience.

Knowledge is enabled by the conditions of experience, *space and time*, and by the concepts of the understanding, also called the *transcendental categories*. The first section of the Transcendental Aesthetic inquires into how we "represent to ourselves objects outside us, and all as in space" (A22/B37). Space is not an empirical concept derived from experience; rather, experience already requires that objects be represented spatially or in space. "Thus the representation [*Vorstellung*] of space cannot be obtained from the relations of outer appearance through experience, but this outer experience is itself first possible only through this representation" (A23/B38). This point turns from public, empirical experience as the *sine qua non* of human knowledge, to the cognitive conditions that make such experience possible. I should note parenthetically that the term representation (*Vorstellung*), which appears in many guises in Kant's writings, is a crucial one. Here it explicates the cognitive structuring of all human experience.[6] The point is definitely *not* the solipsistic one that there is nothing real except our mental representations, but rather that external reality as we experience and know it is cognitively structured. Because of this necessary structuring, Kant refers to reality as represented to human beings in certain organized ways, in this case spatially. It is in this sense that space "is therefore to be regarded as the condition of the possibility of appearances, not as a determination dependent on them, and is an *a priori* representation [*eine Vorstellung a priori*] that necessarily grounds outer appearances" (A24/B39). The cognitive structuring of experience leads to an additional point. "The transcendental concept of appearances in space … is a critical reminder that absolutely nothing that is intuited in space is a thing in itself [*Ding an sich*], and that space is not a form proper to anything in itself" (A30/B45). This is a logical consequence of the argument that human experience is given spatial organization through *a priori* operations. Most importantly, this means that just as we cannot have experience or knowledge that completely eschews sensory input, so reciprocally are we incapable of knowledge that abstracts

---

[6] As Guyer explains, "Intuitions and concepts are two different species of the genus 'representation' (*Vorstellung*), Kant's most general term for any cognitive state." Guyer, *Kant*, p.53 (citing A320/B376–77). Later, we will see that Kant *also* comes to employ the term *Vorstellung* to describe culturally produced representations (narratives, symbols, images) that convey collective values and worldviews.

from the operation of our cognitive faculties. In other words, we cannot know *things in themselves*. There are several implications to this line of argument; however, before pursuing them let us turn to the concept of time, the other subjective condition of sensibility.

As with the representation of space, "time is not an empirical concept that is somehow drawn from an experience. For simultaneity or succession would not themselves come into perception if the representation of time [*die Vorstellung der Zeit*] did not ground them *a priori*. Only under its presupposition can one represent that several things exist at one and the same time (simultaneously) or in different times (successively)" (A30/B46). The same argument applies as in the case of the spatiality of experience: temporal structuring is not the result of having had specific experiences, but rather *precedes* and informs all experience. The organizing structures of space and time are generated as we encounter sensory input. Moreover this model applies not only to objects in the world, but even, *mutatis mutandis*, to our inner intuitions, a point to which I return. Reality as experienced by human beings, that is, as structured by our cognitive faculties, is defined as *appearance*. This is contrasted with the accompanying hypothesis of the unknown thing-in-itself (as both inner and outer), upon which experiences are predicated. The key point is that human beings cognitively structure their intuitions of given objects; what reality might be apart from this structuring activity is an empty question. Kant addresses this point in appraising the Leibnizian–Wolffian model of metaphysics: "what the things may be in themselves I do not know, *and also do not need to know*, since a thing can never come before me except in appearance" (A276–77/B332–33; italics added). Such comments show that the cognitively structured nature of intuitions does not pose a problem for questions of empirical truth. Our experience of reality (appearances) is subject to shared criteria of verifiability and falsifiability. The application of these criteria may be somewhat more difficult in the case of inner intuitions, which by definition are private. However, any claims concerning such experiences must be represented through language or other shared media, and hence they become public and subject to discussion in that manner. Kant does not make this point, but it is consistent with his epistemological model, and also follows from his recurring statements concerning the importance of open speech in the public domain. This criterion of publicity has epistemological and political implications that can work both ways; i.e., I have a right to express my personal views and experiences openly, but in making these public I also subject myself to the shared criteria of truthfulness, verifiability, and lawfulness.

With regard to the status of appearances, Kant emphasizes that these are quite *real*. In the second ("B") edition he makes this point emphatically: "If I say: in space and time intuition represents both outer objects [*Objecte*] as well as the self-intuition of the mind as it **appears**, that is not to say that these objects would be mere **illusion** [*Schein*]" (B69). Kant is responding to the confusion of transcendental idealism with philosophies that dispute the reality of the external world, or which make empirical experience secondary to a presumed immediate intellectual experience. It is rather the case that appearances *are* reality, as presented to us according to our cognitive faculties (which must be strictly differentiated from innate ideas).[7] Human beings have knowledge of appearances only because the forms of intuition, in combination with the categories of the understanding, give structure to experience. As Henry Allison argues, this model does not lead to relativism or skepticism that would question the validity of external experience. He emphasizes that Kant makes "the epistemological claim about the dependence of human knowledge on certain *a priori* conditions which reflect the structure of the human cognitive apparatus." These cognitive abilities express "the universal and necessary conditions in terms of which alone the human mind is capable of recognizing something as an object at all."[8] I am going to take these points as given, since my concern is not with debates about the comprehensiveness and incorrigibility of the Kantian epistemological model, but rather with its implications for a critical approach to metaphysics and theory of religion.

However, other complexities emerge with regard to temporality. For example, because appearance is not equivalent to illusion, Kant reiterates that he is assuming "the empirical reality of time, i.e., objective validity in regard to all objects that may ever be given to our senses" (A35/B52). This view is consistent with an empirically oriented and public approach to knowledge. Additionally, because time, like space, is a transcendental condition of the experience of objects, rather than a concept derived from empirical intuitions, Kant wishes to "dispute all claim of time to absolute reality, namely where it would attach to things absolutely as a condition or property without regard to the form of our sensible intuition"

---

[7] The point is articulated by Pinkard, who, after summarizing Kant's position that categories are presupposed in order for us to "have any conscious experience at all," continues: "Those concepts were, moreover, not innate but were generated by the spontaneous activity of the human mind itself as it shaped experience into judgmental form." Terry Pinkard, *German Philosophy 1760–1860: The Legacy of Idealism* (Cambridge University Press, 2002), p.36.
[8] Henry Allison, *Kant's Transcendental Idealism* (New Haven: Yale University Press, 1983), p.9.

(A35/B52). This point, probably directed at Newtonian ideas of absolute space and time, also remains consistent with the general orientation of the Transcendental Aesthetic.[9] We cannot overstep the bounds of our possible experience as informed by the subjective conditions of sensibility, i.e., space and time. We cannot attribute temporality, or spatiality, "absolutely" to reality, that is, to things as they might be without the structuring effects of our cognitive faculties. Kant proposes a principle of intellectual modesty that ensues from this epistemological approach.[10] Yet at certain points Kant himself seems to go further in his conclusions than is warranted by this model. For example, he claims: "In this therefore consists the **transcendental ideality** of time, according to which it is nothing at all if one abstracts from the subjective conditions of sensible intuition, and cannot be counted as either subsisting or inhering in the objects in themselves (without their relation to our intuition)" (A36/B52). As long as Kant is stating that we simply have no knowledge of things in themselves apart from our human ways of intuiting, and therefore cannot know if they are in themselves characterized by spatiality, temporality, or by the categories of the understanding, he is consistent with his claims to intellectual modesty. However, insofar as he insists that neither space nor time can inhere in things-in-themselves, but must only be the subjective conditions of sensible intuition, he is making a (negative) knowledge claim about things-in-themselves, thus overstepping his epistemological framework.[11] Despite these rare lapses, what remains essential is the general model in which *a priori* faculties of human beings interact with

---

[9] For a discussion of Newton's theory of "absolute time and space," see Jonathan Israel, *Enlightenment Contested: Philosophy, Modernity, and the Emancipation of Man 1670–1752* (Oxford University Press, 2006), pp.206ff.

[10] The term "modesty" characterizes Kant's eschewal of unmediated as well as all-encompassing systems of explanation. However, I also agree with George di Giovanni that Kant's critical project is certainly *not* modest insofar as it represents a radical departure from traditional thought worlds. As di Giovanni emphasizes, "Kant was putting an end to any naïve representational theory of knowledge." Moreover: "It was not just a matter of scaling down earlier claims to knowledge, but of altering the meaning of 'knowledge' itself." George di Giovanni, *Freedom and Religion in Kant and His Immediate Successors* (Cambridge University Press, 2005), pp.35–36.

[11] See Guyer, *Kant*, p.70. Guyer quotes Kant to the effect that "the understanding is itself the source of the laws of nature" (p.72, citing A127). Guyer concludes that in this type of statement "Kant overstates the force of our cognitive autonomy" (p.72). This comment, in offering a mild criticism, also indicates the larger stakes in the Kantian project of autonomy. This builds from epistemology to include concerns with cultivating autonomy on ethical and political levels. Guyer concludes that "the transcendental theory of experience which we have gleaned from Kant's writings … can be accepted without automatic commitment to the doctrine that space and time do not represent genuine features of reality." Paul Guyer, *Kant and the Claims of Knowledge* (Cambridge University Press, 1987), p.344.

INNER SENSE AND THE SUBJECT OF APPERCEPTION

In discussing the spatial and temporal structuring of experience, Kant alludes to the question of *inner experience*. He explains that "consciousness of itself (apperception) is the simple representation of the I [*die einfache Vorstellung des Ich*], and if all of the manifold of the subject were given **self-actively** through that alone, then the inner intuition would be intellectual" (B68). However, a purely intellectual auto-apperception, which would be immediate and transparent, is *not* the way human beings actually experience their own inner being, i.e., the "I" of self-consciousness. Instead, "in human beings this consciousness requires inner perception of the manifold that is antecedently given in the subject, and the manner in which this is given in the mind [*im Gemüte gegehen wird*] without spontaneity must be called sensibility on account of this difference" (B68). Two major points are indicated here: (1) concerning the distinction between apperception and inner sense (or "inner perception of a manifold"); (2) concerning the parallel of this inner sense with the cognitive shaping of outer experience. With regard to the first issue, Allison remarks that "inner sense and apperception, for Kant, are two distinct *yet complementary* forms of self-consciousness."[12] In the case of apperception, this self-consciousness concerns awareness that "I am," or consciousness of the act of thinking. However, as Kant explains, "I am conscious of myself not as I appear to myself, nor **as** I am in myself, but only **that** I am. This **representation** [*Vorstellung*] is a **thinking**, not an **intuiting**" (B157). I am aware of my own existence as a center of consciousness, but there is no specific content associated with this apperception. The notion of *inner sense*, on the other hand, is formulated as parallel to the *outer sense* by which I have representations of objects in the world. With regard to this second point, Allison notes that "feelings, together with other mental items, such as desires and volitions, can be represented as 'subjective objects'."[13] Although Allison observes that the parallel with outer sense is inexact, the key point is that it is equally the case that no unmediated, unstructured knowledge of inner objects and states is possible.

---

[12] Allison, *Kant's Transcendental Idealism*, pp.260, 272; italics added.
[13] *Ibid.*, p.261.

Inner sense and the subject of apperception 77

In the first ("A") edition of the *Critique*, in the context of explicating transcendental apperception Kant explains the unity of consciousness as follows: "no cognitions can occur in us, no connection and unity among them, without that unity of consciousness that precedes all data of intuitions, and in relation to which all representation of objects is alone possible" (A107). For experience to be coherent, it must be related to a conscious subject who has a sense of continuous identity. Kant builds on this point in stating: "All possible appearances belong, as representations, to the whole possible self-consciousness. But from this, as a transcendental representation, numerical identity is inseparable, and certain *a priori*, because nothing can come into cognition except by means of this original apperception" (A113). This affirms the unity of the subject in apperception as the prerequisite for coherent experience. Although the unity of consciousness is posited *a priori*, there is no indication that this unity is immediately known. This line of argument emerges in greater detail when Kant engages the metaphysical schools of his era under the rubric of rational psychology. The unity of thought accompanying experience cannot be reified into a substance with definite knowable properties as in metaphysical doctrines concerning the substantial nature of the soul. Rather, the continuity of the "I think" is presented in *active* rather than *essentialist* terms; it is posited as the necessary presupposition for the unity of experience. Hence, transcendental apperception leads directly to the argument that the manifold of intuition, as represented to a unitary consciousness, is brought under conceptual laws. This argument is augmented by Kant's transcendental deduction of the categories, which I will discuss shortly.

Later in the text, in the course of the Refutation of Idealism added to the second edition, Kant supplements this argument about the coherence of the knowing subject:

the representation **I am** [*die Vorstellung: Ich bin*] which expresses the consciousness that accompanies all thinking, is that which immediately includes the existence [*Existenz*] of a subject in itself, but not yet any **cognition** of it, thus not empirical cognition, i.e., experience; for to that there belongs, besides the thought of something existing, intuition, and in this case inner intuition, i.e., time, in regard to which the subject must be determined, *for which outer objects are absolutely requisite, so that inner experience itself is consequently only mediate and possible only through outer experience.* (B277; italics added)

While some sense of "I" accompanies thinking, actual cognition requires inner intuitions, and these are predicated upon the experience of outer intuitions. With regard to this point, commentators have noted that Kant made certain changes in his discussion of inner and outer sense from the first to the second edition of the *Critique*. As Beiser remarks in discussing the Refutation of Idealism: "While in the first edition of the *Kritik* Kant argued for the *parity* of inner and outer sense ... in the second edition he makes a case for the priority of outer over inner sense."[14] This prioritization of outer sense is associated with an important criticism of solipsistic models of subjectivity, which is further strengthened in the second edition. In this regard, Beiser summarizes Kant's argument formulated against Cartesianism: "the condition of self-consciousness is the consciousness of something permanent in space outside me." This builds upon Kant's insistence on the public, empirically verifiable character of our knowledge of reality: "inner experience is possible only through outer experience, because an inner experience will be determinable in time only through a spatial framework."[15]

In addition to overturning the subject-centered epistemology of Cartesianism, this argument has implications for our wider agenda: it strengthens the interconnection between self-knowledge and public experience. Beiser makes the point incisively: "Kant holds that we can know our inner states in time – we can say that we had an experience at a certain moment – only if we can somehow locate them within a single public space." The external space that we access through outer sense forms the framework within which inner temporal experience can be located. Following through on the implications of this point, Beiser further notes that in direct contrast to idealism, for Kant "intersubjective order precedes or makes possible the subjective order of my inner consciousness."[16] Although the subject is active in forming experience, this dependency of inner sense upon outer sense also undergirds Kant's epistemology. This argument with regard to the prioritization of spatial experience is also supported by Guyer: "Kant clearly perceived that there was some inescapable connection between self-knowledge and knowledge of objects, and this completely undermined the Cartesian assumptions that we could have determinate knowledge of our inner states without any knowledge of the external world at all."[17] These comments clarify the distinction

---

[14] Beiser, *German Idealism*, p.105.
[15] *Ibid.*, p.109.
[16] *Ibid.*, p.110.
[17] Paul Guyer, "Transcendental Deduction of the Categories," in Paul Guyer, ed., *The Cambridge Companion to Kant* (Cambridge University Press, 1992), p.155. Reciprocally, Guyer also concludes that Kant's model "completely undermined the Lockean and Humean project of discovering the

between apperception, in which the *I am* is thought of as accompanying all inner and outer representations, and *inner sense* as pertaining to internal objects of consciousness. The latter includes an experience of representations of mental objects in time, the capacity for which is ultimately predicated upon prior outer experience. In this way, the solipsistic approach of Cartesianism is *reversed*; although the cognitive resources shaping our representations are given *a priori*, the experience of outer objects informs that of inner objects. These formulations undermine any reified model of the self. As Allison summarizes: "the I (soul, mind, or self) is not itself an object of inner experience or inner sense."[18] This model has profound implications for Kant's inquiries into the interrelated issues of freedom, will, conscience, and self-deception. Most significantly, the interdependency of inner and outer forms of knowledge establishes the dynamic epistemology subtending Kant's broader interpersonal and political investigations. This inter-mediation of inner and outer will be played out in another register, with regard to practical concerns on both ethical and political levels.

LOGIC AND JUDGMENT

Kant develops the theme concerning how "our cognition arises from two fundamental sources in the mind." The first of these is the "the receptivity of impressions," which has been outlined in terms of the representations of space and time that organize sensory input. The second is "the faculty for cognizing an object by means of these representations," and so shifts the inquiry from *Transcendental Aesthetic* to *Transcendental Logic*. Kant stipulates that "through the former [the aesthetic] an object is **given** to us, through the latter [logic] it is **thought** in relation to that representation" (A50/B74). The concepts of the understanding are introduced to explain how we make conceptual sense of intuitions, spontaneously organizing them according to logical categories. Both intuitions and concepts fall under the headings of "**empirical**, if sensation (which presupposes the actual presence of the object) is contained therein" and "**pure** if no sensation is mixed into the representation." In this way, Kant introduces mediations offsetting the distinction between *a priori* and *a posteriori*, with the pure or *a priori* being limited to "merely the form" under which

---

foundations of all knowledge and belief in the empirical input of sensation and reflection alone" (*ibid*.).
[18] Allison, *Kant's Transcendental Idealism*, p.263.

something is either intuited or thought. Empirical input is therefore explicitly included not only in intuition, but in thinking: "only pure intuitions or concepts alone are possible *a priori*, empirical ones only *a posteriori*" (A51/B75). Pure intuitions and concepts concern form, whereas the empirical involves sensory input organized by our faculties.

Kant continues to devise an interactive epistemological model, layer by layer. He calls "the receptivity of our mind [*Receptivität unseres Gemüts*] to receive representations insofar as it is affected in some way **sensibility**." He then specifies that the "faculty for bringing forth representations itself, or the **spontaneity** of cognition [*Spontaneität des Erkenntnisses*], is the **understanding**" (A51/B75). This spontaneity parallels that of the imagination; in each case, an active role in experience and knowledge is emphasized. This crucial point is reiterated at several places in the *Critique*: the understanding alone, because it engages sense-based intuitions, gives rise to representations. Here we might note Kant's propensity for establishing various faculties of the mind pertaining to different functions. In addition to sensibility, the understanding, imagination, and judgment, he also introduces the faculty of reason (discussed in the next chapter). These categorizations should be taken heuristically, i.e., as a way to organize our various mental activities and abilities. Most importantly, this organizing model helps structure an inquiry into how we experience reality, and ultimately what can be assessed as valid knowledge claims. Beiser notes that in differentiating our various faculties Kant was "deliberately thwarting any attempt to reduce them to a single source and function." This is because the proliferation of faculties works against any sort of "foundationalist program," such as that of Descartes (who often forms a foil against which Kant's innovative thinking is explicated).[19] The proliferation of various faculties is commensurate with a dynamic model requiring interplay between cognitive faculties and sensibly received intuitions. This resists tendencies to locate agency, or truth, or reality in a single source or ground, offsetting models of a self-contained subject that ignore the communicative and interpersonal nature of knowledge.

At this point in his explication, Kant reiterates that these mental operations, however spontaneous they may be, are necessarily predicated upon the reception of sensory input: "It comes along with our nature that **intuition** can never be other than **sensible**, i.e., that it contains only the way in which we are affected by objects" (A51/B75). Kant scrupulously eliminates consideration of non-sensible intuitions, which would not be

---

[19] Beiser, *German Idealism*, p.7.

based on possible objects in the external world. "Without sensibility no object would be given to us, and without understanding none would be thought. Thoughts without content are empty, intuitions without concepts are blind" (A51/B75; and cf. A92/B125). This articulates a dynamic model of experience and understanding. While intuitions require our cognitive faculties to be represented coherently, reciprocally knowledge of reality cannot be based on concepts alone. Without sense-based intuitions, ontological claims derive from the mere manipulation of concepts. This *dialectical* procedure of making knowledge claims on a purely conceptual level might produce a specious sense of logical coherence, but in relation to reality remains devoid of truth value.

Kant continually mediates between conceptual structuring and the specific sensory content of intuitions. Along these lines, he introduces a distinction between general and particular logic, expressed in the following way. The logic of the general use of the understanding "contains the absolutely necessary rules of thinking, without which no use of the understanding takes place." At this level, there is no reference to differences among various types of objects conceptualized. However, as differentiated from these general rules, Kant specifies "the logic of the particular use of the understanding," which "contains the rules for correctly thinking about a certain kind of objects" (A52/B76). In commenting on this distinction, Béatrice Longuenesse remarks that distinct forms of logic pertain to the rules "in connection with a particular content of knowledge," and in a note she gives as an example that "mathematical proof has rules of its own."[20] In addition to this differentiation among particular logics, Kant divides general logic into pure or applied. The term *pure* designates that which "has to do with strictly *a priori* principles," and therefore pertains "to what is formal in their use, be the content what it may" (A53/B77). However, Kant highlights applied logic, which provides the rules for the use of the understanding "*in concreto*, namely under the contingent conditions of the subject, which can hinder or promote this use, and which can all be given only empirically" (A54/B79). Applied logic pertains to the use of the understanding in organizing experience under variable conditions.

A comment introduced at this juncture has clear implications for our theme. Kant indicates an analogy between two types of distinction, that between pure and applied *logic* and that between pure and applied

---

[20] Béatrice Longuenesse, "Kant on *a priori* Concepts," in Guyer, ed., *The Cambridge Companion to Kant and Modern Philosophy*, p.137, and p.163 n.7.

morality: "pure logic is related to it [applied logic] as pure morality, which contains the necessary moral laws of free will in general [*die notwendigen sittlichen Gesetz eines freien Willens überhaupt enthält*], is related to the doctrine of virtue [*Tugendlehre*] proper, which assesses [*erwägt*, also meaning 'considers'] these laws under the hindrances of the feelings, inclinations, and passions to which human beings are more or less subject" (A54–55/B79). In addition to establishing parallel structuring paradigms for comprehending both logical and moral judgments, Kant addresses the need for general moral laws to be considered in relation to the definite features of human beings. These issues, especially the relation of rational to non-rational aspects of human existence, and the need for judgments involving a wide range of variables, will be discussed in greater detail as we proceed. I note this comment because it shows continuity among the various subdivisions of the critical philosophy. In thinking ahead to issues of mediating formal moral principles in relation with specific life situations, Kant affirms that the focus on experience and application paramount in his epistemology carries over to his ethics. The language may indicate a priority of the pure and formal, but for addressing ethical dilemmas, applications requiring autonomous judgments in context are equally necessary.[21]

This stress on application in a contingent world of experience, decisively opposed to the classical tradition of metaphysics, means that logic does not reflect an ontological order. Longuenesse therefore differentiates the first *Critique* from rationalist metaphysics, such as that of Leibniz and Wolff. These systems, she emphasizes, held that "the most general principles of logic also defined the most general structures of *being*."[22] In correlating logic and being in this way, classical metaphysics creates self-enclosed and self-justifying thought-systems that lack a capacity for corrigibility through application within variable experiential contexts. There is no conceptual space for accommodating critical feedback based on new experience. As Longuenesse summarizes, "Kant intends both to debunk Leibnizian-Wolffian direct mapping of forms of thought upon forms of being, and to redefine, on new grounds, the grip our intellect

[21] A related point is made by Onora O'Neill. She contrasts Kant with rationalists who expected logic to provide "rules that offer complete instructions for handling every case that falls under them" and cites Kant's insistence that "general logic can supply no rules for judgment" (A135/B174). From this it follows that logic "cannot provide the foundation for thinking, for doing, or for the structure of hope that Kant believes articulates modes of unity between the domains of thought and action" ("Vindicating Reason," in *The Cambridge Companion to Kant*, p.304).
[22] Longuenesse, "Kant on *a priori* Concepts," p.137.

can have on the structural features of the world."[23] The critical relationship to metaphysics and onto-theology demands that we relinquish total knowledge claims. It is therefore difficult to sustain in the face of our predisposition to metaphysics, i.e., the human need for comprehensive explanatory frameworks. In this respect, Longuenesse also notes that after Kant this correlation of logic and being is *reinstated* by Hegel, who attempts to reconcile knowledge and being within a historicized metaphysics. "Hegel takes the [logical] relation to be a fact about being itself, and the structures thus revealed to be those of being itself, whereas Kant takes the relation between judging and the structures of being to be a fact about the way human beings relate to being."[24] Because we exercise autonomous judgment within interpersonal and societal contexts, Kant's thinking maintains a space allowing both empirical diversity and a critical amelioration of conceptual models through feedback. The agonizing speculative dilemmas of Hegelianism, such as seeking to resolve specific histories, political systems, and forms of human knowledge into a systematic whole that correlates with the logical unfolding of *Geist*, are simply not a concern for Kant. The principle of intellectual modesty allows an agnostic stance with regard to traditional ontological and theological issues, while focusing decisively on human ethical dilemmas within variable socio-political frameworks.

Finally, Kant turns to the subdivision of general logic into *analytic* and *dialectic*, where additional important points arise. This begins with a discussion of the standard definition of truth as "agreement of cognition with its object," which is "granted and presupposed" (A58/B82). This definition reiterates the point made in the Transcendental Aesthetic that we ascertain truth only insofar as concepts and judgments can be related to possible experience. In establishing the truth of any proposition, we engage objects given through intuitions against which our judgments can be assessed: "if truth consists in the agreement of a cognition with its object, then this object must be distinguished from others; for a cognition is false if it does not agree with the object to which it is related even if it contains something that could well be valid for other objects" (A58/B83). This falsifiable model of truth in which general propositions must be tested against particular cases incorporates the interplay of intuitions and categories of the understanding. A judgment that might correctly apply, or be deemed true, in one context, might be false in another. Kant succinctly elaborates

---

[23] Béatrice Longuenesse, *Kant on the Human Standpoint* (Cambridge University Press, 2005), p.88.
[24] Longuenesse, "Kant on *a priori* Concepts," p.154.

the point a few pages later: "For without intuition all of our cognition would lack objects [*Objecten*], and therefore remain completely empty" (A62/B87). Through acts of judgment, we test knowledge claims within varying empirical situations; this provides the feedback necessary for the critical modification of ideas.

However, Kant also adds an analytic to this model of truth. He describes this as the procedure that analyzes "the entire formal business of the understanding and reason into its elements, and presents these as principles of all logical assessment of our cognition" (A60/B84). This procedure establishes a negative criterion of truth, insofar as incorrect logical procedures can invalidate an argument prior to its being tested against sensible intuitions. This analytic part of logic is "at least the negative touchstone of truth," since it concerns rules for the examination and evaluation of the "form of all cognition" preceding an investigation as to "whether with regard to the object it contains positive truth" (A60/B85). Therefore, in addition to endorsing a modified correspondence theory of truth requiring the agreement of concepts and statements with specific objects in the world, Kant formulates an analytic of the concepts of the understanding to determine the rules of their use. This analytic procedure cannot determine a proposition to be true, but it can determine its untruth by internal contradiction and incoherence. This establishes a twofold model of negative truth (by which analytic procedures invalidate improper uses of concepts), and positive truth (the correspondence of concepts with objects). This model is central to Kant's epistemology, and it carries over into his ethical and political thinking (where, for example, the virtue of truthfulness is paramount).

At this point, Kant begins to explore the metaphysical *misuse* of concepts more deeply. He notes that "general logic, as a putative organon, is called **dialectic**." From examining the "actual use" of dialectic among the ancients, one can determine that "it was nothing other than the **logic of illusion** – a sophistical art for giving to its ignorance, indeed even to its intentional tricks, the air of truth, by imitating the method of thoroughness, which logic prescribes in general, and using its topics for the embellishment of every empty pretension" (A61/B86). Howard Caygill notes that Kant's definition of dialectic is "resolutely Aristotelian," and cites the *Topics* as distinguishing between "demonstrative (scientific) and dialectical reasoning, with the former reasoning from premises that are 'true and primary' and the latter reasoning 'from opinions that are generally accepted'."[25] Kant extrapolates on this Aristotelian sense of dialectic as mere opinion and sophistry. The critique of dialectic addresses misuses of general logic disengaged from any application to specific objects. In the sophistical arts, pure rules of the understanding are manipulated in ways that have the air of intellectual elegance and precision, but which are in fact disconnected from any empirical reference that might ground them in publicly observable and discussable reality. Kant therefore notes "the effrontery of using it as a tool (organon) for an expansion and extension of its information [*Kenntnisse*], or at least the pretension of so doing," and he roundly declares that such activity "comes down to nothing but idle chatter [*Geschwätzigkeit*], asserting or impeaching whatever one wants with some plausibility" (A62/B86). Undisciplined speculation "dares to synthetically judge, assert, and decide about objects in general with the pure understanding alone" (A63/B88), i.e., without reference to experience or intuitions. This constitutes the metaphysical tendency to generate *dialectical illusion*. Kant evocatively refers to the "art of dogmatically arousing such illusions" as a "highly prevalent art among the manifold works of metaphysical jugglery" (A62/B86).

The Transcendental Dialectic is of primary significance for our inquiry, insofar as it explains how the conceptual operations of traditional metaphysics produce specious knowledge claims. Kant also indicates how traditions comprised of such fallacious reasoning take shape and become perpetuated. The necessity for intuitions is the basis for Kant's explication of the dialectical misuse of these categories and principles derived from them by dogmatic metaphysics and theology. However, before turning to this critical undertaking in detail, let us delve somewhat further into the Transcendental Analytic, where the much-discussed tables of judgments and categories are presented.

IMAGINATION AND CONCEPTS OF THE UNDERSTANDING

The Analytic of Concepts further develops the interplay of concepts and intuitions in experience. Here Kant pursues "the pure concepts into their first seeds and predispositions [*Keimen und Anlagen*] in the human understanding, where they lie ready, until with the opportunity of experience they are finally developed and exhibited [*dargestellt*] in their clarity by

---

[25] Howard Caygill, *A Kant Dictionary* (Oxford: Blackwell, 1995), p.157. Caygill cites Aristotle, *Topics*, 100a, 28–30. Also see *Topics*, 105b, 30–31: "For purposes of philosophy we must treat of things according to their truth, but for dialectic only with an eye to opinion." *The Complete Works of Aristotle*, ed. Jonathan Barnes (Princeton University Press, 1984), vol. 1, p.176.

the very same understanding, liberated from the empirical conditions attaching to them" (A66/B91). Hence the *predisposition* to form concepts of the understanding is but a *seed*: it is brought to fruition only through experience. As this occurs, the concepts structuring experiences can then retrospectively be discerned and analyzed. The capacity to judge is a meta-representational activity applying these concepts: "judgment is therefore the mediate cognition of an object, hence the representation of a representation of it [*die Vorstellung einer Vorstellung desselben*]" (A68/B94). Along these lines, Kant further explains that "the **understanding** in general can be represented as a **faculty for judging** [or 'a capacity to judge'; *ein Vermögen zu urteilen vorgestellt werden kann*]" (A69/B94). Through the understanding, the concepts which are "predicates of all possible judgments, are related to some representation of a still undetermined object." These concepts require application to sensible intuitions in specific acts of judgment. In order to delineate the conceptual structures within which judgments occur, he outlines a Table of Judgments under four headings, each of which has three subcategories: (1) *Quantity* (universal, particular, singular); (2) *Quality* (affirmative, negative, infinite); (3) *Relation* (categorical, hypothetical, disjunctive); and (4) *Modality* (problematic, assertoric, apodictic) (A70/B95).

Kant then turns to the notion of *synthesis*, in which a manifold of intuitions is brought into a single cognition. He notes that "synthesis in general is, as we shall subsequently see, the mere effect of the imagination [*Einbildungskraft*], of a blind though indispensable function of the soul without which we would have no cognition at all, but of which we are seldom conscious" (A78/B103). Here the role of imagination in bringing sense data into organized combinations is stated in somewhat restricted terms, although this is subsequently developed more fully. Kant argues that "all intuitions are nothing for us and do not in the least concern us if they cannot be taken up into consciousness, whether they influence it directly or indirectly, and through this alone is consciousness possible" (A116). Consciousness is predicated on sense intuitions, but reciprocally these intuitions are formless for us unless actively organized by the understanding, via the imagination. In the course of this explication, Kant distinguishes between "the productive synthesis of the imagination" which occurs *a priori*, and "the reproductive synthesis" that "rests on conditions of experience" (A118). This conception of a synthesizing activity occurring *a priori* gives greater emphasis to the creative dimensions of imagination. It is the medium for integrating sense impressions, but it already exceeds these impressions in generating unified images.

The B edition of the *Critique* adds several important points clarifying the productive role of the imagination for our capacity to judge. Kant opens the Deduction of the Pure Concepts of the Understanding by highlighting the representational activity intrinsic to mental processes. His over-determined use of the term *representation* appears quite sharply in these passages: "the manifold of representations [*das Mannigfaltige der Vorstellungen*] can be given in an intuition that is merely sensible, i.e., nothing but receptivity." Yet the form given to these intuitions lies "*a priori* in our faculty of representation [*a priori in unserem Vorstellungsvermögen liegen*]." He emphasizes that "the **combination** (*conjunctio*) of a manifold in general can never come to us through the senses," but that this grouping is "an act of the spontaneity of the power of representation [*Actus der Spontaneität der Vorstellungskraft*]" which one must call "understanding" (B129–30). Additionally, as a correlate to the unifying qualities of representing, "the **I think** must **be able** to accompany all my representations; for otherwise something would be represented in me that could not be thought at all" (B131–32). In his second attempt at describing "the **transcendental synthesis of the imagination**," Kant strongly highlights the point that "***Imagination*** is the faculty for representing [*Vermögen … vorzustellen*] an object even **without its presence** in intuition" (B151). Allison, while noting that Kant does not really develop this important comment, extrapolates on the argument to illustrate how "the imagination is required for the representation of time and space as they are described in the Transcendental Aesthetic." This capacity to represent what is *not* immediately present is essential to our everyday orientation within temporally and spatially structured experience. This occurs whenever we position a specific experience within more encompassing frameworks of space and time. Allison notes that every moment takes on its temporal structure by being located within a larger flow of anterior and posterior moments: "in order to represent the particular portion of time, and myself as engaged in that activity during that time, I must be able to represent past and future time. In other words, I must be able to represent times that are not 'present' … this is what the imagination enables me to do."[26] Cognizing an intuition within a wider contextual framework occurs through the productive activity of imagination.

Kant refers to the operation of imagination in acts of synthesis as the "**reproductive** imagination," and specifies that this is "subject solely to empirical laws." This reproductive function is characterized as

---

[26] Allison, *Kant's Transcendental Idealism*, p.160.

"determinable," i.e., directly shaped by sense-based intuitions. This is differentiated from "an exercise of spontaneity, which is determining and not, like sense, merely determinable." As distinct from empirically based representational activity, the "**productive** imagination" is characterized by precisely this quality of spontaneity (B151–52). These comments demonstrate imagination as mediating given intuitions with the understanding, locating these immediate intuitions within more encompassing referential contexts, and also exhibiting a spontaneous generation of images. Hence Kant describes "an active faculty of the synthesis of this manifold in us, which we call imagination, and whose action exercised immediately upon perceptions I call apprehension. For the imagination is to bring the manifold of intuition into an **image** [*Bild*]; it must therefore antecedently take up the impressions into its activity, i.e., apprehend them" (A120). This indicates two key features of the imagination: it apprehends and brings a manifold of impressions into a *unity*, and it presents this unity in an *image*. The imagination mediates between the understanding which enables "the unity of its intellectual synthesis," and "sensibility for the manifoldness of apprehension" (B164; B180–81). The significance of this model extends beyond merely organizing experience. The reproductive role of the imagination shows that the understanding, as a conceptual faculty, has recourse to the figurative resources of imaginative activity.[27]

Although we are not yet ready for a discussion of the productive imagination, a few preliminary points are in order. This image-generating capacity becomes increasingly significant in engaging questions of creativity. This can take the form of art, as discussed in the *Critique of the Power of Judgment*, but does not only relate to individual creativity. The generating power of the imagination also pertains to cultural activity in the production of shared symbol systems and representations. This latter concern is tremendously important insofar as it subtends Kant's inquiries into the ethical and political significance of historical representations. Additionally, we should note the question of what might be termed *pathologies* in the productive imagination's spontaneously transgressing the restraints of sensory input. This critical issue appears in the *Prolegomena*, which discusses how the imagination may be "excused if it daydreams [*schwärmt*] every now and then, i.e., if it does not cautiously hold itself inside the limits of experience" (PR, 4:317). Although Kant clearly values the activities of an imagination that is "enlivened and strengthened through such free flight," he nevertheless stresses that the understanding

[27] See *ibid.*, p.163.

should "moderate its [the imagination's] boldness." The understanding "is supposed to think" rather than merely daydream or enthuse. This is because "all assistance in setting bounds, where needed, to the revelry [*Schwärmerei*, better translated as "enthusiasm"] of the imagination depends on it [the understanding] alone" (PR, 4:317). This important comment highlights the double-edged nature of imagination as productive: while invaluable for creative activity, if undisciplined by principles and rules it is also a source of unbridled enthusiasm. When Kant investigates illusion and delusion on cultural levels of representation such as religious traditions, the link with the figurative resources of the imagination is essential. In fact, these cultural representations, for example in traditional and popular forms of religion, are far more potent, humanly and politically, than the relatively rarefied pathologies of dialectical argument he discerns in classical metaphysics.

At this stage of the exposition, the imagination receives preliminary discussion as a non-conscious process of synthesizing sense data, and as mainly reproductive. The task of mediating intuitions and the understanding is also discussed in terms of the *schematism*, which I turn to below. However, it is the understanding which brings the synthesis generated by the imagination into the form of logical concepts. Although the process occurs virtually instantaneously in acts of sensory perception and representation, for purposes of clarification Kant analyzes the general order in which representations of sense intuitions are formed: (1) "the **manifold** of pure intuition," (2) "the **synthesis** of this manifold by means of the imagination," (3) "the concepts that give this pure synthesis **unity**," which "depend on the understanding" (A78–79/B104). With these points in mind, we may turn to the transcendental deduction of the categories, which establishes the logical basis of the concepts of the understanding and their application. Transcendental deduction is the procedure for establishing the general concepts necessary to knowledge, which does not rule out the formation of concepts based on specific experiences. Kant makes the distinction as follows: "I therefore call the explanation of the way in which concepts can relate to objects *a priori* their **transcendental deduction**, and distinguish this from the **empirical** deduction, which shows how a concept is acquired through experience and reflection on it" (A85/B117). Kant follows Aristotle in calling these concepts *categories*, and he proceeds to outline them in a Table of Categories.[28] The general headings are basically the same as in the Table of Judgments, but with

---

[28] With regard to Kant's appropriation of Aristotelian categories, also see PR, 4:323.

different subheadings. These are: (1) *Of quantity* (unity, plurality, totality); (2) *Of quality* (reality, negation, limitation); (3) *Of relation* (of inherence and subsistence, of causality and dependence, of community); and (4) *Of modality* (possibility–impossibility, existence–non-existence, necessity–contingency) (A80/B106).

Kant's general model outlines the organization of sense-based intuitions, through judgment, by means of an array of organizing rules, in the form of categories of the understanding. However, many commentators who accept the overall epistemological model of the critical philosophy also question whether Kant establishes a definitive table of categories. For example, Paul Guyer asks if *all* the categories are actually required.[29] Elsewhere, he draws on Kant's *Reflections* to demonstrate different sets of possible categories. In one instance, he specifies only five of the twelve categories as necessary: "*magnitude, reality, subject, ground,* and *whole.*"[30] He then cites another *Reflection* indicating that only *three* are really necessary: "substance, causality, and composition or wholeness or the relation of part to whole – in other words, just the three categories *of relation.*"[31] As Guyer concludes:

We really do not need to prove the objective validity of twelve distinct *a priori* concepts of objects in general, but only of five general concepts: reality, magnitude, substance, cause, and the fluctuating fifth category, sometimes described as just the general idea of a whole made of parts and sometimes described as the more particular idea of interaction among the parts of a whole.[32]

While questioning a set of precisely twelve categories, Guyer accepts a more restricted group of concepts operative in acts of judgment. Likewise, Allison questions "Kant's notorious claim regarding the completeness and systematic nature of his list of categories."[33] However, as a general response to such concerns, Allison offers a balanced assessment. He summarizes Kant's achievement as "having shown that the activity of judgment presupposes a set of *a priori* concepts which, because of their essential role in judgment, deserve categorical status."[34]

---

[29] Guyer, *Kant*, p.77.
[30] Guyer, "Transcendental Deduction of the Categories," in *The Cambridge Companion to Kant*, p. 134 (citing R4385; 17:528.)
[31] *Ibid.*, p.135; Guyer cites R4476; 17:565.
[32] *Ibid.*, p.136. Longuenesse is also skeptical about Kant's precise table of categories: "contrary to Kant's claim, logic did not emerge in its completed and perfected form from Aristotle's mind" ("Kant on *a priori* Concepts," p. 158, citing Bviii).
[33] Allison, *Kant's Transcendental Idealism*, p.128.
[34] *Ibid.*, p.129.

Imagination and concepts of the understanding 91

It is also significant that the transcendental deduction is a key place in the first *Critique* where metaphors derived from a judicial model appear; for example, that of a tribunal that assesses the legitimacy of concepts. This is important because it further distinguishes Kant's model from a concern with fixed foundational concepts. As Terry Pinkard points out, "Kant had intended his 'deduction' of the categories not to be a derivation of conclusions from absolutely certain first premises; Kant's use of the term, 'deduction', had more in common with legal usage of the term than with the purely logical use of deriving conclusions from premises."[35] Allen Wood also explores the significance of these juridical terms and methods. He remarks that in developing his epistemological model, "Kant compares the task here to the task you would face as a prosecutor (in a Roman-based legal system) who is trying to make a legal case against a defendant."[36] The meaning of deduction is consequently understood as "that which is to establish the entitlement or legal claim" in the use of the concept (A84/B116). This comment is extremely significant, because it relates the legitimate deduction of the categories to the critical issue of exposing invalid uses of concepts.

Therefore, the transcendental deduction is essential to the task of differentiating a logically and empirically informed approach to knowledge from the self-referential paradigms of metaphysics. In the same way, it also serves to assess the more popular explanatory modes generated by heteronomous sources that circulate in all cultures, and hence in the minds of those who internalize such cultural worldviews. In a statement rich with significance for the wider scope of his critical inquiry, Kant discusses popular explanatory concepts people often invoke to make sense of the tribulations of life:

But there are also concepts that have been usurped [*usurpirte Begriffe*], such as *fortune* and *fate*, which circulate with almost universal indulgence, but that are occasionally called upon to establish their claim by the question *quid juris*, and then there is not a little embarrassment about their deduction because one can adduce no clear legal ground for an entitlement to their use either from experience or from reason. (A84–85/B117; also see LM, 29:862)

This highly important comment indicates that *deduction* involves a reflective capacity to test out our explanatory concepts and models through logic and/or experience, rather than simply establishing a fixed table of definitive categories. It is this active process of testing and assessing

[35] Pinkard, *German Philosophy 1760–1860*, p.100.
[36] Allen Wood, *Kant* (Oxford: Blackwell, 2005), p.47, citing A84/B116.

that makes the deduction akin to a juridical endeavor. Equally importantly, this passage connects the transcendental deduction to a critique of illicit culturally based explanatory concepts. Kant mentions non-rational, popular explanatory concepts such as *fortune* and *fate*, to which might be added a host of others that circulate in cultural worlds. Hence the critical intent of establishing logical concepts is to differentiate these from pseudo-concepts originating in the mists of time and persisting from custom and habit. This concern reappears in Kant's subsequent discussion of "invented concepts" (A222/B269), and it links his epistemology to the critical inquiry into culture that comes to fruition in his engagement with historical religions.[37] To be sure, the first *Critique* largely brackets the subsidiary issue of how cultural modalities such as languages and belief systems superimpose themselves on the basic categories.[38] Yet such issues are indirectly indicated in the recurring endeavors to clear away unfounded, but heretofore culturally dominant systems, modes of cognition, and explanatory pseudo-concepts, as is evident in the critiques of metaphysics, dogmatic theology, and historical religions. Kant differentiates the structuring forms of the categories from culturally constructed knowledge systems that fail the tests of logical consistency, reference to sense experience, and susceptibility to public evaluation. The implication is that these spurious ideas inform how we perceive and think beyond the basic organizational structures of the categories; insofar as these pseudo-concepts affect our sense of self and relations with others, they also have significant practical consequences.

The conjunction of ordering capacities with sensory input is one of the basic safeguards against undisciplined and enthusiastic explanatory systems, whether in popular or more rarefied metaphysical form. This concern is evident in Kant's repeated emphasis that the categories of the understanding require intuitions in order to generate knowledge: "the

---

[37] The ethical and political significance of assessing popular concepts circulating in cultures can be gleaned from the examples given by Halbertal and Margalit. They refer to "imaginary reifications such as 'race', 'nation', 'class', 'blood and earth', and the many other reifications that populate ideologies." Moshe Halbertal and Avishai Margalit, *Idolatry* (Cambridge, MA: Harvard University Press, 1992), p.114. This important reference occurs in the course of a discussion of Kant, and how the Enlightenment critique of religion develops into "criticism of ideology as a type of collective illusion" (*ibid.*).

[38] A more explicit treatment of the cultural shaping of representational activity is developed by the neo-Kantian Ernst Cassirer. In a representative passage, Cassirer outlines how the interplay between cognition and object in Kant's epistemology carries over to the structuring resources he classifies as "symbolic forms." This applies most especially to language: "Like cognition, language does not merely 'copy' a given object; it rather embodies a spiritual attitude which is always a crucial factor in our perception of the objective." Ernst Cassirer, *The Philosophy of Symbolic Forms*, vol. 1, *Language* (New Haven: Yale University Press, 1955), p.158.

categories that have just been adduced are nothing other than the **conditions of thinking in a possible experience**, just as **space** and **time** contain the **conditions of the intuition** for the very same thing" (A111). In each case, experience is the *sine qua non* by which these cognitive conditions generate verifiable knowledge. There are two crucial aspects to establishing the parameters of legitimate knowledge: it must include intuitions, and it must involve the correct use of concepts:

> We cannot **think** any object except through categories; we cannot **cognize** any object that is thought except through intuitions that correspond to those concepts. Now all our intuitions are sensible, and this cognition, so far as its object is given, is empirical. Empirical cognition, however, is experience. Consequently, **no *a priori*** cognition is possible for us except solely of objects of possible experience. (B165–66)

The categories are rules that can only be applied to intuitions arising from sensory input; "they do not have any use at all if they are separated from all sensibility" (A248/B305). In other words, the categories do not in themselves generate knowledge. On the basis of such arguments, Kant concludes that "the proud name of an ontology, which presumes to offer synthetic *a priori* cognitions of things in general in a systematic doctrine (e.g. the principle of causality), must give way to the more modest one of a mere analytic of the pure understanding" (A247/B303). Intellectual modesty involves drawing back from the comprehensive but insupportable ontological claims of traditional metaphysics and theology. In all the innovative boldness of his thinking, Kant redirects our inquiries from fruitless speculation to practical application.

PRINCIPLES, JUDGMENT, AND SCHEMATISM

Kant now explores how transcendental categories are *mediated* in relation to empirical intuitions. This is first addressed in terms of the relation between logical categories and sensory experience, but also has important implications for acts of judgment. "The **analytic of principles**," Kant specifies, "will accordingly be solely a canon for the **power of judgment** [*Urteilskraft*] that teaches it to apply to appearances the concepts of the understanding, which contain the condition for rules *a priori*" (A132/B171). Kant employs prosopopoeia to describe the power of judgment as "taught" by the canon of principles. Nevertheless, these cognitive capacities are employed by persons who must exercise judgment within specific contexts. In discussing how "the power of judgment is the faculty for **subsuming** under rules," Kant indicates that every rule would need other rules to show how it is applied, leading to a potentially infinite regress. At some point, we require a capacity to apply rules in context: "the power of judgment [*Urteilskraft*] is a special talent that cannot be taught but only practiced. Thus this is also what is specific to so-called mother-wit [*Mutterwitzes*], the lack of which cannot be made good by any school" (A133/B172). This language resists over-formalization; judgments, including ethical judgments, require a capacity that must be cultivated through practice and cannot be pre-formulated. We are also reminded of Kant's disparagement of the mechanical use of precepts and formulae as the "ball and chain of an everlasting minority."

A concern with *judgments in context* continues to be addressed in a variety of interconnected ways. Kant poses the general epistemological question: how is "the **application** of the category to appearances possible, since no one would say that the category, e.g., causality, could also be intuited through the senses and is contained in the appearance?" (A137–38/B176–77). Such questions indicate the need for "a transcendental doctrine of the power of judgment [*Urteilskraft*]" (A138/B177), which further explicates interstitial concepts such as the schematism. The capacity to judge, as Longuenesse translates "*Vermögen zu urteilen*" (as employed, for example, at A69/B94), is central not only to Kant's epistemology and ethics, but also appears in the *Critique of the Power of Judgment* in relation to aesthetic and purposive (teleological) apprehensions of nature. Longuenesse calls the capacity to judge "that structured, spontaneous, self-regulating capacity characteristic of human minds that makes them capable of making use of concepts in judgments, of deriving judgments from other judgments in syllogistic inferences, and of systematically unifying all of these judgments and inferences in one system of thought."[39] The capacity to relate general concepts to particular cases is essential to acts of judgment, further distinguishing Kant's inquiry from a focus on static *a priori* concepts.

With regard to conceptual resources for making judgments in experience, Kant introduces the notion of *schematism*:

Now it is clear that there must be a third thing [*ein Drittes*], which must stand in homogeneity with the category on the one hand and the appearance on the other, and makes possible the application of the former to the latter. This mediating representation [*vermittelnde Vorstellung*] must be pure (without anything empirical) and yet **intellectual** on the one hand and **sensible** on the other. Such a representation is the **transcendental schema**. (A138/B177)

---

[39] Longuenesse, "Kant on *a priori* Concepts," p.142.

Principles, judgment, and schematism 95

Logical concepts do not immediately reduplicate the structures of empirical reality, and hence can only indirectly be applied thereto. Mediating forms of conceptualization are required. As Guyer observes: "the categories have merely *logical* content," whereas experience "presents itself in spatio-temporal terms."[40] Taking the category of "substance" as an example, Guyer explains that the relevant temporal schema would be "something that endures through the change of its properties," and the concepts of cause and effect would "be applied to experience through the temporal 'schema' of states of affairs that follow one another in time in accordance with a rule."[41] Schematization mediates the conceptual and the empirical, and in this way overlaps with the function of imagination. In fact, Kant stresses that "the schema is in itself always only a product of the imagination." However, the schema is not to be conflated with an image as such; it is not like "five dots in a row" that can provide "an image of the number five." Rather, it is more wide-ranging, such as the thinking of "a number in general," which might then be applied to "five or a hundred." With reference to any ordering of "a multitude" Kant specifies that the schema is distinguished from an image. It is another form of meta-representational activity that encompasses various specific images: "more the representation of a method [*die Vorstellung einer Methode*] for representing a multitude in an image (e.g., a thousand) [*eine Menge (z.b. Tausend) in einem Bilde vorzustellen*] in accordance with a certain concept than the image itself [*als Bild selbst*]" (A140/B179; translation modified). The schema is not the image as such but a mediating of concept and image: "this representation of a general procedure of the imagination [*Einbildungskraft*] for providing a concept with its image [*Bild*] is what I call the schema of the concept" (A140/B179–80). Hence schematization is part of the dynamic process of conceptually ordering our intuitions, bringing them under rules and into unities by mediating imaging with concepts. Kant provides an overview of this interactive model that reconfirms the epistemological boundaries it generates: "the schemata of the concepts of pure understanding are the true and sole conditions for providing them with a relation to objects [*Objecte*], and thus with **significance** [*Bedeutung*], and hence *the categories are in the end of none but a possible empirical use*" (A146/B185; italics added).[42]

As with imagination, Kant recognizes some obscurity surrounding the function of schematism. He writes of "a hidden art in the depths of the

---

[40] Guyer, *Kant*, p.96. [41] Ibid., p.98, citing A144/B183.
[42] Allison, who also quotes this passage, amplifies this comment concerning the logical categories taking on significance only through schematization by arguing that "what Kant is providing here is a set of translations of logical into real modalities." *Kant's Transcendental Idealism*, p.189.

human soul, whose true operations we can discern from nature and lay unveiled before our eyes only with difficulty" (A141/B181). There is an element of non-transparency to our subjective operations; they are indirectly reconstructed on the basis of the "mere form" of appearance presented to us. To summarize:

> We can say only this much: the **image** [*Bild*] is a product of the empirical faculty of productive imagination, the **schema** of sensible concepts (such as figures in space) is a product and as it were a monogram [*ein Monogramm*] of pure *a priori* imagination, through which and in accordance with which the images first become possible, but which must be connected with the concept. (A141–42/B181)

The term "monogram" is used in the sense of a "sketch or outline," which Kant later refers to as "constituting more a wavering sketch, as it were, which mediates between various appearances, than a determinate image, such as what painters and physiognomists say they have in their heads" (A570/B598; I return to this passage in the next chapter, with reference to the transcendental ideal). The schema is a rather indefinite intermediary activity linking concepts, through the activity of the imagination, to empirical intuitions.

Kant also introduces the "principles of the pure understanding" to describe the schematically mediated application of categories in judgments of experience. While the imagination and related schematism explain the figurative features of representation, principles explain the application of rules. The faculty of the pure understanding is "the source of the principles [*der Quell der Grundsätze*] in accordance with which everything (that can even come before us as an object) necessarily stands under rules, since, without such rules, appearance could never amount to cognition of an object corresponding to them" (A159/B198). This reiterates that the understanding generates concepts in response to experience, whereby experience becomes ordered for our faculties. This in itself is crucial, since Kant later emphasizes that the faculty of reason, while taking up concepts generated by the understanding and using them without empirical reference, cannot produce its own concepts and principles. There must be sensible input for the spontaneous ordering capacities (predispositions) of the mind to come into play. Only secondarily are these expanded by reason either as regulative principles for theoretical and practical purposes, or misapplied to putative supersensible entities. To indicate the application of concepts of the understanding in making empirical judgments, Kant defines principles as "rules of the objective use of the categories." He then provides another four-part table to illustrate the general groupings of these principles: (1) *Axioms of intuition*; (2) *Anticipations of perception*; (3) *Analogies of experience*; (4) *Postulates of empirical thinking in general* (A161/B200).[43] Additionally, Kant subdivides this group of four, so that numbers (1) and (2) fall under the heading of "mathematical principles" which are "capable of an intuitive certainty," and numbers (3) and (4) fall under the heading of "dynamical principles [*dynamischen Grundsätze*]" which "are only capable of a discursive certainty" (A162/B201). He stipulates that the mathematical principles are "constitutive," for example in "the determination of appearances as magnitude." In contrast to this, the dynamical principles are said to be "merely regulative" (A178/B221). Longuenesse clarifies this distinction in stating that "'mathematical' combination … is constitutive of its object and arbitrarily produced," while "'dynamical' combination … is only regulative and produced under the condition of an empirical given."[44] Hence, mathematical principles *constitute* their objects through logical procedures alone, without reference to anything empirical; they therefore are "unconditionally necessary, i.e., apodictic." Dynamical principles do not constitute their own objects but are merely rules for ordering objects presented to us through sense intuition: they function "only under the condition of an empirical thinking in an experience, thus only mediately and indirectly" (A160/B199).

For the purposes of our inquiry, we are interested mainly in dynamical principles and their regulative function in relation to experience. Kant explains that "an analogy of experience will therefore be only a rule in accordance with which unity of experience is to arise from perceptions … and as a principle it will not be valid of the objects (of the appearances) **constitutively**, but merely **regulatively**" (A180/B222). Immediately following this point, he adds that "the very same thing will also hold for the postulates [*Postulaten*] of empirical thinking in general, which together concern the synthesis of mere intuition (of the form of appearance), of perception (of its matter), and of experience (of the relation of these perceptions), namely, that they are only regulative principles" (A180/B223). As dynamical principles, both the analogies and the postulates are rules for processing sense intuitions; they concern the relation of cognition to intuition, not things in themselves either in the form of intellectual intuitions or unmediated objects of intuition.

---

[43] With regard to this table, Allison summarizes how principles are judgments that make use of schematized categories: "each of these Principles can be characterized as a synthetic *a priori* judgment which asserts that a particular schema functions as a necessary condition of the possibility of experience." *Kant's Transcendental Idealism*, p.195.

[44] Béatrice Longuenesse, *Kant and the Capacity to Judge* (Princeton University Press, 1998), p.43.

Subsequently we will see that regulative principles, introduced here with regard to the operations of the understanding, become equally crucial for explaining how we can rationally formulate practical laws guiding our autonomous willing and acting. The distinction between constitutive and regulative also has a critical function, insofar as it helps us understand the illusions arising when these regulative principles are mistaken for constitutive ones (positing supersensible objects on the basis of ideas alone, as in metaphysics and rational theology). The role of regulative principles at this stage of the exposition can be understood in light of Longuenesse's comments that conceptual categories do not mirror an ontological order. This severing of logic from a constitutive relation to ontology can initially be discussed with regard to the third type of principle, "analogies of experience." Kant specifies of these that "their principle [*Princip*] is: **Experience is possible only through the representation** [*durch die Vorstellung*] **of a necessary connection of perceptions**" (B218). The task of mediating independently presented sense perceptions is central. Allison emphasizes the significance of the term "analogy" in this regard: "that category and schema (and therefore Principle) are *merely* 'analogous' to one another, rather than being identical, is a direct consequence of Kant's transcendental distinction between sensibility and understanding."[45] Thought and being are not strictly homologous; an order of ideas does not necessarily reflect an order of reality. For valid acts of judgment to occur, we must actively engage sensibly generated intuitions and experience. Allison further emphasizes that the error of rationalist philosophy in conflating logical and temporal relations "leads to the 'transcendental illusion' by means of which these pure concepts are seen as themselves the source of metaphysical principles that are applicable to 'real' objects."[46] In this illusion-governed approach, the need to *translate* experience into judgments is abrogated, and interpretation and mediation collapse into a *literal* imposition of conceptual systems upon speculatively constituted supersensible objects.

The section on the Postulates of Empirical Thinking in General (*Die Postulate des empirischen Denken überhaupt*) is also significant in clarifying how principles provide rules for structuring and assessing our cognitions of phenomena. Kant divides these postulates into three groupings: "1. Whatever agrees with the formal conditions of experience (in accordance with intuition and concepts) is **possible** [*möglich*]. 2. That which

[45] Allison, *Kant's Transcendental Idealism*, p.196.
[46] Ibid., p.197.

is connected with the material conditions of experience (of sensation) is **actual** [*wirklich*]. 3. That whose connection with the actual is determined in accordance with general conditions of experience is (exists) **necessarily** [*notwendig*]" (A218/B265–66). The regulative status of these principles is immediately evident: they are guiding rules for assessing the validity of our thinking about any experience. Most importantly, the critical function of the postulates of empirical thinking is explicated with reference to what Kant terms "invented concepts [*gedichtete Begriffe*]" (A222/B269); this picks up the earlier discussion of *fate* and *fortune* as "concepts that have been usurped," i.e., taken over without any valid claim (A84–85/B117). He introduces this assessment in the course of explicating the "postulate of possibility," which "requires [of things] that their concept agree with the formal conditions of experience in general" (A220/B267). These conditions include the absence of contradiction in the concept as well as the synthesis involved in the empirical cognition of objects. Kant illustrates how thinking might stray from adherence to these formal conditions: "if one wanted to make entirely new concepts [*gar neue Begriffe*] of substances, of forces, and of interactions from the material that perception offers us, without borrowing the example of their connection from experience itself, then one would end up with nothing but figments of the brain [*Hirngespinste*, also meaning 'fantasies']" (A222/B269). This clearly indicates some of the thought-objects of traditional metaphysics, theology, and popular lore formulated without reference to observable empirical laws. These have the status of "invented concepts" not grounded in coherent empirically tested rules for cognizing experience. To further clarify, Kant refers to "a substance that was persistently present in space without filling it" (i.e., *non-material entities*), or "a special fundamental power of our mind to *intuit* the future (not merely, say, to deduce it)" (i.e., *pre-cognition*), or "a faculty of our mind to stand in community of thoughts with other men (no matter how distant they may be)" (i.e., *telepathy*). Each of these specious formulations indicates "concepts the possibility of which is entirely groundless, because it cannot be grounded in experience and its known laws, and without this it is an arbitrary combination of thoughts [*eine willkürlich Gedankenverbindung*]" (A222–23/B270). Kant notes that any serious endeavor to grasp the laws governing reality requires that we "get help from experience," and that this endeavor "does not concern the form of the relation that one can always play with in fictions [*in Erdichtungen spielen*]" (A223/B270). As with the former examples of fortune and fate, invented concepts such as non-material entities, precognition, or telepathy circulate freely through cultural histories in various guises. Unless these specious explanatory ideas are brought to trial by the exercise of empirically informed principles, they distort and falsify our grasp of reality and of ourselves.

In the same vein, with regard to "the postulate of the actuality of things," Kant reiterates that this "requires perception." This stipulation further undermines the metaphysical practice of manipulating concepts without reference to sensory phenomena to construct elegant speculative systems. As Kant observes: "in the mere concept of a thing [*in dem bloßen Begriffe eines Dinges*] no characteristic of its existence can be encountered at all" (A225/B272). This important argument resurfaces later in the *Critique*, as Kant assesses the validity of the ontological proof for the existence of God. It is also noteworthy that here, as a subdivision of the section on the postulate of actuality, Kant introduces the Refutation of Idealism into the B edition of the *Critique* (B274–79). As I have noted, Kant illustrates how many features of the idealist thought of Descartes or Berkeley cannot survive the trial of reason in accordance with critical principles. Knowledge and experience are predicated on cognitively structured representations interacting with a highly diversified sensible world. This approach does not establish a mental ground for knowledge; in fact, it relinquishes foundationalism altogether. Hence, Collins notes that Kant's model requires sense experience based on real objects (though not known "in themselves"), and therefore "gives up the very idea of ultimate evidence as unworkable."[47] Nor does Kant follow a Cartesian approach of combating doubt by invoking a benevolent God who guarantees our knowledge of the world. Because of its reliance on a divine guarantor, Guyer states, "'Cartesian skepticism' was the model of a *non*-autonomous conception of human knowledge."[48] This returns us to the interface of epistemology, religion, and the political: an autonomous model of knowledge does not invoke any heteronomous reference or guarantor, nor is it disconnected from a publicly available interpersonal world of experience accessed in open, discursive forms of judgment.

PHENOMENA AND NOUMENA

The categorical structuring of intuitions demonstrates the mind's active role in empirical knowledge. It is from this *a priori* structuring ability, interacting with intuitions arising from a world "outside us," that Kant

---

[47] Collins, *Possible Experience*, p.84; cf. Guyer, *Kant*, pp.120–22.
[48] Guyer, *Kant*, p.121.

begins to draw what he calls "important consequences." In the Guyer and Wood edition of the first *Critique*, a footnote is appended to this comment, indicating that Kant added the words "against enthusiasm" at this point in his own copy (A238/B297n.*e*). As we saw, "enthusiasm" designates the undisciplined assertion of supersensible knowledge taking the form of "individual illuminations." This notion is crucial to Kant's critique of metaphysics and religion, where it continues to resonate with epistemological, ethical, and political implications.

Kant reminds us that the categories "do not have any use at all if they are separated from all sensibility, i.e. they cannot be applied to any supposed object at all [*keinen angeblichen Gegenstand*]" (A248/B305). Therefore, there can be no valid assertion concerning any object established through the categories alone without sensory input. However, many types of these "supposed objects" do in fact arise and take on collective meaning within intellectual and cultural histories. The very same productive faculties of human minds that govern epistemology also make it possible for us to speculate without reference to sense experience, and to create thought objects devoid of intuitive input. It is here that the likelihood of "a deception that is difficult to avoid" arises. To explain this deception, Kant recapitulates the way objects intuited by us in the form of appearances can be termed "beings of sense (*phaenomena*), because we distinguish the way in which we intuit them from their constitution [*Beschaffenheit*] in itself" (B306). In Kant's use, the term "phenomenon" is basically synonymous with the term "appearance"; these describe intuited sense objects as ordered through the conditions of sensibility and the categories. However, the antithetical correlate of phenomena would then be objects conceived as they might be in themselves, without any human cognitive structuring. We can undertake a thought experiment and imagine reality apart from the organizing activity contributed by our cognitive faculties, but these indirectly conceptualized things-in-themselves are necessarily unknowable. As we have seen, Kant dismisses metaphysical preoccupations with the pursuit of a chimerical reality-in-itself as a waste of time. The concept of things-in-themselves does, however, serve a critical function; it helps us cultivate awareness that in cognizing phenomenal appearances we do *not* have knowledge of reality as such, unmediated by our faculties interacting with sensible intuitions.

Kant now explores a different way of conceiving the conceptually generated opposite to the phenomena actually intuited by us. Generally, the expression "thing-in-itself" designates everyday objects, imagined as they might be without our cognitive structuring. This is also linked with the concept of the *noumenal*, which also can be thought only negatively: "the doctrine of sensibility is at the same time the doctrine of noumenon in the negative sense, i.e., of things that the understanding must think without this relation to our kind of intuition, thus not merely as appearances but as things in themselves" (B307). The hypothesis of the noumenal can serve a critical function in inhibiting our conflation of appearances with things-in-themselves. It indirectly reveals that phenomenal experience has been cognitively ordered. As Kant puts it: "the concept of a *noumenon* is therefore merely a **boundary concept** [*blos ein Grenzbegriff*], in order to limit the pretension of sensibility, and therefore only of negative use" (A255/B311). We become aware not only that we have not grasped the whole of reality, but also that there may be other ways of cognizing the same objects.

However, a distinction can be made between the noumenal thing-in-itself as an object apart from the sensory and cognitive experience of human beings, and reified metaphysical concepts of the noumenal. To imagine this latter form of noumenal, we might theoretically posit "other possible things, which are not objects of our senses at all, and call these beings of understanding (*noumena*)" (B306). Here the term "noumenal" indicates possible non-sensible realities such as God or the immortal soul, which can never be intuitively experienced by humans. Focusing on these conceptual creations as if they were objects, and explicating them through illegitimately applying various categories such as *reality, magnitude, substance, cause* generates metaphysical speculation disconnected from any possible appearances. This misapplication forms the basis for the "supersensible objects that traditional metaphysics thought could be grasped by reason alone."[49] We can speculatively construct such supersensible entities by giving them the attributes of actual phenomena, such as having temporal coordinates, or as operating in terms of cause and effect. However, the essential difference is that these speculatively constructed entities arise from the operations of reason without experience; they are the product of *thought alone* rather than the understanding interacting with sense-based intuitions.

Kant proceeds to explain the nature of the crucial deception and concomitant potential for unbridled enthusiasm that arises from positing noumena as the non-sensible counterparts to the cognitively structured phenomena we can actually experience. One "is thereby misled into

[49] Pinkard, *German Philosophy 1760–1860*, p.41n.33.

taking the entirely **undetermined** concept of a being of the understanding, as a something in general outside our sensibility [*als einem Etwas überhaupt außer unserer Sinnlichkeit*], for a **determinate** concept of a being that we cognize through the understanding in some way" (B307). Legitimately, we can have a general, undetermined conception of non-sensible objects as the negative correlate of our intuitively restricted understanding. However, we can never know what these *noumena* might be in any specifically determinate way; we can make no definite knowledge claims concerning any such entities. The positive sense of the noumenal employed by metaphysics corresponds to a determinate concept and would assume "an object of a non-sensible intuition," also called an "intellectual intuition" (B307). Kant stresses that "such an intuition, namely an intellectual intuition, lies absolutely outside our faculty of cognition"; this is where the critical epistemology is decisive in questioning the very procedures and presuppositions constitutive of metaphysics and rational theology. Therefore, he again stresses that his own use of the term noumenon radically departs from these misguided traditional renderings: "that which we call noumenon must be understood to be such only in a **negative** sense" (B308–09). In the same vein, Kant also ascribes what he terms a "problematic" status to intelligible objects: "the domain outside of the sphere of appearances is empty (for us), i.e., we have an understanding that extends farther than sensibility **problematically**, but no intuition, indeed not even the concept of a possible intuition" (A255/B310). This point, while ceding no ground to those claiming knowledge of intelligible entities, also indicates a capacity for conceptual expansion, albeit only negatively. It indicates that there are limits to the range of the understanding, but can generate no knowledge concerning whatever might be beyond those limits:

Thus the concept of pure, merely intelligible objects is entirely devoid of all principles of its application, since one cannot think up any way in which they could be given, and the problematic thought, which leaves a place open for them, only serves, like an empty space, to limit the empirical principles, without containing and displaying any other object of cognition beyond the sphere of the latter. (A259–60/B315)[50]

---

[50] Wood states that "we may call such concepts 'empty' or 'problematic' concepts: they are 'empty' because they possess no determinate intuitive content; and they are 'problematic' because none of the judgments in which they are predicated of objects can ever be verified or falsified. Our concepts of objects as noumenal or things-in-themselves are all concepts of this sort. So are the ideas of reason which generate the problems of the Dialectic." Allen Wood, *Kant's Rational Theology* (Ithaca, NY: Cornell University Press, 1978), p.48.

In this way, Kant employs the concept of the noumenal as a correlate to establishing the boundaries of the range of our understanding; this concept can be inferred only negatively or problematically, but not actually known in any determinate sense.

Disclaimers concerning our ability to make meaningful statements about noumenal or intelligible objects reappear throughout Kant's critical writings. For example: "If by a merely intelligible object we understand those things that are thought through pure categories, without any schema of sensibility, then things of this sort are impossible" (A286/B342).[51] These unequivocal statements warn us not to conflate Kant's thinking with traditional metaphysical paradigms. His use of concepts such as noumenon, held in a classical binary relation to phenomenon, is in fact radically innovative. Indeed, these reconfigurations of metaphysical constructs have a clear anti-metaphysical function, because they deny speculative claims concerning supersensible knowledge, while indicating the conceptual procedures that give rise to these claims. It is crucial for considering Kant as a theorist of religion and theology that the critical epistemological model stipulates that no knowledge without empirical intuitions, hence no supersensible knowledge, is possible for us. We are able to *think of* such noumenal objects as ideas of reason rather than objects of the understanding that generate actual knowledge.[52] Hence, while denying direct knowledge of the supersensible, Kant retains an indirectly articulated conceptual space for discussing the noumenal. As we shall see, this capacity to think beyond the confines of given intuitions, without making supersensible knowledge claims, is also crucial for a practical approach to ideas of reason.

In order to assess metaphysical and religious concepts, which share common features, Kant must first establish crucial distinctions between his own critical discourse and the "empty trafficking with words" he discerns in metaphysical inquiries into an intelligible world (A257/B312). To develop this theme, Kant discusses an intellectually sophisticated version of this tendency in the work of G. W. Leibniz. The metaphysics of Leibniz, Kant notes, lacked a "reflection [*einer Überlegung*]" determining whether a representation originates from the pure understanding, or is

---

[51] To call the noumenon such an object, Kant continues, "signifies precisely the problematic concept of an object for an entirely different intuition and an entirely different understanding than our own, which is problematic in itself" (A287/B343–44).
[52] "Kant holds that through the pure categories we can *think* objects which can never be *known* by us because no sensible intuition of them can ever be given." Wood, *Kant's Rational Theology*, p.48.

"given in appearance by sensibility" (A269/B325). The term "reflection" indicates a critical assessment of knowledge claims, and it has affiliations with the juridical procedures of the transcendental deduction. "Without this reflection," Kant continues, the theorist is led to "a transcendental amphiboly, i.e., a confusion of the pure object of the understanding [*Verstandobjects*] with the appearance." Because he lacked these critical distinctions, "Leibniz constructed an **intellectual system of the world**" by which he "compared all things with each other solely through concepts." He did not engage the question of "the conditions of sensible intuitions, which bring with them their own distinctions," i.e., specific intuitions of objects in the world. For Leibniz sensibility was not understood as "original," i.e. as an independent source of intuitions and representations. Rather, "sensibility was only a confused kind of representation [*eine verworrene Vorstellungsart*] for him and not a special source of representations [*eine besonderer Quell der Vorstellungen*]" (A270/B326).[53] Within the framework of Leibnizian metaphysics, a theorist can make purely conceptual connections without reference to specific features of actual experience, which is merely secondary.

A consequence of this mode of thinking is that a purely "logical" conceptual system can be used to explain away the evils and injustices of the world by interpreting them as mere "negations" inherent in the limited nature of finite beings. To illustrate this problem, Kant provides the telling example of the metaphysical *principle of non-contradiction* formulated by Leibniz. This holds "that realities (as mere affirmations) never logically oppose each other." Kant argues that this is an "entirely true proposition about the relations of concepts," but such a proposition nevertheless "signifies nothing at all either in regard to nature nor overall in regard to anything in itself (of this we have no concept)" (A273/B329). The first problem concerns the procedure of jumping from logically established relations to putative ontological truths, without any intervention of experience. Additionally, this logical principle of non-contradiction leads in practice to the applied principle that "all ills are nothing but the consequences of the limits of created beings, i.e., negations" (A273–74/B329–30). This type of explanation makes it easy to avoid the daunting problem of confronting the particular sources of these ills, for example in human social-political institutions, attitudes, and actions. This vital point, which is somewhat

---

[53] As Beiser clarifies, "the specific target of [Kant's] criticism is Leibniz's doctrine that sense perception is illusory insofar as it is sensory." According to Beiser this is an accurate representation of Leibniz's views (*German Idealism*, p.80).

understated here in the *Critique*, resurfaces with much greater force in Kant's crucial, non-metaphysical and non-theological engagement with the problem of radical evil and its interconnection with social-political realities in *Religion*.

Kant provides another instance of dubious metaphysical procedures that have direct implications for rational theology. According to the same purely conceptual method of understanding the world, the Leibnizian-style metaphysics of Kant's time holds that it is "not merely possible but natural to unite all reality in one being without any worry about opposition" (A273–74/B329–30). This is another example of ideas being wrought into a self-contained conceptual system that might elegantly cohere on a purely abstract level. However, this neat intellectual construct fails to engage the messy contradictions of actual experience (which may, as Kant observes, offer opposition to such conceptual unity). This type of approach can generate intellectual and even emotional satisfaction, but it tells us nothing about the world within which we live out our lives. These criticisms of metaphysics already indicate an *ethical* as well as an *epistemological* set of concerns. There is a danger of consoling metaphysical systems glossing over morally significant conflicts and evils, diverting intellectual attention from engaging actual human experience in its diversity, complexity, and frequent discord. This brief but significant discussion of some representative problems in classical metaphysics indicates various distinctive features of Kant's approach. The very idea of a comprehensive intellectual system of understanding, attained without reference to empirical experience, not only becomes completely untenable but also feeds into a human tendency to shy away from confronting the evils and contradictions of life, papering these over with comforting explanatory systems. Subsequently, in summarizing the pitfalls of metaphysics, Kant emphasizes that the misapplication of problematical understanding to supersensible entities leads to *transcendental illusion*. In relation to this error, Kant clarifies his conceptual position and differentiates it from strictly epistemological concerns with establishing the certainty of empirical representations: "Our concern here is not to treat of empirical (e.g. optical) illusion … rather, we have to do only with transcendental illusion [*mit dem transcendentalen Scheine*], which influences principles whose use is not ever meant for experience" (A295/B352). Illusion is not simply a matter of misrepresenting the nature of empirical reality. Rather, it is precisely the transcendental categories of understanding, when misconceived and misdirected toward hypostasized supersensible objects detached from sensible intuition, which generate transcendental illusions.

These arguments form an indispensable groundwork for Kant's analyses of theology and religion, and they also begin to indicate the multifaceted quality of his critical approach. Transcendental principles *do* have meaningful uses, such as regulative and symbolic ones that are especially pertinent to practical reason, but they cannot provide knowledge of supersensible objects. This twofold relationship to metaphysics, involving both critique and constructive, non-literal reinterpretation, establishes a pattern that remains consistent throughout Kant's analyses of both theology and historical religions. One of the essential dimensions of this model is the distinction between categories of the understanding and *ideas of reason*. This provides additional conceptual support for an interpretive program that begins in the first *Critique* and plays out through a number of subsequent writings.

CHAPTER 4

Illusions of metaphysics and theology

IDEAS OF REASON

The Transcendental Dialectic turns from the ordering of intuitions by the understanding to our faculty of reason. This investigation delves deeper into the sources of illusion in metaphysics and theology, which are intertwined with a predisposition toward comprehensive explanation. Kant begins with an overview integrating the understanding with the unifying faculty of reason: "All our cognition starts from the senses, goes from there to the understanding, and ends with reason, beyond which there is nothing higher to be found in us to work on the matter of intuition and bring it under the highest unity of thinking" (A298/B355). Reason is the *highest* faculty because its procedures are the most abstracted from experience. But reason in itself, without the understanding's ordered reception of sense intuitions, cannot generate knowledge of reality. The entities hypothesized by metaphysics and theology are emblematic of the endeavors of reason to make ontological assertions disconnected from intuitions.

The understanding is the "faculty of rules" by which intuitions are organized, whereas reason is defined as a "faculty of principles" (A299/B356). Kant describes reason as a "cognition from principles [*Principien*]" in which "I cognize the particular in the universal through concepts" (A300/B357). We have seen that concepts are generated as the understanding organizes sense intuitions. Through the faculty of reason, we can *take up* these concepts and employ them in more far-ranging ways. Reason expands concepts to their maximum range, producing principles that exceed a mere ordering of given intuitions. Each of these faculties has a role in unifying a manifold of information. With the understanding this occurs in relation to a manifold of *intuitions* (for which the unifying capacity of imagination is crucial). In the case of reason, the manifold of the *rules of the understanding* is unified under these more encompassing principles. "If the understanding may be a faculty of unity of appearances by means of rules, then reason is the faculty of the unity of the rules of understanding under principles" (A302/B359). Reason, while dependent on the understanding, is therefore the seat of principles or ideas. Kant further explains his terminology as follows: "Just as we called the concepts of understanding 'categories', we will ascribe a new name to the concepts of pure reason and call them 'transcendental ideas'" (A311/B368). Later in the *Critique*, when discussing the "cosmological ideas" of reason, Kant clarifies the development of ideas from the categories:

[I]t is only from the understanding that pure and transcendental concepts can arise, that reason really cannot generate any concepts at all, but *can at most only free a concept of the understanding from the unavoidable limitations of a possible experience*, and thus seek to extend it beyond the boundaries of the empirical [*die Grenzen des Empirischen*], though still in connection [*Verknüpfung*] with it. (A409/B435; italics added)

In outlining how reason abstracts the categories from their organizing function in relation to sensible intuitions, this passage also illustrates both the value and the hazards of transcendental ideas. The constructive aspect concerns ideas that have wider, more universal practical significance than anything derived from sense experience, including historical and political realities. Moreover, ideas and principles can impact meaningfully upon social and political worlds (and this is the crucial significance of Kant's stating that the concepts *freed* by reason nevertheless remain *in connection with* the empirical world).

More immediately relevant are the *dangers* in reason's pursuit of unconditioned ideas. Kant inquires whether reason is itself a "genuine [*eigener*] source of concepts and judgments," or if it is "merely a subordinate [*subalternes*] faculty that gives to given cognitions a certain form, called 'logical' form" (A305/B362). The basis for this question is that reason is the faculty for unifying concepts of the understanding under a smaller number of more universal concepts called ideas or principles. This means that reason in itself "deals only with the understanding and its judgments" and "is therefore not the unity of a possible experience"; i.e., it does not directly relate to sensible intuitions, and its operations provide no knowledge thereof (A307/B363). Because of this ancillary status, "no adequate empirical use can ever be made of" the supreme principle of pure reason (A308/B365). While indicating a capacity for conceptual expansiveness serving practical purposes, Kant eschews metaphysical illusion, whereby ideas of reason are conflated with knowledge claims about the nature of reality. This dialectical misuse of reason generates "misinterpretations and delusions [*Mißdeutungen und Verblendungen*]" (A309/B366). From the expanding and unifying quality of rational judgments, traditional metaphysics hypothesizes a totality in empirical conditions existing with reference to reality (as in Leibniz's principle of non-contradiction). Because of their association with the speculative excesses of traditional metaphysics, the "concepts of reason" are introduced in the first book of the Transcendental Dialectic (with "dialectic," as we have seen, designating a sophistical use of logic).

To develop his inquiry, Kant immediately turns to Plato's theory of ideas. He recounts that "Plato made use of the expression **idea** in such a way that we can readily see that he understood by it something that not only could never be borrowed from the senses, but that even goes far beyond the concepts of the understanding" (A313/B370). As he summarizes core elements of Platonic thought, it is clear that Kant simultaneously distances himself from this tradition: "Ideas for him [Plato] are archetypes of things themselves [*Urbilder der Dinge selbst*], and not, like the categories, merely the key to possible experiences" (A313/B370). As we shall see, Kant repeatedly utilizes the term *Urbild*, variously translated as archetype, prototype, or original image, to classify representations of ideals of reason with a practical function (e.g., the Sage, the philosopher, the human being pleasing to God). This function is strictly differentiated from a metaphysical conception of ideas as the forms or templates of physical objects. However, before articulating their differences more explicitly, Kant first presents Platonic ideas as prefiguring the practical interpretation he later gradually develops. "Plato found his ideas preeminently in everything that is practical, i.e. in what rests on freedom, which for its part stands under cognitions that are the proper product of reason" (A314–15/B371). Kant's relationship to Plato is complex; he appropriates the insight that ideas do not simply mirror sensible realities, and that they can have a transforming impact upon reality (i.e., upon the social-political worlds we create and inhabit). A key feature is the linking of ideas and *freedom*: ideas are a means whereby we can actively modify our environments. Yet both the way ideas are conceptualized and the type of moral-political order to which they give rise are quite distinct in their Platonic and Kantian formulations. An important footnote explains that Plato "also extended his concept to speculative cognitions, whenever they were pure and given wholly *a priori*." Kant eschews this prototypical metaphysical approach linking ideas with direct knowledge of reality: "I cannot follow him in this, just as little as I can in the mystical deduction [*in der mystichen Deduction*] of these ideas or in the exaggerated way in which he hypostasized them" (A314/B371n.). This is a crucial disclaimer separating the practical function of ideas from any ontological claims. Kant highlights his radical departure from both metaphysical speculation and from the enthusiasm that neglects empirically founded concepts by straying into the vague territory of mystical illuminations.[1]

It is crucial that the disconnection from sense-based intuitions, so problematic for knowledge claims, actually becomes a constructive resource for ethics. "Whoever would draw the concepts of virtue from experience, whoever would make what can at best serve as an example [*als Beispiel*] for imperfect illustration into a model [*als Muster*] for a source of cognition (as many have actually done), would make virtue an ambiguous non-entity, changeable with time and circumstances, useless for any sort of rule" (A315/B371). If ideas and principles are derived from empirical sources, then ethics and politics become limited by contingent experience, not only on the individual level, but on the levels of history and tradition. Kant is also careful to stipulate that the unity and systematicity exhibited by ideas cannot be *imposed* upon reality, which is one of the errors of speculative metaphysics. Ideas are regulative with regard to autonomous ethical-political practice, serving as guidelines for judgment and action. "For it is only by means of this idea [of virtue] that any judgment of moral worth or unworth is possible; and so it necessarily lies at the ground of every approach to moral perfections" (A315/B372). We recognize virtue (or its antithesis) by applying principled criteria for this determination to experience. Hence the inquiry shifts from the world of intuitions yielding knowledge, to the experiential realm as social and historical, wherein practical choices and actions occur.

To be sure, social-political worlds already incorporate ideational elements; they offer ready-made ideologies that are to varying degrees limited and parochial. Hence the *completeness* and *systematic unity* of ideas of reason indicates a possible expansion of our ethical vision to vistas more inclusive, i.e., more universal, than the "empirical cognitions" of existing societies. Kant limits the scope of knowledge in the understanding, while expanding the range of ethical principles beyond the constraints of individual and cultural experience. At this juncture we may note the

---

[1] In his *Lectures on Metaphysics* Kant also describes Plato's approach to ideas of reason as "mystical" (LM, 29: 950–57). He clarifies his definition as follows: "mysticism, or the presupposition of an intuitive intellect <*intellectus intuitivi*> or intellectual intuition <*intuitus intellectualis*>, i.e., the possibility that purely intellectual *a priori* concepts <*conceptus a priori mere intellectuales*> rest on immediate intuition of the understanding" (LM, 29:953).

parallelism in Kant's engagement with traditional metaphysics and with traditional ethical worldviews. In each case he questions the heteronomy of received authority in order to disclose possibilities for fresh lines of thinking. An ethical norm derived from social-political sources would likely have only partial validity; it would serve the interests of some and not others, and would therefore fail the criterion of universality (discussed in the next chapter).

It is therefore apposite that Kant cites the idea of "the **Platonic Republic**," thereby linking his inquiry with definite social and political concerns. He points out that many interpreters find Plato's conception of the ideal Republic to be impracticable; it "has become proverbial as a supposedly striking example of a dream of perfection that can have its place only in the idle thinker's brain" (A316/B373). However, without defending the specifics of Plato's political vision, Kant strongly advocates the political value of ideas in his own terms:

A constitution providing for the **greatest human freedom** according to laws that permit **the freedom of each to exist together with that of others** (not one providing for the greatest happiness, since that would follow of itself) is at least a necessary idea, which one must make the ground not merely of the primary plan of a state's constitution but of all the laws too; and in it we must initially abstract from the present obstacles, which may perhaps arise not so much from what is unavoidable in human nature as rather from neglect of the true ideas [*der ächten Ideen*] in the giving of laws. (A316/B373)

Here Kant employs an ethical-political idea that is more his own than Plato's: that of the social contract establishing laws permitting the greatest freedom of all insofar as this does not violate the freedom of others. He does not develop a template for an ideal Republic, but his focus on mutual autonomy is in many respects significantly different from the Platonic model.[2] Since the political thinking of both Plato and Aristotle contributes to the heteronomous and hierarchical models predominant in Western history and elsewhere, it is imperative that we do not mistakenly assimilate Kant into this more traditional framework. The reference to happiness in this passage is also noteworthy. Kant does not *base* ethical-political laws on the principle of happiness, which privileges individual gratification, but claims that maximum happiness will ensue from the application of just principles. This reference to the happiness of all

---

[2] For example, Plato's "noble falsehood" concerning the division of humanity into four classes ordered according to gold, silver, bronze, and iron sustains hierarchical models in which different rules and laws apply to different groups of people according to a pre-given structure (see *Republic*, Book III, 414–15). This is the antithesis of a Kantian model of universal laws.

balanced with that of others bears fruit in the regulative idea of a realm of ends.

Reciprocal freedom and the pursuit of shared happiness under laws of autonomy form the heart of Kant's ethical and political thinking. He augments this point toward the end of the *Critique*, arguing in the tradition of social contract theory that "the state of nature is a state of injustice and violence, and one must necessarily leave it." However, Kant's vision of the lawful state differs significantly from that of Hobbes, for example. In leaving the hypothetical "state of nature," where each person is pitted against the other, striving for personal gain and pre-eminence in relations of ungoverned force, we need not give ourselves over to the hegemony of the Leviathan. Rather, the individual relinquishes the lawlessness of the state of nature "in order to submit himself to the lawful coercion which alone limits our freedom in such a way that it can be consistent with the freedom of everyone else and thereby with the common good" (A752/B780; and cf. TP, 8:291–97). Kant is not describing historical facts concerning the emergence of the rule of law in specific political units. This model of relinquishing a state of nature characterized by brute force clarifies how, at least ideally, the institution of ethical and political laws takes account of the rights and freedoms of all persons. The idea of mutually beneficial and equally applicable laws also emphasizes the free public expression of diverse and critical views. Consequently, Kant adds this essential point: "to this freedom, then, there also belongs the freedom to exhibit [*auszustellen*] the thoughts and doubts which one cannot resolve oneself for public judgment [*öffentlich zur Beurteilung*] without thereupon being decried as a malcontent and a dangerous citizen" (A752/B780). To be sure, Kant's advocacy for freedom of speech must be held in balance with his equal emphasis on mutually applicable laws, as well as with his overriding concern with truth on all levels (as emphasized in his above reference to "true ideas"). Therefore, freedom of speech cannot mean the lawless freedom of the state of nature, in which one might say anything at all (including hate speech, slander, misleading and untruthful claims on the part of businesses, politicians, or their surrogates, etc.). Freedom of speech means freedom to uncover truth. In this way, ideas of reason also form the counterpart to Kant's empirically informed epistemology and its focus on assessing truth claims. As the correlate to basing knowledge on publicly accessible sense intuitions, practical ideas are not derived from any given experience, but they impact upon the phenomenal, in the form of the political, through autonomous, principled judgments occurring in public forums.

Kant's discussion of ideas emphasizes the necessity to "abstract from present obstacles." This refers to the conditions of extant states, where the egalitarian ideal of mutual freedom under just laws may be nowhere in evidence. He notes that these less than ideal states of affairs do not result from something "unavoidable in human nature," hence his explanation is not deterministic. Rather, unjust conditions "result from neglect of the true ideas in the giving of laws"; they are the result of *contingent historical processes*. A series of errant choices made collectively or by authorities over great spans of time have genealogically constituted existing states of affairs in the form of the unjust societies predominating in the world. Following these comments, Kant then elaborates on this crucial theme of the historical production of so-called *facts* on the level of politics and the political: "nothing is more harmful or less worthy of a philosopher than the vulgar appeal to allegedly contrary experience, *which would not have existed at all if institutions had been established at the right time according to ideas*, instead of frustrating all good intentions by using *crude concepts* [*rohe Begriffe*] in place of ideas, just because these concepts were drawn from experience" (A317/B373; italics added). This powerful argument develops an indispensable dimension of Kant's ethical-political analysis. His approach to the institutions that shape human existence is even more dynamic than his epistemological model. It is a temporal-historical model, including the volitional activities of those who have instituted policies and laws over a series of generations.

As we saw in the previous chapter, Kant employs the postulates of empirical thinking in general to differentiate between testable, empirically grounded concepts and "invented concepts" such as fate, fortune, telepathy, and precognition. Here, he makes a parallel distinction between *true ideas of reason* and *crude concepts* drawn from experience. He indicates that conceptual frameworks of some variety will play a role in ordering and rationalizing existing institutions and mores; the question becomes that of assessing these inherited conceptual frameworks concerning their truth and legitimacy. What *ought to be* should not be reduced to, or derived from, what *is* (or, to better emphasize the historical contingency of political realities, what *happens to be*):

> For when we consider nature, experience provides us with the rule and is the source of truth [*der Quelle der Wahrheit*]; but with respect to moral laws, experience is (alas!) the mother of illusion [*die Mutter des Scheins*], and it is most reprehensible to derive the laws concerning what I **ought to do** from what **is done**, or want to limit it to that. (A318–19/B375)

Kant's approach to problems of knowledge is explicitly reversed with regard to practical concerns, where the pursuit of *ethical truth* is paramount. Whereas in epistemology ideas without reference to possible experience generate dialectical illusion, for ethical-political questions it is often the predominant socially conditioned norms nurtured by those seeking power over others that yield crude principles. In contrast to parochial codes instituting hierarchy and favoritism, for example, ideas of reason represent the maximum of inclusivity and universality. They have the same relation to the crude concepts formed by the power dynamics of political histories as does the moral law to exclusive conventional codes. At each level, the idea serves as a critical resource for judging and modifying such crude concepts and potentially rectifying existing institutions and practices. This dynamic interplay of ideal and real through autonomous judgments occurring over the span of histories is central to Kant's ethical, political, and religious thinking.

The challenge is to instantiate ethical ideas through critically judging existing cultural systems. Kant realistically allows that any actualization of ideas of freedom and justice will necessarily be partial and imperfect, and will involve us in incessant labors. Yet true ideas should on no account be dismissed because of their lofty and seemingly unrealizable nature. To make his case, immediately following his discussion of the Platonic Republic, Kant explicates the idea of freedom in what he calls its *maximum* articulation (meaning its widest conceptualization as a regulative principle of the greatest possible freedom for all under mutual laws). "Even though this may never come to pass, the idea of this maximum [*dieses Maximum*] is nevertheless wholly correct when it is set forth as an archetype [*zum Urbilde aufstellt*], in order to bring the legislative constitution of human beings ever nearer to a possible greatest perfection" (A317/B374). Here ideas are portrayed as generating foundational representational forms, i.e., *Urbilder*, with an explicitly practical function. Unlike the Platonic forms, in Kant's usage archetypes are not ontologically grounded, but rather constructed by the operations of reason and given an exemplary form drawn from phenomenal and cultural factors.[3] A few lines later, Kant notes that any actual human being may have little

---

[3] An archetype is therefore a representation of an ideal, i.e., the maximum conceivable realization of an idea within a given frame of inquiry (some of Kant's examples are: the wise man or sage, the philosopher, the ethical human being). In his *Lectures on Metaphysics*, Kant also specifies that "the greatest <*maximum*> is a relative concept, i.e., it does not give me a determinate concept" (LM, 28:568). This point further differentiates Kant's usage of the concept of the maximum from any ontological pretensions to establishing an absolute standpoint.

congruence with "the idea of humanity that he bears in his soul as the archetype of his actions [*das Urbild seiner Handlungen in seiner Seele trägt*]" (A318/B374). Nevertheless, although no person can fully embody the ideal, it is practically possible to approximate it in the course of our lives. This is "where ideas become efficient causes (of actions and their objects), namely in morality [*im Sittlichen*]" (A317/B374). The ideal archetype is a representational configuration of an idea of perfectibility generated by reason, which we can each approximate through autonomous efforts. Kant frequently links ideas of reason presented through ideals with various representational forms transmitted historically, while also utilizing ideas to interpret and assess the moral worth of these culturally informed images. All Kant's subsequent discussions of ethical and religious models, representations, and archetypes are rooted in the first *Critique*'s formulation of ideas and ideals of reason and how these are represented.

Transcendental ideas are concepts of the understanding detached from intuitions and extended to their maximum conceptual range (sometimes also called the unconditioned). Because something unconditioned can be thought, but never actually known, these are ideas "to which no congruent object can be given in the senses." They do not concern matters of knowledge and cannot be correlated with entities of any kind. Nevertheless, "they are not arbitrarily invented [*nicht willkürlich erdichtet*], but given as problems [*aufgegeben*] by the nature of reason itself" (A327/B383–84). With reason, we possess a capacity to generate ideas that surpass the range of possible experience. As indicated in Kant's discussion of the just Republic, these ideas have their potential application mainly in practical concerns, rather than epistemologically. By providing regulative guidelines, ideas are "the indispensable condition of every practical use of reason" in making ethical and political judgments. Kant also specifies with reference to the practical application of an idea that "its *execution* [*Ausübung*; also meaning "performance"] is always bounded and defective, but within bounds that cannot be determined" (A328/B385). Practical ideas cannot be applied without reference to the variable social-historical worlds we inhabit; yet, while these contexts affect our capacity to implement them, the degree to which this might occur remains unpredictable and non-deterministic. Hence, application is not mechanical, but requires *acts of judgment* taking into account features unique to every situation. Nevertheless, ideas can have ameliorative impact on our actions, even if only incrementally: "the practical idea is always fruitful in the highest degree and unavoidably necessary in respect of actual actions [*der wirklichen Handlungen*]. In it practical reason even has the causality actually to bring forth [*das wirklich hervorzubringen*] what its concept contains" (A328/B385). In this sense ideas such as truth and justice can become real in affecting existing states of affairs, insofar as our actions guided by the idea can lead to improvements in ethical-political conditions. However, ideas as such lack direct intuitive representation: "we can never project it in an image [*niemals im Bilde entwerfen können*]" (A328/B384). This is why Kant introduces the notions of *ideals* that, by contrast, offer more individualized representations of ideas, as in his associated use of the term *Urbild*. Ideals and archetypes convey rational ideas in intuitively accessible form, and therefore assist us in implementing abstract ideas under actual social-political conditions.

This approach is not idealistic in a facile sense of being disconnected from political realities. Nor does it involve a utopian vision of unidirectional or uniform progress. Yet, through actively applying practical ideas of reason *in situ*, we can have a constructive impact on the dominant worldviews and institutions shaping human reality within specific societies, thereby generating ongoing political realization of freedom under just laws. Just as Kant's active epistemological model opposes any construal of human beings as merely passive recipients of sense impressions, in a similar way we are not merely molded by the established norms of existing ethical and political traditions. We have the potential to critically engage these parochial sets of norms through the resources of reason, by which we can assess the "crude" ideas operative in societies against criteria like truth, justice, inclusivity and universality.

DIALECTICAL CONSTRUCTIONS OF SOUL, COSMOS, AND GOD

A constructive ethical-political vision predicated on autonomy unfolds only incrementally in Kant's work. Much of the remainder of the first *Critique* interrogates traditional forms of metaphysics and theology that stray beyond the range of the understanding and embroil themselves in unsustainable ontological speculations. However, Kant's approach to these traditional sources is also dynamic: he questions their literal validity, while simultaneously opening up alternative lines of reinterpretation. In accordance with this twofold project, Kant outlines the three major classes of transcendental ideas elaborated in traditional metaphysics: "the **first** contains the absolute (unconditioned) **unity** of the **thinking subject**, the **second** the absolute **unity** of the **series** of **conditions of appearance**, the **third** the absolute **unity** of the **condition of all objects of thought** in general" (A334/B391). These three classes of transcendental ideas correspond to traditional metaphysical formulations of the *soul*, the *cosmos* or world-whole, and the highest being or *God*. The first, the "thinking subject," is the "object of **psychology**," indicating the branch of metaphysics called "rational psychology," which proffers a "transcendental doctrine of the soul." The second consists of the "sum total of appearances (the world)" and is "the object of **cosmology**," which offers a "transcendental science of the world" explaining the total order of reality. Finally, "the being of all beings" is "the object of **theology**," which sought to establish a "transcendental cognition of God" as the origin and ordering principle of all that is (A334–35/B391–92). These three areas of metaphysical inquiry stray into supersensible speculation and thereby transgress legitimate uses of reason. However, the three classes of transcendental ideas also form the basis for three ideas of reason subsequently developed by Kant. They therefore become crucial to the ethical interpretation of traditional concepts, for example in the postulates of practical reason.

There are two main ways of understanding these ideas of reason. For example, Guyer notes that in Kant's explication "the traditional metaphysical concepts of the soul, of the world-whole, and of God are not supposed to be the arbitrary inventions of philosophers, but the natural product of the human faculty of reason."[4] To be sure, such arguments for the spontaneous generation of ideas by reason seem to disregard historical and cultural influences upon the formation of concepts. At the same time, Kant is drawing upon a historical tradition of metaphysical and theological speculation, i.e., the Western European and Christian one, and offering an innovative understanding of these traditional concepts. Accordingly, Guyer also indicates a historical-critical procedure when he refers to Kant's explication of the ideas of reason as "an elaborate reconstruction of the contents of traditional metaphysics."[5] Kant is critically reinterpreting inherited notions of *completion*, *unity*, and *absoluteness* as they have been applied to the concept of a unitary subject, a world-whole, and an ultimate being. He refutes arguments that confuse concepts of

---

[4] Paul Guyer, *Kant* (London: Routledge, 2006), p.132.
[5] *Ibid.*, p.133. The two ways of reading the *Critique* on the issue of rational metaphysics are not strictly incommensurable. The one highlights an abstracted reason generating ideas, disregarding the cultural histories that show a diversified range of potentially universalizable ideals. The second reading, which is followed here, retains the sense of reason's capacity to generate practical ideas, but understands this process as intertwined with specific cultural and intellectual histories, so that variations in the representations of ideals are also considered.

Dialectical constructions of soul, cosmos, and God 119

totality with corresponding supersensible objects, while simultaneously reconceiving them as regulative principles.

In Kant's approach to ideas of reason the impetus toward totality, as Guyer notes, is rendered in such a way that it "derives from some *practical* rather than *theoretical* objective." Guyer then asks the vital question: "But *what* practical law of reason is it that requires the representation of anything unconditioned?"[6] In responding to this question Guyer cites one of Kant's "Reflections" that refers to "the absolute unity of reason" and "the harmony of the sum of all purposes."[7] The notion of a harmony of the sum of all purposes, Guyer proposes, "represents some sort of constraint on the rationality of one's actions by requiring their compatibility with, or even advancement of, the harmonious achievement of the aims of all, thus an anticipation of the conception of the categorical imperative as the universal law of nature."[8] This corresponds with Kant's formulation of ethical-political laws that sustain the freedom of each person in harmony with that of all others. However, before this practical reworking of regulative ideas can be further developed, the critical task of clearing away the misconceptions of traditional metaphysics is far from complete. The problem of the deceptions engendered by dogmatic metaphysics is given its most detailed treatment in relation to ideas of reason. Each of the three classes of transcendental ideas produces specious dialectical inferences without reference to objects of possible experience. These speculative constructions lead to "an unavoidable illusion" by which we presume to "give objective reality" to mere ideas. Kant refers to these as "sophistries not of human beings but of pure reason itself" (A339/B397), to emphasize a misuse arising from the operations of reason when it has not been subjected to the disciplining of critique. With these concerns, Kant is not merely engaging his predecessors and contemporaries in the field of rationalist metaphysics, such as Descartes, Leibniz, Wolff, *et al*. Insofar as we are generally drawn toward comprehensive explanations of self and reality in any form, we also fall into the typical errors of the classical metaphysicians and theologians. An interface exists between the highly abstracted speculations of metaphysics and the more culturally influential ideas of theology and religion. In the latter, the dialectical tendencies of reason are reinforced by other needs, such as a longing for certainty and consolation

---

[6] Paul Guyer, *Kant and the Claims of Knowledge* (Cambridge University Press, 1987), p.397; italics added.
[7] *Ibid.*, p.398, citing R4849; 18:5–6.
[8] *Ibid.*

on a personal level, as well as deference to authority and group cohesion on social-political levels.

To make his case, Kant presents "three species of ... dialectical syllogisms," i.e., three forms of fallacious reasoning expanding upon the core ideas of metaphysics. Accordingly, the transcendental concept of the *subject* gives rise to a "*transcendental paralogism*"; the transcendental concept of *absolute totality in a series* gives rise to dialectical inferences called the "*antinomy of pure reason*"; and the *absolute synthetic unity of all conditions for the possibility of things* gives rise to the inference of "a being of all beings" for which there is "no concept at all," leading to the dialectical syllogism called "*the ideal of pure reason*" (A340/B398). Each of these interrelated metaphysical constructs is treated in a separate chapter of the Transcendental Dialectic. I will outline Kant's main arguments following the order in which they are formulated.

PARALOGISMS AND ANTINOMIES

Kant defines "paralogism" as "the falsity of a syllogism due to its form" (A341/B399). The paralogisms of pure reason concern the hypostatization of the concept of the soul into an entity, and the attribution of definite characteristics to this entity. The rational psychologists have a single basis upon which to build their edifices: they commence from the introspective experience of a thinking being: "**I**, as thinking, am an object of inner sense, and am called 'soul'" (A342/B400). Here Kant returns to the nature of *apperception* as a general awareness of the process of thinking: "this inner perception is nothing beyond the mere apperception **I think**, which even makes all transcendental concepts possible"; however, this "inner experience cannot be regarded as empirical cognition" (A343/B401). In other words, there is no intuitively given object corresponding to the awareness of thinking as such. Nevertheless, following the "guide of the categories," the rational psychologists devise "the pure doctrine of the soul, without any other principle being cognized in the least" (A345/B403). The pure rules of the understanding, suitable only for organizing cognition of empirical objects, are used illegitimately for conceptualizing a non-intuitive supersensible entity. The inner apperception of oneself *as thinking* is converted into the substantialized form of a thing that thinks (*res cogitans*). Drawing on the rules of the understanding, the metaphysicians attribute qualities to the entity called soul such as immateriality, incorruptibility, personality, and immortality. By contrast, Kant insists that we cannot characterize our unified thought processes as an entity.

He accordingly describes the "wholly empty representation **I** [*gänzlich leere Vorstellung: Ich*], of which one cannot even say that it is a concept, but a mere consciousness that accompanies every concept" (A346/B404). Kant retains an empty place at the core of the subject, which he calls "the transcendental subject of thoughts = x ... about which, in abstraction, we can never have even the least concept" (A346/B404).[9]

The first edition of the *Critique* explicates the problem in considerable detail, outlining how qualities of substantiality, simplicity, and personality are attributed to the soul. With reference to the unknown "x" of human subjectivity, Kant argues that "this Something is not extended, not impenetrable, not composite, because these predicates pertain only to sensibility and its intuition, insofar as we are affected by such objects (otherwise unknown to us)" (A358). Here the work of the Transcendental Aesthetic, showing that knowledge requires intuitions organized by the categories, becomes crucial in combating the systemic errors of metaphysics. Because no intuitions are provided by consciousness as such, "we can have little hope of broadening our insights through mere concepts [*durch bloße Begriffe*] without any relation to possible experience (still less through the mere subjective form of all our concepts, our consciousness)" (A361). In discussing the third paralogism of personality, a similar refutation is directed at dogmatic assertions concerning the unity of the person. However, in this section Kant adds a key point anticipating the arguments of his ethics: "the concept of personality" expressing "a unity of the subject which is otherwise unknown to us" is nevertheless "necessary and sufficient for practical use" (A365–66). This practical value of the concept of personality is linked with freedom and the capacity to recognize and act upon the moral law. Finally, Kant formulates a refutation of "the ideality of outer relation" attributed to Descartes. He defines this position as that of the "idealist," who "does not admit that [external objects of sense are] cognized through immediate perception and infers from this that we can never be fully certain of their reality from any possible experience" (A368–69). Kant recapitulates the empirically oriented element of his epistemology, for which "external things exist as well as my self, and indeed both exist on the immediate testimony of my self-consciousness." This immediate perception "is at the same time a sufficient proof of their reality" (A371). Therefore, he emphasizes that "the real in outer

---

[9] Kant is consistent in this respect. He allows only a negative characterization of the noumenon, and is willing to posit a thing in itself that can never be known apart from appearances. Here the "I" is left in abeyance as a "something = x," and we shall see that a parallel approach is taken with regard to the idea of an ultimate being.

appearances is thus actual only in perception, and cannot be actual in any other way" (A376). With these arguments, Kant repeatedly distances himself from possible misleading associations with various forms of pre-critical idealism.

These investigations trace the operation whereby the faculties of understanding and reason generate illusions from the fabric of their own structuring concepts:

> Thus every dispute about the nature of our thinking being and its conjunction with the corporeal world is merely a consequence of the fact that one fills the gaps regarding what one does not know with paralogisms of reason, making thoughts into things and hypostatizing them [*man seine Gedanken zu Sachen macht und sie hypostasirt*]; from this arises an imagined science [*eingebildete Wissenschaft*]. (A395)

The metaphysical propensity for total explanation, for example concerning the "something = x" of human subjectivity, generates illusory constructs to fill the gaps in speculative knowledge. "Everyone either presumes to know something about objects about which no human being has any concept, or else makes his own representations into objects [*seine eigene Vorstellungen zu Gegenständen macht*], and thus goes round and round in an eternal circle of ambiguities and contradictions" (A395). In this way, representations deriving from the categories (quantity, quality, cause and effect, etc.), and from ideas generated by reason's progression toward maximum explanation, are disconnected from the testing-ground of experience. As Kant summarizes: "One can place all **illusion** [*Schein*] in the taking of a **subjective** condition of thinking for the cognition of an **object**" (A396). The illusion of rational psychology is to interpret this transcendental unity of thinking as an objectified "subject of these thoughts," which Kant also calls a "hypostatized consciousness (*apperceptionis substantiate*)" (A402).

Before moving to the next dialectical syllogism, a further observation on the concept of the soul is in order. Summarizing his findings concerning "this transcendental illusion of our psychological concepts," Kant notes that three "dialectical questions" arise within rational psychology. The first concerns "the possibility of the community of the soul with an organic body," or the relation of the soul to the body; i.e., the so-called mind–body problem. The second concerns "the beginning of this community, i.e., of the soul in and before the birth of the human being." The third dialectical question concerns "the end of this community, i.e., of the soul in and after the death of the human being (the question concerning immortality)" (A384; also see B395n.). The speculative problems encapsulated in these questions are based on the fundamental error of metaphysics, whereby ideas and apperceptions are misconstrued as distinct objects. This generates specious questions which simply cannot be answered. However, of these "dialectical questions," the problem of the *immortality of the soul* returns with some significance as a practical postulate disconnected from all knowledge claims. This practical orientation is indicated in the second edition of the first *Critique*; Kant asks his readers to join him in an endeavor to "turn our self-knowledge away from fruitless and extravagant speculation toward fruitful practical uses, which, even if it is always directed only to objects of experience, takes its principles from somewhere higher [i.e., from reason], and so determines our behavior, as if our vocation extended infinitely far above experience, and hence above this life" (B421). I note this issue because of its significance for Kant's ethics and interpretation of religion, especially with regard to an ethical vocation that calls us to a more principled relation to others.

The second type of dialectical syllogism is defined as a "contradiction in the laws (antinomy) of pure reason" (A407/B434). Here Kant addresses the speculative claims of traditional metaphysics and theology concerning the origins and nature of the world (cosmology). He begins by noting that, "just as the paralogism of pure reason laid the ground for a dialectical psychology, so the antinomy of pure reason will put before our eyes the transcendental principles of an alleged pure (rational) cosmology" (A408/B435). To illustrate the speciousness of any proof or disproof concerning speculative constructs unrelated to intuitions, Kant outlines a series of four opposing stances on these questions. In each instance, both the positive argument (thesis) and the negative counter-argument (antithesis) have a degree of conceptual plausibility, yet each transgresses the limits of the understanding. In this way, the opposing arguments cancel each other out, forming *antinomies* that illustrate the groundlessness of all metaphysical assertions and counter-assertions concerning supersensible realities. In brief, the four cosmological antinomies can be summarized as follows: (1) that the world does/does not have a beginning in time; (2) that every substance is/is not composed of simple parts; (3) that in addition to the causal laws of nature there is/is not another causality through freedom; and (4) that there is/is not a "necessary being" either in the world or outside the world as its cause (A426–61/B454–89). Of immediate noteworthiness is that the third antinomy concerning freedom relates to issues of central import to Kant's ethical, political, and religious thinking. The fourth antinomy, concerning a *necessary being*, links directly to the third species of dialectical syllogism, *the ideal of reason* (wherein traditional proofs for God's existence are examined). We will return to these important themes at the appropriate points in the exposition.

DOGMATISM VERSUS EMPIRICISM

The opposing conceptual tendencies concerning the cosmological antinomies are grouped under the general headings of *dogmatism* and *empiricism*. Kant's overview of these paradigms builds on the imagery of the warring factions discussed in chapter 2, and adds conceptual detail to the analysis. He opens by noting "the glittering pretensions [*glänzenden Anmaßungen*] of reason to extend its territory beyond the bounds of experience [*über alle Grenzen der Erfahrung*]" (A462/B490). Such pretensions occasion "this disunity of reason with itself" (A464/B492), as illustrated in the arguments mounted both for and against every cosmological assertion. Kant outlines both positions as preliminary to establishing a fresh mode of inquiry. In each instance, the *thesis* has "intellectualistic starting points" and is characterized by a "**dogmatism** of pure reason" (A466/B494). However, Kant also notes some additional characteristics of this dogmatic approach, the foremost of which is "a certain practical interest." While the viability of proofs concerning ontological assertions is rejected, a certain practical value is discerned in the dogmatic views concerning the beginning of the world, the unity and freedom of the soul or self, and the claim "that the whole order of things constituting the world descends from an original being, from which it borrows its unity and purposive connectedness." Kant recognizes that "these are so many *cornerstones of morality and religion*," while "the antithesis robs us of these supports, or at least seems to rob us of them" (A466/B494; italics added). Kant argues that, if properly interpreted, these cosmological ideas form a world picture (i.e., a set of culturally influential representational resources) that potentially supports human beings, singly and collectively, in their autonomous ethical endeavors.

Before turning to the antitheses, Kant notes two other areas of consideration with regard to dogmatism. He refers to a "speculative interest" whereby reason seems to require an exploratory grasp of the whole (i.e., the cosmos) that offers a degree of "stability and support from a self-sufficient thing as an unconditioned original being" (A467/B495). This procedure anticipates the notion of regulative principles, whereby reason follows autonomously generated rules to progress from conditioned to unconditioned (to the maximum extent possible within a given sphere of inquiry). However, Kant's approach offers no support for the literal validity of dogmatic arguments, but rather indicates important psychological and practical needs to which these ideas respond. The third point with regard to dogmatism takes up precisely this theme, while indicating the questionable aspects of our desire for total explanation. Kant notes that "this side has the merit of **popularity** [*Popularität*]" because it satisfies "the common understanding," by which he implies a general intellectual need among the public not confined to academic specialists. This common understanding finds no difficulty "in the idea of an unconditioned beginning for every synthesis." Kant then elaborates upon some of the psychologically attractive features of these speculative constructs: "in the concept of something absolutely first [*den Begriffen des absolute Ersten*] (about whose possibility it does not bother itself) it finds both comfort [*Gemächlichkeit*] and simultaneously a firm point [*einen festen Punkt*] to which it may attach the reins guiding its steps" (A467/B495). Hence, dogmatic explanatory systems are extremely enticing, insofar as they rationalize the difficulties and conflicts of existence while offering a comprehensive orientation for life. This idea of a *firm point of reference* should be juxtaposed with Kant's advocacy for engaging *multiple standpoints* in our ethical thinking and practice; this latter is a more laborious approach but also one more likely to achieve balance and breadth or inclusivity of vision. Hence, dogmatism's intellectual attraction for Kant is at best qualified. It caters to a human need for comforting worldviews that can orient and guide us in the course of life. However, this need can feed into illusion and enthusiasm that not only oppose the quest for genuine knowledge, but are also ethically and politically regressive. Subsequently, lest there be any doubt about his position on these matters, Kant insists that the cosmological questions concern "*an object that can be given nowhere but in our thoughts*, namely the absolutely unconditioned totality of the synthesis of appearances" (A481/B509; italics added). On the other hand, the unconditioned ideas of reason offered by dogmatism remain valuable if reconceived and reclaimed as regulative procedures for conceptualizing ethical principles.

The antithesis, wherein the speculative cosmological arguments are disproved, draws upon the methods of empiricism. Kant immediately indicates a negative feature of this line of thinking. Empiricism refutes claims of an original being, envisages the world as without a beginning or an author, sees the will as empirically conditioned and hence as essentially *not free*, and the soul (i.e., the human personality) as divisible and corruptible like matter. Because these metaphysical concepts serve to convey practical principles, the danger is that a comprehensive empiricist demolition of rational ideas can adversely affect our ethical reasoning: "**moral** ideas and principles lose all validity, and they collapse along with the **transcendental** ideas that constitute their theoretical support" (A468/B496). The empiricists, in reducing all reality to derivations from matter following deterministic laws of nature, undermine ideas of reason and eliminate transcendental and practical freedom from consideration. While raising this practical concern, Kant nevertheless endorses the empiricist argument that knowledge requires sense experience: "with empiricism the understanding is at every time on its own proper ground, namely the field solely of possible experiences, whose laws it traces, and by means of which it can endlessly extend its secure and comprehensible cognition" (A468/B496). This testing of knowledge claims with reference to observable phenomena serves to "strike down the impertinent curiosity and presumptuousness" of those who misapply ideas of reason to metaphysical realities. For Kant, empiricism therefore provides "a maxim for moderating our claims" (A470/B498). With reference to the conjunction of empiricism and skepticism, Kant also indicates the critical value of "the skeptical method," which he sharply differentiates from dogmatic skepticism per se. The latter takes this interrogative method to an extreme, thereby becoming an ideological system in itself. In this form, skepticism "undermines the foundations of all cognition" and so leaves "no reliability or certainty anywhere" (A424/B451). Empiricism is also capable of overextending itself, for example in making sweeping negative claims concerning matters that cannot be known. When this over-extension occurs "empiricism itself becomes dogmatic," and therefore "itself makes the same mistake of immodesty" as does speculative dogmatism (A471/B499). By contrast, "the skeptical way of treating the questions that pure reason puts to pure reason" provides the means for one to "exempt oneself from a great deal of dogmatic rubbish, and put in its place a sober critique which, as a true cathartic, will happily purge such delusions [*Wahn*] along with the punditry [*Vielwisserei*] attendant on them" (A486/B514). This striking comment anticipates Kant's evocation, in the *Prolegomena*, of Hume awakening him from "dogmatic slumbers." The empiricist and skeptical methods can be used critically to clear away the unfounded knowledge claims of metaphysical systems, opening the way to addressing practical issues.

This analysis is a key instance, not only of Kant thinking beyond the confines of the established schools of his time, but of his even-handed avowal of intellectual modesty. He resists all ideologically driven tendencies to explain everything within a single method or system; these tendencies give rise to unfounded assertions, severely limited interpretive horizons, and closed intellectual attitudes. Later, Kant therefore positions the critical philosophy as a *third stage* of intellectual history in respect to these two main types of predecessor. As he summarizes: the "first step in matters of pure reason, which characterizes its childhood, is **dogmatic**." Reacting against this, the "second step is skeptical, and gives evidence of the caution of the power of judgment sharpened by experience [*Erfahrung gewitzigten Urteilskraft*]" (A761/B789). This focus on judgment tempered by experience is crucial for every aspect of Kant's thought, especially ethics. However, while Kant acknowledges the valuable influence of empiricism in this respect, he also argues that it only submits "the *facta* of reason to examination." This procedure is merely "the censorship of reason," leading to "**doubt** about all transcendent use of principles" (A760/B788). The failure to demarcate practical from speculative use of principles leads to skeptical doubts affecting ethical reasoning. In superseding these endeavors, Kant examines not only the *facts* presented by reason, "but reason itself, as concerns its entire capacity and suitability for pure *a priori* cognitions" (A761/B789). He characterizes the critical philosophy as an "adult power of judgment"; it strictly demarcates practical reasoning from the excesses of dogmatic speculation. Hence Kant is not interested in evaluating specific conceptual claims as much as the entire nature and scope of the faculty of reason. In this way, his critical analyses establish "not merely the **limits** [*Schranken*] but rather the determinate **boundaries** [*Grenzen*]" of reason (A761/B789). This distinction between limits and boundaries is important. Subsequently, in the *Prolegomena*, Kant points out that "boundaries [*Grenzen*] (in extended things) always presuppose a space that is found outside a certain fixed location, and that encloses that location; limits [*Schranken*] require nothing of the kind, but are mere negations that affect a magnitude insofar as it does not possess absolute completeness" (PR, 142; 4:352). That is, boundaries, while circumscribing the scope of what can be known, nevertheless indicate something remaining outside of that circumscription. This approach to metaphysical and religious questions allows us to think beyond what can be objectively known, although only along practical lines.

If we follow the principle of intellectual modesty, and avoid the unfounded speculative claims of dogmatism and sweeping denials of skepticism, then the practical significance of ideas of reason can become more clearly manifest. "For in such a case intellectual **presuppositions** and **faith** on behalf of our practical concern would not be taken from us;

only one could not put them forward with the title and pomp of science and rational insight, because real speculative **knowledge** can encounter no object anywhere except that of experience" (A470/B498). The precise nature of the faith critical inquiry allows remains unclear at this point; we should not, however, misleadingly read into it any of the familiar tenets of traditional belief systems. The key point is that a path to the ethical reinterpretation of religious and metaphysical ideas is held open just as unfounded claims transgressing the boundaries of knowledge are denied. Kant's recognition of lasting contributions from both camps, if their ideas are appropriately modified, combined with his emphasis on open inquiry, is indicative of a fresh path of practical thinking. Neither the dogmatic metaphysicians nor the skeptical empiricists can lay claim to an exhaustive grasp of reality. The reflective approach that gives each side an impartial hearing, applies the principle by which one should commit to "publicly communicating his remarks to others for their judgment" (A475/B504). The seemingly abstract conflicts of those who sustain and those who oppose systems of metaphysics converge in a political concern for open inquiry guided by the principle of truth. The introduction of this point is not fortuitous; these inquiries into the resources of reason also intersect with the task of critically engaging the social-political worlds informing human mores.

REGULATIVE PRINCIPLES

Before turning to the issue of freedom, another key conceptual innovation requires further clarification. In the course of elucidating the antinomies, Kant notes that the "cosmological principle of totality," while disconnected from anything that can be attested in experience, nevertheless is "given as a problem." Problems posed by reason can arise from the reliance of a given concept on prior concepts, leading to something like a genealogical analysis: "the concept of the conditioned already entails that something is related to a condition, and if this condition is once again conditioned, to a more remote condition, and so through all the members of the series" (A498/B526). Once again, the task of following the logical movement of these problems is strictly differentiated from knowledge claims about objects of possible experience. Kant is concerned with the mental operations by which we proceed from particular ideas to more encompassing concepts that include those particulars.

The procedural order of regress from any conditioned concept to its intellectual condition generates a key interpretive tool used to reconfigure metaphysical and theological concepts, that of regulative principles. As I noted in chapter 3, these are dynamical principles that, unlike mathematical ones, do not make determinate judgments about reality (i.e., they do not constitute their own objects of knowledge). This notion formalizes the function of ideas of reason as providing rules for thinking: they guide us in conceptually moving from more circumscribed to more encompassing concepts. This type of rational procedure is now described as "a logical postulate [*Postulat*] of reason to follow that connection of a concept with its conditions through the understanding, and to continue it as far as possible, which already attaches to the concept itself" (A498/B526). Kant employs the term "postulate" to describe a requirement arising from the nature of a given principle; it begs explanation in terms of antecedent generative principles (I will discuss the etymological link of postulating with *requesting* or *demanding* in explaining the practical postulates in the following chapter.) Kant adds clarity to the connection between postulating and regulative principles in the course of discussing "the principle of reason," which he explains as follows:

> Thus it is not a principle of the possibility of experience and of the empirical cognition of objects of sense, hence not a principle of the understanding … nor is it a **constitutive principle** of reason [*constitutives Princip der Vernunft*] for extending the concept of the world of sense beyond all possible experience … It is a principle of reason which, as a **rule**, postulates [*welches als Regel postulirt*] what should be effected by us in the regress [of a series from conditioned to conditions], but **does not anticipate** what is given in itself **in the object** prior to any regress. Hence I call it a **regulative** principle of reason [*ein regulatives Princip der Vernunft*]. (A509/B537)

Regulative principles offer guidelines for thinking from particulars to limited concepts, and from these to more general concepts. Their application follows the procedures of the postulates of empirical thinking in general, but extends beyond the conceptual ordering of phenomenal experience through the categories of the understanding. In this way, they provide a dynamic procedure for conceptualizing "the whole," or the maximum, i.e., for postulating a more encompassing explanatory framework within which specific particulars can be understood. This capacity for expanding the parameters of thinking, Kant insists, is strictly differentiated from "a constitutive cosmological principle, the nullity of which I have tried to show." As with all dialectical formulations, these misconstrued constitutive principles undertake "the ascription of objective reality [*objective Realität*] to an idea that merely serves as a rule" (A509/B537). By contrast, regulative principles give conceptual shape to principles of totality or completion without making *knowledge claims*, as do constitutive principles.

Regulative procedures emerge within various domains of inquiry, whenever one concept logically entails a more inclusive antecedent or consequent. Guyer enumerates some of the general principles Kant outlines in this respect: "the principle of *homogeneity*, which dictates that we should always seek to subsume more specific concepts of natural forms or laws under more generic ones" (summarizing A652–55/B680–03); "the principle of *specificity*, which dictates that under whatever concepts of species of forms or forces we have formed we should seek to find further subspecies" (summarizing A655–57/B683–85); "the principle of the *affinity* or *continuity* of all concepts, which dictates that we should always seek to find a 'graduated increase of varieties' among our conceptions of natural laws and forces" (summarizing and quoting A657–58/B685–86).[10] Having noted this range of possible applications, we will mainly be interested in regulative principles as related to practical reason, including both ethical and political applications. This is in fact the predominant domain in which Kant utilizes them.

Kant refers to regulative principles as postulating an antecedent condition for any conditioned concept. This association of regulative principles with postulates points directly to practical reason, where these concepts play a strategic role. Although the practical postulates are not fully formulated until the second *Critique*, Kant already establishes this connection between postulates and ethics in the first *Critique*. He differentiates between "theoretical cognition as that through which I cognize **what exists**, and practical cognition as that through which I represent what **ought to exist** [*ich mir vorstelle, was dasein soll*]" (A633/B661). This practical concern with what *ought to be* either has a "determinate condition" that is "absolutely necessary for it," or the conditioned result can be "presupposed as only optional [*beliebig*]." Kant follows the procedure of regulative principles proceeding from a given concept to that which is required by that concept both antecedently and prospectively (e.g., as presupposed by the concept, as grounding the concept, or as necessary to the possibility of practically applying the concept). Just as a concept analytically postulates an antecedent concept, so too with regard to a practical principle that indicates that something *should happen*: if "a certain determinate condition" is "absolutely necessary for it" then "the condition is postulated [*postulirt*] (*per thesin* [by thesis])" (A633/B661). Here Kant

---

[10] Guyer, *Kant*, p.166.

applies the procedure of regulative principles to indicate a movement, not from a given to an antecedent concept, but from an *ought* or *imperative* to that which is required for the fulfillment of that imperative, and he calls this movement a form of postulating. "Since there are practical laws that are absolutely necessary (the moral laws), then if these necessarily presuppose any existence as the condition of the possibility of their binding force, this existence has to be **postulated** [*dieses Dasein postulirt werden*]" (A634/B662). Anticipating arguments taken up in the second *Critique*, Kant indicates a future task: "we will show about the moral laws that they not only presuppose the existence of a highest being, but also, since in a different respect they are absolutely necessary, they postulate this existence rightfully but, of course, only practically [*nur praktisch postuliren*]" (A634/B662). These passages, supported by arguments running through the critical writings, make it clear that our capacity to generate ideas of the highest being is interlinked with the moral law. Regulative procedures are intrinsic to practical reasoning, in which the demand ensuing from a practical principle leads us to postulate further ideas necessary to the fulfillment of the practical principle. The idea of a highest being results from this practical postulating. Kant states this further on in the *Critique*: "The ideal of the highest being [*des höchsten Wesens*] is, according to these considerations, nothing other than a regulative principle of reason [*ein regulatives Princip der Vernunft*]" (A619/B647). I develop this point later in this chapter in discussing the *ideal of reason* and in the next two chapters. For the moment, I merely note the interdependency of regulative principles, practical reason, postulates, and the ideal of reason. This series of alignments definitively separates Kant's inquiries from the constitutive knowledge claims of traditional metaphysics and theology.

In every practical application of ideas, this demarcation between regulative and constitutive principles is crucial. Traditional metaphysics, which makes determinate claims about the ultimate order of reality based on ideas alone, mistakes regulative principles for constitutive ones. By contrast, when used correctly regulative principles guide us along the path of thinking from particulars to more comprehensive concepts, while retaining awareness that we are dealing with concepts alone.[11] In this way, we strive to "think the whole" without finalizing the process, i.e., without falsely designating an empirically conditioned formulation as ultimate.

---

[11] In the second *Critique*, Kant retains this critical distinction. However, he adds the qualification that practical principles can *also* be *immanently constitutive* insofar as their object, the highest good or realm of ends, can be constituted in the world through the intentions and actions of human beings in accordance with the moral law.

This is why Kant insists that regulative principles serve to guide a *"regressus in indefinitum,"* i.e., an indefinite regress that prevents reason from remaining fixated in given empirical conditions, including social ones, but which does not culminate in a known object. This indefinite conceptual movement "can be distinguished clearly enough from the regress *in infinitum* [infinite regress]" that vainly tries to conceptualize infinity (A520/B548). Expanding the parameters of our thinking and concepts toward the whole or maximum, without declaring objects beyond possible experience, is profoundly interconnected with widening the conceptual vistas informing our practical thinking. It leads Kant's ethics in the direction of shared representations of an inclusive humanistic and cosmopolitan vision. In this regard regulative principles are strategic conceptual resources in matters pertaining to ethics, religion, and the more encompassing ends of reason in social-political contexts.

In his "critique of all speculative theology," Kant notes the detrimental effects of theological ideas when taken hypostatically, i.e., as designating underlying ultimate substances. At the same time, he indicates a potential for constructive practical employment: "the transcendental ideas too will presumably have a good and consequently **immanent use**, even though, if their significance is misunderstood and they are taken for concepts of real things [*Begriffe von wirklichen Dingen*], they can be transcendent in their application and for that very reason deceptive [*trüglich*]" (A643/B671). Strictly demarcated from a specious application of ideas to putative supersensible realities, the immanent use pertains to practical action in the world. Kant reiterates that "the transcendental ideas are never of constitutive use, so that the concepts of certain objects would thereby be given, and in case one so understands them, they are merely sophistical (dialectical) concepts" (A644/B672). This clarifies that the manner in which we utilize ideas generated by reason, either as constitutive or as regulative, is definitive of their status as either sophistical or practically valuable. A clear definition of the regulative use of these ideas and principles ensues:

[H]owever, they have an excellent and indispensably necessary regulative use, namely that of directing the understanding to a certain goal [*einem gewissen Ziele zu richten*] respecting which the lines of direction of all its rules converge at one point, which, although it is only an idea (*focus imaginarius*) – i.e., a point from which the concepts of the understanding do not really proceed, since it lies entirely outside the bounds [*den Grenzen*] of possible experience – nonetheless still serves to obtain for these concepts the greatest unity alongside the greatest extension. (A644/B672)

A more precise explication of these "immanent goals" for which regulative principles provide guidelines will take shape as we proceed. I will also return to the way ideas are related to a *focus imaginarius* with reference to collective representations guiding ethical practice. These goals of ethical and political amelioration require another key idea, that of *freedom*. Once again, in discussing a concept associated with metaphysics, Kant simultaneously resists traditional ontological assumptions while opening a practical line of interpretation.

FREEDOM AND ETHICS

The idea of freedom, or more precisely autonomy, has unequaled significance for Kant's ethical, religious, and political thinking. Kant initially discusses the issue of freedom with reference to the second cosmological idea concerning "the totality of the derivation of occurrences in the world." As a way to illustrate both the dogmatic and the skeptical sides of the argument in the sharpest terms, Kant sets up a dichotomy between explanations of occurrences as being "either according to **nature** or from **freedom**" (A532/B560). Nature, which Kant often renders as "laws of nature" or even "natural law," signifies the model of modern natural science as he knew it, which establishes "the connection of a state with a preceding one in the world of sense according to a rule." This form of explanation, restricted to sense experience understood within a generally Newtonian model, requires a causal sequence of explanation. In contrast to this type of explanatory model, Kant defines "freedom in the cosmological sense" as "the faculty of beginning a state **from itself**, the causality of which does not in turn stand under another cause determining it in time in accordance with the law of nature" (A533/B561). Consequently, freedom involves a capacity for self-generated goals and actions that circumvent causal chains of explanation (i.e., in terms of antecedent determinable causes producing our ideas, desires, and actions as effects).

Kant explains that freedom and causality operate on different levels of explanation. "Freedom in this signification is a pure transcendental idea, which, first, contains nothing borrowed from experience, and second, the object of which also cannot be given determinately in any experience, because it is a universal law – even of the possibility of all experience – that everything that happens must have a cause." In other words, freedom is not a principle that can be used to explain occurrences in the natural world in a way that disregards or overrides observable causal factors. However, the concept of freedom arises from our inability to conceptualize exhaustively the totality of natural causes. Since "no absolute totality of conditions in causal relations is forthcoming, reason creates the idea of spontaneity, which could start to act from itself" (A533/B561). Freedom is a transcendental idea that eludes the web of an explanatory system positing the sum total of causal relations extending to infinity. It does not arise from sense experience, and it cannot be used, in a way that would contradict verifiable findings of empirical research, to explain experiential phenomena. Hence these arguments are not compatible with any form of theological voluntarism, in which a hypostatized transcendent being freely intervenes in the working of nature and the world.[12] Freedom always coexists with the known laws of nature. However, if freedom does not offer an alternative explanation of natural phenomena contrary to those of the natural sciences, what then is its value?

Immediately, Kant turns to the issue of primary significance for his inquiry: relating freedom to *human will* and our capacity for ethical choice. "It is especially noteworthy that it is this **transcendental** idea of **freedom** on which the practical concept of freedom is grounded." The transcendental idea of freedom is the more general principle, which includes practical freedom as a subset. However, the subset is actually Kant's foremost concern, and he now proceeds to explicate it: "**Freedom in the practical sense** is the independence of the power of choice [*Willkür*] from **necessitation** by impulses of sensibility" (A534/B562). The power of choice or *Willkür* is a key concept for addressing ethical decision-making within the contexts of inner-worldly social and political interactions. In *Religion* and other late writings, Kant clarifies this distinction between *Willkür* and *Wille*, with the latter indicating the transcendental free will that subtends practical decision-making. At present, he is emphasizing a freedom that is "sensible," and hence related to practical decisions in the public world of shared human interactions, and this falls under the heading of *Willkür*. "The human power of choice [*Willkür*] is indeed an *arbitrium sensitivum* [sensible power of choice], yet not *brutum* [animal] but *liberum* [free], because sensibility does not render its action necessary, but in the human being there is a faculty of determining oneself from oneself, independently of necessitation by sensible impulses" (A534/B562). The power of choice is defined as *sensible*; hence, *Willkür* interconnects with interpersonal, social, and political realities. Choosing occurs within phenomenal and social worlds shared with others. At the same time, the

---

[12] Later in the *Critique*, Kant specifically rejects theological voluntarism; see A819/B847; compare G, 4:443 and CJ, 5:460.

power of choice is not compelled by sensibly intuited phenomena or sensible impulses.[13]

Kant's discussion of human freedom unambiguously reveals the practical import of the distinction between noumenal (or intelligible) and phenomenal (or sensible). In following through on the antinomy of pure reason related to freedom, he exploits the opening generated by the opposition between speculative and empiricist approaches to uphold freedom without contradicting the known laws of nature. Transcendental freedom is linked with practical freedom, i.e., the capacity to make ethical choices not predetermined by heteronomous physical or social-political forces. "The abolition of transcendental freedom would also simultaneously eliminate all practical freedom. For the latter presupposes that although something has not happened, it nevertheless **ought** to have happened" (A534/B562). Our capacity for free will is linked with autonomy as a capacity to act according to ethical imperatives; in terms of ideas concerning what *ought to be*. Kant goes further, and proposes that only transcendental idealism, because it distinguishes things as they appear to us from things as they are in themselves, is compatible with transcendental freedom: "For if appearances are things in themselves, then freedom cannot be saved" (A536/B564). The essential point is that if appearances are exhaustive of things as they are, and if these appearances present nature as "an inexorable law," this would "bring down all freedom if one were stubbornly to insist on the reality of appearances" (A537/B565). Following from this general distinction between a world of appearances determined by mechanistic laws and a noumenal thing in itself not subject to these determinations, Kant focuses his analysis on the issue of ethical autonomy.

It is crucial that Kant applies the distinction between phenomenal and noumenal specifically to human beings (A546/B574). He defines "intelligible" as "that in an object of sense which is not itself an appearance," and notes:

[I]f that which must be regarded as appearance in the world of sense has in itself a faculty which is not an object of intuition through which it can be the cause of appearances, then one can consider the causality of this being in two aspects [*zwei Seiten*], as **intelligible** in its **action** as a thing in itself, and as **sensible** in the **effects** of that action as an appearance in the world of sense. (A538/B566)

This is a decisive comment in many respects. We are phenomenal beings who live and interact in a world of sense, but we also have a "faculty that

---

[13] This definition of the power of choice is also developed in the concluding discussions of practical freedom in the Canon of Pure Reason (A800–02/B828–30).

is not an object of intuition" (i.e., which cannot be directly perceived). As intelligible beings we actively formulate ideas that can have effects in the phenomenal world via the power of choice. Moreover, the distinction between phenomenal and noumenal indicates *two aspects*, i.e., two ways of understanding the very same being. Kant therefore refers to humanity as having a "double aspect [*doppelte Seite*]" (A538/B566). We are embodied beings affected by and affecting the sensible world, but also intelligible beings, who can reason, formulate principles, and make free choices that impinge upon reality. This continuity within our twofold natures is indicated by the fact that the intelligible activity of willing can influence the public world of phenomenal experience. "Of the faculty of such a subject we would accordingly form an empirical and at the same time intelligible concept of its causality, both of which apply to the same effect" (A538/B566). The heart of Kant's ethical and political thought is encapsulated here: intelligible causality introduces ideas of reason into the world through willing and acting. However, willing must also take account of the empirical conditions under which ideas are applied.

Kant develops this argument with an illuminating discussion of human *character*, which has both empirical and intelligible aspects. Empirical character concerns those observable aspects of human beings by which our "actions, as appearances stand through and through in connection with other appearances, in accordance with constant natural laws" (A539/B567). This notion is perhaps made more complex by Kant's use of the term "appearances" to discuss observable interactions in a shared physical world. The point nevertheless is clear and important: the laws of nature known through the ongoing findings of the sciences cannot be casually bypassed by alternative metaphysical or mystical forms of explanation. Continuing with his explication of the two-aspect model, Kant describes persons as possessing an empirical character "in appearance," while also having an intelligible character "as a thing in itself" (A539/B567). Human beings form a differentiated continuum spanning intelligible and sensible. Moreover, unlike empirical character as an object of sense experience, intelligible character "does not stand under the conditions of time" (A539/B567). Temporality is a necessary form of intuition in the human experience of the world, but human free will is not subject to the cause-and-effect relations associated with temporality. Our ethical decisions and actions are not directly determined by temporal events occurring under phenomenal conditions. With specific regard to ethical decisions, these cannot be understood exclusively in terms of influences such as genetics, upbringing, physical coercion, or political indoctrination. While these factors can influence us to varying degrees, we are also capable of making ethical choices irreducible to past practices, to any series of preceding forces and events, or to immediate causal pressures. Therefore, our intelligible character stands *out of time* in this very important respect: it can interrupt the flow of determining influences with regard to our attitudes and actions.

It is very important that while Kant establishes these critical distinctions to illustrate our capacity for autonomous ethical choice, his model is not dissociated. Our intelligible character can "never be known immediately," yet it is *inferred* through the empirical character we manifest in the world. We can only perceive appearances; therefore, the intelligible character "would have to be **thought** in conformity with the empirical character" (A540/B568). The intelligible can only be thought (but not actually known) insofar as it becomes manifest through observable actions. This means that the intelligible and empirical aspects of character are not dichotomized, but are in fact a continuum; therefore Kant describes empirical character as "a mere appearance of the intelligible character" (A541/B569). Calling intelligible character the "transcendental cause" of empirical character, he insists that this is "entirely unknown, except insofar as it is *indicated through* the empirical character as only its *sensible sign* [*durch den empirischen als das sinnliche Zeichen desselben angegeben wird*]" (A546/B574; italics added). The indicating or signifying of the intelligible through the empirical shows their continuity in a single being; but what exactly does it mean? How does this indication occur?

To explicate this, Kant discusses the way reason, as a faculty constituting intelligible character, impacts upon sensible reality: "that this reason has causality, or that we can at least represent [*vorstellen*] something of the sort in it, is clear from the **imperatives** that we propose as rules [*als Regeln*] to our powers of execution in everything practical" (A547/B575). Hence the key instance in which the intelligible interfaces with the empirical is described in terms of reason setting practical rules (i.e., regulative principles) or imperatives. The imperative is described as an *ought*; Kant stipulates that "this 'ought' expresses a possible action, the ground of which is nothing other than a mere concept [*ein bloßer Begriff*]" (A547/B575). Any action ensuing from the imperative "must be possible under natural conditions"; hence no abrogation of natural causal laws is proposed. At the same time, "these natural conditions do not concern the determination of the power of choice [*Willkür*] itself, but only its effect and result in appearance" (A548/B576). Ethical imperatives, subsequently explicated in terms of the *categorical imperative*, are intelligible in the sense that they are formulated regulatively through reason; they are not simply the result of empirical conditioning (for example in the form of inherited social codes and mores). At the same time, the effects of these rational imperatives occur nowhere but in the phenomenal world. Kant proposes that we "assume it is at least possible that reason does have causality in regard to appearances: then even though it is reason it must nevertheless exhibit [*zeigen*] an empirical character" (A549/B577). Reason and intelligible character are described in synonymous terms: both are indicated or exhibited through the actions of our empirical character. The Kantian subject is indeed *doubled*, but it is definitely not *schizoid*. There is an interrelationship between what we *will* intelligibly and what we *do* and *are* in the world of observable interrelationships. Our intelligible character cannot be known directly, but it can be discerned through the *signs* of our empirical character. Because Kant does not understand ethics as *only* a matter of what is observable in a person's character and actions, because he focuses on autonomously generated laws and principles as guiding our wills, the interface between intelligible and empirical emphasized here is often overlooked. Without pursuing this issue at present, this interplay between intelligible principles and empirical actions shows that our ethical dispositions are indirectly known through the cumulative fruits of our worldly activities.

The interconnection between the empirical and the intelligible character is not uncomplicated. Since the intelligible is by definition unknowable in itself, our interior motivations are inferred only indirectly through outer signs. Kant extrapolates on the argument that the empirical character (in the mode of sense, *Sinnesart*), is all we can discern in a human being; the intelligible character (in the mode of thought, *Denkungsart*), is something "we are not acquainted with … but it is indicated [*bezeichnen*] through appearances" (A551/B579). An appended note elaborates on how empirical conditions also affect the manifestation of one's character in the world. Anticipating his later discussions of self-deception and the inner lie, Kant strikingly maintains that "the real morality of actions (their merit and guilt), even that of our own conduct, therefore remains entirely hidden from us." There is always an element of circumstance, he continues, such as "innocent defects of temperament," or its "happy constitution," operative in shaping our visible actions (A551/B579n.). Therefore no direct correlation between act and intention is possible. Nevertheless, the intelligible ground of ethical or unethical decisions partially manifests in the visible actions of a person. Kant also writes of "the intelligible character, of which the empirical one is only the sensible schema" (A553/B581).

As we have seen, schematism describes mediating structures between the logical concepts of the understanding and objects of sense intuition. Here the term "schema" is used in an analogous manner to express mediations between the intelligible and the empirical characters of human beings.[14]

Our intelligible and empirical aspects are differentiated yet interconnected. Kant reserves the term "intelligible" for inner states such as intentions and dispositions, while recognizing these as partially manifesting phenomenally. This is a vital element of Kant's innovative redeployment of traditional concepts, and it is a major feature of his discussions of free will, radical evil, and responsibility. Intelligible character is correlated with autonomy, meaning the capacity to conceive non-arbitrary ethical laws that are efficacious within phenomenal conditions. The significance of the concept of intelligibility for ethics is clearly evident in this section of the text:

> [R]eason does not give in to those grounds which are empirically given, and it does not follow the order of things as they are presented in intuition, but with complete spontaneity it *makes its own order according to ideas, to which it fits the empirical conditions* and according to which it even declares actions to be necessary that yet **have not occurred** and perhaps will not occur, nevertheless presupposing of all such actions that reason could have causality in relation to them; *for without that, it would not expect its ideas to have effects in experience.* (A548/B576; italics added)

---

[14] In addressing the issue of representing ideas that lack corresponding objects, Kant sometimes expresses himself this way, for example in the subsequent discussion of how we cognize the idea of "the regulative principle of the world's systematic unity, but only by means of a schema of that unity, namely of a supreme intelligence that is its author through wise intentions" (A697/B725). In this case, the idea of a supreme intelligence becomes the *schema* of the comprehensive unity of reality. However, elsewhere Kant restricts the discourse of schematism to the mediation of the understanding with empirical intuitions. In the second *Critique*, he states that the moral law is "applied to objects of nature" through the understanding, and continues: "what the understanding can put under an idea of reason is not a *schema* of sensibility but a law" (CPrR, 5:69). Here he proposes the term "type" to indicate the form of the moral law, adding that this "typic," in representing yet not being identical with the morally good, "also guards against *mysticism* of practical reason, which makes what served only as a *symbol* into a *schema*" (CPrR, 5:70). Similarly, in the third *Critique*, he differentiates between two modes of "making something sensible." The first is "**schematic**, where to a concept grasped by the understanding the corresponding intuition is given *a priori*," and the second is "**symbolic**, where to a concept which only reason can think, and to which no sensible intuition can be adequate, an intuition is attributed with which the power of judgment proceeds in a way merely analogous to that which it observes in schematization" (CJ, 5:351). Here the symbolic representation is analogous to the function of schematism, but without any supporting intuition. In *Religion*, Kant distinguishes between "*schematism of object-determination*," which corresponds to schematism proper, and "*schematism of analogy*," which corresponds to what he terms *symbolic* in the third *Critique* (see R, 6:65n.). I will return to these concepts in discussing Kant's efforts to make the moral law more intuitive through traditional symbolic representations.

As we temporarily put aside issues of freedom, a matter of tremendous import for Kant's ethical and political thinking has been clarified: ideas can have practical value in altering the political worlds wherein we live and interact. In concluding this section on the third antinomy, Kant explains that he has not been "trying to establish the **reality** of our freedom." Indeed, whether this assumption of transcendental freedom can lay claim to any form of *proof* remains ambiguous (however, at A802/B830 he claims that "practical freedom can be proved through experience," such as in cases where we act, based on principles, in opposition to immediately compelling influences). At this juncture, Kant confines himself to the observation that "freedom is treated here only as a transcendental idea." Nevertheless, he insists that "this antinomy" between freedom and natural causation "rests on mere illusion [*Scheine*], and that nature at least **does not conflict with** causality through freedom" (A558/B586). These aspects coexist in human beings as both phenomenal and intelligible.

The fourth and final antinomy concerns the concept of a "necessary being." Since Kant treats of this very briefly within the context of the cosmological antinomies, and then develops a detailed analysis in the ensuing discussion of the *ideal of reason*, I will turn directly to the latter section.

THE IDEAL OF REASON

Chapter 3 of Book 2 of the Transcendental Dialectic is entitled "The Ideal of Pure Reason." This discusses traditional proofs for the existence of God, as well as counter-arguments showing the failure of these proofs. Kant has already explained why all claims to knowledge must be based on intuitions structured by the understanding, thereby excluding supersensible knowledge. Moreover, his discussion of human freedom has forged a new pathway for interpreting traditional metaphysical and theological concepts. Rather than making knowledge claims about supersensible entities, ideas of reason provide regulative guidelines for our ethical reflection and practice. However, Kant leaves no stone unturned in establishing that we must relinquish traditional modes of speculation, so as to be better able to employ ideas and ideals of reason autonomously in addressing ethical and political concerns. He therefore turns to the primary arguments of rational theology, which exemplify the speculative procedures of metaphysics and provide the point of departure for his subsequent analyses of historical religions. The critical engagement with the time-worn proofs of

The ideal of reason

traditional onto-theology is a further step in reconceptualizing the meaning and function of theological and religious discourses.

A twofold relation to traditional modes of thinking is evident from the start of this section, and in the very rubric of the ideal of reason under which the question of God is addressed. Kant now augments his earlier explication of ideas, along with the ideals and *Urbilder* giving them representational form. He emphasizes that:

> **Ideas**, however, are still more remote from objective reality than **categories**; for no appearance can be found in which they may be represented [*vorstellen*] *in concreto*. They contain a certain completeness that no possible empirical cognition ever achieves, and with them reason has a systematic unity only in the sense that the empirically possible unity seeks to approach it without ever completely reaching it. (A567/B595)

Ideas do not designate objects of experience, but because they have a comprehensiveness not found in actual entities they can guide practical thought toward more inclusive horizons (sometimes called the "maximum"). Within this interpretive framework, ideals are defined as specific representations of a concept or set of concepts: "But something that seems to be even further removed from objective reality than the idea is what I call the **ideal**, by which I understand the idea not merely *in concreto* but *in individuo*; i.e., as an individual thing which is determinable, or even determined, through the idea alone" (A568/B596). Kant presents ideals as distinct conceptual figures embodying an idea of reason. Hence, an ideal is a concrete universal; although ideas cannot be directly represented, they can be indirectly indicated through such exemplars. The ideal is at once more concrete and more individualized, but also, as Kant emphasizes, even further removed from objective reality. This is an indispensable qualification: because the ideal is more individuated, and hence more likely to be informed by specific characteristics derived from the world of sense (such as ones based on human features and cultural values), it is essential not to conflate it with an existing entity or with parochial, culturally determined ideals in the colloquial sense.

In this context, Kant discusses "humanity in its entire perfection," which would include both the "idea of perfect humanity" in congruence with its ends (e.g., ethical realization), and "also everything besides this concept that belongs to the thoroughgoing determination of the idea" (A568/B596). In other words, the mere idea or concept of a perfect human being is enhanced through being portrayed in terms of the various non-contradictory qualities or predicates that would constitute such a being. These qualities, such as virtue, are also ideas when taken in themselves:

"Virtue, and with it human wisdom in its entire purity, are ideas." He then turns to the representation of ideas in an ideal of moral perfection: "the sage (of the Stoics) is an ideal [*der Weise (des Stoikers) ist ein Ideal*], i.e., a human being who exists merely in thoughts, but who is fully congruent with the idea of wisdom" (A569/B597). Hence the Sage is an individual representation that unifies ideas such as virtue and wisdom into a single coherent image of perfected humanity. Moreover, there need not be, nor ever have been, any actual person corresponding to this Sage in order for the ideal to have practical significance. Importantly Kant now reiterates how his interpretation of ideals must be distinguished from that of Platonic idealism: "human reason contains not only ideas but ideals, which do not, to be sure have a creative power like the **Platonic** idea, but still have **practical** power (as regulative principles) grounding the possibility of perfection of certain **actions**" (A569/B597). The point could not be clearer: neither ideas nor ideals have ontological status, and they do not refer to supersensible entities. Yet they provide non-arbitrary rules guiding *our* actions in the world, and in this sense, through the medium of autonomous human willing, judging, and acting, can have a profound impact upon the social-political worlds we inhabit.

Elsewhere, Kant clarifies how ideals make ideas of reason more accessible for practical endeavors. In his *Lectures on the Philosophical Doctrine of Religion* (from the mid 1780s), he asks: "How does an idea of reason differ from an *ideal of imagination*? An idea is a universal rule *in abstracto*, whereas the ideal is an individual case which I bring under this rule" (LPR, 28:994). Here the ideal is related to imagination, further indicating its status as a *figurative representation of ideas*. Reason and imagination work in tandem to provide symbolically configured guidelines for human ethical endeavor. In the first *Critique*, although this link with imagination is not explicitly stated, Kant similarly links ideals with archetypes (*Urbilder*) that incorporate an image-making function. He makes the point while explicating the ideal of the Sage as a human being of perfected wisdom:

> So the ideal in such a case serves as the **original image** for the thoroughgoing determination of the copy [*zum Urbilde der durchgängigen Bestimmung des Nachbildes*], and we have in us no other standard for our actions than the conduct of this divine human being, with which we can compare ourselves, *judging ourselves and thereby improving ourselves*, even though we can never reach the standard. These ideals, even though one may never concede them objective reality (existence), are nevertheless not to be regarded as mere figments of the brain [*Hirngespinste*]; rather, they provide an indispensable standard [*ein*

The ideal of reason

unentbehrliches Richtmaß] for reason, which needs the concept of that which is entirely complete in its kind, in order to assess and measure the degree and the defects of what is incomplete. (A569/B597)

As with the *ideal Republic* and the corresponding archetypes of *maximum freedom* and the *idea of humanity* (A317/B374), Kant is rethinking the function of traditional metaphysical concepts. Ideas and their representations through ideals and archetypes do not have ontological status, but nor are they figments of the brain like the delusory products of fantasy and enthusiasm. Their reality is practical, and the rational generation of ideals and archetypes forms a reference point for critically reflecting upon ourselves and our institutions in pursuing ethical and political amelioration.[15] The "ideal of reason," Kant continues, "always rests on determinate concepts and must serve as a rule and an original image [*zur Regel und Urbilde*], whether for following or for judging" (A570/B598). This crucial point indicates the conjunction of regulative principles with the faculty of imagination as a resource for furthering ethical endeavor. Hence, just as imagination mediates sensible intuitions for the understanding, it reciprocally *mediates ideas of reason for practical employment in the world of sense*.

However, if the power of imagination is disconnected from the guidance of regulative principles, we can drift into fantasy and illusion. In contrast with rationally generated ideals, "it is entirely otherwise with the creatures of the imagination [*den Geschöpfen der Einbildungskraft*], of which no one can give an explanation or an intelligible concept; they are, as it were, **monograms**, individual traits, though not determined by any assignable rule, constituting a mere wavering sketch [*schwebende Zeichnung*], as it were, which mediates between various appearances, than a determinate image [*ein bestimmtes Bild*]." Kant also compares these monograms or "wavering sketches" to an "*incommunicable silhouette*

---

[15] Later in the *Critique*, Kant mentions "the system of all philosophical cognition" as "the archetype [*Urbild*] for the assessment [*Beurteilung*] of all attempts to philosophize, which should serve to assess [*beurteilen*] each subjective philosophy" (A838/B866). This is followed by a reference to a "**cosmopolitan concept** [*Weltbegriff*] (*conceptus cosmicus*)" that is "personified and represented as an archetype [*Urbild*] in the ideal of the **philosopher**." He stresses that the philosopher is "the legislator of human reason," and that "it would be very boastful to call oneself a philosopher in this sense and to pretend to have equaled the archetype [*dem Urbilde*], which lies only in the idea" (A839/B867). The archetypes of philosophy and the philosopher formed by reason provide regulative guidelines for judging any endeavor to approximate these ideals. Similarly, in the *Critique of the Power of Judgment*, Kant formulates a parallel model with regard to judgments of taste: "**Idea** signifies, strictly speaking, a concept of reason, and **ideal** the representation [*Vorstellung*] of an individual being as adequate to an idea. Hence that archetype [*Urbild*] of taste, which indeed rests on reason's indeterminate idea of a maximum, but cannot be represented [*vorgestellt*] through concepts, but only in an individual presentation [*Darstellung*], would better be called the ideal of the beautiful" (CJ, 5:232).

[*nicht mitzuteilendes Schattenbild*, which could also be translated as *incommunicable shadow image*]" (A570/B598). These remarks further differentiate between the disciplined uses of the imagination in conjunction with principles of reason, and undisciplined uses of the imagination that are arbitrary and idiosyncratic. The latter may be harmless in the forms of creative fantasy or artistic production, but are damaging if confused with constitutive representations of reality or even with regulative ideals (in other words, if we take culturally conditioned ideals as regulative for our practice, our lives might be governed by merely parochial values such as servility, cunning, or ruthlessness. Hence it is very important that this section begins with guidelines concerning the status of ideals: even before introducing the question of God in its traditional forms, Kant establishes the rigorous conceptual framework within which the ideal of the highest being is addressed. Like the ideal as archetype of the human embodiment of wisdom, such as the Sage, this serves a regulative and reflective function in our ethical endeavors by providing an individualized presentation of universalizable ideas of reason. By contrast, an unregulated use of the imagination in religion and theology leads to parochialism, superstition, enthusiasm, and other regressive aberrations.

There is nevertheless a significant difference between ideals such as that of the Sage and the individualized idea of God as the *transcendental ideal* (also called *Prototypon transcendentale*; A571/B599). The transcendental ideal embraces the most encompassing features conceivable, thereby extending well beyond what could be attributed to any human being, no matter how idealized. As he did with the *Urbild* of perfected humanity in the Sage, Kant utilizes the rationalist notion of thoroughgoing determination (*durchgängige Bestimmung*) to explicate this comprehensive set of ideas: "in order to cognize a thing completely one has to cognize everything possible and determine the thing through it, whether affirmatively or negatively." However, unlike the rationalist metaphysicians, Kant makes no ontological claims on the basis of this principle, but instead attributes a regulative status to the idea. "Thoroughgoing determination is consequently a concept that we can never exhibit [*darstellen*] *in concreto* in its totality, and thus is grounded on an idea which has its seat solely in reason, which prescribes to the understanding the rule [*die Regel*] of its complete use" (A573/B601). This conceptualization of completeness gives us the "idea of the **sum of all possibility**, insofar as it grounds the condition of every thing as the condition of its thoroughgoing determination." This idea is "still indeterminate," yet "as an original concept [*als Urbegriff*], excludes a multiplicity of predicates, which, as derived through others, are already given, or cannot coexist with one another." By logical refinement, we arrive at "the concept of an individual object that is thoroughly determined merely through the idea, and then must be called an **ideal** of pure reason" (A574/B602). The ideal of reason therefore encapsulates the most comprehensive set of compatible ideas within a single coherent super-representational form.

After further elaboration of "the idea of an All of reality (*omnitudo realitatis*)," Kant refers to "an *ens realissimum* [most real being]" as "the concept of an individual being" in which the predicate "which belongs absolutely to being, is encountered in its determination" (A575–76/B603–04). He calls this the "transcendental ideal which is the ground of the thoroughgoing determination that is necessarily encountered in everything existing," and states that this is "the one single genuine ideal of which human reason is capable, because only in this one single case is an – in itself universal – concept of one thing thoroughly determined through itself, and cognized as the representation [*als die Vorstellung*] of an individual" (A576/B604). It is characteristic of Kant to take a formulation of traditional metaphysics, in this case the *ens realissimum*, and to reconceptualize it within a new frame of reference. This ideal is unique because it subsumes the most comprehensive ideas of completeness and universality into a single image-concept not predicated upon anything else; hence it is "thoroughly determined through itself." Although he stresses that this is the only genuine ideal of reason, it is significant that this is introduced following his discussion of the Sage of Stoicism and the related issue of archetypes and regulative guides for human ethical amelioration. The ideal of the *ens realissimum*, like the Sage, offers a conceptual and imaginative reference point for human self-reflection, ethical action, and even political judgment.

Kant quickly discredits a possible misreading of the transcendental ideal along any traditional onto-theological lines: "reason *does not presuppose the existence of a being* conforming to the ideal, but only the *idea of such a being*" (A577–78/B605–06; italics added).[16] It is important for understanding this section of the first *Critique* that Kant has

---

[16] Longuenesse explains Kant's divergence from rationalist metaphysics in this regard. The rationalists fall prey to "dialectical reasoning" by which "this *totum realitatis* is then posited as a distinct being, the ground of all finite reality: the *ens realissimum* of rational theology." Béatrice Longuenesse, *Kant on the Human Standpoint* (Cambridge University Press, 2005), p.212. By contrast, "in the critical context this *totum realitatis* remains a mere idea: there is no given totality of positive predicates, the mere limitation of which would give us the complete determination of each singular thing" (p.220).

already explicated the regulative function of ideas and ideals. Some of his comments may *echo* the discourse of metaphysics, as in his statement that "for reason the ideal is thus the original image (*prototypon*) of all things [*das Urbild (Prototypon) aller Dinge*], which all together, as defective copies (*ectypa*), take from it the matter for their possibility" (A578/B606). This, however, is not like Platonic idealism, which makes metaphysical claims concerning the ideational basis of reality. In contrast to metaphysics, the transcendental ideal or prototype has a regulative function in relation to our conceptual activity. Kant indicates his renunciation of ontological claims just as he continues to link this ideal with traditional nomenclature such as "**original being** (*ens originarium*)," "**highest being** (*ens summum*)," and "the **being of all beings** (*ens entium*). Yet all of this," he reiterates, "does not signify the objective relation of an actual object to other things, but only that of an **idea** to **concepts**, and as to the existence of a being of such preeminent excellence it leaves us completely in ignorance" (A578–79/B606–07). The ideal of reason represents a comprehensive set of maximally extended rational principles; it tells us nothing concerning the existence of any actual corresponding being.

Therefore, the concern of traditional modes of theology with establishing the existence of a highest being corresponding to rationally generated perfections is a distortion of the genuine problem of the ideal of reason. Kant argues that "if we pursue this idea [of the highest being] of ours so far as to hypostatize it," then we arrive at "**God** thought in a transcendental sense, and thus the ideal of pure reason is the object of transcendental theology" (A580/B608). However, Kant discredits these literal theological claims that misappropriate the ideal; he insists: "this use of the transcendental idea would already be overstepping the boundaries of its vocation [*die Grenzen ihrer Bestimmung*] and its permissibility" (A580/B608). Concerning theological endeavors to reduce the ideal to something that is "given objectively, and itself constitute a thing," he concludes: "This latter is a mere fiction [*eine bloße Erdichtung*], through which we encompass and realize the manifold of our idea in an ideal, as a particular being; for this we have no warrant, not even for directly assuming the possibility of such a hypothesis" (A580/B608). While the transcendental ideal cannot be translated into an entity with a causal relationship to material reality, neither is this *mere fiction* synonymous with falsity. A later comment explicitly draws associations among concepts, mere ideas, and regulative principles; all serve "as heuristic fictions [*als heuristische Fictionen*]" (A771/B799). As such, these fictions do not refer to objects, but if used correctly they have regulative value in guiding our practical thinking and activity in the world.

The tendency to objectify these heuristic fictions also explains reason's dialectical misuse of ideas and the concomitant production of metaphysical and theological illusions (A581/B609). Here Kant reiterates that "no other objects except those of sense can be given to us, and they can be given nowhere except in the context of a possible experience [*einer möglichen Erfahrung*]" (A582/B610). However, the problem of "natural illusion [*natürlichen Illusion*]" arises when we abstract the principle from its regulative function in ordering possible experience, and "hypostatize this idea of the sum total of all reality" (A582/B610). Through a process of "transcendental subreption," we confuse concepts generated by the understanding and ideas of reason with "the concept of a thing that stands at the summit of the possibility of all things, providing the real conditions for their thoroughgoing determination" (A583/B611).[17] An ideal that can help guide our inquiry and practice in the world is turned into the highest entity responsible for the physical order of reality. In a footnote, Kant further explicates the fallacious reasoning that turns the ideal into an entity: "This ideal of the supremely real being, even though it is a mere representation [*eine bloße Vorstellung*], is first **realized**, i.e., made into an object, then **hypostatized**, and finally … through a natural process of reason in the completion of unity, it is even **personified**." Because "the regulative unity of experience rests … on the connection of its manifold by the understanding (in one apperception)," then the unity of the highest reality "seems to lie in a highest understanding, hence in an **intelligence**" (A583/B611n.). In this way rational theology transforms the ideal of reason into an anthropomorphized entity with specific phenomenally conditioned attributes.[18]

QUESTIONING PROOFS OF GOD'S EXISTENCE

Only after developing this reinterpretation of the highest being as the transcendental ideal does Kant turn to traditional proofs for God's existence. Unfortunately, these important features of the text, whereby

---

[17] "Subreption" is "the fallacy of confusing what is sensible with what belongs to the understanding." Howard Caygill, *A Kant Dictionary* (Oxford: Blackwell, 1995), p.380.
[18] Longuenesse refers to "the transformation of the never-ending progress of the discursive use of the understanding into the (illusory representation of) a given totality of conceptual determinations of objects of experience. This illusory representation of a 'collective whole of realities' is ultimately hypostatized (posited as a distinct being) into the representation of an *ens realissimum*, as the single ground of all reality" (*Kant on the Human Standpoint*, p.222).

the analysis of theological arguments is carefully contextualized within a detailed practical reinterpretation, are often ignored. In fact, as Kant introduces the cosmological argument, it is noteworthy that he begins with preliminary observations that further contextualize his analysis. He first reiterates that reason has a propensity to seek comprehensiveness in explaining specific facts, and ultimately reality as a whole. This tendency, which parallels reason's pursuit of "the maximum" within an area of inquiry, generates regulative principles. However, if these rational procedures are misconstrued as offering comprehensive ontological grounding, reason then seems to establish the origins and purpose of existing entities by tracing them to a prior cause (logically and temporally).

In summarizing this type of theological reasoning, Kant notes that every etiological explanation "itself floats without support if there is still only empty space outside and under it, unless it fills everything, so that no room is left over for any further **Why?** – i.e., unless it is infinite in its reality" (A584/B612). The principle governing exhaustive explanation is that "if something, no matter what, exists, then it must also be conceded that something exists necessarily" (indicating the cosmological argument). It is this conceptual movement toward a speculative first cause, set in play by this line of regressive questioning, "on which reason grounds its progress to the original being" (A584/B612). The concept of an original, necessary being "contains within itself the 'Because' to every 'Why?'." It is therefore a concept "which is in no part or respect defective," and "which is in all ways sufficient as a condition" (A585/B613). Kant outlines the steps by which rational procedures produce this necessary being resolving all ontological questions. Once reason has been convinced of "the existence of **some** necessary being … it seeks for the concept of something independent of all conditions, and finds it in that which is the sufficient condition for everything else, i.e., in that which contains all reality." This necessary condition is conceptualized as "the All without limits" and as "absolute unity" (A586–87/B614–15). In this way, the comprehensiveness attributed to the ideal of reason is embodied within the concept of an Absolute Being. As we might expect, Kant remains dubious about this type of reasoning and its claims to generate metaphysical knowledge. He sharply states that "this argument has not produced for us even the least concept of the properties of a highest being, and has in fact achieved nothing at all" (A588/B616). However, Kant continues to weave metaphysical discourse into his own argument, reiterating that this concept remains necessary for practical purposes. Thus, we "would be without any incentive [*Triebfedern*], if a highest being were not presupposed who could give effect and emphasis to the practical laws" (A589/B617). While this is a strong statement concerning the practical necessity of the transcendental ideal, it remains very far removed from any onto-theological claims.[19]

Only after these preliminary inquiries does Kant address traditional theological arguments, determining whether efforts to ground theology in reason can withstand scrutiny. He insists that there are only three types of argument establishing the comprehensive Being of Beings. We may begin with the sensible world and ascend to the highest cause outside the world, which forms the *physico-theological proof*. We can begin with "an experience that is only indeterminate," i.e., the existence of any given particular thing, and proceed to some necessary being as the basis for such contingent things, producing the *cosmological proof*. Finally, we may take a transcendental approach and "abstract from all experience and infer the existence of a highest cause entirely *a priori* from mere concepts," as with the *ontological argument* (A590/B618). Kant immediately confirms the reader's suspicions that these proofs will be found wanting: "I will establish that reason accomplishes just as little on the one path (the empirical) as on the other (the transcendental), and that it spreads its wings in vain when seeking to rise above the world of sense through the mere might of speculation" (A591/B619). Here we should recall that the entire critical epistemology already invalidates such arguments before Kant even assesses them, and this may explain why his treatment bears marks of impatience.[20]

Under the heading of "the impossibility of an ontological proof of God's existence," Kant stipulates that "from the foregoing one easily sees that the concept of an absolutely necessary being is a pure concept of reason, i.e., a mere idea, the objective reality of which is far from being proved by the fact that reason needs it" (A592/B620). Having established the parameters of his analysis in showing that reason has a propensity to attempt comprehensive explanation without reference to empirical

---

[19] Kant similarly proclaims that "without a God and a world that is now not visible to us but is hoped for, the majestic ideas of morality are, to be sure, objects of approbation and admiration but not incentives for resolve and realization" (A813/B841).

[20] Wood emphasizes that the epistemology established in the *Critique* undermines traditional metaphysical and theological arguments: "The idea of God could represent to us something like a true and immutable nature only if we possessed an intuitive understanding, a capacity to produce concepts wholly a priori without any reliance on sensibility to supply their contents." Following this, Wood concludes that "the critical philosophy, therefore, involves epistemological restrictions which are sufficient to bar the way to any pretended intuition of the true and immutable nature of God, and thus to any ontological proof of the Cartesian type." Allen Wood, *Kant's Rational Theology* (Ithaca, NY: Cornell University Press, 1978), p.123. Also see Peter Byrne, *Kant on God* (Farnham, UK: Ashgate, 2007), pp.23ff.

intuitions, Kant dispenses with this proof, as well as the two following proofs, in a summary fashion. The proof, as succinctly rendered by an imaginary interlocutor representing a traditional theological position, holds that there is one case, and one concept, "where the non-being or the cancelling of its object is contradictory within itself, and this is the concept of a most real being." Since, this argument continues, "existence is also comprehended under all reality," it therefore "lies in the concept of something possible. If this thing [existence] is cancelled, then the internal possibility of the thing is cancelled, which is contradictory" (A596/B624). In this rendering, the necessary being by definition includes the quality of existence; it would therefore be contradictory to claim that it does not exist. Following this summary, Kant responds tersely to his interlocutor. "You have already committed a contradiction when you have brought the concept of its existence, under whatever disguised name, into the concept of a thing which you would think merely in terms of its possibility … you have won the illusion [*Scheine*] of a victory, but in fact you have said nothing; for you have committed a mere tautology" (A597/B625). This is because "**Being** is obviously not a real predicate, i.e., a concept of something that could add to the concept of a thing" (A598/B626). In defining a concept, one might render it in terms of predicates such as comprehensiveness, consistency, and so forth, but one cannot simply add the predicate of existence in the same way and from this definition prove that a being necessarily exists. "Thus whatever and however much our concept of an object may contain, we have to go beyond it in order to provide it with existence" (A601/B629). This *going beyond* the mere concept is what we do when we turn to experience, to the public world of empirical examination, in order to confirm or controvert conceptual claims. Having dispensed with the objective claims of the ontological argument, Kant reaffirms that "the concept of a highest being is a very useful idea in many respects; but just because it is merely an idea, it is entirely incapable all by itself of extending our cognition in regard to what exists" (A601/B629).

Kant had already formulated a more detailed rebuttal of the ontological argument in *The Only Possible Argument in Support of a Demonstration of the Existence of God* (1763). This pre-critical analysis attends more closely to Descartes' specific version of the ontological proof, which as Peter Byrne notes, entails "a clear and distinct perception of the idea of God."[21] Kant specifies, in response to the Cartesian notion of perfections (taken over

---

[21] Byrne, *Kant on God*, p.23.

from scholasticism), that "existence is not a predicate at all, and therefore not a predicate of perfection either."[22] In essence, the earlier argument is much the same as that of the first *Critique*, although more attention is given to the details of the Cartesian version. Byrne summarizes Kant's conclusions as follows: "for finite knowers such as us, existential claims, and indeed claims about what is really possible, can only be established through experience." In light of this, we can grasp Kant's argument in response to Descartes as establishing that "our understanding of God's nature can never be such as to enable us to prove God's existence from that understanding."[23] Kant clearly has such rationalist proofs in mind in this section of the *Critique*, and he concludes by referring to both Leibniz and Descartes. Hence, "the famous Leibniz was far from having achieved what he flattered himself he had done, namely gaining insight *a priori* into the possibility of such a sublime ideal being." Again, the point is that ontological claims cannot be made on the basis of ideas alone: "the famous ontological (Cartesian) proof of the existence of a highest being from concepts is only so much trouble and labor lost, and a human being can no more become richer in insight from mere ideas than a merchant could in resources if he wanted to improve his finances by adding a few zeroes to his cash balance" (A603/B631).

The next section is entitled "On the impossibility of a cosmological proof of God's existence" (A603/B631). This proof is not concerned with the particular features of objects in the world (i.e., it does not need to discern order and purpose in observable reality, as in the physico-theological proof or argument from design). Rather, it is a general argument from the contingency of the world to a necessary non-contingent origin: "if something exists, then an absolutely necessary being also has to exist" (A605/B632). This line of reasoning starts with the contingency of experienced reality, and tries to ground itself by getting, as Kant puts it, "a footing in experience." In this way, its proponents can claim that it is "distinct from the ontological proof" (A606/B634). However, Kant discerns in this theological stratagem a multitude of "sophistical principles," such that, as he emphatically expresses it, "speculative reason seems to have summoned up all its dialectical art so as to produce the greatest possible transcendental illusion [*transcendentalen Schein*]" (A606/B634). The illusion consists in this cursory use of experience "only to make a single step, namely to the

---

[22] Kant, *The Only Possible Argument in Support of a Demonstration of the Existence of God* (2:156); also quoted in Byrne, *Kant on God*, p.24.
[23] Byrne, *Kant on God*, p.29.

existence of a necessary being in general." The grounding in experience is specious, because there is nothing in experience itself that generates a line of reasoning from contingency to necessity. This is rather a *purely conceptual* procedure, following reason's propensity to move from the particular to the more general. Moreover, the issue of what specific properties this necessary being might possess is completely disconnected from anything experience can confirm. Hence, "reason says farewell to it [experience] entirely and turns its inquiry back to mere concepts: namely, to what kinds of properties in general an absolutely necessary being would have to have" (A607/B635). Grounding the cosmological argument in the contingency of experience is a mask covering a decisive reliance on concepts alone. Therefore, the cosmological argument covertly depends upon the procedures of the ontological argument with its strictly *a priori* reasoning (A607/B635). Human experience of the world provides no grounds for justifying a conceptual progression from contingency to necessary origin, and certainly not to a being exhibiting all imaginable perfections. This progression occurs only in an order of concepts, which is artificially grafted onto known reality as a response to contingency.

By contrast, the regulative use of ideas restricts them to the status of "subjective principles of reason" (A616/B644). That is, they serve to guide our thinking as we pursue questions of ends, but do not designate objective realities. In this discussion, Kant specifies two of the regulative principles he employs:

> The one says that you should philosophize about nature **as if** [*als ob*] there were a necessarily first ground [*ersten Grund*] for everything belonging to existence, solely in order to bring systematic unity into your cognition by inquiring after such an idea, namely an imagined first [or supreme] ground [*eingebildeten obersten Grunde*]; but the other warns you not to assume any single determination dealing with the existence of things as such a first [*obersten*] ground, i.e., as absolutely necessary, but always to hold the way open to further derivation [*immer den Weg zur ferneren Ableitung offen zu erhalten*] and hence always to treat it as still conditioned. (A617/B645)

The strictly regulative status of a necessary first ground is unmistakable. Moreover, the guiding rules of reason not only instruct us to think of the maximum possible order governing the world of nature. They also counteract tendencies to artificially terminate the reflective process when we think it has brought us to a satisfactory conclusion (i.e., to the idea of an ultimate ground that is intellectually elegant and emotionally reassuring). Whatever concept of a first ground we are able to arrive at remains a *determined* one.

Assuming that there is necessity in the way things are, and welding this to a fixed conceptual structure, creates a smothering heteronomous worldview inimical to open inquiry and to possible amelioration of ethical-political conditions. Therefore, for Kant the notion of a possible ultimate ground of reality serves a critical rather than a dogmatic function. This is evident in his remark that "the unconditioned necessity, which we need indispensably as the ultimate sustainer of all things, is for human reason the true abyss [*der wahre Abgrund*]" (A613/B641). It remains an abyss because it exceeds the boundaries of what can be known; but its abyssal nature also sustains freedom of inquiry by not foreclosing questions of meaning and purpose within heteronomous frameworks. Kant's approach to ultimate questions eschews the debilitating effects of skepticism by providing orientating regulative frameworks, while retaining an intellectual openness that fosters ongoing questioning and change.

PHYSICO-THEOLOGY, TELEOLOGY, AND DESIGN

The physico-theological proof is in many respects a precursor to more recent proposals concerning *intelligent design*; hence it will be well to discuss the arguments in somewhat greater detail. As Jonathan Israel notes, physico-theology was mainly developed by Newtonians "claiming Sir Isaac's science as the best way to demonstrate divine providence." This produced "a highly integrated physico-theological system encompassing not only science, religion, and philosophy but also history, chronology, Bible criticism, and moral theory."[24] It is also significant that Newtonian physico-theology is welded to a form of *theological voluntarism*. "The regularity, purposeful intricacy, and coherence of the universe, held Newton, are in themselves proof of supernatural agency in its design: 'this most beautiful system of the sun, planets, and comets, could only proceed from the counsel and dominion of an intelligent and powerful being'."[25] Importantly, this emphasis on the universe's dependence on the will of an anthropomorphic God poses the same problems of arbitrariness and heteronomy that Kant attacks in his critique of theological voluntarism in connection with ethical and political thinking.

Kant's criticisms of physico-theology again focus on how an argument that claims to be empirically based is actually derived from a preconceived

---

[24] Jonathan Israel, *Enlightenment Contested: Philosophy, Modernity, and the Emancipation of Man 1670–1752* (Oxford University Press, 2006), p.203.
[25] *Ibid.*, pp.207–08 (citing Newton, *Philosophia naturalis principia*).

order of ideas. The physico-theological approach begins with a "determinate experience, that of the things in the present world, their constitution and order" (A620/B648). Features of the natural world typically cited to substantiate claims of a necessary divine creator and sustainer include order, intricate detail, and magnificence. It is not insignificant that Kant expresses a reverence for nature in a condensed but evocative statement: "everywhere in the world there are clear signs of an order according to determinate aim, carried out with great wisdom, and in a whole of indescribable manifoldness of content as well as of unbounded magnitude in scope." However, design arguments go well beyond marveling at the vastness and complexity of the known world, claiming that examples of intricacy must signify "a principle of rational order grounded on ideas" (A625/B653). This interpretation imposes an anthropomorphic model on reality, wherein order must indicate intelligence. Based on this assumption, the argument concludes that there must be "a sublime and wise cause" of this world, since the notion of an all-powerful nature working though "blind fecundity" (i.e., non-intelligent generation) seems an inadequate explanation. That this cause possesses unity, Kant continues, is "inferred from the unity of the reciprocal relation of the parts of the world as members of an artful structure." The crucial interpretive tool utilized here is *analogy*: the great mechanism of the natural world, grasped as a unified system, is seen as the product of a single intelligent artificer. This assumption is based on an analogy with complex mechanisms and structures known to be the product of the intelligent designs produced by humans (A626/B654). Clearly, Kant is impressed by the awe-inspiring spectacle of the natural world, and this receptivity to the power of nature is linked to moral experience and endeavor, for example through the notion of the sublime in the *Critique of the Power of Judgment*. However, even in those analyses Kant is clear that the experience of the sublime is a response within us evoked by the experience of power and magnificence in nature:

The disposition of the mind [*die Stimmung des Gemüts*] to the feeling of the sublime requires its receptivity to ideas; for it is precisely in the inadequacy of nature to the latter, thus only under the presupposition of them, and of the effort of the imagination to treat nature as a schema for them, that what is repellent for the sensibility, but which is at the same time attractive for it, consists, because it is a dominion that reason exercises over sensibility only in order to enlarge it in a way suitable for its own proper domain (the practical) and to allow it to look out upon the infinite, which for sensibility is an abyss [*Abgrund*]. (CJ, 5:265)

Experiences of the sublime highlight our intellectual response to the power of the natural world; indeed, it is the disjunction between the comprehensiveness of our ideas and our actual experience of nature that generates sublimity. This disjunction encourages ethical reflection, i.e., a movement toward universality in our practical principles, for which the expansiveness presented by nature serves as an imaginative schema. It is another matter altogether to construct a proof that proceeds from awe-inspiring features of nature to a necessary being possessing the attributes claimed by speculative theology.

Kant supports an "as if" or regulative approach to teleological views, although only insofar as this abets our investigation into the *ends of humanity* in accordance with the known laws of nature (CJ, 5:437). By contrast, traditional theology uses the analogical method to jump from humanly constructed artifacts to the hypothesis of an intelligent designer of nature, making literal assertions about reality. Most importantly, Kant argues that this rigid theological use of analogy "*does violence to nature* and constrains it not to proceed in accordance with its own ends but to *bend it to ours* (the similarity of nature's ends to houses, ships and clocks)" (A626/B654; italics added). Kant does not pursue the issue except to note that this type of thinking also makes human faculties of understanding and willing, transposed to a highest being, fundamental to nature. We derive the ground of nature "from another though superhuman art, which sort of inference [*welche Schlußart*] perhaps might not stand up to the sharpest transcendental critique" (A626/B654). In other words, analogical reasoning merely projects human attributes upon a superhuman entity posited as the ground of reality. There is a strong narcissistic element in such worldviews, and in *Religion* Kant returns to the theme of self-love manifest in anthropomorphized notions of the divine.

Later, Kant augments these illuminating points concerning the imposition of human perspectives upon natural reality. He offers a trenchant critique of what he calls "perverted reason (*perversa ratio*)," which takes the regulative principle of the unity of nature and misuses it literally for "grounding things hypostatically on the actuality of a principle or purposive unity." This hypostatic rendering of the principle of unity formulates a determinate substantial ground ordering all reality. Most crucially, beyond making unfounded ontological claims, attempts to establish ultimate principles in a reified mode serve to block rather than foster open inquiry into the workings of nature: "because it is entirely inscrutable, the concept of such a highest intelligence is determined anthropomorphically, and then *one imposes ends on nature forcibly and dictatorially* [*dictatorisch*], instead of seeking for them reasonably on the path of physical investigation" (A692/B720; italics added). This argument correlates with Kant's explication of the highest being as an unknown abyss for reason, and it shows how we project anthropomorphic characteristics onto a conceptualized ultimate being to fill an explanatory void.[26] This is a crucial augmentation of Kant's critique of physico-theological arguments. They are not only ungrounded, they not only make illicit leaps from selected features of empirical reality to a purely intellectual explanatory system, but moreover they display a *perverted reason* that undermines open inquiry. With the dictatorial imposition of a fixed explanatory framework upon reality, "teleology, which ought to serve only to supplement the unity of nature in accordance with universal laws, not only works to do away with it, but even deprives reason of its end" (A692/B720). The regulative function of reason in formulating principles guiding our practical actions (its proper end), is distorted into a dialectical endeavor to establish onto-theological dogmas. These comments indicate Kant's sensitivity to the problem of imposing human perspectives on the world, whether through forced reasoning in accordance with preconceived explanatory systems, or through the endeavors of instrumental reason. This is not an isolated remark; it correlates with Kant's sustained critique of the dogmatic tendencies of metaphysics, theology, and religion, on the one hand, and with all mechanistic explanatory systems on the other. Each strives to impose closed models on reality, including human reality, and in this way impedes both progression toward greater knowledge and practical cultivation.

On a different level, Kant uses figurative language and analogical reasoning in the form of *as if* and fictional approaches to the natural world as meaningful for human experience. However, these comments are not meant to prove anything about the origins and purpose of the natural world; they are heuristic and regulative, and they correlate with the use of symbolism to express ideas of reason. Kant's teleological formulations are not arguments at all, but rather serve to indicate the wider vistas of significance (i.e., the ends) within which inquiries into the amelioration of ethical and political conditions can occur. In criticizing objectifying approaches to analogical reasoning, Kant therefore applies a crucial

---

[26] Kant does not explicitly employ the concept of *projection* in these arguments, but it conveys his concern with the imposition of preconceived notions upon reality. In the *Critique of the Power of Judgment*, he is more explicit with regard to our imposition of ideas of objective purposiveness upon nature: "even experience cannot prove the reality of this to us unless it has been preceded by some sophistry that has merely projected [*hineinspielt*] the concept of the end into the nature of things but has not derived it from the objects and the experiential cognition of them" (CJ, 5:359–60). A more general comment concerning the projective operations of reason is found in *Opus Postumum*: "reason precedes, with the projection [*der Entwerfung*] of its forms (*forma dat esse rei*) because it alone carries necessity" (OP, 21:15).

distinction between the ontologically constitutive and the practically regulative uses of principles.

To take the discussion somewhat further, we should also note that there is a disconnection, if not a chasm, between observable indications of order in the world and the far-reaching claims concerning a perfect designer proffered by traditional theology. Although he does not pursue this line of thinking as thoroughly as does Hume, Kant notes the limited and imperfect features of the world as we know it. On this basis he observes that:

> [T]he proof could at most establish a highest **architect of the world**, who would always be limited by the suitability of the material on which he works, but not a **creator of the world**, to whose idea everything is subject, which is far from sufficient for the great aim that one has in view, namely that of proving an all-sufficient original being. (A627/B655)

Kant seems reluctant to dismiss the design argument out of hand, perhaps because he remained open to features of natural reality that might stimulate wider inquiries and moral endeavors, as in the experience of the sublime. He is content to show that the evidence can at best sustain a truncated and qualified claim: not an omnipotent creator as represented in biblical terms, but a finite architect hampered by inadequate materials! However, Kant also takes a different tack to refute the comprehensive claims of design arguments. He notes the relative and perspectival nature of all human assessments of reality, using this to question the speculative leap from the imperfect world we actually experience to a perfect intelligible source. "For the predicates **very great**, or 'astonishing', or 'immeasurable power' and 'excellence' do not give any determinate concept at all, and really say nothing about what the thing in itself is, but are rather only relative representations [*Verhältnißvorstellungen*], through which the observer (of the world) compares the magnitude of the object with himself and his power to grasp it" (A628/B656). This is a crucial point: a subjective experience of greatness or magnificence, for example in an ocean, forest, or mountain range, on the part of finite beings such as we humans cannot warrant a conceptual leap to an ultimately perfect being. This issue is augmented in the third *Critique*, where Kant also questions our right to "arbitrarily expand" into an all-wise infinite being the "artistic intelligence" (but not wisdom) one might discern in nature, based on "my limited knowledge of the world." For this to happen, "it would presuppose omniscience in myself in order to have insight into the entire nexus of the ends of nature." We cannot validly leap from our necessarily partial and perspectival knowledge of nature to a comprehensive explanation necessitating "an intelligence that is infinite in every respect" (CJ, 5:441).

Many of these points echo Hume's decisive refutations of the argument from design. Hume stresses the correlation between the actual features of the observable world (rather than some highly selective and idealized rendition thereof), and the comprehensive theological claims supposedly made on this basis. As he remarks: "every argument, deduced from causes [God] to effects [an ordered world], must of necessity be a gross sophism; *since it is impossible for you to know anything of the cause, but what you have antecedently, not inferred, but discovered to the full, in the effect.*"[27] The qualities and virtues attributed to the creator cannot exceed those evident in the actual creation. As Hume graphically illustrates, the universe as we know it is flawed; despite its vastness, intricacy, and beauty, it is rife with suffering, imperfection, and injustice on multiple levels. These features typify physical nature, as well as the relations among human beings and societies; thus the imperfection of the world includes both physical and moral evil.[28] One cannot logically leap from this imperfect world to positing a perfect, omnipotent, benevolent creator as its source. Hume acutely indicates some "antecedent inference" operative in these assertions; i.e., those who make these claims have already begun with a notion of an omnipotent creator before they ever turn to the world of nature for substantiating evidence.

Hume argues for a direct proportionality between the qualities we observe in the world and those we infer in an assumed creator, prefiguring Kant's scaling back of the claims of onto-theology. "As the universe shows wisdom and goodness, we infer wisdom and goodness. As it shows a particular degree of these perfections, we infer a particular degree of them, precisely adapted to the effect which we examine."[29] These arguments for proportionality between observed effects and purported cause can allow for the possibility of some form of first cause to the world. However, based on the evidence at hand, Hume irreverently proposes through the character of Philo that this flawed world might just as well be "the work of some dependent, inferior Deity" (a view reminiscent of certain forms

---

[27] David Hume, *An Enquiry Concerning Human Understanding*, Section XI, in *Dialogues and Natural History of Religion*, ed. J. C. A. Gaskin (Oxford University Press, 1993), p.18; italics added.
[28] Hume, *Dialogues Concerning Natural Religion*, in *Dialogues and Natural History of Religion*, pp.112–14.
[29] Hume, *An Enquiry Concerning Human Understanding*, Section XI, p.21.

of Gnosticism). Or perhaps, he further speculates, "it is the production of old age and dotage in some superannuated deity."[30] Elsewhere, Hume proposes a polytheistic worldview as better corresponding to observable reality than does a single omnipotent deity. The world "is so full of variety and uncertainty, that, if we suppose it immediately ordered by any intelligent beings, we must acknowledge a contrariety in their designs and intentions, a constant combat of opposite powers, and a repentance or change of intention in the same power, from impotence or levity."[31] The ironic tone evident here, so different from Kant's more respectful engagements with theological matters, should not obscure the importance of Hume's refutation. If we really seek to base theological conclusions on the evidence of the world of nature, including human existence, then some form of imperfect or conflicted original source better corresponds to the product than do the idealized portraits proffered by natural theology. These reflections provide a somewhat more graphic reinforcement of the line of questioning Kant pursues, showing that there is no necessary logical connection between the empirical world with its flaws and conflicts, and the perfections attributed to a creator deity by design arguments.

Although Kant refrains from imagining what kinds of original source might be indicated by the order and disorder of the world as we know it, in other respects he goes beyond Hume. For example, Kant emphasizes the chasm between the causal connections observable in the world and a logical order of concepts formulated according to ideas of reason. The latter provide critical resources unavailable to strict empiricism for analyzing the dialectical errors of metaphysics and theology in transposing ideational systems onto physical reality. Moreover, in illustrating how an allegedly empirical argument actually follows a conceptually generated chain of reasoning, Kant shows how physico-theology, just like the cosmological argument, covertly bases itself upon the ontological argument. "I assert that the physico-theological proof can never establish the existence of a highest being alone, but must always leave it up to the ontological proof" (A625/B653). Observations of the phenomenal world are insufficient for the claims made by physico-theology; as the attributes of nature fail to establish a necessary being, the argument slides over into an emphasis on the *contingency* of the world.

After one has gotten as far as admiring the magnitude of the wisdom, power, etc., of the world's author, and cannot get any further, then one suddenly leaves

---

[30] Hume, *Dialogues Concerning Natural Religion*, p.71.
[31] Hume, *The Natural History of Religion*, in *Dialogues and Natural History of Religion*, p.139.

this argument carried out on empirical grounds of proof and goes back to the contingency that was inferred right at the beginning from the world's order and purposiveness. Now one proceeds from this contingency alone, to the existence of something absolutely necessary ... Thus the physico-theological proof, stymied in its undertaking, suddenly jumps over to the cosmological proof, and since this is only a concealed ontological proof, it really carries through its aim merely through pure reason. (A629/B657)

This conclusion adds another plank to Kant's refutation: since the ontological argument has been undermined, the ultimate reliance upon it of both the cosmological and physico-theological proofs indicates that they are likewise flawed. The key point is that an antecedent *order of ideas* is operative in all these arguments. Indirectly, Kant is providing us with an answer to Hume's reference to the "prior inferences" subtending arguments from design. These arguments, along with all other theological proofs, are founded on orders of ideas without the syntheses that occur only with sensible intuitions ordered through the understanding.[32] At the same time, Hume likely discerned cultural and historical influences, specifically those derived from biblical tradition and church doctrines, predetermining the conclusions of the natural theologians. Kant strengthens this analysis by detailing the conceptual operations driving the movement to comprehensive explanation.

While Kant does not entirely ignore historical and cultural influences on theology, these are given only passing reference in the first *Critique*. For example, in assessing theological arguments, Kant notes that theology, as "the cognition of the original being [*Urwesens*] ... is either from pure reason (*theologia rationalis*) or from revelation (*revelata*)" (A631/B659). Although he says little about the revelatory source of theology, this issue is taken up in *Religion*, where *revelation* is engaged in terms of the historically transmitted scriptures and institutional forms of religion. I will return to these issues in discussing Kant's hermeneutics of religion, but the immediate point is that Kantian epistemology and ethical theory can provide no support for literally understood religious and metaphysical worldviews. Regulative principles can provide rules for theoretical and practical endeavors, but these must be applied in varying real-world contexts though the autonomous use of reason and judgment. Finally, I

---

[32] As we know from the Transcendental Aesthetic, intuitions are required for synthetic judgments providing knowledge. "For all synthetic principles of understanding are of immanent use; but for cognition of a highest being a transcendent use of them would be required, for which our understanding is not equipped at all" (A636/B664). The idea of an unconditioned being is an idea of reason precisely because it cannot correspond to anything derivable from experience, which presents us only with conditioned beings.

should reiterate that Kant's critique of metaphysics and theology is also the starting point for his *constructive* inquiry into the moral possibilities of humanity. Far from exhibiting a despairing stance at losing the consoling edifices of traditional thinking, for Kant this relinquishing of heteronomous worldviews signals our liberation from illusion. This is a necessary step in generating a fresh inquiry into the possibilities of autonomous ethical-political amelioration guided by ideas of reason. Kant has illustrated that the dogmatic truth claims of theology and metaphysics can be supported neither rationally nor empirically. This failure happens to be beneficial. The clearing away of traditional ontology is simultaneously a clearing away of some of the dominant conceptual resources supporting heteronomy in the ethical and political spheres. The hope we invest in supersensible worlds and in the authorities who proclaim them should be redirected toward ethically transforming the political worlds in which we live. Kant has made considerable headway in retrieving some of the conceptual resources of these speculative systems for an autonomous, humanly oriented program of ethical and political inquiry, and he continues to follow through on this project over the final two decades of his life.

CHAPTER 5

Autonomy and judgment in Kant's ethics

FROM METAPHYSICS TO PRACTICAL REASON

Throughout the *Critique of Pure Reason*, as Kant contests the objective validity of metaphysical and theological systems, he also begins to reinterpret them in practical terms. The main epistemological liability of traditional metaphysics, i.e., its tendency to construct worldviews based on orders of ideas without reference to experience, becomes a constructive resource for expanding the parameters of ethical-political thinking. To function in support of practical reason, ideas must be liberated from any pretense to ontological claims. As part of this restructuring, Kant also develops an innovative model of human subjectivity that is crucial to his ethical-political inquiries. Most importantly, our capacity for autonomy resists closed metaphysical systems that fix the status of human beings within hierarchical ordering structures. Autonomy is equally resistant to the mechanistic theories of scientific materialism. The subject traverses both reason and nature, and it is this dynamic twofold quality that allows us to apply practical ideas within existing states of affairs.

As we saw in the previous chapter, intelligible character cannot be known directly, but is indicated through empirical character. Along similar lines, the *Groundwork* approaches human beings from "two standpoints [*zwei Standpunkte*]" (G, 4:452) and "in this twofold [*zweifache*] way" (G, 4:457). To reiterate, this is *not* a classically dualistic model. Kant reworks traditional categories to describe human beings as, at one and the same time, subject to phenomenal influences (heteronomy), and yet able to exercise free will and formulate rational laws (autonomy). These are two ways of grasping the very same being: "both not only *can* very well coexist but also must be thought as *necessarily united* in the same subject" (G, 4:456). The conjunction of phenomenal and intelligible aspects expresses our ability to will and act in accordance with an imperative, and to introduce this idea-guided willing into phenomenal reality. "The moral '*ought*' [*Das moralische Sollen*] is then his own necessary '*will*' [*notwendiges Wollen*] as a member of an intelligible world, and is thought by him as 'ought' only insofar as he regards himself at the same time as a member of the world of sense" (G, 4:455). The language of an intelligible world, conveying our autonomous capacity to conceptualize and act in accordance with shared moral laws, should not divert us into a retrogressive path of metaphysical speculation. Most crucial is the conjoining of freedom and duty: the moral ought is generated autonomously by principles of practical reason. This autonomous willing directs an *ought to be* toward a world of sense that is not governed by these imperatives.[1]

In the Preface to the *Groundwork*, Kant takes this distinction between nature and freedom as a point of departure. Based on this division, he differentiates between material philosophy, which "is concerned with some object," and formal philosophy or logic which concerns "the universal rules of thinking in general." He notes that material philosophy is divided into two types of determinate objects and the laws to which they are subject: "For these laws are either laws of **nature** or laws of **freedom**. The science of the first is called **physics**, that of the other is **ethics;** the former is also called the doctrine of nature [*Naturlehre*], the latter the doctrine of morals [*Sittenlehre*]" (G, 4:387). Laws of nature represent physical forces understood deterministically, and laws of freedom indicate the human capacity to will and act autonomously according to an imperative. Kant stipulates that, unlike logic, both "natural as well as moral philosophy can each have its empirical part." For moral philosophy, this empirical component is necessary insofar as we are concerned with "taking into account the [material] conditions under which it [what ought to happen according to laws] very often does not happen" (G, 4:387–88). Following this emphasis on material factors obstructing our capacity to realize ethical ideas in the world, Kant addresses the relationship from the opposite direction. He rejects efforts to *base* moral principles on the particulars of experience: "I ask only whether the nature of science does not require that the empirical part always be carefully separated from the rational part" (G, 4:388). He follows this point by asking: "is it not thought to be of the utmost necessity to work out for once a pure moral philosophy, completely cleansed of everything that may be only empirical and that

---

[1] The point is summarized by Patrick Riley: "There is a great deal of force in Kant's notion that no conception of 'ought' is conceivable as long as men are considered merely as parts of a system of nature who act according to laws – such as physical laws that cause appetites – but not according to the conception of laws." *Will and Political Legitimacy* (Cambridge, MA: Harvard University Press, 1982), p.59.

belongs to anthropology?" (G, 4:389). This preliminary step of purging formal ethical concepts of empirical influence is a crucial one. Ultimately, however, the *application* of these purified concepts on anthropological levels is equally essential.

An emphasis on *a priori* moral laws accords with autonomy; we reason for ourselves and work out universalizable principles, rather than simply accept principles derived *a posteriori*. Nevertheless, this language can create misconceptions concerning rigid divisions between pure and impure, rational and material, *a priori* and *a posteriori*. Kant seems to sustain such dichotomies as he argues that moral philosophy originates in "the *pure part of reason*," and that "when it is applied to the human being it does not borrow the least thing from acquaintance with him (from anthropology) but gives to him, as a rational being, laws *a priori*" (G, 4:389). Yet, the illusion of a self-contained moral position is quickly dispelled as we follow the train of Kant's argument. He immediately adds that these moral laws "no doubt still require a judgment sharpened by experience, partly to distinguish in what cases they are applicable and partly to provide them with access to the will [*Eingang in den Willen*] of the human being and efficacy for his fulfillment of them; for the human being is affected by so many inclinations that, though capable of the idea of a practical pure reason, he is not so easily able to make it effective *in concreto* in the conduct of his life" (G, 4:389; compare A133/B172). This shows that Kant divides the pure from the impure as a preliminary strategic move to offset the conditioning of ethical principles by empirical forces, especially in the form of parochial traditions. After articulating the formal structure of universalizability in the categorical imperative (discussed in detail below), he brings these conceptually refined moral ideas into interrelation with phenomenal existence through human willing. This is a template for ethical practice that works to ameliorate rather than merely sustain existing conditions. It is also noteworthy that Kant repeatedly stresses that the application of moral ideas in the course of human lives is a difficult task, undertaken in the face of many obstacles. He recognizes that moral principles must be applied by finite, fallible human beings, subject to a variety of competing influences and inclinations.

Kant uses the term "anthropology" to describe various empirical features of personal and collective existence; it therefore incorporates a range of both psychological and cultural factors, as well as their interplay. Much of Kant's ethical philosophy brackets these anthropological features in order to restrict their influence on the formation of ethical concepts. The influence of culturally conditioned concepts has already been indicated in the first *Critique*'s discussion of the *crude and invented concepts* operative throughout human history. This bracketing is a necessary step, because any claim to universality in ethics cannot be based on rules and norms that have only a subjective, culturally contingent, or exclusive status. In the overview Kant understands human beings both rationally and anthropologically, just as he sees their intelligible and empirical characters as interrelated in a dynamic continuum. In the *Groundwork* he argues that "because moral laws are to hold for every rational being as such," we must therefore seek "to derive them from the universal concept of a rational being as such, and in this way to set forth completely the whole of morals." However, after again abstracting ethical principles from contingent influences, Kant immediately describes ethics as that "which needs anthropology [*der Anthropologie bedarf*] for its *application* [*Anwendung*] to human beings" (G, 4:412). The formal structure of moral laws is first established as conceptually distinct from empirical influences, i.e., from anthropology including its cultural and political manifestations. These more encompassing universalizable ideas, having been pushed to their maximum inclusivity though regulative procedures, are then reapplied within the world.[2] Kant's focus on the issue of interests guiding our will, on the need for pedagogical resources including ideals, models, and images, and his strategy of critically reinterpreting the representational resources of inherited traditions are all associated with the application of moral principles within shared social-political worlds.

JUDGMENT AND ETHICAL PRACTICE

Our capacity to make principled judgments in relation to specific dilemmas and contexts is essential to ethical practice. There is a parallel structure in the linkage of *rules* with *judgment*, and moral *laws* with *autonomy*. In each case, concepts require independent decision-making and application. In the second *Critique*, under the heading of the "Typic of Pure Practical Judgment" Kant discusses the "concepts of good and evil" that

---

[2] It is noteworthy that Kant understands critical abilities as cultivated through historical experience. The "Idea for a Universal History" employs the concept of unsocial sociability (*ungesellige Geselligkeit*) to discuss how conflict in human relations can foster moral reasoning (IH, 8:20). Kant emphasizes that over time moral judgments based on material constraints give way to ones based on principles: "through progress in enlightenment, a beginning is made toward the foundation of a mode of thought [*Denkungsart*] which can with time transform the rude natural predisposition [*Naturanlage*] to make moral distinctions into determinate practical principles and hence transform a *pathologically* compelled agreement to form a society finally into a *moral* whole" (IH, 8:21).

"determine an object of the will [*dem Willen*]." These concepts "stand under a practical rule of reason [*unter einer praktischen Regel der Vernunft*]," indicating their status as regulative guides. The task of judgment requires independent reflection in context, concerning whether or not an intended action is good or evil: "whether an action possible for us in sensibility is or is not a case that stands under the rule requires practical judgment [*praktische Urteilskraft*], by which what is said in the rule universally (*in abstracto*) is applied to an action *in concreto*" (CPrR, 5:67).[3] Kant specifies that ethical rules require individual acts of judgment for application in the phenomenal world. Sensory input (arising from cultural and political influences) does not determine our rules; yet the point of these rules is to guide decisions and actions in the world. Having established in the first *Critique* that the sensible world provides intuitions necessary to all knowledge, and that we live within political worlds wherein the public testing of norms is a crucial task, it would be a gross contradiction to omit these cornerstones of the critical philosophy in formulating an ethics. Just as Kant's epistemology is predicated on receptivity to sense intuition, in a reciprocal manner his ethics is ultimately directed toward modifying the sensible (public and political) world.

Abstracting moral principles from contingent anthropological features is designed to counter non-universalizable influences on practical reasoning and decision-making. Most obvious in this regard is *self-love*. Kant notes that "principles of self-love can indeed contain universal rules of skill (for finding means to one's purposes)," but that "practical precepts based on them can never be universal because the determining ground of the faculty of desire is based on the feeling of pleasure or displeasure, which can never be assumed to be universally directed to the same objects" (CPrR, 5:25–26). The subjective elements of personal happiness and self-love invalidate them as valid sources of ethical principles. In fact, if maxims based on happiness were made into universal laws "the most extreme opposite of harmony would follow, the worst conflict, and the

---

[3] Allen Wood notes that the "typic" has a role in practical reasoning "analogous to the 'schemata' for the categories of pure understanding." The typic "relates a law to concrete conditions of action in the natural world by representing the lawfulness of morality as the lawfulness belonging to nature." *Kant's Ethical Thought* (Cambridge University Press, 1999), p.79. Wood also emphasizes the indispensable role of judgment: "Kant holds that every application of a general rule or concept to a particular case involves an act of judgment that eludes formulation in generalizations" (p.151). The need to cultivate a capacity for judgment is discussed by Barbara Herman under the rubric of *moral literacy*, which she defines as "a basic, learned capacity to acquire and use moral knowledge in judgment and action." Barbara Herman, *Moral Literacy* (Cambridge, MA: Harvard University Press, 2007), p.80.

complete annihilation of the maxim itself and its purpose" (CPrR, 5:28). Rather than fostering ethical interrelations among persons, maxims based on self-love pit each against the other, leading to conflict in the quest for ascendency. To be sure, Kant is not entirely insensitive to human needs for happiness; ultimately he is concerned to bring the pursuit of happiness for all people into harmony with the moral law.

The issue of self-love therefore spans the individual and political. It appears in cultural mores catering to specific interests and therefore not susceptible to universalization. Hence, Kant insists that the "ground of obligation ... not be sought ... in the circumstances of the world in which [we are] placed, but *a priori* simply in concepts of pure reason" (G, 4:389). A similar argument appears in the second *Critique*: "To substitute subjective necessity, that is, custom [*Gewohnheit*, also indicating *habit*], for objective necessity, which is to be found only in *a priori* judgments, is to deny to reason the ability to judge [*urteilen*] an object, that is, to cognize it and what belongs to it" (CPrR, 5:12). Established norms are conditioned by cultural and political factors that are no less subjective for being collectively operative.[4] The test of universalizability is designed to counteract the parochialism of rank, custom, and habit, which often tend to support a status quo characterized by favoritism and injustice.

Autonomous principles guide ethical judgments concerning existing states of affairs; they support the human right to reform existing social-political conditions. In "Toward Perpetual Peace," Kant argues that "if there were no freedom and no moral law based upon it and everything that happens or can happen is instead the mere mechanism of nature, then politics (as the art of making use of this mechanism for governing human beings) would be the whole of practical wisdom, and the concept of right would be an empty thought" (PP, 8:372). Kantian ethics and politics are distinct yet interrelated, with ethical laws operating along legislative lines, and political thinking in large part forming an application and extrapolation of ethical principles on collective and institutional levels. In this vein, Kant notes the need for "political wisdom" to "make reforms in keeping with the ideal of public right its duty." He differentiates such lawful reforms from the potential for anarchy lurking in revolutions, and further stresses the need "to bring about fundamental reforms of a lawful constitution based on principles of freedom" (PP, 8:373n.). This emphasis

---

[4] Barbara Herman emphasizes "the constraining facts of the world in which one acts." She continues: "the roles and institutions present in our social world preconfigure our possibilities, some in ways that are hospitable to what moral value allows, some not" (*Moral Literacy*, p.284).

on lawful reform is the logical correlate of Kant's qualified support for the French Revolution: it emphasizes amelioration based on principles, undertaken in harmony with those principles. Elsewhere this right to reform in accordance with an imperative generated by practical reason is advocated with specific respect to religious reform (MM, 6:327). The interrelationship of ethics, politics, and religion centers on the ethical amelioration of existing conditions. In this context, the conjunction of intelligible and phenomenal nature in the same being expresses our ability to transform reality, interpersonally and politically, by applying formal principles through acts of autonomous judgment. Kant's ethical approach retains the focus on inner-worldly interactions that characterizes his epistemology. Ideas and principles are regulative, offering guiding rules for our autonomous judgment under phenomenal conditions.

Metaphysical and theological worldviews have often subtended the imposition of parochial ethical principles based on closed relations of authority and obedience. With regard to this issue, J. B. Schneewind argues of Kant that "his own work emerged from consideration of several alternatives to earlier conceptions of morality as obedience." Schneewind offers a trenchant summary of heteronomous ethics as well as the social-political attitudes it sustains:

> Those conceptions were almost without rivals until the late seventeenth century. They had two essential components. One concerns the proper human stance in relation to God. As created beings, we are required to show deference and gratitude as we obey our Creator's commands, which cover morality as well as religious worship. The other concerns human moral abilities. Most people are unable to think well enough to give themselves adequate moral guidance; most people are also too weak-willed and too strongly driven by their desires and passions to behave decently without credible threats of punishment for transgression and promises of reward for compliance. The majority, therefore, must defer to the exceptional few whom God has enabled to understand, follow, and teach his moral orders.[5]

Schneewind details how theological, ethical, and political forms of heteronomy reinforce each other. An order of reality grounded in a hypostatized image of God instantiates fixed codes of conduct that include social-political norms in addition to strictly ethical ones. The model is clearly hierarchical, and includes both traditional feudal societies and the absolutist monarchical states of the early modern period. As discussed in

---

[5] J. B. Schneewind, *The Invention of Autonomy: A History of Modern Moral Philosophy* (Cambridge University Press, 1998), p.509.

chapter 2, both *ancien régime* France and the Prussia of Kant's time are prime examples of these hierarchically structured absolutist states. They represent social orders and systems of mores founded on inherited authority and fixed codes of conduct based on rank. Evolving out of feudalism, they continued to group their populations into rigid hereditary orders, with the vast majority barred by their subservient status from a full range of rights and from exercising autonomous choice. Only the elite were endowed with the right to guide and command others.

In a related vein, Charles Taylor has outlined some features of traditional pre-modern worldviews or *social imaginaries*. He explains the legitimizing influence of Plato's *Republic*, in which the "non-self-sufficiency of the individual" is seen to necessitate "an order of mutual service," i.e., one in which the various fixed strata of society work in cooperation to sustain each other. This social-political ordering is understood as ontologically fixed, so that the social strata and the relations among them are rendered virtually immutable. Taylor notes that "this order is meant to stand in analogy and interaction with the normative order in the soul," indicating the intermeshing of metaphysical and political orders. Moreover, political structures of this sort weld themselves to an *order of virtues*, so that people learn to attribute a normative quality to their allotted rank: "the mutual service that classes render to each other when they stand in the right relation includes bringing them to the condition of their highest virtue."[6] This worldview, augmented by Aristotle's hierarchical model of natural law and often fused with Roman and biblical influences, subtends hierarchical ethical-political orders within Western intellectual and social history.[7]

As I have noted, Kant was deeply influenced by Rousseau's critique of these oppressive systems, and it is Rousseau who pinpoints the errors

---

[6] Charles Taylor, *Modern Social Imaginaries* (Durham, NC: Duke University Press, 2004), p.13. As noted in chapter 2, Taylor discusses how the absolutist states of early modern Europe retained the hierarchical models and theological legitimizations of pre-modern societies. *A Secular Age* (Cambridge, MA: Harvard University Press, 2007), pp.127–29. He notes that "hierarchy serves the end of order by allocating to everyone their proper situation and role, and by putting in place a chain of command through which the impulses from the top can be carried down through the whole of society." Taylor also reminds us that "this hierarchical, command conception of order drew on a doctrine of Providence. In obeying this kind of sovereign one was following God's will, most clearly in the variant of this notion which still is notorious today, the theory of the Divine Right of Kings" (p.128).

[7] It is also the case that the Bible has provided resources for counteracting unjust social and political hierarchies. See Blandine Kriegel, *The State and the Rule of Law* (Princeton University Press, 1995), pp.34–35, 60–61, 150. Kant ultimately addresses both sides of religious sources in regard to an autonomous ethical-political model.

in metaphysical legitimizations of inequality. He observes how "Aristotle, before all the others [i.e., before Hobbes, Grotius, and other early modern political theorists], had also said that men are by no means equal by nature, but that some were born for slavery and others for domination. Aristotle was right, but *he took the effect for the cause*."[8] In other words, some people are *made* into slaves by the ideologies and practices of unjust societies; they are not ontologically predetermined to this dehumanized status. While slavery may be the extreme case of institutionalized injustice, Rousseau's critique applies as well to any political order with in-built discrimination based on class, gender, wealth, or other variables. In the same way, Kant works to undermine ideological legitimation of injustice. He excoriates the activities of "despotizing moralists," arguing that "instead of the *practice* [*Praxis*] of which these politically prudent men boast, they deal in *machinations* [*Praktiken*], inasmuch as their only concern is to go along with the power now ruling (so as not to neglect their private advantage)" (PP, 8:373). This support of an unjust status quo is self-serving, winning favor and privilege for its proponents. Hence Kant rigorously opposes heteronomous ethical theories that reinforce "despotically given coercive laws" (PP, 8:374). He disassociates practical principles from any ontological order, and opposes the political heteronomy correlated with hierarchical models of reality. Kantian autonomy questions the assumptions of inherited heteronomous systems of mores. Autonomy simultaneously addresses ethical concerns with respect for the rights of all persons, and political concerns with the institutions that either foster or suppress these rights. Autonomously formed moral laws do not necessarily invalidate the mores deriving from heteronomous traditional sources, but they provide an autonomous method for assessing and modifying them.[9]

---

[8] Jean-Jacques Rousseau, *The Social Contract*, in *The Basic Political Writings*, trans. Donald A. Cress (Indianapolis: Hackett, 1987), Book I, Chapter II, p.142; italics added. With regard to the metaphysical legitimating of slavery, Luc Ferry points out that classical political philosophy "insofar as it assumed that politics is an imitation of the natural order was inegalitarian: the Greek universe – in both its cosmology and politics – was naturally hierarchical." Luc Ferry, *Political Philosophy 1: Rights – The New Quarrel between the Ancients and the Moderns*, trans. Franklin Philip (University of Chicago Press, 1990), p.20. See Aristotle, *Physics*, IV, 1–4, in *Complete Works of Aristotle*, ed. Jonathan Barnes (Princeton University Press, 1984), vol. I, pp.354–61, for descriptions of the hierarchically ordered universe. The dire ethical-political implications of this worldview are spelled out in Aristotle's assertion in the *Politics*: "from the hour of their birth, some are marked out for subjection, others for rule." *Politics*, I: 4, 1254a, 22–23, in *Complete Works of Aristotle*, vol. II, p.1990.

[9] Lewis White Beck notes that "in rejecting heteronomy … Kant does not reject the moral political, social, religious, and physical goods which the philosophers of heteronomy had rightly commended. They are all affirmed, but under the condition that their pursuit be regulated by a formal principle." *A Commentary on Kant's Critique of Practical Reason* (University of Chicago

Practical principles can expand the parameters of our thinking, assisting us in setting ethically guided laws and ends (e.g., progressing from parochial models of justice and rights for *some* and not others to a truly inclusive model). Autonomous principles are formulated through reason (and are in this sense *a priori*), but it remains our responsibility to make judgments in context. The ethical laws formulated under the rubric of the categorical imperative have this expansive and inclusive quality, fostering a greater capacity to think from the standpoints of others in accordance with formal principles. This capacity to think and imagine within wider frameworks helps liberate intentionality from immediate motivations (e.g., my personal needs and assumptions, or the exclusive well-being of those closest to me or most like me, or the norms transmitted by a specific tradition in which I happen to participate, and so forth). Since autonomous willing and acting involve my attitudes toward and relationships with other people within social-political frameworks, it is clear that autonomy has nothing in common with the solipsism and closure of *autarky*.

Moral laws are non-arbitrary constructions of reason; they arise from our capacity to think along lines of consistency, reciprocity, and greater inclusivity, but they are not innate or encoded. As Kant puts it, philosophy should act as "sustainer of its own laws, not as herald of laws that an implanted sense or who knows what tutelary nature whispers to it" (G, 4:425).[10] Autonomy, practical reason, and the moral law, are therefore intertwined, to the point of being virtually synonymous: "autonomy of the will [*die Autonomie des Willens*] is the sole principle of all moral laws and of duties in keeping with them" (CPrR, 5:33). Autonomy manifests when we intentionally act according to the formal guidelines of the moral law; it is not just "freedom in the negative sense," which Kant also characterizes as "*independence*" (CPrR, 5:33). This distinction is clarified in

---

Press, 1960), p.107. The critical method of adjudicating moral claims is based on practical reason; if traditional mores pass this test they are not rejected simply by virtue of having been derived heteronomously (e.g., from tradition). However, heteronomous norms cannot be sustained by the force of authority, and if they cannot pass the tests of universality and inclusivity they must be modified or rejected. Barbara Herman emphasizes the latter point: "We get the wrong lessons about justice if the source of authority in ruler or tradition has evaluative precedence over the facts of justice. The facts of justice cannot then play the right role in autonomous judgment; the flexibility of sound rationale is lost in the appeal to authority" (*Moral Literacy*, p.127).

[10] Allen Wood argues that "what is *a priori* is produced by our faculties, not *given to* them, whether through sensation or otherwise. This means that for Kant *a priori* cognition is utterly different from innate cognition, whose existence Kant emphatically denies." *Kant's Ethical Thought*, p.59. Towards the close of the second *Critique*, Kant notes that by the deduction of the categories "we can be prevented from taking them, with Plato, to be innate and basing them on extravagant pretensions and theories of the supersensible to which we can see no end, thereby making theology a magic lantern of chimeras" (CPrR, 5:141).

The Metaphysics of Morals: "*Freedom* of choice is this independence from being *determined* by sensible impulses; this is the negative concept of freedom. The positive concept of freedom is that of the ability of pure reason to be of itself practical" (MM, 6:213–14). Hence autonomy is not mere independence from external influences or constraints (sometimes called "lawless freedom"). Autonomy, as "freedom in the *positive* sense," is associated with a capacity for "lawgiving on its own on the part of pure and, as such, practical reason" (CPrR, 5:33).

Autonomy and heteronomy are two modalities of subjective and social-political orientation (paralleling the noumenal and phenomenal aspects of persons). The second *Critique* describes human beings as concurrently autonomous and yet subject to heteronomous influences: "The sensible nature of rational beings in general is their existence under empirically conditioned laws and is thus, for reason, *heteronomy*. The supersensible nature of the same beings, on the other hand, is their existence in accordance with laws that are independent of any empirical condition and thus belong to the *autonomy* of pure reason" (CPrR, 5:43). The difference between autonomy and heteronomy consists in *how* we orient ourselves in relation to any type of incentive, influence, or authority. That which opposes autonomous willing could be external, but it can also be internalized to become part of our subjective ways of thinking. In contrast to autonomy, Kant initially defines "heteronomy of choice [*Heteronomie der Willkür*]" as "dependence upon the natural law [*Naturgesetze*] of following some impulse or inclination" (CPrR, 5:33). Subsequently, Kant lists "happiness … perfection … moral feeling … the will of God" as being "in every case heteronomy" (CPrR, 5:64). This indicates a very wide range of potentially heteronomous forces, including not just somatic and egotistical ones such as those based on self-gratification, but even fixed ideas and norms insofar as these are accepted without critical reflection. As soon as we give priority to an extra-moral point of reference, even traditional notions of *God's will*, the danger arises of judgment becoming compromised by non-moral factors.

Although Kant often employs religious as well as metaphysical discourse to express practical ideas, it is essential that he rebukes theological literalism just as he eschews metaphysical objectivism. An objectified God-image, augmented by the authority of ecclesiastical institutions, diverts us from practical reasoning to heteronomous reference points. This is why Kant insists that rational grounds for morality are "always better than the theological concept [*theologische Begriff*], which derives morality from a divine, all-perfect will" (G, 4:443). The literalism of theological voluntarism has no more viable basis in experience or reason than the speculative constructions of metaphysics. Moreover, making ethics subject to the will of an anthropomorphized higher being sustains ethical parochialism. Kant trenchantly observes how our grasp of the divine will is made up "of the attributes of desire for glory and dominion [*herrschaftbegierde*] combined with dreadful representations [*furchtbaren Vorstellungen*] of power and vengefulness," and how these qualities "would have to be the foundation for a system of morals [*System der Sitten*] that would be directly opposed to morality [*Moralität*]" (G, 4:443). Beyond indicating a concept of projection in which we transfer the attributes of worldly authorities onto our idea of the divine, this comment shows that Kantian ethics is not simply preoccupied with abstract principles in isolation. It is directed toward applying these principles in the world, and hence toward critically engaging heteronomous systems of all kinds.

Distinguishing between theological literalism and the practical influence of religious representations is central to Kant's ethical-political project. This distinction is illustrated in a discussion of various duties, including "the *duty of religion*." He emphasizes that

> this is not consciousness of a *duty to God*. For this idea proceeds entirely from our own reason and we ourselves make it, whether for the theoretical purpose of explaining to ourselves the purposiveness in the universe as a whole or also for the purpose of serving as the incentive [*Triebfeder*] in our conduct. Hence we do not have before us, in this idea, a given being to whom we would be under obligation … Rather, it is the duty of the human being to himself to apply this idea, which presents itself unavoidably to reason, to the moral law in him, where it is of the greatest moral fruitfulness. (MM, 6:443–44)

This is the antithesis of the heteronomous obedience outlined by Schneewind. A key feature is the firm rejection of the literalism and anthropomorphism subtending religious manifestations of heteronomy.[11] Nevertheless, the idea of God gives expression to an omnilateral, inclusive perspective providing regulative guidelines in accordance with

---

[11] The second *Critique* similarly addresses heteronomous representations of God. Kant notes four classes of heteronomy: that of "punishments and rewards as mere machinery in the hands of a higher power"; that assuming "a certain special moral sense which, instead of reason, determines the moral law"; that of "material principles of morality"; and finally "the will of God … taken as the object of the will without an antecedent practical principle independent of this idea" (CPrR, 5:38–41). Kant also rejects theological voluntarism in the first *Critique*: "we cannot in turn regard these [moral laws] as contingent and derived from a mere will, especially from a will of which we would have had no concept at all had we not formed it in accordance with those laws. So far as practical reason has the right to lead us, we will not hold actions to be obligatory because they are God's commands, but will rather regard them as God's commands because we are internally

autonomous judgment.[12] Kant readily employs discourse concerning God, modeled after his explication of the transcendental ideal in the first *Critique*, as a means of articulating maximally extended principles and laws. Rather than representing a subjective will writ large, as in theological voluntarism, the idea of God exemplifies an *omnilateral will* actualizing the universalizability and inclusivity of moral laws.

As we have seen, the "Enlightenment" essay criticizes rote uses of reason that inhibit our capacity to question and think for ourselves. This links the rational capacity to arrive at *a priori* principles with the exercise of autonomous faculties, as opposed to any heteronomous imposition of norms. Allen Wood emphasizes that "Kant associates *a priori* practical principles both with the idea of autonomy and with the maxim of enlightenment: always to think for oneself."[13] The *a priori* generation of ideas is preliminary; it still requires critical reflection and the public use of reason. "Rational capacities themselves open our nature to modification by being the source of perfectibility. For reason is precisely our capacity for an indeterminate mode of life, one that is open-ended and self devised, in contrast with the life of other animals, which is fixed for them by instinct."[14] Developing this indeterminacy of the human condition, Wood harmonizes reason and the *a priori* moral law with openness to diversity and historical change: "we badly misunderstand Kant's theory if we suppose he thought the *a priori* principle of morality (in any formulation) could determine what to do *apart from empirical principles of application*." An autonomous capacity to apply principles within situations and contexts is essential to ethical practice. Wood also notes that "the intermediate premises connecting FH [the Formula of Humanity] with conduct are *hermeneutical* in nature: they involve interpreting the *meaning* of actions regarding their respect or disrespect of the dignity of human

---

obligated to them" (A819/B847). Wood stresses the incompatibility of Kantian ethics with voluntarism in any form, including religious ideas: "In its theological form, voluntarism is an unenlightened, authoritarian, slavish view." Allen W. Wood, *Kantian Ethics* (Cambridge University Press, 2008), p.110.

[12] I have drawn the notion of an omnilateral will from Arthur Ripstein, *Force and Freedom: Kant's Legal and Political Philosophy* (Cambridge, MA: Harvard University Press, 2009). In discussing Kant's views of the state, Ripstein notes that "fundamental human rights are constitutional, then, because they are the conditions of the state constituting itself as an omnilateral will" (p.218). Subsequently he discusses public institutions as "creating a standpoint through which omnilateral public law replaces unilateral private choice" (p.308). On a different level of analysis, i.e., in terms of cultural resources and their capacity to give expression to ideals and principles that are at once ethical and political, the transcendental ideal of God symbolizes this function of an omnilateral will taking into account the rights of all.

[13] Wood, *Kant's Ethical Thought*, p.60; citing OT, 8:146.

[14] Ibid., p.199; citing CB, 8:111–15.

nature."[15] This reference to hermeneutical procedures is very important. It distinguishes our application of ethical principles from mechanical or instrumental forms of reasoning. It shows that we must learn to read and assess unique situations in order to judge ethically.

Moral laws are not like recipes to be followed automatically. As Onora O'Neill expresses it, "there are and can be no algorithms for applying rules or principles in particular situations."[16] Algorithms indicate mechanical applications of principles; by contrast, ethical principles require autonomous judgments within the variable historical and political contexts wherein human interactions occur. Ethical ideas and laws have their own internal logic and coherence, insofar as they represent universalizable principles such as justice, fairness, and equality applicable within given contexts. But they are not rigidly prescriptive. We must apply moral laws in situations where new, unforeseen ethical issues arise, or where competing ends are at stake.[17] Moreover, subjecting our judgments to rational deliberation requires open interaction with others, and this practice in turn must be supported by public laws and institutions. Kant makes this point in the *Anthropology*, arguing against what he terms *logical egoism*. Referring to the need for freedom of the press, he insists: "if this freedom is denied, we are deprived at the same time of a great means of testing the correctness of our own judgments, and we are exposed to error" (A, 7:128–29). This point again shows that ethical judgment does not occur in

---

[15] *Ibid.*, p.154 (some italics added). The hermeneutical nature of moral judgment is developed in Wood's subsequent work. He argues that moral rules can be derived, but not rigorously deducted from the principles of the categorical imperative. "Instead [of rigorous deduction], we should think of the relation between the two as interpretive or hermeneutical in character. Rules or duties result when the basic value and fundamental principle are *interpreted* in light of a set of general empirical facts about human nature, perhaps also so modified by cultural or historical conditions" (*Kantian Ethics*, p.60).

[16] Onora O'Neill, *Constructions of Reason* (Cambridge University Press, 1989), p.160.

[17] The global environmental crisis is a prime example of an ethical and pragmatic issue requiring new ways of responding. Activities previously not understood as having ethical implications, such as unrestricted fuel consumption, are now fraught with serious consequences for the well-being of future generations. The need for judgments in context is further indicated by cases where different kinds of duties might come into conflict. Kant argues that because "the law can prescribe only the maxim of actions, not actions themselves, this is a sign that it leaves playroom (latitude) for free choice in following (complying with) the law." He therefore introduces the notion of "wide duties" indicating "permission to limit one maxim of duty by another (e.g., love of one's neighbor in general by love of one's parents), by which in fact the field for the practice of virtue is widened" (MM, 6:390; cf. MM, 6:410). Also see Roger J. Sullivan, *Immanuel Kant's Moral Theory* (Cambridge University Press, 1989), where these passages are discussed on pp.52–53, as well as 73–74. As Sullivan concludes: "What Kant has in mind here is the necessary and ineluctable role of judgment in the application of moral rules" (p.74).

a vacuum; an open public space of information in which competing ideas can be assessed fairly is required. Apart from showing that Kantian ethics is not as rigid as some caricatures render it, these concerns also indicate the importance of cultural and political institutions directed toward cultivating, rather than suppressing, autonomous ethical judgment among individuals and peoples.

DUTY, DISPOSITIONS, AND SELF-DECEPTION

The *Groundwork* presents moral judgment as arising from the procedures of practical reason: the maxims governing my intentionality are assessed with reference to the universalizability of the moral law. Kant calls this compliance with the moral law *duty*. Although this term has generated considerable misunderstanding, it emphasizes that cultivating ethical dispositions is *not* automatic or fully attainable for human beings, finite and fallible as we are. This consideration of ineliminable human imperfection already appears in Kant's description of "the concept of duty [*den Begriff der Pflicht*], which contains that of a good will under certain subjective limitations and hindrances [*subjectiven Einschränkungen und Hindernissen*]" (G, 4:397). The very concept of duty assumes that living according to ethical principles is laborious and impeded by obstacles endemic to the human condition. Section II of the *Groundwork* clarifies the hindrances to cultivating an ethical disposition. If one were to look to experience alone, "no certain example can be cited of the disposition [*Gesinnung*] to act from pure duty" (G, 4:406). In the second *Critique*, in discussing religious notions of moral perfection, Kant specifies that these regulative guides can be approximated, but never fully realized:

> But no creature can ever reach this stage of moral disposition [*moralischen Gesinnung*]. For, being a creature and thus always dependent with regard to what he requires for complete satisfaction with his condition, he can never altogether be free from desires and inclinations which, because they rest on physical causes, do not of themselves accord with the moral law. (CPrR, 5:84)

This crucial passage anticipates Kant's explication of *radical evil*. It shows that fallibility is built into the human condition, by the conjunction of free power of choice with strong drives and receptivity to social-political conditioning. The moral disposition is an ideal we may strive to approximate in the course of our lives, but it is not fully attainable as such.

In the first *Critique*, *Gesinnung* is used to express the disposition, cast of mind, or fundamental attitude specific to every person.[18] The rich valences of *Gesinnung*, only partially captured by the term "disposition," indicate inner ethical states actively cultivated through choices made over a lifespan.[19] This is a crucial concept, because it makes the locus of ethical endeavor synonymous *with the entirety of one's life path*, rather than reducing ethics to discrete dilemmas faced only occasionally. The *Gesinnung* is neither innate nor immutable along the lines of classical models of the soul, but it conveys the biographical continuity of our personal decisions and actions. Employing this dynamic concept, Kant differentiates our inner ethical states from anything that can be assessed by merely behavioral criteria. For example, ethical duty is differentiated from conformity to socially determined ends such as honor or prestige, and analogously inner moral religion is differentiated from rote conformity to external dogmas and practices.

Focusing on the state of one's disposition figures prominently in distinguishing "whether an action in conformity with duty is done *from duty* or from a self-seeking purpose" (G, 4:397). Only in the former case is there moral worth, because we have grasped the principles of the moral law and attempted to apply them autonomously. It is crucial that we learn to cultivate a good disposition out of freely chosen respect for ethical principles. If legally or ethically acceptable actions are undertaken only out of habit, fear, or a desire for reward, this engenders what Kant calls "a mixed doctrine of morals, put together from incentives of feeling and inclination and also of rational concepts." This mixed set of priorities "must make the mind waver between motives that cannot be brought under any principle, that can lead only contingently to what is good and can very often also lead to what is evil" (G, 4:411). This point anticipates Sigmund

---

[18] For example, Kant discusses a "disposition to rectitude" at B425, and "moral dispositions" at A813/B841ff.

[19] As John R. Silber explains: "The disposition is thus the enduring aspect of *Willkür* [power of choice]; it is *Willkür* considered in terms of the continuity and fullness of its free expression. It is the enduring pattern of intention that can be inferred from the many discrete acts of *Willkür* and reveals their ultimate motive." "The Ethical Significance of Kant's *Religion*," in Immanuel Kant, *Religion within the Limits of Reason Alone*, trans. Theodore M. Greene and Hoyt H. Hudson (New York: Harper & Row, 1960), p.cxvii. Whether by design or not, Kant's disposition parallels Hume's notion of *enduring character*. Despite Hume's overall predilection for a utilitarian stance, he yet emphasizes: "If any action be either virtuous or vicious, 'tis only as a sign of some quality or character. It must depend upon durable principles of the mind, which extend over the whole conduct, and enter into the personal character." David Hume, *A Treatise of Human Nature*, ed. L. A. Selby-Bigge (Oxford University Press, 1965), p.575.

Freud's trenchant observations of 1915, when, in the midst of the Great War, he wondered at the ease with which the veneer of civilized morality was stripped away from many European nations and individuals alike. In response, he noted that civilizations impose external constraints upon a populace, without necessarily affecting their inner beings: "this or that action which is 'good' from the cultural point of view may in one instance originate from a 'noble' motive, in another not."[20] In other words, even among those who may be acting in apparently the same good way, it is possible to discern a profound difference between those acting from selfish motivations and those acting from principled motivations and dispositions. Freud therefore describes one acting according to law merely from self-serving interests as a "hypocrite" who masks their true feelings and attitudes with seemingly ethical behavior. "It is undeniable," Freud continues, "that our contemporary civilization favours the production of this form of hypocrisy."[21] The ready way in which so many seemingly civilized people revert to barbarism under the conditions of war is indicative of this merely external, hypocritical form of morality. This is why addressing our deeper motivations and dispositions is utterly crucial to genuine ethical pedagogy.

From another angle, Kant counters the view that no such inner disposition toward the good even exists. Perhaps every seemingly good action, he reflects, can be ascribed "to more or less refined self-love." In engaging this concern, Kant acknowledges that in the overview human experience gives little evidence of good dispositions. He notes how pessimistic thinkers "spoke with deep regret of the frailty and impurity of human nature," and how human weakness inhibits our endeavors to follow practical reason. Kant is by no means denying the massive presence of ethical imperfection; indeed he proceeds to extrapolate on these concerns. In keeping with his "Enlightenment" essay and the first *Critique*, Kant notes the *deformation* of reason itself, whereby we use reason, which should serve "for giving law, only to look after the interests of the inclinations" (G, 4:406). This perversion of reason directly connects with the theme of self-deception. We cannot establish, by means of experience, "a single case in which the maxim of an action otherwise in conformity with duty rested simply on moral grounds." Delving into this problem, Kant proposes that even with "the keenest self-examination … it cannot be inferred with certainty that no

---

[20] Sigmund Freud, "Thoughts for the Times on War and Death," in *The Standard Edition of the Complete Psychological Works of Sigmund Freud*, vol. XIV (London: Hogarth Press, 1957), p.283.
[21] Ibid., p.284.

Duty, dispositions, and self-deception 179

covert impulse of self-love, under the pretense of that idea [of the moral ground of duty], was not actually the real determining cause of the will." In outlining the psychological needs and associated deception generating a specious sense of self-worth, he notes that "we like to flatter ourselves by falsely attributing to ourselves a nobler motive, whereas we can never, even by the most strenuous self-examination, get entirely behind our covert incentives [*geheimen Triebfedern*]" (G, 4:407).[22] These comments indicate the range and complexity of Kant's model of human personalities. The rational subject potentially capable of willing and acting autonomously is also one whose self-love leads to distortions and deceptions, not only externally but even within self-assessments. Looking more closely at our "intentions and aspirations … we everywhere come upon the dear self [*das liebe Selbst*], which is always turning up" (G, 4:407). Narcissism surreptitiously interferes with our approximating good dispositions.

In explaining these obstructions to recognizing and following the moral law, Kant anticipates the more intensive analyses of radical evil and the complacent conscience developed in *Religion*. In fact there are numerous direct references to human evil in Kant's ethical writings.[23] He emphasizes that the categorical imperative guides human wills that are *by*

---

[22] In discussing dispositions in the first *Critique*, Kant notes "a certain dishonesty in human nature" which he characterizes as "an inclination to hide its true dispositions [*wahre Gesinnungen*] and to make a show of certain assumed ones that are held to be good and creditable." He observes that "through this propensity [*Hang*] to conceal themselves as well as to assume an appearance that is advantageous for them humans have not merely **civilized** themselves but gradually **moralized** themselves to a certain degree, since no one could penetrate the mask of respectability, honorableness, and propriety" (A747–48/B775–76).

[23] The second *Critique* specifies that "the only objects of a practical reason are therefore those of the *good* and the *evil*" (CPrR, 5:58). This indicates free choice as the basis for both ethical and unethical maxims: "good or evil always signifies a reference to the will [*den Willen*] insofar as it is determined by the law of reason to make something its object" (CPrR, 5:60). Kant also specifies that "good or evil is, strictly speaking, referred to actions," indicating continuity between willing and acting. He continues: "it would be only the way of acting [*die Handlungsart*], the maxim of the will, and consequently the acting person himself as a good or evil human being, that could be so called" (CPrR, 5:60). Later, he argues that we are accountable "for every action intentionally performed," because these express one's character and arise "from one's choice [*Willkür*]." It is clear that our power of choice enables us to choose *evil*: "these actions, on account of the uniformity of conduct, make knowable a natural connection that does not, however, make the vicious [*arge*] constitution of the will necessary but is instead the consequence of evil and unchangeable principles freely [*freiwillig*] adopted, which make it only more culpable and deserving of punishment" (CPrR, 5:100). In the first *Critique*, Kant reflects concerning the postulates of "divine existence and a future" that even if uncertain these might have an effect upon one who is "separated from the moral interest by the absence of all good dispositions." He recognizes that holding to these ideas would constitute only a "negative belief" which "would not produce morality and good dispositions," but this might at least "powerfully restrain the outbreak of evil dispositions" (A830/B858). In light of such recurring comments, it is strange

180 *Autonomy and judgment in Kant's ethics*

no means routinely in conformity with ethical laws. The imperative "represents a practical rule in relation to *a will that does not straightaway do an action just because it is good*, partly because the subject does not always know that it is good, partly because, *even if he knows this, his maxims could still be opposed to the objective principles of a practical reason*" (G, 4:414; italics added). As rational beings, we have the capacity to form autonomous laws, yet in actual practice we usually remain ignorant of these laws. Additionally, even when the moral law has been systematized for us, e.g. by an ethical tradition or thinker, competing inclinations and maxims such as those based on self-love are routinely prioritized. We can always choose *not* to follow the moral law, even when its injunctions are clear. Or we may deceive ourselves about what really guides us, disguising self-love as somehow serving altruistic purposes. It is here, at the heart of ethical choosing, that the theme of radical evil arises.

Duty expresses a relation with the moral law that is arduous, fraught with deception, and never fully realizable. The "moral ought" remains an ideal we are enjoined to emulate, but the best we can do is bring ourselves into greater harmony with this ideal. This is why Kant contrasts the relation to duty on the part of fallible humans with that of a hypothetical perfect will:

> A perfectly good will would, therefore, equally stand under objective laws (of the good), but it could not on this account be represented [*vorgestellt*] as *necessitated* to actions in conformity with law since of itself, by its subjective constitution, it can be determined only through the representation [*Vorstellung*] of the good. Hence no imperatives hold for the *divine* will and in general for a *holy* will: the "ought" is out of place here, because volition is of itself necessarily in accord with the law. Therefore imperatives are only formulated expressing the relation of objective laws of volition in general to the subjective imperfection [*Unvollkommenheit*] of the will of this or that rational being, for example, of the human will. (G, 4:414)

Although Kant's rendering of the moral law is sometimes dismissed as idealistic, these passages confirm that the moral law is a regulative guideline for imperfect subjective wills prone to the influences of contingent forces. In the second *Critique*, Kant likewise discusses "holiness of the will" as "a practical *idea* which must necessarily serve as

---

that commentators have responded with surprise and dismay to Kant's inquiry into radical evil, as if it had no basis in his ethical thinking. To the contrary, since the entirety of Kantian ethics is predicated on autonomy actualized within phenomenal conditions, and on the need to bring our maxims into greater conformity with duty, freely chosen unethical maxims and therefore human radical evil are assumed from the beginning.

a *model* [*zum Urbilde dienen muß*] to which all finite beings can only approximate without end" (CPrR, 5:32). Here the crucial term *Urbild*, usually translated as "archetype" or "original image," describes the regulative function of practical ideas. The divine or holy will exemplifies the moral law; it also highlights the fact that human wills *do not* fall into this ideal category. We *require* imperatives if we are to make moral progress.

We should keep in mind that *law as such* is the logical application of the regulative principle of seeking maximum inclusiveness and consistency within the realm of ethics. The moral law is a conceptual template for working out the most egalitarian and just guidelines for willing, providing a formal procedure of universalization. "Hence, nothing other than the *representation* [*Vorstellung*] *of the law* in itself, *which can of course occur only in a rational being*, insofar as it and not the hoped-for effect is the determining ground of the will, can constitute the preeminent good we call moral" (G, 4:401). This rational representation of the law is interconnected with the individual will showing "*pure respect* for this practical law," adopting a "maxim of complying with such a law even if it infringes upon all my inclinations" (G, 4:400–01). A degree of conflict is built into these formulations; here it is depicted as occurring between moral law and inclinations, indicating that there is nothing simple or automatic about ethical choices. An attached footnote defines a maxim as "the subjective principle of volition." These subjective maxims are measured in relation to "the objective principle (i.e., that which would also serve subjectively as the practical principle for all rational beings if reason had complete control over the faculty of desire)," which "is the practical *law*" (G, 4:401n.). Here, both maxims and laws are described as *principles*. In the second *Critique*, Kant states the definition more precisely. Practical principles are "propositions that contain a general determination of the will, having under it several practical rules." These practical principles "are subjective, or *maxims*, when the condition is regarded by the subject as holding only for his will," or they are "objective, or practical *laws* when … holding for the will of every rational being" (CPrR, 5:19).[24] Principles are the more inclusive term. These can take the form of maxims having only subjective or goal-specific value. They might prioritize personal needs and goals, and therefore might very well be immoral and in conflict with universalizable laws. On the other hand, principles can represent laws formalizing moral

---

[24] Later, in the *Metaphysics of Morals*, Kant sharpens the distinction by stating that "laws proceed from the will [*von dem Willen*], maxims from choice [*von der Willkür*]" (MM, 6:226).

guidelines applicable to all. The moral law provides the rational criterion against which subjectively chosen maxims and principles are adjudicated.

In contrasting subjective maxims with universalizable principles, Kant does not only address blatantly unethical maxims and actions. He also articulates a more subtle distinction between universalizable moral laws and seemingly ethical mores serving specific individual and group interests. For example, maxims adopted from duty (i.e., from principle) are differentiated from those based on socially defined criteria, such as "the inclination to honor [*der Reigung nach Ehre*]" (G, 4:398). This indicates the interface of the ethical and the political, insofar as it shows that furthering ethical principles requires that we engage and assess the actual institutions and practices shaping our lives. The full import of this analysis is only gradually developed. For the moment we can note that the problem is not that customary mores based on rank and honor are necessarily bad. Rather, if these parochial ends are prioritized they can easily displace universalizable ethical principles (e.g., my concern with honor might lead me to disparage or harm another person).[25] Therefore, Kant differentiates the moral law from narrowly prescribed ends of any kind. He frames moral criteria in terms of the deeper motivations of our dispositions:

[A]ction from duty has its moral worth *not in the purpose* to be attained by it but in the maxim in accordance with which it is decided upon, and therefore does not depend upon the realization of the object of the action but merely upon the *principle of volition* [*Princip des Wollens*] in accordance with which the action is done without regard for any object of the faculty of desire. (G, 4:399–400)

The focus is on the principles guiding intentionality. However, Kant does *not* posit a will completely abstracted from the human interrelations

---

[25] Elsewhere, Kant refers to "the semblance of morals in love of honor and external propriety" (IU, 8:26; and cf. A748/B776). Manfred Kuehn notes that Kant's contemporary Christian Garve had published a treatise in which "honorableness" was proposed as a key virtue. This emphasized acting "with a view to how we will appear to others," specifically within the norms of late eighteenth-century Prussian society. Kuehn argues that in contrast to these parochial views, Kant "was not worried so much about the particularities of Prussian or even European society as *he was concerned with the destiny of humanity as a whole*" (Manfred Kuehn, *Kant: A Biography* [Cambridge University Press, 2001], pp.280–81). Sullivan also articulates what is at stake here: "Kant's entire moral philosophy can be understood as a protest against distinctions based on the far less important criteria of rank, wealth, and privilege, and perpetuated by religious and political force and fear. Kant's is an ethics of the people, of moral egalitarianism. Nowhere is this more evident than in his second formula. 'Respect' is radically different from the notion of 'honor', which rests on societal roles and prudential distinctions" (*Immanuel Kant's Moral Theory*, p.197). Yet, Kant is able to see the "impulse to honor" as something that might be harnessed for ethical ends. Insofar as this leads us to respect the views of others, "this drive leads us to compare our judgments concerning our knowledge with the opinion of others. This is the touchstone that we subject our knowledge to the judgment of many heads" (LE, 27:411).

wherein ethical judgments occur. Willing guided by principles is conjoined with recognition that we are mentally and physically affected by external conditions. This is expressed in the distinction between free will as such (*Wille*) and the power of choice (*Willkür*) undertaking decisions under phenomenal conditions. We need clear ethical criteria precisely because of the sometimes overwhelming presence in our lives of multifarious determining forces not derived from ethical principles, i.e., material principles or heteronomous influences.

Kant stresses the discord between maxims determined by inclination (honor, privilege, profit) and those guided by the moral law. This emphasizes the efficacy of the moral law in helping us assess non-moral or immoral inducements. To illustrate this, Kant describes a reflective procedure by which the form of law is used to interrogate one's subjective maxims: "the law contains no condition to which it would be limited, nothing is left with which the maxim of action is to conform but the universality of a law as such; and this conformity alone is what the imperative properly represents [*vorstellt*] as necessary" (G, 4:421). Universalizability is the formal structure of moral law. Critical reflection in accordance with universalizable principles can bring us into greater approximation to moral laws, and this reflection is also predicated on our exercise of free will. "Autonomy of the will is the property of the will by which it is a law to itself (independently of any property of the objects of volition). The principle of autonomy is, therefore: to choose [*wählen*] only in such a way that the maxims of your choice [*seiner Wahl*] are also included as universal law in the same volition" (G, 4:440). This emphasis on willing and choosing is of strategic importance: it shows that genuine morality cannot be imposed heteronomously but must be freely cultivated.

Kantian ethics develops strategies for bringing our prevailing maxims into consciousness so that we are better able to adjudicate and modify them. The categorical imperative provides resources for critically reflecting on the maxims and dispositions we have already cultivated.[26] In this way, the categorical imperative formulae are regulative principles for inclusive

---

[26] Kant describes the application of the categorical imperative as a reflective procedure: "I ask myself only: can you also will that your maxim become a universal law? If not, then it is to be repudiated (G, 4:403). Concerning these issues, Béatrice Longuenesse observes that "the role of the categorical imperative is mainly negative, and comes in after maxims have already been adopted." *Kant on the Human Standpoint* (Cambridge University Press, 2005), p.241n.8. Subsequently, she notes that the categorical imperative's "role is to evaluate the rules we already have, resulting from the hypothetical premises expressing prudential and instrumental relations of ends and means" (p.251).

and mutually applicable ethical laws.[27] Systematizing autonomy under inclusive egalitarian laws provides the quintessential principles regulating ethical judgment. Moreover, the categorical imperative as a guideline for critical reflection assumes that all persons already are willing and acting according to maxims of some kind. Far from being disconnected from the specificities of individual and cultural life, the categorical imperative helps us engage the maxims we have already chosen or internalized from heteronomous sources (e.g., parents, teachers, religious and political authorities, mass media, and so on). Therefore, Kant's approach to ethics does not assume a fully rational subject whose maxims are transparent. He assumes quite the opposite: we are embodied, culturally and politically formed beings, subject to a multitude of heteronomous influences. To develop ethical clarity we must bring these already operative maxims into greater awareness and make them more susceptible to critical adjudication.

QUINTESSENCE OF MORAL JUDGMENT

The categorical imperative constitutes several interrelated formulations of universalizable laws of practical reason. This diversification provides complementary guidelines for critical reflection on our existing maxims in relation to universalizability, consistency or non-contradiction, inclusivity, justness, and equality. The *Groundwork* presents the first and best-known formula, what Allen Wood calls the Formula of the Universal Law,[28] as follows: "*I ought never to act except in such a way that I could also will that my maxim should become a universal law.*" In commenting on this formulation, Kant specifies: "Here mere conformity to law as such, without having as its basis some law determined for certain actions, is what serves the will as its principle, and must so serve it, if duty is not to be everywhere an empty delusion [*ein leerer Wahn*] and a chimerical concept" (G, 4:402). The universalizability of principles counteracts purely subjective norms and parochial cultural mores; these can be "determined for certain actions," in which they are focused on limited ends. This reduces the scope of these norms to hypothetical imperatives with only

---

[27] In the first *Critique*, Kant writes of "the imperatives that we propose as rules [*als Regeln*] to our powers of execution in everything practical" (A547/B575). The second *Critique* discusses practical rules at CPrR, 5:67. The third *Critique* describes pure reason "as a faculty [or capacity, *Vermögen*] for determining the free use of our causality by means of ideas (pure concepts of reason)"; this contains "a regulative principle [*ein regulatives Princip*] for our actions in the moral law" (CJ, 5:453).

[28] Wood, *Kant's Ethical Thought*, p.17.

relative value in relation to specific goals (e.g., currying favor, personal gain, attaining social success). This formulation of the categorical imperative, emphasizing universality, is restated somewhat differently several pages later: "There is, therefore, only a single categorical imperative and it is this: *act only in accordance with that maxim through which you can at the same time will that it become a universal law*" (G, 4:421). Kant also adds the phrase "a **universal law of nature**" to this formulation, indicating the analogy with nature conceived as operating under inviolable laws that do not make arbitrary exceptions. Wood describes this supplementary Formula of the Law of Nature as the more intuitive variant of the formula of universality, bringing the law into closer relation with phenomenal experience.[29] In fact, Kant's initial rendition of the imperative is gradually supplemented by a series of incrementally more intuitive variants.

The capacity to universalize is the essential guideline for assessing maxims. Regulative ethical principles are rigorous, in that they cannot be altered to cater to subjective or parochial needs. Immoral acts violating the autonomy and dignity of myself and others cannot be universalized because they always involve some form of privileged, inequitable, or discriminatory judgment. This is why Kant presents ethics in the form of laws that do not allow us to make special exceptions for ourselves (G, 4:424; CPrR, 5:28). This crucial feature has also been stressed by Onora O'Neill: "In restricting our maxims to those that meet the test of the Categorical Imperative we refuse to base our lives on maxims that necessarily *make of our own case an exception*."[30] In his analyses of both politics and religion Kant is intent on counteracting this fundamental principle of self-love: to privilege ourselves over others and accordingly to seek favored treatment from worldly or otherworldly authorities. This criterion of ethical universalizability is a non-negotiable feature of moral imperatives. At the same time, the formulations are general enough to be applicable in a potentially infinite number of circumstances and to allow space for critical judgment.[31] O'Neill attributes "wide scope" to these formal

---

[29] Allen W. Wood, "The Supreme Principle of Morality," in Paul Guyer, ed., *The Cambridge Companion to Kant and Modern Philosophy* (Cambridge University Press, 2006), p.358. In Kant's words, the formulae of the categorical imperative are "three ways of representing [*vorzustellen*] the principle of morality"; as these unfold they "bring an idea of reason closer to intuition" (G, 4:436).
[30] O'Neill, *Constructions of Reason*, p.156; italics added.
[31] Longuenesse draws on the distinction between the two types of judgment (determining and reflecting) made in the third *Critique* and applies it to Kant's model of ethical judgment. She notes that the moral law serves as "the unconditioned principle" of moral judgment, and specifies that this applies "whether determining (answering the question: what should I do?) or

universals; i.e., they are structural guidelines with sufficient flexibility to be applied under highly variable conditions.[32] They are therefore distinguished from the positive laws of distinct societies and communities, which are more narrowly focused and which often lack universalizability. We can understand the categorical imperative as a set of guiding rules for ethical practice in varying circumstances. In his *Lectures on the History of Moral Philosophy*, John Rawls also counteracts views of the moral law as rigidly shaping judgment: "In his moral philosophy, Kant seeks self-knowledge: not knowledge of right and wrong – that we already possess – but a knowledge of what we desire as persons with the powers of free theoretical and practical reason."[33] Rawls focuses on how Kant's ethics encourages a reflective process fostering self-knowledge. He argues that "as ideally reasonable persons, we have the capacity to stand above and to assess our object-dependent desires." That is, while we do not necessarily know how to find the ideal answer to all ethical problems, we have the capacity to question ourselves, to reflect on our motivations and how they impact upon others, and to take some critical distance from them. What assists us in this reflective operation, Rawls states, is "the CI-procedure, as I shall call it."[34] This emphasizes a dynamic approach to the application of the categorical imperative: not imposing norms heteronomously, but offering critical resource taken up in autonomous judgment. These judgments pertain not only to specific ethical decisions, but to the overall trajectories of our lives.

Considered this way, the categorical imperative helps us take the position of others acting on similar maxims or affected by such maxims. The person engaging in ethical reflection "must always take his maxims from

---

reflecting (answering the question: 'is this action, and the will of this agent, morally good or evil?')" (*Kant on the Human Standpoint*, p.237; and see CJ, 5:179).

[32] As she states: "if universal principles are abstract they will underdetermine action, and so will not prescribe uniform action. Neither universal form nor wide scope entails uniform requirement." Onora O'Neill, *Bounds of Justice* (Cambridge University Press, 2000), p.68.

[33] John Rawls, *Lectures on the History of Moral Philosophy* (Cambridge, MA: Harvard University Press, 2000), p.148.

[34] *Ibid.*, p.152. While reflective functions are stressed in Rawls' explication of the CI-procedure, it emphasizes the more abstract Formula of the Universal Law over more intuitive formulations. For this point see Wood, *Kant's Ethical Thought*, p.337n.3. Subsequently, Wood notes with reference to "a 'CI-procedure' or 'procedural conception of practical reason'" that "from a properly Kantian point of view, however, *objectivity* can never be the outcome of any subjective volitions, stances, or procedures" (*Kantian Ethics*, p.108). This is clearly correct; if the CI-procedure is understood as a procedure for *generating* moral laws it is, as Wood stresses, "still only *subjectively* valid" (*Kantian Ethics*, p.108). Where the approach of Rawls and his followers is helpful, however, is in relation to the question of working with and *applying* the objective moral law, in other words, in mediating the objective and the subjective.

the point of view [*Gesichtspunkte*] of himself, and likewise every other rational being, as lawgiving beings (who for this reason are also called persons)" (G, 4:438). This indispensable point correlates with the formulations of the third *Critique* describing how an ethical person "reflects on his own judgment from a **universal standpoint** [*allgemeinen Standpunkte*] (which he can only determine by putting himself into the standpoint of others)" (CJ, 5:295). Kant also writes of "universal, i.e., valid for everyone" and "universal, i.e., knowable for all subjects" (CJ, 5:354). As we have seen, this capacity to reflect from the standpoints of others requires open communication. These comments illustrate that universality here means *inclusivity*: it requires a process of assessing and augmenting our particular views with reference to the standpoints of others, guided by formal principles.

The categorical imperative is a conceptual resource assisting us in engaging our maxims with reference to a fully reciprocal, egalitarian, and inclusive set of regulative criteria. Law as such is characterized by this capacity for universalizability. However, the principles formulated through practical reason simply guide the reflective judgments of autonomous individuals and communities. It is always *we* who choose to act ethically or unethically; the responsibility rests with us. Universality also means that principles of respect for all persons are built into this formulation: it can never privilege a specific individual, group, or class, because all equally are lawgivers and persons. In this regard, one commentator notes: "one of the best ways in which to understand the categorical imperative is to think of it as the *antithesis of tyranny*. Tyrants use other people as their property, merely as things for their own private purposes, and have no respect for the rights or intrinsic worth of their subjects."[35] Even here the political implications of Kantian ethics are evident. However, as Kant extrapolates from the initial formulation, he strives continuously "to bring an idea of reason closer to intuition … and thereby to feeling" (G, 4:436). Layer by layer, he adds sufficient specificity to the imperative to facilitate judgment on phenomenal levels, without abrogating the formal principle of universality. As this occurs he increasingly focuses on the social and political forces intertwined with our ethical priorities and decision-making.

Questions of ethics arise whenever my actions impact directly or indirectly upon others. Therefore, as a logical unfolding of the other-directedness of the categorical imperative, Kant introduces a second

---

[35] Sullivan, *Immanuel Kant's Moral Theory*, p.259; italics added.

imperative known as the Formula of Humanity as End in Itself.[36] This arises from the first formulation when we ask: *who* is able to generate such universal moral laws? *To whom* do they apply? *To what ends* are they directed? Since these are laws of reason generated by autonomous rational beings and applying equally to all, Kant's response is unequivocal: "Now I say that the human being and in general every rational being exists as an end in itself [*als Zweck an sich selbst*], not merely as a means to be used by this or that will at its discretion [*nicht blos als Mittel zum beliebigen Gebrauch*, conveying arbitrary use]" (G, 4:428). Not reducing humans to something *used* is most essential here, and it is simultaneously an ethical and a political injunction. Kant insists that "rational beings are called *persons* [*Personen*] because their nature already marks them out as an end in itself" (G, 4:428). He distinguishes persons as objective ends ("the existence of which is in itself an end"), from either "material ends [that] are only relative" or "merely subjective ends" which have worth only "for us." The logic is clear: either we are *all* autonomous beings of worth in ourselves, or we are *all* mere objects to be manipulated, if not literally bought and sold. This formulation is further explicated as follows: "*So act that you use humanity, whether in your own person or in the person of any other, always at the same time as an end, never merely as a means*" (G, 4:429). In emphasizing the humanity of all persons, the anti-tyrannical quality of this principle becomes evident: the universality and egalitarianism built into the categorical imperative now elicit a principle of the inviolability of all persons.[37] This provides a crucial check against the all-too-common tendency to compromise human rights in the name of rigidly construed ideologies, with their accompanying grand schemes and policies. In relation to these totalizing systems, the anti-tyrannical nature of Kantian principles is palpable. It is equally evident in the face of the more subtle

---

[36] See Wood, *Kant's Ethical Thought*, pp.18–20. Elsewhere, Wood proposes "FUL [Formula of the Universal Law] as the starting point of the process, thus the most abstract, most provisional, and (in that sense) the least adequate of the three formulae. And this thought turns out to be right; for it is FH [the Formula of Humanity as an End in itself], not FUL, which is Kant's formula of choice for applying the moral principle in the *Metaphysics of Morals*." Allen W. Wood, "Kant's Practical Philosophy," in Karl Ameriks, ed., *The Cambridge Companion to German Idealism* (Cambridge University Press, 2000), p.63.

[37] Wood highlights the use of the term *humanity* in this formulation. In *Religion* Kant distinguishes three general gradations in the human being: personality, humanity, and animality. Wood notes that "personality seems 'higher' than humanity in that it has essential reference to moral value, moral responsibility, and the 'positive' concept of freedom, where humanity includes none of these." This is significant because focusing on our humanity means that respect is inclusive of the full range of human being, not just humans insofar "as they are virtuous or obedient to moral laws" (*Kant's Ethical Thought*, p.120). This is also stressed in the *Metaphysics of Morals*: "it is in itself his duty to make the human being as such his end" (MM, 6:395).

forms of manipulation and dehumanization arising from obeisance before the idols of the marketplace: profit, consumerism, technological proliferation, and market forces. When we prioritize these goods, we take mere means to an end (e.g., wealth or technology as means to human well-being) to be ends in themselves.

Before proceeding, I should note an important strategy Kant employs with regard to the first two formulations of the categorical imperative. After outlining the formula of universality, Kant presents four *test cases* concerning unethical decisions: to commit suicide when life brings more unhappiness than happiness; to borrow funds under false pretenses (when one knows one cannot repay the loan); to waste one's talents; and to refuse to assist others who are experiencing "great hardships" (G, 4:422–23). In each case, willing that the maxim governing our actions were to become a universal law would lead to gross contradictions making human existence absurd and coexistence unworkable. He notes that "this is the canon of moral appraisal [*Beurteilung*, which I will henceforth translate as "judgment"] of action in general" (G, 4:424). The criteria of universalizability and non-contradiction are initially presented as sufficient in guiding our capacity for judgment. Nevertheless, after explicating his correlated principle of treating all persons as ends in themselves, Kant reviews the same four examples with reference to this ethical criterion (G, 4:429–30). In each case, respect for humanity, in the person of myself and others, is *also* violated by the actions of suicide, false promises, waste of potential, and failure to assist those in need. Most importantly, he specifies with regard to the last instance that "there is still only a negative and not a positive agreement with humanity as an end in itself unless everyone also tries, as far as he can, to further the ends of others" (G, 4:430). Reviewing the same four cases from the different vantage points of the first and second formulations illustrates the need for autonomous reflective procedures. The multiplication of regulative principles shows that the application of the categorical imperative is anything but automatic. Ethical questions need to be assessed from multiple standpoints and through complementary regulative criteria; they cannot be resolved by purely codified or instrumental reasoning. Kant also emphasizes that the cultivation of the principle of humans as ends in themselves requires that we further the *ends of others*. We have a duty to establish conditions that allow others to realize their potential as autonomous beings to the maximum extent possible. In this way the second set of formulations opens into a more explicit politically oriented vision: we are obliged to assist others in having the resources and opportunity to cultivate their own potential, and we all possess the right to be given these opportunities. This form of obligation cannot be undertaken entirely by individuals working in isolation, but requires the establishment of just institutions. The ethical-political quality of the categorical imperative is already evident in the principle governing interrelations; in furthering the ends of all in conformity with moral laws, *we are each limited in relation to the autonomy of others*. This point plays a strategic role in Kant's ethical writings: "this principle of humanity, and in general of every rational nature, *as an end in itself*... is the supreme limiting condition of the freedom of action of every human being" (G, 4:431). The mutual limitation of autonomy by that of others forms the template for an ethical-political analysis of the interplay of rights and obligations under omnilateral laws. This includes material well-being as its necessary but not sufficient basis, and ultimately requires conditions that further autonomy for all. However, respecting the autonomy of each requires that we avoid positing ends *for* others. Other-directedness is neither moralistic as in much religious ethics, nor based on subjective desires as in utilitarianism. The second formula clearly arises from the first, since it is predicated on the potential for autonomous ethical judgment in all persons, and it similarly opens into additional supplementary formulations.

The Formula of Autonomy emerges directly from the universal worth of all persons. Kant clarifies that "the subject of all ends is every rational being as an end in itself," which generates "the third principle of the will, as supreme condition of its harmony with universal practical reason, the idea *of the will of every rational being as a will giving universal law* [*allgemein gesetzgebenden Willens*]" (G, 4:431). This refines the principle of humanity as an end in itself, focusing on persons as generating autonomous laws (again, in opposition to heteronomy, where the one or the few impose laws upon the many).[38] Subsequently, Kant augments this imperative by focusing on the criterion it provides for willing: "The principle of autonomy is, therefore: choose only in such a way that the maxims of your choice are also included as universal law in the same volition" (G, 4:440). This principle assumes that our maxims are normally *not*

---

[38] Without law in some form, there would be no autonomy, only the anarchic condition classical theorists called *the state of nature*. Hence Pinkard notes that "a being that did not act in accordance with laws would not be free but only chaotic, random, pushed around by the laws of chance like a hapless ball in a roulette wheel." In a condition of lawlessness, not only would one be subject to chaos, but to relationships based on physical force. To act autonomously, one needs laws, but "these laws had to be self-imposed, that is, the agent was moved only by laws of which he first formed a representation and then applied it to himself." Terry Pinkard, *German Philosophy 1760–1860: The Legacy of Idealism* (Cambridge University Press, 2002), p.48.

structured according to autonomy and universality; this is evident as well in Kant's statement that "in accordance with this principle *all maxims are repudiated* that are inconsistent with the will's own giving of universal laws" (G, 4:431; italics added). Hence, the formulae provide guidelines for assessment and potential amelioration of existing maxims and practices. Kant makes a general observation about reflective judgment similar to what he stated concerning the first and second formulae, now with regard to the formulae of autonomy and of the realm of ends. In doing so he also explicates the transition from one to the other: "The concept of every rational being as one who must regard himself as giving universal law through all the maxims of his will, so as to judge [*beurteilen*] himself and his actions from this point of view, leads to a very fruitful concept dependent on it, namely that *of a realm of ends* [*eines Reichs der Zwecke*] (G, 4:433; translation modified).[39] Extrapolating on rational laws applying to all, the ensuing formulation of the realm of ends unfolds in an unambiguously social-political direction:

> By a realm [*einem Reiche*] I understand a systematic union of various rational beings through common laws. Now since laws determine ends in terms of their universal validity, if we abstract from the personal differences of rational beings as well as from all the content of their private ends we shall be able to think of a whole of all ends in systematic connection (a whole both of rational beings as ends in themselves and of the ends of his own that each may set himself), that is, a realm of ends, which is possible in accordance with the above principles. (G, 4:433)

Wood understands this as the more intuitive variant of the formula of autonomy: it brings the principle still closer to sensible manifestation.[40] This is a formula for the lawful structure of an ethical-political

---

[39] I have substituted "realm" for the translation of *Reich* as "kingdom," and will make this substitution throughout. The editors of the Cambridge Edition note that *Reich* might also be translated as "commonwealth" (*Practical Philosophy*, p.83. editors' note *j*). Elsewhere, Paul Guyer argues: "Kant's expression *Reich der Zwecke* is frequently translated as 'kingdom' rather than 'realm' of ends. It seems to me that nothing could be more misleading, since the idea of a kingdom implies that there is one agent free to give laws to others who are not equally free." Paul Guyer, *Kant on Freedom, Law, and Happiness* (Cambridge University Press, 2000), p.142n. Apart from issues of translation, the very notion of a "kingdom" of any kind being prescribed as an ideal ethical community is highly problematic, given that any political model based on an inherited status such as kingship or nobility is diametrically contrary to the fundamental principles of democracy, freedom, and equality. Since Kant's social and political thinking is firmly in the "republican" tradition (although he has a problematic relationship to democracy), it is conceptually misleading to employ the term "kingdom of ends."

[40] Wood, "The Supreme Principle of Morality", p.358; and see Wood, *Kant's Ethical Thought*, pp.17–18.

commonwealth; it is therefore a key instance where the ethical and the political flow into each other.

This should not be misunderstood as a utopian blueprint imposed on reality. As with the autonomous application of the categorical imperative in assessing individual maxims and dispositions, the realm of ends is neither more nor less than a regulative guideline for critical reflection upon existing conditions.[41] It provides a conceptual means for assessing our maxims as these relate to social-political institutions and mores: "every rational being must act as if [*als ob*] he were by his maxims at all times a lawgiving member of a universal realm of ends [*allgemeinen Reiche der Zwecke*]" (G, 4:438). At this level, the potential movement from idea to reality (by which institutions can better approximate the regulative idea) is apparent. If we begin by acting as if we were members of an ethical realm of ends, we can contribute in some way toward actually bringing about social-political conditions more closely resembling such a realm. This is the *grassroots* element in Kant's ethical-political thought. The imperative connects the way we imagine ourselves (the "wider vistas" informing our identities and interrelations), and the actual forms of law-governed interrelations we construct socially and politically.

For, all rational beings stand under the law that each of them is to treat himself and all others never merely as means but always at the same time as ends in themselves. But from this there arises a systematic union of rational beings through common objective laws, that is, a realm [*Reich*], which can be called a realm of ends [*Reich der Zwecke*] (admittedly only an ideal) because what these laws have as their purpose is just the relation of these beings to one another as ends and means. (G, 4:433).

The realm of ends represents a shared ethical-political condition under universalizable moral laws, providing a further regulative guideline for judgment and practice under variable phenomenal conditions.

---

[41] Kant's model elides any sharp distinction between what Amartya Sen calls "arrangement focused" and "realization focused" approaches to justice (*The Idea of Justice* [Cambridge, MA: Harvard University Press, 2009], p.7). Sen analyses John Rawls' work in this respect, asking how the "consistent and coherent political model" Rawls formulates "will translate into guidance about judgments of justice in the world in which we live, rather than in the imagined world with which Rawls is here primarily concerned" (p.79). However, Kant's model and method cannot be conflated with those of Rawls. If we examine the realm of ends in these terms, it is both a "transcendental ideal" quite distinct from anything we might encounter in the world, and yet also a regulative guideline that can help shape the priorities and behavior of actual persons seeking to advance justice under less than ideal conditions.

ENGENDERING THE REALM OF ENDS

Many formulations that appear inattentive to the consequences ensuing from our maxims are in fact directed toward resisting a utilitarian calculus of worth. As an example of this ostensible inattention, Kant asserts: "the essentially good in the action consists in the disposition [*in der Gesinnung*], let the result be what it may" (G, 4:416).[42] The focus on inner motivation or disposition often leads Kant to frame ethical value in opposition to actions determined by external ends. However, ultimately the disposition forms the basis for ethical or unethical actions in the world, so that the apparent dichotomy is superseded. Stressing the inner worth of moral principles is the correlate of both the universalizability of moral laws and the irreducible dignity of persons. Kant argues that "in the realm of ends everything has either a *price* or a *dignity* [*einen Preis, oder eine Würde*]," noting further that "what has a price can be replaced by something else as its *equivalent* [*Äquivalent*]; what on the other hand is raised above all price and therefore admits of no equivalent has a dignity" (G, 4:434). These remarks indicate that the realm of ends is an ideal pertaining to actual social-political transformation. It includes items and actions that "have a price," but prioritizes morality and human dignity as beyond any price. Dignity is distinguished from anything that can be *bought and sold*; this differentiates human worth from barter and exchange value. Kant further distinguishes between that which possesses a "*market price* [*Marktpreis*]" which "is related to general human inclinations and needs," and that which "has a *fancy price* [*Affectionspreis*]," such as what "even without presupposing a need, conforms with a certain taste, that is, with a delight in the mere purposeless play of our mental powers [*Gemütskrafte*]" (G, 4:434–35). It is not simply items that respond to basic needs, such as foodstuffs or "skill and diligence in work," that have a price (market price). Even higher-order cultural activities responding to taste and mental or aesthetic pleasures (Kant offers "wit, lively imagination and humor") can be negotiated in terms of *fancy price* and equivalency.

---

[42] In the second *Critique*, Kant similarly discusses "categories of freedom" which are "directed to the determination of free choice [*freien Willkür*]." This free choice "has as its basis pure practical law *a priori*," also characterized as "the form of a pure will [*eines reiner Willens*] as given with reason." Kant insists that "all precepts of pure practical reason have to do only with the *determination of the will* [*um die Willens*], not with the natural conditions (of practical ability) for *carrying out its purpose*" (CPrR, 5:65–66).

Human dignity and worth are strictly differentiated from either of these forms of exchangeable value: "morality, and humanity insofar as it is capable of morality, is that which alone has dignity." This is further explicated through the following examples: "fidelity in promises and benevolence from basic principles (not from instinct) have an inner worth." Kant reiterates that "nature, as well as art, contains nothing that, lacking these [moral principles], it could put in their place" (G, 4:435). One cannot substitute any other activity or goods, even those higher-order cultural activities with a fancy price, for ethical dispositions. Kant adds a further decisive point concerning ethical principles: "their worth does not consist in the effects arising from them, in the advantage and use [*im Vorteil und Nutzen*] they provide, but in dispositions [*in den Gesinnungen*], that is, in maxims of the will that in this way are ready to manifest themselves through actions, even if success does not favor them [*der Erfolg sie nicht begünstigte*]" (G, 4:435). This encapsulates a series of crucial points. First, in minimizing consequences, Kant is concerned with effects in the world associated with advantage and use, emphasizing the distinction between ethical principles and a utilitarian calculus. Further, having distinguished a disposition guided by principles from measurable effects, Kant insists that *actions in the world, guided by ethical dispositions*, are ultimately very much at stake. This articulates a complex relation between disposition and actions. The latter do not directly reveal the inner depths of our being, but they none the less provide a sensible sign or indicator of these inner states. Here Kant says of actions that they "need no recommendation from any subjective disposition [*Disposition*] or taste, so as to be looked upon with immediate favor [*Gunst*[43]] or delight." Rather, what is crucial is that "they present the will [*stellen den Willen … dar*]" (G, 4:435). Actions and the results they engender cannot be the sole gauge of morality, nor can the immediate favor they elicit (for example, from public opinion or persons in authority) be the gauge of their worth. However, it is crucial that actions are the medium through which the good will or disposition is realized in the world, specifically in relations with others. A variety of contingent factors may affect the results of our intended actions, but only dispositions guided by universal principles can reliably yield ethical results over the long term.

---

[43] These remarks about *expecting to be favored* as a manifestation of subjective attitudes are important. They take on added significance in light of Kant's repeated critiques of any ethical or religious worldview directed toward *gaining favor* (*Gunst*) or privileged status in some form.

In the course of discussing dispositions, Kant develops the social-political direction of his ethics. He describes the value of "a morally good disposition, or virtue" as justified in terms of "the *share* it affords a rational being *in the giving of universal laws*." This emphasis on actively participating in the giving of laws, and on having a stake in these laws, is significant in itself. Moreover, it is this lawgiving capacity that makes us "fit to be a member of a possible realm of ends" (G, 4:435). This is essential because the morally good disposition is inseparable from an autonomous will in accordance with universal laws. The capacity to give and follow laws for ourselves is the *sine qua non* of the realm of ends: "*Autonomy* is therefore the ground of the dignity of human nature and of every rational nature" (G, 4:436). The realm of ends is the collective instantiation of the autonomy characterizing rational beings.

In the second *Critique*, Kant stresses this connection between being individually guided by the categorical imperative and the capacity to reform societies in accordance with moral principles. The moral law "transfers us, in idea, into a nature in which pure reason, if it were accompanied with suitable physical power, *would produce the highest good*, and it determines our will *to confer on the sensible world* the form of a whole of rational beings" (CPrR, 5:43; italics added). The ultimate end of the moral law is to bring about the highest good within the sensible world. Once again, Kant distinguishes between the material conditions (which take various forms) in which "objects must be the causes of the representations [*Vorstellungen*] that determine the will," and our willing in accordance with principles of practical reason, in which "*the will is the cause of objects*" (CPrR, 5:44; italics added). While the maxims directing our wills should not be predicated on material conditions, Kant repeatedly describes the will as *causing* objects or impacting upon material conditions. In the same vein, he discusses the "immanent use" of reason, "in which reason is by means of ideas itself an efficient cause in the field of experience" (CPrR, 5:48). Free will, guided by ideas of reason, can modify human interrelations, including existing ethical-political conditions in a given society. However, the ethical value of our maxims is not to be judged by the actual power we have to effect political transformation. On an ethical level, it is the maxim governing my will which is at stake, rather than a calculus of effects in the world which may vary wildly based on social position and resources. Some may be better equipped than others to realize good dispositions in beneficial social-political activities, but this favorable positioning does not determine one's ethical worth.

SOVEREIGNTY IN THE REALM OF ENDS

Since the realm of ends is not based on contingent laws favoring some and excluding others, all persons are in principle members: "a rational being belongs as a member to the realm of ends when he gives universal laws in it but is also himself subject to these laws." However, to this comment, which follows directly from the autonomous generation of universalizable laws, Kant adds a somewhat cryptic remark: "He belongs to it as sovereign [*als Oberhaupt*] when, as lawgiving, he is not subject to the will of any other" (G, 4:433). All members of the realm of ends both give laws and are subject to them. Who then is the sovereign raised above determination by other wills? Is this invocation not at risk of undermining the universalizability upon which the moral law is founded? To add to the puzzle, Kant defines the sovereign as one who is "a completely independent being, without needs and with unlimited resources [or capacity: *Vermögen*] adequate to his will" G, 4:434). This comment would rule out any human being as a candidate for the role of sovereign: fortunately, even the most powerful tyrant would still fall short of the criteria of "complete independence" and "unlimited capacities."

In a series of remarks, Kant sketches the conceptual lineaments of the realm of ends and begins to clarify the meaning of sovereignty. He first recapitulates the grassroots perspective concerning how each of us can facilitate progression toward this realm under phenomenal conditions: "Now, such a realm of ends would actually come into existence through maxims whose rule the categorical imperative prescribes to all rational beings if they were universally followed" (G, 4:438). Our autonomous judgments, based on the categorical imperative applied within specific contexts, contribute to a society under mutual laws. However, in discussing the possibility of actualizing the realm of ends through following the prescriptions of the categorical imperative, Kant adds an important qualification that unfolds into several seminal points. He notes that even someone scrupulously following the moral law "cannot for that reason count upon every other to be faithful to the same maxim nor can he count on the realm of nature [*Reich der Natur*] and its purposive order to harmonize with him." Our individual moral efforts are not likely to be met with reciprocity by others, nor can we expect our moral endeavors to bear fruit directly in terms of concrete results such as justice and well-being. One who thinks along lines of being rewarded for moral endeavors expects reality to respond by "favoring [*begünstigen*] his expectation of happiness" (G, 4:438). This warning that we should not expect "favor" from any source (human or otherwise) is well in line with Kant's egalitarianism, with his refutation of traditional onto-theology with its voluntarism and heteronomy, and with ethical principles not predicated upon consequences.

Kant then imagines a hypothetical harmonization of the realm of ends with the realm of nature (the idealized state of affairs he has just described as unattainable). He observes that "even if the realm of nature as well as the realm of ends were thought as united under one sovereign [*unter einem Oberhaupte*], so that the latter would *no longer remain a mere idea* but obtain true reality, it would no doubt gain the increment of a strong incentive but never any increase of its inner worth" (G, 4:439; italics added). This clarifies that, apart from this hypothetical unification of the realms of nature and of ends, *the ideal sovereign remains a mere idea.* This first point provides us with an initial response to the dilemma raised by Kant's earlier comments. That is, the sovereign in a realm of ends cannot be any particular human being, but is rather the practical idea, *the moral law itself,* which can guide human willing and acting as not determined by phenomenal conditions. The final point made in these comments is that even if an instantiation of the realm of ends in the world were imagined as realized, the sovereign would not compel obedience by coercive means: "even this sole absolute lawgiver [*Gesetzgeber*] would, despite this, still have to be represented [*vorgestellt*] as judging [*beurteilte*] the worth of rational beings only by their disinterested conduct, prescribed to themselves merely from that idea" (G, 4:439). Hence the idea of the moral law remains the true sovereign, to be followed autonomously. An external sovereign, even one fully attuned to the moral law, cannot compel morality heteronomously but can at best serve as a facilitator for actualizing the moral law we ourselves generate through practical reason. Hence, Kant's model resists arbitrary subjectivist models of sovereignty.[44] It requires autonomous judgment occurring within regulative guidelines of universalizability and inclusivity.

---

[44] This is the failure of the concept of sovereignty formulated by Carl Schmitt in his *Political Theology* of 1922. Schmitt argued that "all law is 'situational law'," and because of this "the sovereign produces and guarantees the situation in its totality. He has the monopoly over the last decision." Carl Schmitt, *Political Theology*, trans. George Schwab (University of Chicago Press, 1985), p.13. Schmitt develops this authoritarian model of sovereignty to address "states of exception" indicating emergencies where the homogenous medium required for the application of codified laws (as he understood it) does not apply. "The exception confounds the unity and order of the rationalist scheme" (p.14). Interestingly, he notes that "emergency was no law at all for Kant" (p.14), which is quite right: for Kant legitimate sovereignty works within and applies the moral law, which requires decision but not willful abrogation of the law. Judgments must

Kant is concerned to show that the moral law provides regulative guidance extending into shared institutions. The ethical idea remains paramount: it is not overridden by the arbitrary authority of any sovereign or by parochial customs and traditions. Yet, Kant is sufficiently realistic to recognize that existing mores and power structures, however inadequate these may be, cannot simply be swept away. Therefore, issues of mediating the moral law, of bringing it closer to intuition and facilitating our moral capacities for judgment and critical reform in context, are decisive. In this respect, two different but related types of mediation are considered.

The first concerns the relationship of human sovereigns and governmental institutions to moral laws. This approach follows the path we saw with regard to Kant's assessment of the French Revolution. While supporting progressive reform of social-political conditions toward greater approximation of the principles of freedom, equality, and human dignity, he advocates a lawful approach to such transformation, lest the means undermine the end. For example, *The Metaphysics of Morals* emphasizes that the relations among sovereigns and citizens should develop toward concordance with the model of the realm of ends. Thus Kant emphasizes that the notion of property might hold with regard to animals, but that "it simply cannot be applied to human beings, especially the citizens of a state" (MM, 6:345). This argument against treating humans as property is likely directed against Aristotle, who explicitly defends slavery under the heading of property rights.[45] Kant's opposition to ownership of others is directly linked to the formulations of the categorical imperative: "For they [citizens] must always be regarded as colegislating members of a state (not merely a means, but also ends in themselves), and must therefore give their free assent, through their representatives" (MM, 6:345). Finally, this relationship of co-legislation involves "the duty of the sovereign to the people (not the reverse)" (MM, 6:346). Hence, relations of sovereign and people are regulated by moral laws: the sovereign's duty to the people involves bringing institutions and legislation into greater conformity with universalizable principles.

The second issue concerns *symbolic representations* of moral principles. This builds on the arguments that ideas of reason can be made

---

respond to emergencies and exceptional states, but these do not justify the abolition of rightful law. By contrast, Schmitt's model of sovereignty, in overriding law, provides no regulative guidelines for the political, let alone for ethical-political existence. It opens the door to legitimizing the arbitrary willfulness of the dictator. As Tracy B. Strong notes of Schmitt's affiliation with the Nazis: "*his understanding of law required that he support Hitler*" ("Foreword," to Schmitt, *Political Theology*, p.xxxi).

[45] Aristotle, *Politics*, Book I, 4, 1253b, 24ff. (*Complete Works of Aristotle*, vol. II, pp.1989–90).

more readily applicable under phenomenal conditions through ideals and archetypes. Only the transcendental ideal, as representing universal moral laws, could fulfill the criteria of sovereignty Kant has adumbrated: complete independence, ability to judge the inner disposition of all, and unrestricted capacity. This approach plays a central role in harnessing religious representational systems as a resource for collectively instantiating the moral law, as we shall see in the next chapter. Kant draws from religious and theological discourse, while resisting literal interpretations. Most importantly, he rejects any form of theological voluntarism that projects human willfulness onto the transcendental ideal. The distinction is explained in *The Metaphysics of Morals*:

> One who commands (*imperans*) through the law is the *lawgiver* (*legislator*). He is the author (*autor*) of the obligation in accordance with the law, but not always the author of the law. In the latter case the law would be positive (contingent) and chosen [*willkürlich*] law. A law that binds us *a priori* and unconditionally by our own reason can also be expressed [*ausgedrückt werden*] as proceeding from the will of a supreme lawgiver, that is, one who has only rights and no duties (hence from the divine will); but this signifies [*bedeutet*] only the idea of a moral being whose will is a law for everyone, without his being thought as the author of the law. (MM, 6:227)[46]

The idea of God relates to the legislator who "has only rights and no duties."[47] It is clear that this view is not compatible with theological voluntarism which, as with Carl Schmitt's notion of sovereignty in his *Political Theology*, makes laws secondary to the arbitrary will of the sovereign. Hence Schmitt appropriates the absolutism of theological voluntarism as a template for human dictatorship. In sharp contrast to this, Kant understands the idea of the divine as representing a will fully in accordance with the moral law, so that lawfulness taking the form of universalizability is not vitiated by the arbitrary willfulness characterizing anthropomorphic renderings of God. In fact, because it provides the quintessential depiction of a *higher law* transcending the specificity

---

[46] The same approach is developed in the third *Critique*. Kant proposes with regard to "the original being" that "we must not conceive of it merely as an intelligence and as legislative for nature, but also as a legislative sovereign in a moral realm of ends" (CJ, 5:444). The value of this representation is that it helps us conceive and work towards "a final end," i.e. the realization of human ethical potentiality in the world: "this final end can be nothing other than **the human being under moral laws**" (CJ, 5:445).

[47] In his *Opus Postumum*, Kant also links the idea of God with the sovereign who legislates but is not subject to laws: "Now *a being which has only rights and no duties is* **God**" (OP, 22:120). Kant remains consistent in noting of God that "it is not a *substance* outside myself ... but the concept of duty (of a universal practical principle) is contained identically in the concept of a divine being as an ideal of human reason for the sake of the latter's law giving" (OP, 22:123).

of human vantage points (as in representations of an omnilateral will), religious discourse can *potentially* work to counteract the narrowness and injustice of parochial positive laws and legislators. This is where the task of critically interpreting religious modes of representation in accordance with universalizable principles becomes decisive.

If all our wills conformed to the moral law, this would ideally bring about the realm of ends. However, there is a far more complex interrelation between our individual identities and the social-political worlds we inhabit, so that amelioration must occur on the level of political institutions and collective mores as well as individual wills. This means that the types of human legislators we empower, and the types of positive laws they legislate, are as ethically crucial as attention to our inner dispositions. These approaches to the reform of existing conditions – through inner awakening and through more direct engagement with existing ethical-political conditions – are mutually complementary.

INTEREST, MOTIVATION, AND POSTULATES

From out of the regulative structure of the formal model of lawfulness, more concrete representations of a possible life in common are derived. This movement toward intuition and hence phenomenal application is crucial. Intellectually recognizing the universal law is the indispensable prerequisite for establishing clear principles. Nevertheless, mental recognition is still far removed from actually being able to judge and act in accordance with the moral law, individually and collectively, within variable circumstances. Obstructions to cultivating moral dispositions appear on several mutually reinforcing levels. They concern our susceptibility to drives or inclinations directed toward personal gain, our propensity for self-love in various manifestations, our capacity to deceive ourselves about our motivations and maxims, our fear of power and authority, and our receptiveness to parochial traditions and institutions. In response to the multiple problems generated by these sources, Kant delves more deeply into the way cultural and political mores are internalized by the power of choice. He also explores how publicly accessible resources such as traditions, symbol systems, and institutions can help maximize our capacity to recognize and be motivated by moral laws. This requires a more explicit focus on historically transmitted shared representations as resources that can be brought into the service of practical reason and that contribute to judgment *in concreto*.

Toward the end of the *Groundwork*, Kant returns to the *anthropological* factors conducive to making ethical judgments in context. He relates freedom of the will to "an *interest* [*ein Interesse*] which the human being can take in moral laws" (G, 4:460).[48] An attached footnote explains that "an interest is that by which reason becomes practical, i.e., becomes a cause determining the will." In these passages, interest is associated with the capacity of rational beings to direct their wills (their *Willkür* or power of choice) according to a moral end. Interest is therefore differentiated from the capacities of non-rational creatures who "feel only sensible impulses" (G, 4:460n.). Following these comments, we are reminded that "it is not *because the law interests* us that it has validity for us (for that is heteronomy and dependence of practical reason upon sensibility)" (G, 4:460–61). Granting this point, the issue concerns the transition from rationally formulated lawfulness to embodied beings invested in actualizing that law in the world. *Interest* is a subjective factor (anthropological and psychological) intrinsic to this mediation.

This concern with awakening interest in the moral law opens a discussion of the idea of the intelligible world. As we have seen, human beings are both sensible (affected by and affecting the phenomenal world) and intelligible (capable of formulating and willing according to reason and moral principles). On this basis, Kant figuratively speaks of an intelligible world of which we are "members." He cautiously notes that this is an idea about which we "might indeed revel [or *enthuse* about, *herumschwärmen*]" but, "even though I have an *idea* of it, which has its good grounds, yet I have not the least *cognizance* of it nor can I ever attain this by all the efforts of my natural faculty of reason. It signifies only a 'something' [*sie bedeutet nur ein Etwas*] that is left over when I have excluded from the determining grounds of my will everything belonging to the world of sense" (G, 4:462). Kant reminds us that the moral law cannot be derived from empirical experience, but also argues that neither should reason "impotently flap its wings without moving from the spot in space, which is empty for it, of transcendent concepts called the intelligible world, and

---

[48] Earlier in the *Groundwork*, Kant insists that categorical imperatives are distinguished from hypothetical imperatives by "the renunciation of all interest, in volition from duty" (G, 4:431). He adds that "just because of the idea of giving universal law it is based on no interest" (G, 4:432). These remarks differentiate the moral law from parochial or subjectively determined mores governed by limited ends; i.e., they serve the interests of myself and/or of favored others, but are not universalizable. In the later sections I am now discussing, however, Kant explores resources for bringing the "purified" moral law into active effect within our subjective dispositions and actions in the world. He is now addressing interest in the service of the moral law.

so lose itself in phantoms [*Hirngespinsten*]" (G, 4:462). Resisting the lure of supersensible knowledge claims, Kant returns to the theme of interest. In this respect, the intelligible world remains

a useful and permitted idea for the sake of rational belief [*vernünftigen Glaubens*], even if all knowledge stops at its boundary – useful and permitted for producing in us a lively *interest* [*ein lebhaftes Interesse*] in the moral law by means of the noble ideal of a universal realm [*Reich*] of *ends in themselves* (rational beings) to which we can belong as members only when we conduct ourselves in accordance with maxims of freedom as if they were laws of nature. (G, 4:462–63)

The initial point concerns awakening an interest in following and actualizing the moral law. Here the theme of *rational belief* concerns motivating our ethical willing and acting. There is no mention of God, immortality of the soul, or other traditional Christian ideas: it is the noble ideal of a universal realm of ends in which we all participate, towards which our belief and interest are directed. This theme is also anticipated in the first *Critique*, where Kant cites Leibniz's notion of a "realm of grace [*Reich der Gnaden*]" conveying the notion of "rational beings and their interconnection in accordance with moral laws under the rule of the highest good" (A812/B840). While we live in a "realm of nature" where some might act according to moral laws and yet "cannot expect any success for their conduct except in accordance with the course of nature in our sensible world," the realm of grace remains "a practically necessary idea of reason" (A812/B840). It is a regulative idea sustaining us in the face of the injustices and contingencies of life and guiding us in contributing toward a more ethical condition. Kant links the ideas of intelligible world, moral world, and realm of grace in writing: "intelligible, i.e., moral world (*regnum gratiae* [*realm of grace*])." He further specifies with regard to these ideas that "the world must be represented [*vorgestellt*] as having arisen out of an idea if it is to be in agreement with that use of reason without which we would hold ourselves unworthy of reason, namely the moral use which depends throughout on the idea of the highest good" (A815–16/B843–44). An important aspect of this idea is that it responds to human needs for happiness and well-being. It brings the autonomous moral law into combination with these needs, without succumbing to the lure of heteronomous principles. It presents our pursuit of happiness as interdependent with, if secondary to, our endeavors to follow moral laws, and in this way integrates happiness with a more encompassing ethical-political vision.

This wider vision is established in an early section of the second *Critique*. While emphasizing that moral laws cannot be determined by specific ends (such as my own happiness), Kant also introduces a pivotal comment concerning the reconciliation of the moral law with the pursuit of happiness. "Let the matter be, for example, my own happiness. This, if I attribute it to each (as, in the case of finite beings, I may in fact do) can become an *objective* practical law only if I include in it the happiness of others" (CPrR, 5:34). The pursuit of happiness is recognized as an essential element in human life.[49] However, my pursuit of happiness can be reconciled with moral law only in being *universalized*, i.e., expanded to include the happiness of all others. This universalization also establishes limiting conditions for my personal pursuit of happiness; if this is undertaken at the expense of others, for example by exhausting resources for future generations, then it is morally insupportable. A related argument is presented in "Theory and Practice," five years after the second *Critique*. Kant describes the goal of ethical-political endeavor in the following terms: "to work to the best of one's ability toward the *highest good* possible in the world (universal happiness combined with and in conformity with the purest morality throughout the world)" (TP, 8:279). This description of the highest good leaves no doubt that it represents an inclusive ethical-political vision; it addresses not my own individual happiness conceived in isolation from others, but the *happiness of all* within the framework of just ethical-political laws. In responding to our needs for happiness as well as our potential for autonomy, the highest good points toward a political ideal of justice and fairness. Even if this ideal is not fully realizable, it offers rules guiding our individual and collective practice under phenomenal conditions. Here it also becomes evident that happiness is irreducible to the passing sensuous enjoyments of atomized individuals. It rather opens into much deeper questions concerning *the quality of the interactions among human beings, and of the types of socio-political worlds within which these interactions occur*. Regulative ideas such as the realm of ends, immortality, and the highest being reinforce and supplement the categorical imperative, providing conceptual resources for cultivating moral sensibility and judgment. The use of representational supports guiding ethical practice is central to these considerations. These express ideals of reason, but they are also informed by cultural and historical factors, as we saw in the examples of various archetypes. This interface of reason and historical

---

[49] Later in the second *Critique*, Kant reiterates this point: "It can even in certain respects be a duty to attend to one's happiness, partly because happiness (to which belong skill, health, and wealth) contains the means for fulfillment of one's duty and partly because lack of it (e.g., poverty) contains temptations to transgress one's duty" (CPrR, 5:93). This comment emphasizes the interplay of inner dispositions and social-political conditions. Poverty and injustice create conditions where the probability of choosing unethically (e.g. stealing) becomes far more likely.

life makes Kant's analyses of religious representations an integral part of his ethical-political thinking.

The *postulates of practical reason* concerning freedom, God, and immortality of the soul serve a practical function similar to the idea of a realm of ends: to motivate and guide our autonomous choices based on moral laws. The postulates of practical reason are directly related to realizing the realm of ends, i.e., the highest good as the conjunction of morality with the happiness of all. These postulates were introduced in the first *Critique* as presupposed by the moral law. Referring to the idea of a highest being, Kant writes that moral laws "postulate this existence rightfully but, of course, only practically [*nur praktisch postuliren*]" (A634/B662). Throughout the three *Critiques* and other mature writings, Kant never wavers from the position that we can have no knowledge of supersensible entities, and he repeats this point many times. Hence the postulates are not proofs in any sense that claims objectified knowledge of supersensible realities. In chapter 4 I discussed the postulates of empirical thinking in general, and we saw that these are classified as dynamical and regulative, rather than mathematical and constitutive principles.[50] Subsequently, I discussed regulative principles with regard to ideas of reason such as the cosmological ideas. In the present context, I want to stress Kant's association of practical regulative principles with the act of postulating (see A509/B537), which is sharply differentiated from constitutive principles involving knowledge claims beyond the scope of possible human experience. Like regulative principles generally, the postulates of practical reason guide a progressive movement of mental operations; in this case, a progression in our cultivation of ethical dispositions and correlated ethical activity in the world.

Later in the first *Critique*, Kant establishes that the practical reality of the postulates concerns ethical actions. He links "**the ideal of the highest good**" with "an intelligible, i.e. **moral** world." Most crucially, he notes that "we must assume the moral world to be a *consequence of our conduct*

---

[50] We may recall that in the first *Critique* the term "postulate" initially appears with respect to empirical thinking in general, and then migrates over to practical thinking. With regard to the first, Cassirer remarks that "they concern the content of objective appearance less than the place we ourselves give it in empirical thinking." Ernst Cassirer, *Kant's Life and Thought* (New Haven: Yale University Press, 1981), p.189. Although the objects of concern are different in each case, what unifies the two uses of the term "postulate" is that both involve our mental operations. In neither case is Kant concerned with objects disconnected from subjective processes; hence, postulates are regulative of practical activity and not constitutive of supersensible objects. They are, however, *also* constitutive in the specific sense of directing us toward the realization of the realm of ends.

in the sensible world" (A810–11/B838–39; italics added). Once again, the apparent dualism of intelligible and sensible worlds is resolved: the first is an ideal that regulates our autonomous practical activity in the latter. More precisely, the intelligible world and the corresponding intelligible character of human beings are formed by the rationally generated ideas of the categorical imperative. The formulae of practical reason also generate supporting ideals, such as archetypes and postulates, which if properly understood can help us bring practical ideas into phenomenal reality. Hence, after discussing the ideal of the highest good, Kant immediately returns to the postulates. He notes that "without a God and a world that is now not visible to us but is hoped for, the majestic ideas of morality are, to be sure, objects of approbation and admiration but not incentives [*Triebfedern*] for resolve and realization" (A813/B841). The practical reality of these ideas means they can *become* real through our ethical activity in the world. Reciprocally, ideas of reason help us cultivate interest in the moral law; they provide incentives and guidance for our imperfect efforts to realize a moral world. Similar arguments are presented in the second *Critique*. For example, Kant states that "supersensible nature, so far as we can make for ourselves a concept of it, is nothing other than a nature under the autonomy of pure practical reason." He describes "this pure world of the understanding" as "the *archetypal* [*urbildliche*] *world* (*natura archetypa*) which we cognize only in reason, whereas the latter [the natural world] could be called the *ectypal* [*nachgebildete*] *world* (*natura ectypa*) because it contains the possible effect of the idea of the former as the determining ground of the will" (CPrR, 5:43). The intelligible or archetypal world accords with the moral law, i.e., it represents the realm of ends. Traditional metaphysical discourse is reconceptualized to describe autonomous ethical-political transformation in accordance with universalizable principles.

In the first *Critique* Kant also clarifies his position with regard to "**moral belief**" (A828/B856). He reiterates that

no one will ever be able to boast that he **knows** that there is a God and a future life … No, the conviction is not **logical** but **moral** certainty, and, since it depends on subjective grounds (of moral disposition) I must not even say "**It is** morally certain that there is a God", etc., but rather "**I am** morally certain" etc. (A828–29/B856–57)

This could not be clearer in linking moral faith with our subjective attitudes and dispositions concerning ethical endeavor. Kant is not discussing knowledge of supersensible objects existing outside us; the focus is on ideas and ideals intrinsic to ethical progress. This point also differentiates moral faith from any form of fantasy, wishing, or enthusiasm, all of which slide over from practical ideas to unfounded assertions about reality.[51] Moral faith becomes real through the progress of our dispositions, regulated by the moral law and manifested in the course of life through activity in the world. The postulates of practical reason regulatively guide progress toward instantiating the realm of ends. Therefore, they are *also* constitutive in a special sense; i.e., insofar as moral principles are actualized in the world through our autonomous activity, new social and political realities are brought into being.

The second *Critique* develops the practical significance of the postulates in considerable detail. Early on, Kant emphasizes the concept of freedom as the "*keystone* ... of pure reason and even speculative reason." He continues: "and all other concepts (those of God and immortality), which as mere ideas remain without support in the latter, now attach themselves to this concept and with it and by means of it get stability and objective reality, that is, their *possibility* is *proved* by this: that freedom is real, for this idea reveals itself through the moral law" (CPrR, 5:3–4). Rather than being heteronomous, the idea of God is founded on freedom (i.e., moral autonomy), and is postulated with reference to the ends of morality. This point also confirms that freedom manifests in ethical dispositions and actions in the world. This constitutes the form of proof with which Kant is concerned: insofar as we bring moral principles into our individual and collective lives they are proven in experience and hence become real. Moreover, in subsequently discussing this "pure rational belief," Kant emphasizes that "it is not to be understood by this that it is necessary to assume the existence of God *as a ground of all obligation in general* (for this rests, as has been sufficiently shown, solely on the autonomy of reason itself)" (CPrR, 5:125–26). He rejects making morality contingent upon religious belief in its multifarious forms; rather, religious conceptions can further morality insofar as they give expression

---

[51] Kant specifies that "moral theology is therefore only of immanent use, namely for fulfilling our vocation here in the world by fitting into the system of all ends, not for fanatically [*schwärmerisch* – more strictly translated as "enthusiastically"] or even impiously abandoning the guidance of a morally legislative reason in the good course of life in order to connect it immediately to the idea of a highest being, which would provide a transcendental use but which even so, like the use of mere speculation, must pervert and frustrate the ultimate ends of reason" (A819/B847). Besides clarifying that the practical significance of theological ideas concerns our actions in the world, Kant makes a move he develops in *Religion*: enthusiastic ventures into transcendental speculation are not only unfounded, they are *impious* in relation to the genuine religious calling of good life-conduct.

to freedom directed toward the ends of reason. Kant specifies that "in the highest good which is practical for us, that is, to be made real through our will [*durch unsern Willen wirklich zu machenden*], virtue and happiness are thought as necessarily combined." He also reiterates of the highest good that "it concerns a practical good, that is, one that is possible through action [*durch Handlung*]" (CPrR, 5:113). Hence a connection of moral realization with actively modifying phenomenal and political conditions is made explicitly clear.

However, there is no necessary correspondence between our dispositions and the laws of cause and effect. We may strive with the utmost integrity to achieve moral dispositions, yet nevertheless suffer hardships, injustice, and unhappiness. This observation generates the Antinomy of Practical Reason: "if therefore the highest good is impossible in accordance with practical rules, then the moral law, which commands us to promote it, must be fantastic and directed to empty imaginary ends and must therefore in itself be false" (CPrR, 5:114). This comment is important in confirming the stoical element in Kant's thinking: we cannot expect inner moral cultivation to be favored by external rewards. Yet the claim that the impossibility of full realization of the highest good somehow undermines the principles of the moral law is problematic as a rigorous argument or even as a psychological analysis. In any case, Kant immediately responds to the antinomy of practical reason by invoking the distinction between phenomenal and noumenal aspects of human beings. Proceeding from phenomenal to noumenal, it remains "*absolutely false*" that "the endeavor after happiness produces a ground for a virtuous disposition." Yet, from the other direction, the proposition "that a virtuous disposition necessarily produces happiness, is false *not absolutely* but only insofar as this disposition is regarded as the form of causality in the sensible world" (CPrR, 5:114). Hence, after emphasizing that the pursuit of happiness cannot produce virtue, Kant then indicates a different quality of happiness or well-being, one not predicated on material conditions. This does not mean that the latter are neglected, but rather that a full correspondence of ethical disposition and phenomenal contentment is not required for my happiness as an intelligible being. A few paragraphs later, Kant expresses this deeper understanding of happiness as internally connected with virtue: "If a human being is virtuous he will certainly not enjoy life unless he is conscious of his uprightness in every action, however fortune may favor [*günstig*] him in the physical state of life" (CPrR, 5:116). This is consistent with themes running through the critical philosophy; fortune and accident affecting material conditions do not impinge upon our moral worth, and the pursuit of an ethical disposition should involve no expectation of external favor or reward.

Having established this distinction between virtue and happiness for the purposes of instituting clear criteria and priorities, Kant re-emphasizes the connection between inner dispositions and the phenomenal world. Here the more familiar postulating of a highest being is invoked. Kant notes that

> it is not impossible [*nicht unmöglich*] that morality of disposition should have a connection, and indeed a necessary connection, as cause with happiness as effect in the sensible world, if not immediately yet mediately (by means of an intelligible author of nature), a connection which, in a nature that is merely an object of the senses, can never occur except contingently and cannot suffice for the highest good. (CPrR, 5:115)

This is a somewhat strained argument if its goal is to establish the reality of an "intelligible author of nature."[52] However, given that Kant's focus is the autonomous cultivation of ethical dispositions, perhaps the best way to understand this discussion is again with regard to sustaining interest and motivation. It is in this sense that Kant sometimes writes of postulating as a form of *demand*, which draws on the etymology of the Latin *postulatio* meaning a claim or a demand, or *postulo*, meaning to claim, demand, or request.[53] For example, in stressing of the postulation of God

---

[52] As Byrne observes, "It is hard to think how the existence of a rational, universal need to conceive the highest good as genuinely possible provides good reason for thinking that there is a God." Peter Byrne, *Kant on God* (Farnham, UK: Ashgate, 2007), p.89. Guyer reaches an equally negative conclusion with regard to both the highest being and immortality of the soul: "[Kant's] claim that we must postulate our own immortality in order rationally to attempt this goal [of the highest good] collapses into incoherence, and his argument that we must believe in the existence of God in order to pursue this goal depends on an overly strong interpretation of the conditions of rationality." Paul Guyer, *Kant* (London: Routledge, 2006), pp. 236–37. In his early work, Wood takes a somewhat more favorable view. He discusses this antinomy of practical reason in terms of an "*absurdum practicum*," summarizing the basic line of thinking as follows: "If I deny the existence of God or of a future life, I can be made to deny the validity of the moral law. But I know the moral law to be valid. Therefore, if I am to avoid this contradiction, I must not deny the existence of a God and a future life." Allen W. Wood, *Kant's Moral Religion* (Ithaca, NY: Cornell University Press, 1970), p.26. Wood clarifies this reasoning in noting that "Kant proposes to justify a *belief* in a God and a future life which can never become a form of *knowledge*" (p.104). The status of this moral belief is important; it does not generate knowledge but remains a guide to practical action. In a later piece, Wood draws closer to this interpretation: "Kant's arguments do not show that there is a God and a future life, but only that belief in God and a future life would be very desirable for a moral agent to have, since it would rescue such an agent from a practical paradox." Allen W. Wood, "Rational Theology, Moral Faith, and Religion," in Paul Guyer, ed., *The Cambridge Companion to Kant* (Cambridge University Press, 1992), p.404.

[53] Wood makes the same point with reference to the Greek, referring to "a 'postulate' in something like the Euclidean sense, where the Greek word for 'postulate' (*aitema*) means request." *Kantian Ethics*, p.93.

that "no positive use can now be made of it for theoretical purposes," Kant adds that this putative reference to possible objects "can also not be demanded [*nicht gefordert werden kann*]" (CPrR, 5:134). The third *Critique* similarly emphasizes that the conception of a pure bodiless spirit is "a **sophistical entity**," and that this must be rigorously differentiated from an "**entity of reason**" that is valid "for the practical use of reason, because the latter, which has its own special and apodictically certain principles *a priori* even demands [*erheischt*] (postulates) this" (CJ, 5:468). This sense of postulating as a form of request or demand indicates that it arises from our subjective ethical needs. The ideas of reason that are practically postulated help address our failure of nerve in cultivating ethical dispositions in the face of the setbacks and uncertainties with which we are confronted.

This approach to the postulates as sustaining interest and motivation is supported by the ensuing discussion's explicit turn to the issue of cultivating our interest in ethical improvement. Kant notes that "the virtuous Epicurus ... fell into the error of presupposing the virtuous *dispositions* [*die tugendhafte Gesinnung*] in the persons for whom he wanted first of all to provide the incentive to virtue [*die Triebfeder zur Tugend*]" (CPrR, 5:116). Far from assuming we are habitually virtuous, this emphasizes that we must *work* to cultivate a virtuous disposition. This ethical task is assisted by the psychological possibility of taking pleasure in the determination of the will "directly by reason alone," again indicating a form of pleasure irreducible to sense experience (CPrR, 5:116). In fact, we can take satisfaction in ethical attainment itself: "it is something very sublime in human nature to be determined to actions directly by a pure rational law." Following this, Kant emphasizes that "it is also of great importance to take notice of this property of our personality and to cultivate [*cultiveren*] as much as possible the effect of reason on this feeling" (CPrR, 5:117). The aim is to further our interest in cultivating an ethical disposition; this involves mediation between intelligible ideas and sensible existence (in the form of the feeling of the sublime). The question becomes: *how* do we cultivate such an ethical disposition? This is not merely a matter of imitating right actions externally; actions must be done "from duty, which must be the true end of all moral cultivation [*moralischen Bildung*]" (CPrR, 5:117). Although Kant remains vigilant about our being motivated by anything other than the moral law (hence by heteronomy), he recognizes that the task of ethical cultivation can be assisted by intuitively accessible conceptual resources, such as religious ones, that focus and guide our interest, hence bridging practical reason and phenomenal existence.

Returning to the question of "actions that aim at realizing the highest good," Kant proposes exploring two grounds of that possibility: "first with respect to what is immediately within our power and then, secondly, in that which is not in our power but which reason presents [*darzustellen*] to us, as the supplement [*Ergänzung*] to our inability, for the possibility of the highest good" (CPrR, 5:119). What compensates for our inability to realize the highest good is *an idea* presented to us by reason. This indicates a double function of reason; i.e., it is both the source of formal laws, and also of regulative ideals such as the highest good and the realm of ends that support our active cultivation of dispositions in accordance with those laws. Hence no heteronomous source is invoked (although the human need for media by which ideals of reason are represented and transmitted, e.g., cultural traditions, reopens the question of heteronomy insofar as moral ideas become admixed with various non-moral historical elements. This leads to the problem of interpretation addressed in *Religion*.) Similar strategies appear with regard to the postulate of the immortality of the soul. As we have seen, as rational beings living in the sensible world, we can never achieve holiness (complete conformity of the will with the moral law). Therefore, a viable response to the duty or command to be ethical "can only be found in an *endless progress* as the real object of our will." This ongoing progress seems to require "the presupposition of the *existence* and personality of the same rational being continuing *endlessly* (which is called immortality of the soul)" (CPrR, 5:122). As we shall see, Kant reiterates this theme of ongoing approximation of a moral disposition throughout *Religion*, where he dispenses with the postulate of immortality of the soul, arguing instead that from the standpoint of "one who knows the heart," i.e. God as representing the moral law, ethical progress is equivalent to attaining a moral disposition. In this section of the second *Critique*, Kant actually makes a similar point:

[A]ll a creature can have with respect to hope for this share [in the highest good] is consciousness of his tried disposition [*seiner erprüften Gesinnung*], so that, from the progress he has already made from the worse to the morally better and from the immutable resolution he has thereby come to know, he may hope for a further uninterrupted continuance of this progress. (CPrR, 5:123)

What emerges with respect to the postulates is a way of representing ongoing moral progress as a motivating guide for our fallible wills.

Kant now returns to "The Existence of God as a Postulate [*Postulat*] of Pure Practical Reason" (CPrR, 5:124). The postulate of God follows from (or is demanded by) the impossibility of total ethical realization combined with happiness. "Therefore, the highest good in the world is possible only insofar as a supreme cause of nature having a causality in keeping with the moral disposition is assumed" (CPrR, 5:125). Although this reasoning does not override Kant's prior effort to detach happiness from sense experience, the postulate of God harmonizes ethical dispositions with causality in the natural world. This point is not unlike that concerning the hypothetical sovereign in a realm of ends as reconciled with the realm of nature. In much the same way, the postulate of the highest being reconciling morality and nature assists us in overcoming the hopelessness that might ensue from the dissociation between our moral endeavors and worldly success. Therefore, in discussing the "moral necessity" of postulating a highest being, Kant reiterates that "this moral necessity *is subjective*, that is, a need [*Bedürfnis*], and not *objective*, that is itself a duty" (CPrR, 5:125).[54] Such comments decisively remove the act of postulating from ontological claims: the ideas of God and immortality of the soul arise from our autonomy and are postulated in accordance with realizing our potential as ethical beings in a world that all too often resists those efforts. Kant further reminds us that "it is not to be understood by this that it is necessary to assume the existence of God *as a ground of all obligation in general* (this rests, as has been sufficiently shown, solely on the autonomy of reason itself)" (CPrR, 5:125–26). I have noted that Kant consistently opposes theological voluntarism and heteronomy. The idea of God can assist us in being ethically focused and motivated, but it is not the *basis* for ethics. He insists, concerning the "pure *rational belief* [*reiner Vernunftglaube*]" of practical postulating, that "pure reason alone (in its theoretical as well as in its practical use) is the source [*Quelle*] from which it springs" (CPrR, 5:126). The representationally enhanced ideals of the postulates therefore serve as supplements to the formal procedures of practical reason.

It is highly significant that Kant now directly discusses how representational forms can assist our moral endeavors. In this regard he enters into a brief comparative discussion of Greek and Christian ideas. With regard to the possibility of attaining the highest good, the Epicureans made "the rule of the use which the human will makes of its freedom the sole and sufficient ground of this possibility, without, as it seemed to them, needing the existence of God for it." On this point, Kant unhesitatingly

---

[54] A similar point is made in the third *Critique*: "This moral argument is not meant to provide any **objectively** valid proof of the existence of God, nor meant to prove to the doubter that there is a God ... Hence it is a **subjective** argument, sufficient for moral beings" (CJ, 5:450–51n.).

affirms that "they were indeed correct in establishing the principle of morals by itself, independently of this postulate and solely from the relation of reason to the will" (CPrR, 5:126). This corroborates the derivative status of the practical postulates in relation to moral principles. However, Kant rebukes the Epicureans for another reason: they "had assumed an altogether false principle of morals as supreme, namely that of happiness." He then contrasts this prioritization of happiness with the position of the Stoics. The latter "had chosen their supreme practical principle quite correctly, namely virtue [*die Tugend*], as the condition of the highest good" (CPrR, 5:126). In this case, however, the problem lies in the Stoic way of representing the realization of virtue, which is both unrealistic and one-sided. In making these points, Kant emphasizes the effects on our motivation of the way ethical ideas are portrayed within culturally informed images:

[I]nasmuch as they represented [*vorstellen*] the degree of virtue required by its pure law as fully attainable in this life, they not only strained the moral capacity of the *human being*, under the name of the *sage*, far beyond all limits of his nature and assumed something that contradicts all cognition of the human being, but also and above all they would not let a second *component* of the highest good, namely happiness, hold as a special object of the human faculty of desire but made their *sage*, like a divinity in his consciousness of the excellence of his person, quite independent of nature (with respect to his own contentment), exposing him indeed to the ills of life but not subjecting him to them (at the same time representing him as also free from evil [*als frei vom Bösen darstellten*]). (CPrR, 5:127)

This important passage is illuminating in several respects. Alongside calling attention to collective representational devices as guiding ethical endeavor, thereby further articulating the interface between ethics and culture, it confirms that embodied human beings are the focus of Kant's practical inquiries. The Stoic ideal or archetype of the sage is undisturbed by the forces of nature, unconcerned with happiness and well-being, untainted by evil maxims. This is exactly what actual human beings *are not*. The sage is a representation of human perfection that contradicts all cognition of the empirical possibilities of human beings. Hence, far from enjoining us to imitate these impossible ideals, Kant works within the limitations and imperfections of humans while attempting to expand the envelope of our moral capacity as far as this might reasonably go.

Kant then turns to what he calls the doctrine of Christianity which, "even if it is not regarded as a religious doctrine, gives on this point a concept of the highest good (of the realm of God [*des Reichs Gottes*]) which alone satisfies the strictest demands of practical reason" (CPrR, 5:127). He reiterates that ethical perfection is not a human possibility; the best we can attain is "still only virtue, that is, a disposition conformed *from respect* for law." Respect indicates a desire to follow the moral law conjoined with a sense of distance from it. Respect is connected with "consciousness of a continuing propensity [*Hanges*] to transgression or at least impurity" (CPrR, 5:128; this propensity to transgression is a key feature of radical evil). The combination of striving and unattainability produces feelings of "self-esteem combined with humility," which Kant advocates as the correct moral attitude in contradistinction to the despair generated by the overly lofty image of the sage.[55] The comment about not necessarily regarding Christianity as "a religious doctrine" indicates that its value as an ethical tradition is not predicated upon accepting its representations literally and dogmatically. Kant similarly insists that "the Christian principle of *morals* itself is not theological (and so heteronomy); it is instead autonomy of pure practical reason by itself" (CPrR, 5:129). The key point is that Kant turns to Christianity as a tradition offering culturally established ethical representations. These, unlike either Epicureanism or Stoicism, address our needs for both virtue and happiness (with virtue prioritized), and also foster rather than inhibit ethical endeavor by combining self-esteem with humility. We should not assume a perfect realization of our moral endeavor, but rather remain humble yet hopeful in our efforts.

We may recall that the first *Critique* discusses the Stoic sage as an archetype (*Urbild*) of moral attainment: it is a culturally informed representation of a practical ideal. The second *Critique* extends Kant's analysis of the practical significance of archetypes and other representational forms with reference to both Greek and Christian traditions. In a note appended to the above-cited passage, Kant restates his view of the Stoic sage as one "who, in raising himself above the animal nature of the

---

[55] In the second *Critique*, Kant explores how recognition of the moral law within us can have a *humiliating* effect. He discusses the perversion of self-love into self-conceit, and notes that "what in our own judgment infringes upon our self-conceit humiliates. Hence the moral law unavoidably humiliates every human being when he compares with it the sensible propensity of his nature [*den sinnlichen Hang seiner Natur vergleicht*]. If something represented as a *determining ground of our will* humiliates us in our self-consciousness, it awakens *respect* for itself insofar as it is positive and a determining ground" (CPrR, 5:74). This shows the experience of humiliation in the face of the moral law as a facet of ethical awakening. We are able to conceptualize the principles of the moral law, which is something sublime in all human beings. Yet, when we compare this universalizable law with our flawed and self-serving maxims, our self-conceit is cut down. Humility is therefore ethically important, but it is not equivalent to self-abnegation. It is rather conjoined with respect for the law we ourselves generate.

human being, is sufficient to himself … and is not subject to any temptation to transgress the moral law" (CPrR, 5:127n.). Here he actively rejects the precise stereotype (arid self-sufficiency) with which his ethical theory is often mistakenly identified. He even argues that the Stoics could not have advocated such an ideal of virtue "if they had represented [*vorgestellt*] this law in all its purity and strictness, as the precept of the Gospel does." Kant portrays the Gospel as representing various facets of the moral law. As he emphasizes: "the moral ideas, as archetypes [*als Urbilder*] of practical perfection serve as the indispensable rule [*Richtschnur*, literally *guideline*] of moral conduct and also the standard of comparison." This note concludes with a proposal that the Christian representational system also conveys a strict moral law to which we may lack confidence of being adequate. Yet, the doctrine of Christianity is simultaneously "enabling us to hope that if we act as well as is within our *power*, then what is not within our power will come to us from another source, whether or not we know in what way" (CPrR, 5:127n.). The conjunction of moral rigor with a sense of *hope* corresponds with the motivational effects of the postulates, and also echoes the juxtaposition of self-esteem and humility in our moral dispositions. The reference to a representation of "assistance from another source" as morally valuable also anticipates the discussion of the idea of grace in *Religion*. In *neither* case is Kant venturing into theological speculation. He is concerned with the way inherited doctrines and representations can affect our moral endeavors, while bracketing irresolvable questions concerning any possible objective referents of these representations.

This point is thoroughly borne out by the ensuing discussion in the second *Critique*. Recalling the unattainability of moral perfection conjoined with happiness by finite creatures, Kant notes that "the Christian doctrine of morals now supplements [*ergänzt*] this lack (of the second indispensable component of the highest good) by representing the world [*durch die Darstellung der Welt*] in which rational beings devote themselves with their whole soul to the moral law as a *realm of God* [*als eines Reichs Gottes*], in which nature and morals come into harmony" (CPrR, 5:128). The Christian ideal of a realm of God is an intuitively accessible representation of the realm of ends conjoining morality and happiness. Kant's language is instructive in this respect. Referring to the precepts Christianity presents to members of its community, he notes that "*holiness* of morals is prescribed to them as a guideline [*Richtschnur*] even in this life." This holiness is "the archetype [*Urbild*] of their conduct in every state" (CPrR, 5:129). It is evident that Kant is not concerned with theological doctrines taken literally and dogmatically. Rather, he draws upon the conceptual resources of the Christian tradition as providing representations and archetypes that assist members of a community in ethical practice in the here and now.

In the second *Critique*'s concluding discussion of the postulates, Kant further explains that "these postulates are not theoretical dogmas [*sind nicht theoretische Dogmata*] but *presuppositions* having a necessary practical reference [*in notwendig praktischer Rucksicht*]" (CPrR, 5:132). In other words, the postulates "are quite unable to ground a speculative cognition," and "their use is, instead, limited solely to the practice of the moral law [*die Ausübung des moralischen Gesetzes*]" (CPrR, 5:137, and cf. 5:138). Clearly, no claims concerning knowledge of supersensible realities are made here. In the same vein, Kant reminds us that any ideas of reason, or any ideals or representations based thereon, are "merely *regulative* principles of speculative reason, which do not require it to assume a new object beyond experience" (CPrR, 5:135). Postulates and other representational aids guide our autonomous ethical practice in this world; they do not divert our focus to some other putative reality. As he elaborates how religious representations can assist ethical practice, Kant also remains preoccupied with possible misinterpretations of his comments as supporting objectified and heteronomous forms of theology. It is noteworthy that between CPrR, 5:134 and 138, for example, he reiterates the caveat that the postulates provide no supersensible knowledge at least *twenty-one times*! In the same vein, Kant insists that we should work with ideas of reason "in a negative way … that is, to ward off *anthropomorphism* as the source of *superstition* or specious extension of those concepts by supposed experience, and on the other side *fanaticism* [*den Fanaticism*], which promises such extension by means of supersensible intuition or feelings – all of which are hindrances to the practical use of reason" (CPrR, 5:135). This comment encapsulates the critical approach to religion and theology. While representations of the divine and associated conceptual supports can enliven our interest in cultivating a moral disposition, elements of anthropomorphism, superstition, and fanaticism must be purged. These are not just epistemologically dubious; they are morally harmful in diverting our focus from autonomous ethical practice toward heteronomous reference points.

The reality represented by the postulates comes into being through autonomous human endeavors; it is the ethical-political ideal of the realm of ends. With regard to this, Kant states that the postulates "become *immanent* and *constitutive* inasmuch as they are grounds of the possibility of *making real the necessary object* of pure practical reason (the highest good), whereas apart from this they are *transcendent* and merely *regulative* principles of speculative reason, which do not require it to assume a new object beyond experience" (CPrR, 5:135). This crucial point is reiterated in the third *Critique*, where Kant writes that the regulative principles become, for practical reason, "at the same time **constitutive**, i.e., practically determining" (CJ, 5:457). Ideas of reason are both regulative and constitutive in this sense alone: they provide the rules and guidelines for our autonomous practice according to moral laws, and are directed toward constituting the realm of ends in the phenomenal world.

CULTURE AND ETHICAL PEDAGOGY

The theme of drawing upon cultural resources to assist our ethical endeavors is similarly addressed in the brief concluding part of the second *Critique*, the Doctrine of Method of Pure Practical Reason. Although this is presented as a separate section, it develops many of the themes formulated in the immediately preceding discussion of the postulates. The continuity is evident in that Kant begins by defining the doctrine of method as concerning "the way in which one can provide the laws of pure practical reason with *access* to the human mind [*Gemüt*] and *influence* [*Einfluß*] on its maxims, that is, the way in which one can make objectively practical reason *subjectively* practical as well" (CPrR, 5:151). This comment encapsulates much of the preceding discussion. It shows that the moral law requires mediating operations; we need guidelines and pedagogical resources to bring our subjective maxims and dispositions into greater concord with ethical principles.

The manner in which moral principles are conveyed by cultural figures such as educators is vital to this endeavor: "the immediate representation [*Vorstellung*] of the law and the objectively necessary observance of it must be represented [*vorgestellt*] as the proper incentives to action, since otherwise legality of actions would be produced but not morality of dispositions." This shows that Kant is conjoining external cultural resources and pedagogical endeavors with the task of awakening an internal and autonomous ethical sensibility. He writes of the "presentation [*Darstellung*] of pure virtue" as having "more power over the human mind [*Gemüt*]" and as providing "a far stronger incentive … than all the deceptive allurements of enjoyment … or even all threats of pain and troubles" (CPrR, 5:151). What is interior and invisible, i.e., ethical dispositions, can be partially represented and thereby improved through the assistance of culturally formed media. The last point in this passage also expresses a theme appearing throughout Kant's discussions of religion. He seeks shared resources for cultivating moral dispositions that address our potential for autonomy, rather than heteronomously wielded rewards and punishments that occlude moral principles and reinforce our status as minors. Enlightened pedagogical resources help cultivate the capacities intrinsic to our rational natures. Such an approach "teaches the human being to feel his own dignity" (CPrR, 5:152). This procedure is "the method of founding and cultivating genuine moral dispositions [*die Methode der Gründung und Cultur ächter moralischer Gesinnungen*]" (CPrR, 5:153). The basic idea is that examples of virtue, i.e., of people freely willing and acting in accordance with moral principles, are the best means of evoking that capacity in others. This is not blind imitation, but rather involves cultivating in students this "propensity [*Hange*] of reason to enter with pleasure upon even the most subtle examination of the practical questions put to them" (CPrR, 5:154). This method provides guidelines for the autonomous judgment required for engaging the multiple variables, sometimes taking the form of competing goods, which characterize ethical dilemmas. Moral educators are encouraged to draw from biographies, for example, in order to "have at hand instances for the duties presented, in which, especially by comparison of similar actions under different circumstances, they could well activate their pupils' judgment [*Beurteilung*] in marking the lesser or greater moral import of such actions." In this way, by evaluating not merely abstract codes but actual instances of conduct in relation to changeable circumstances, the student becomes "not a little interested, since he would feel the progress of his faculty of judgment [*den Fortschritt ihrer Urteilskraft fühlt*]" (CPrR, 5:154). This point not only speaks to the issue of awakening our interest in the moral law, but also elaborates upon the crucial function of autonomous judgment. This cannot be instilled by rote training but is sharpened by practice and experience.

One of the crucial features of this discussion is that it addresses the paradox of autonomous morality: this is a capacity we all have, and yet in large part we remain ignorant of it and at variance with it. Towards the end of this section, Kant reiterates his approach in terms of "the lively presentation [*Darstellung*] of the moral disposition in examples" (CPrR, 5:160). He remarks that through these efforts "there is revealed to the human being an inner capacity not otherwise correctly known by himself, the *inner freedom* to release himself from the impetuous importunity of the inclinations" (CPrR, 5:161). These very important comments indicate the inadequacy of ethical models that focus on the solitary individual attaining moral clarity. We require assistance in becoming awakened to our own autonomous capacity for judgment. To this end, Kant harnesses cultural resources in order to work with our potential for autonomy, and in a certain way he elides a sharp demarcation of what is inner and what is outer. Just as heteronomy can be internalized to form part of my personality (as formalized, for example, in Freud's model of the authoritarian super-ego), so too can external resources assist in the cultivation of inner autonomy. Within these inquiries, the issue of giving sensible expression to the inexpressible, i.e., to the moral law and moral dispositions, is also central. Although religion per se is not explicitly discussed in this final section, Kant's approach to religious representations is connected with these endeavors, insofar as he understands traditions as resources with the potential to mediate inner autonomy with public forms of representation.

This section on the doctrine of method for cultivating practical reason and autonomous ethical judgment is not well developed. However, the basic principles are important, and in many ways they distil Kant's approach toward religious representations and the postulates of practical reason. What might seem a weak feature of the critical philosophy when grasped as an attempt to prove immortality and a highest being appears in a different light when understood as addressing our difficulties in becoming more moral, individually and collectively. The *idea* of God, generated by practical reason, does not require reliance on the interventions of an anthropomorphically conceived higher power, nor need it abrogate the integrity of reason by empowering heteronomous authorities claiming to represent such a higher power. It does, however, indicate the need for shared representations that facilitate our reflection and judgment in accordance with moral laws. By the same token, Kant's analysis indicates that collective representations can also *impede* awareness and ethical cultivation. In this respect, the task of *Religion* is both to critique and reinterpret religious representations in order to harness their expressive power for practical purposes. Kant works to bring historical religions, which can have enormous influence over people's inner dispositions and public worldviews, into greater conformity with ideas and ideals generated by practical reason.

CHAPTER 6

Ethics and politics in Kant's Religion

AUTONOMY AND RADICAL EVIL

Kant's inquiry into historical religions does not compromise the epistemological and ethical principles underpinning the critical philosophy. He makes this clear at the opening of the work:

[S]o far as morality is based on the conception of the human being as one who is free [*als eines freien*] but who also, just because of that, binds himself through his reason to unconditional laws, it is in need neither of the idea of another being above him in order to recognise his duty, nor, that he observe it, of an incentive other than the law itself. (R, 6:3)

This decisive statement indicates the full continuity of *Religion* with the critical philosophy. There may be psychological and social reasons to "assume a higher, moral, most holy, and omnipotent being who," as the *summum bonum*, "alone can unite the two elements of this good" (R, 6:5). Nevertheless, this need does not justify heteronomous authority: "what is most important here, however, is that *this idea rises out of morality and is not its foundation*" (R, 6:5; italics added). Hence religious and theological conceptions, *when properly understood*, can assist rather than impede our autonomous efforts at moral improvement. My interpretation of Kant's project therefore differs from that of Mark Lilla, for example. His analysis builds on the idea of a "Great Separation" of theology from the state, initiated in the work of Hobbes.[1] Lilla then views theorists such as Rousseau and Kant as relegitimating political theology: "Though Kant's political philosophy respected the principles of the Great Separation, his religious thought opened the intellectual possibility of bridging it in some way."[2] By contrast, I am claiming that, rather than foster the *return* of

---

[1] Mark Lilla, *The Stillborn God: Religion, Politics and the Modern West* (New York: Knopf, 2007), p.58.
[2] Ibid., p.162.

something rightly purged by secular political thought, i.e., political theology, Kant is working with a social and political *fact*. In Kant's cultural context, the Christian tradition continued to exert widespread influence in education, ethical mores, and in subtending political legitimacy.[3] Much like Spinoza before him, Kant works with this operative influence, interpreting historical religions as collective *representations* or *symbols* of moral ideas.[4] The strategy of ethically interpreting traditions is central to the task of engaging the internalized worldviews and mores that influence many people. This offers a political analogue to Kant's procedure of applying the categorical imperative to interrogate and ameliorate the maxims already operative in our individual lives.

Earlier, I noted that the third *Critique* (1790) distinguishes between schemata and symbols, "the first of which contain direct, the second indirect presentations [*Darstellungen*] of the concept" (CJ, 5:352). Kant also notes how this representational activity pertains to religious concepts: "the poet ventures to make sensible rational ideas of invisible beings, the kingdom of the blessed, the kingdom of hell, eternity, creation, etc." (CJ, 5:314). Subsequently, he emphasizes that "all of our cognition of God is merely symbolic [*blos symbolisch*]" (CJ, 5:353). These comments retain the restriction on knowledge established in the first *Critique*, while furthering the practical interpretation of metaphysical and theological representations. If this representational power "aesthetically enlarges the concept itself in an unbounded way, then in this case the imagination is creative, and sets the faculty of intellectual ideas (reason) into motion" (CJ, 5:315). Hence there are legitimate practical uses of the creative imagination that enliven abstract ideas, making them accessible and effective within phenomenal existence.[5] Building on these analyses, *Religion* formulates an ethically guided hermeneutics, directed mainly toward biblical sources.

---

[3] See Tim Blanning, *The Pursuit of Glory: Europe 1648–1815* (London: Penguin Books, 2007).
[4] Throughout *Religion*, Kant refers to religious teachings as giving representational form to ethical ideas and dilemmas. See, for example, R, 6:59–60, 74, 78, 83, etc.
[5] *The Conflict of the Faculties* describes "the Idea of God, which is derived from morality itself, to give morality influence on man's will to fulfill his duties" (CF, 7:36). Various traditional representations are "different forms in which the divine will is represented sensibly [*sinnlichen Vorstellung*] so as to give it influence on our minds" (CF, 7:36). The *Anthropology* specifies that "it is *enlightenment* to distinguish the symbolic from the intellectual (public worship from religion), the temporarily useful and necessary *shell* from the thing itself. Because otherwise an *ideal* (of pure practical reason) is mistaken for an *idol*, and the final end is missed" (A, 7:192). Similarly, in his *Lectures on Metaphysics* from 1790–91, Kant remarks that historically images precede conceptual thinking. "No people had properly begun to philosophize before the Greeks; everything previously had been represented by images [*vorher stellte man alles durch Bilder vor*], and nothing by concepts" (LM, 28:535). A page later, he reiterates: "Poetry is older than prose, for the first philosophers clothed everything in images [*kleideten alles in Bilder ein*]" (LM, 28:536). This

Kant's explication of religion begins with our *failures* in actualizing moral principles. This emphasis appears in the theme of Part One: "Concerning the Indwelling of the Evil Principle alongside the Good, or, Of the Radical Evil [*das radikale Böse*] in Human Nature." We have the potential for autonomous moral judgment, yet this seems rarely to be exercised; "the world lieth in evil" (R, 6:19; citing John 5:19). Kant accepts the prevalence of evil, if not deterministic notions of the Fall invented by dogmatic theology, noting that this complaint is "as old as that oldest among all fictions [*Dichtungen*], the religion of the priests" (R, 6:19). This reference to fictions evokes symbolic uses of theological concepts for practical purposes. Kant also notes the views of "pedagogues" who proclaim "that the world steadfastly (though hardly noticeably) forges ahead … from bad to better" (R, 6:19). To this he responds: "surely, if the issue is *moral* good or evil (not just growth in civilization), they have not drawn this view from experience, for the history of all times attests far too powerfully against it" (R, 6:20). This shows that recourse to experience is an indicator of moral standing individually and collectively. It also separates progress in civilization, which includes technical advances as well as the cultivation of polite manners, from actual moral progress.[6] Kant is not interested in wrangling with questions of theodicy (consistent with the essay of 1791, "On the miscarriage of all philosophical trials in theodicy"). He is not trying to reconcile human evil and suffering with the idea of a perfectly just, omnipotent deity. He disengages the problem of evil from a theological framework. Within a humanistic focus, radical evil is initially defined as willful moral failure. From the start, the main concern is with human interrelations, i.e., with respect for others

---

chronological priority of poetic images also has significance for understanding religions. In his lectures from 1782–83, Kant notes of the ancient Greeks that "at that time the manner of expressing ideas was to clothe them in images [*in Bilder einzukleiden*] so that as a rule one finds philosophy carried out poetically, which also happened in part in order to impress religion all the better into memory" (LM, 29:758).

[6] This distinction between acculturation and genuine moral development is established in one of Kant's earliest political writings, the "Idea for a Universal History." He notes of European societies of his time that "we are *cultivated* in a high degree by art and science. We are *civilized*, perhaps to the point of being overburdened, by all sorts of social decorum and propriety. But very much is still lacking before we can be held to be already *moralized*. For the idea of morality still belongs to culture; but the use of this idea which comes down only to a resemblance of morals in love and honor and in external propriety constitutes only being civilized" (IH, 8:26). A similar separation of superficial cultivation from moral progress is made by the historian Richard J. Evans; he observes that "if the experience of the Third Reich teaches us anything, it is that a love of great music, great art and great literature does not provide people with any kind of moral or political immunization against violence, atrocity, or subservience to dictatorship." Richard J. Evans, *The Coming of the Third Reich* (New York: The Penguin Press, 2004), p.xxiii.

as ends in themselves. Evil occurs when we violate others directly and indirectly, when we perpetrate violence upon them in any form. As noted in chapter 5, both the *Groundwork* and the second *Critique* assume that most of our maxims and actions will *not* be in accordance with the moral law. Similarly, *Religion* pinpoints *Willkür* or power of choice as the locus of ethical decision: "the ground of evil cannot lie in any object *determining* the power of choice [*Willkür*] through inclination, not in any natural impulses, but only in a rule [*nur in einer Regel*] that the power of choice itself produces for the exercise of its freedom, i.e., in a maxim" (R, 6:21). This concern with the free choice of evil addresses both the source of our misguided decisions, and the possible means of counteracting them.

Although our maxims and actions are not always correlated, there is a relation between the two: patterns of action over a span of time indicate abiding inner dispositions. "We call a human being evil, however, not because he performs actions that are evil (contrary to law), but because these are so constituted that they allow the inference [*schließen lassen*] of evil maxims in him" (R, 6:20). This is also consistent with the arguments of the first and second *Critiques* whereby intelligible character is discerned through our empirical characters. Moreover, in focusing on "underlying maxims" the inquiry into radical evil goes to the heart of what *kinds* of maxims govern a person's life. Kant is less concerned with specific moral and immoral deeds than with the underlying pattern of choosing and prioritizing indicated by these acts. Focusing on the power of choice means that our capacity for evil is "innate [*angeboren*]." However, moral evil is not the product of determining causes rooted in our biological constitutions: "we shall always be satisfied that nature is not to blame for it (if the character is evil), nor does it deserve praise (if it is good), but that the human being is alone its author" (R, 6:21). Subsequently, Kant stresses with regard to "moral evil" that "of all the ways of representing [*Vorstellungsarten*] its spread and propagation through the members of our species and in all generations, the most inappropriate is surely to imagine it as having come to us by way of *inheritance* from our first parents" (R, 6:40). The Christian doctrine of *original sin* is rejected as an explanation; this doctrine locates evil outside our free will and therefore outside of anything that can rightly be called our own.[7] Kant likewise insists that

---

[7] A note specifies three forms of deterministic thinking concerning evil pertaining to medicine, law, and theology: "either as *inherited disease*, or *inherited guilt*, or *inherited sin*" (R, 6:40n.). A similar rejection of inherited sin as explaining human evil occurs in the "Conjectural Beginning of Human History" of 1786. Kant observes with regard to the biblical "representation of an original condition" that "such a presentation of his history is beneficial and serviceable to the human

"the ground of this evil ... cannot be placed, as is commonly done, in the sensuous nature of the human being, and in the natural inclinations originating from it" (R, 6:35). Later, he emphasizes that "*considered in themselves* natural inclinations [*natürliche Neigungen*] are *good*, i.e., not reprehensible, and to want to extirpate them would not only be futile but harmful and blameworthy as well" (R, 6:58). This position is clearly *not* that of the metaphysical dualist who dichotomizes spirit and matter, locating fault in the latter's corrupting qualities. The fact of embodiment within a world shared with others (which goes beyond an individual mind–body problematic to social and political considerations), is a factor that can contribute to our choosing evil maxims.[8] However, embodiment per se cannot override freedom of choice. Evil results from *freedom*, from the power of choice itself. The problem concerns a voluntary incorporation of evil into our maxims, although this is not traceable to specific acts. Therefore "evil ... is to be sought not in ... inclinations, but in ... perverted maxims [*in der verkehrten Maxime*], and hence in freedom itself" (R, 6:58n.). Evil is freely chosen yet entwined with our condition as embodied phenomenal beings. The difference between *Wille* as synonymous with practical reason and *Willkür* as the "power of choice" making decisions within specific life situations is extremely significant.[9] Kant safeguards the law-giving function of willing from the vagaries of human choosing. Therefore, distinguishing *Willkür* from *Wille* gives tremendous leeway to the former with regard to willing evil; this provides a realistic account of the function of the human freedom to choose in actual life-situations. This distinction occurs within a unified model, a continuum spanning noumenal and phenomenal.

It could be argued that the most heinous acts of evil in human history negate the autonomy and thereby the humanity of individuals or groups, making it easier to view them as readily manipulated in the service of ideology. Jonathan Glover makes this point by illustrating common features of National Socialism, Stalinism, Maoism, and other hideous projects of social redesigning of the twentieth century. He characterizes

---

being for his instruction and improvement by showing him that he must not blame providence for the ills that oppress him; that he is also not justified in ascribing his own misdeeds to an original crime of his ancestral parents" (CB, 8:123).

[8] As Michalson observes, "evil arises from what we freely do with what we are naturally given, rather than from what we are naturally given taken by itself." Gordon E. Michalson, Jr., *Fallen Freedom: Kant on Radical Evil and Moral Regeneration* (Cambridge University Press, 1990), p.38.

[9] As Allison clarifies: "Kant uses the terms *Wille* and *Willkür* to characterize respectively the legislative and executive functions of a unified faculty of volition, which he likewise refers to as *Wille*." Henry E. Allison, *Kant's Theory of Freedom* (Cambridge University Press, 1990), p.129.

these tendencies as "grandiose," "coercive," and "inhuman."[10] It is also significant that Glover emphasizes that "the rigidity also came from religious commitments to the cause ... Faith is holding beliefs rigidly. Corrective feedback is irrelevant."[11] Although this use of the terms "faith" and "religion" is partially analogical, the comment has implications for understanding the pathologies of religion per se. Respecting the autonomy and rights of others means taking their varying standpoints and needs seriously; this should lead to a more democratic approach to human interrelations rather than to coercive social engineering. Where I would disagree with Glover is in his blanket assessment that these deterministic worldviews "were in thrall to the Enlightenment."[12] To be sure, others have linked certain trends in Enlightenment social and political thinking, for example that of the Marquis de Condorcet, with "the twentieth century gigantic projects of human engineering with their devastating effects."[13] Nevertheless, as I have argued, the Enlightenment does not represent a monolithic movement; for his part, Kant stands in clear opposition to heteronomous ordering of human relations. Autonomy and mutual respect are central to his thinking; he consistently stresses an open communicative model of reason opposing uniform ordering from above.

The concept of self-love indicates the antithesis of both autonomy and other-directedness (R, 6:45). Those who succumb to self-love have become enslaved to their own desires and egoism.[14] The problem is developed through a threefold categorization of the "predisposition to good." This assumes an original goodness of our nature and focuses on how this becomes corrupted. A predisposition (*Anlage*) given with human nature is differentiated from a disposition (*Gesinnung*) cultivated through a lifetime of decisions. The predisposition to *animality* concerns humans as living beings; Kant refers to this as "mechanical self-love" for which "reason is not required." This is an essential component of human nature necessary to self-preservation and propagation of the species, and includes "the social drive [*der Trieb zur Gesellschaft*]." As with all forms of self-love, this

---

[10] Jonathan Glover, *Humanity: A Moral History of the Twentieth Century* (London: Jonathan Cape, 1999), pp.310–12.
[11] Ibid., p.312.   [12] Ibid., p.310.
[13] Louis Dupré, *The Enlightenment and the Intellectual Foundations of Modern Culture* (New Haven: Yale University Press, 2004), p.210.
[14] In Rousseau's words: "to be driven by appetite alone is slavery, and obedience to the law one has prescribed for oneself is liberty." *The Social Contract*, in *The Basic Political Writings*, trans. Donald A. Cress (Indianapolis: Hackett, 1987), Book I, Chapter VIII, p.151.

predisposition is subject to corruptions, which are "grafted onto this predisposition as root." Vices are distortions of our inclinations, such as the savagery of nature and "wild lawlessness" (R, 6:26–27). This form of self-love concerns immediate somatic needs; its corruptions take the form of unbridled lawlessness rather than evil proper.

Predispositions to humanity include our status as rational beings and self-love that "*involves comparison.*" Kant specifies that "reason is required" for this comparative orientation, indicating that we have moved to a sphere of human interrelations involving freedom of choice. This predisposition is the flowering of the drive to sociality inherent to our animality, and with it there "originates the inclination to *gain worth in the opinion of others*" (R, 6:27). This inclination is related to the reasonable expectation that no one achieves undue ascendancy over others (as within socially constituted hierarchies and power relations). Indeed, this comparative assessment of social status is foundational for a sense of social and political justice. However, our basic predisposition for social coexistence and our desire for equal worth become corrupted by the mutually reinforcing fear that if one does not dominate others, then one will become dominated by them. Hence, each of us fears "the anxious endeavor [*der besorgten Bewerbung*] of others to attain a hateful superiority [*Überlegenheit*] over us." In response, we strive "to procure it for ourselves over them for the sake of security, as preventive measure" (R, 6:27). This remarkable analysis is noteworthy for its astute combination of psychological, social, and political insights. These destructive endeavors after superiority and domination are called "vices of *culture*," because they involve a warping and debasement of a natural tendency for humans to group together and to form cultures. With the predisposition to humanity involving the capacity to calculate and compare ourselves with others, we also encounter evil and violence against others in the form of an endless competition for gain, prestige, and dominance, whatever the ethical cost. Hence rivalry, envy, ingratitude, and other morally reprehensible competitive orientations can be the pretext for other immoral acts such as defamation, lying, and stealing. Unlike "mechanical self-love," vices of culture are based on social relations with others that incorporate their parochial attitudes and priorities as significant to my sense of worth.

Kant's discussion owes much to Rousseau's analyses of the corruptions of socialization, specifically his distinction between *amour-propre* and *amour de soi*. Tzvetan Todorov, drawing on Rousseau's writings, notes that *amour de soi* is "broadly speaking the instinct of self-preservation that primitive man shares with animals. It is 'the sole passion natural to man'.[15] By contrast, *amour-propre* as "a characteristic only of social man, consists of situating oneself in relation to others and preferring oneself to everyone else."[16] Natural self-love is a reference point for evaluating corruptions of self-love occurring in socialization. Yet, some form of socialization is essential to being human. Todorov affirms that "real humanity begins at the moment one can distinguish good and evil," quoting Rousseau's comment that "It is only by becoming sociable that [the individual] becomes a moral being."[17] Kant confirms Rousseau in viewing social relations as stimulating artificial needs based on competition with others. In this form, human relations have little to do with expanding one's ethical orientation beyond narrow parameters. Rather, the refined narcissism of social life augments our neediness in virtually unlimited ways, as identity and personal worth become conflated with possessions, status, and other superficial indicators. With developments of this kind, the other person becomes a means rather than an end. The discussion of predispositions to humanity indicates the *social* influences affecting self-love, our power of choice, and hence our ethical capacities. The predisposition (*Anlage*) to the good in its first two forms is readily susceptible to having various vices grafted onto it (or to being used inappropriately, R, 6:28). By contrast, the third category of *personality* indicates the freedom of will upon which the power to choose is predicated; it is "the susceptibility [or receptivity, *Empfänglichkeit*] to respect for the moral law *as of itself a sufficient incentive to the power of choice* [*Willkür*]" (R, 6:28). This intellectual basis of personality cannot be known, nor can it be rendered as an underlying substance. However, an intelligible aspect of human beings manifests in our capacity for moral autonomy. The personality's receptivity to moral law "does not yet constitute an end of the natural predisposition [*Naturanlage*] but only insofar as it is an incentive of the power of choice [*Triebfeder der Willkür*]" (R, 6:27). The predisposition to personality does not make us good; it must be realized through our power of choice, and this cultivation constitutes "a good character." Importantly, Kant emphasizes that "this character, as in general every character of the free power of choice, is something that can only be acquired" (R, 6:27).

---

[15] Tzvetan Todorov, *Imperfect Garden: The Legacy of Humanism* (Princeton University Press, 2002), p.82 (citing Rousseau, *Émile*).

[16] Todorov, *Imperfect Garden*, p.83. Todorov corrects a common misunderstanding of Rousseau's ideas by emphasizing that "the 'state of nature' [associated with *amour de soi*] is not situated in time" (p.84).

[17] Ibid., p. 85, citing Rousseau, *Political Fragments*. Later, Todorov cites Rousseau's "Lettre sur la vertu," which emphasizes that "good and evil flow from the same source" (p.194).

The development of character (good or evil) is the product of choices made over the course of a human lifetime.

In "Concerning the Propensity to Evil [*Von dem Hange zum Bösen*] in Human Nature," a *propensity* is defined as "the subjective ground of the possibility of an inclination ... insofar as this possibility is contingent for humanity in general" (R, 6:29). Although one's choices are subjective, they occur in relation to propensities inherent to the human condition (R, 6:30). Choosing evil comes with our status as free beings who are embodied and receptive to interpersonal and societal influences. The point is articulated in the twofold understanding of propensity as either *physical*, wherein "it pertains to a human's power of choice [*Willkür*] as natural being," or *moral*, which "pertains to a human's power of choice [*Willkür*] as moral being" (R, 6:31). Evil arises from the moral propensity, because moral evil (*Moralisch-Bösen*) "must originate from freedom" (R, 6:31). The distinction between power of choice at the levels of natural being and moral being indicates that *Willkür*, unlike *Wille*, straddles our phenomenal and noumenal aspects. This confounds traditional associations of evil with matter and the body. Propensities to evil are associated with the free choice that enables morality, and the seemingly oxymoronic expression "moral evil" evinces this mixing.[18] This focus on freedom also governs Kant's concerns with conscience. *Religion* defines conscience (*das Gewissen*) "as the moral faculty of judgment, passing judgment upon itself" (R, 6:186). Our capacity for ethical reflection is frequently associated with the idea of God as crystallizing the omnilateral will. However, interactions with our own consciences can be distorted (as noted in chapter 5; see G, 4:406–07). *The Metaphysics of Morals*, before comparing conscience to being accountable to God, refers to our capacity to perpetrate an "inner lie [*die innere Lüge*]." From this "rotten spot ... the ill of untruthfulness spreads into his relations with other human beings as well" (MM, 6:430).[19] Moreover, from this deceit one can derive "peace of conscience

---

[18] Hume also distinguishes between "natural evil" indicating misfortune stemming from accidents of nature, and "moral evil" stemming from human choice and action. See *Dialogues Concerning Natural Religion*, Parts XI–XII in *Dialogues and Natural History of Religion*, ed. J. C. A. Gaskin (Oxford University Press, 1993), pp.112ff. and 122ff.

[19] Kant discusses a person who deceives himself into professing belief in "a future judge of the world, although he really finds no such belief within himself." He persuades himself that "it might even be useful to profess in his thoughts to one who scrutinizes hearts a belief in such a judge, in order to win his favor [*seine Gunst zu erheucheln*] in case he should exist" (MM, 6:430). This indicates self-deception within internal professions of belief, and it also links this mendacity with the recurring ethical and political theme of gaining favor. Similarly, in "On the miscarriage of all philosophical trials in theodicy," Kant refers to "the impurity that lies deep in

[*Gewissenruhe*]" (R, 6:38).[20] This peace is synonymous with complacency; it allows us to rest comfortably with an abnegation of ethical responsibility. As with the discussion of the inner lie in *The Metaphysics of Morals*, the false peace of conscience builds from an individual level toward interpersonal and political concerns: "this dishonesty, by which we throw dust in our own eyes and which hinders the establishment in us of a genuine moral disposition, then extends itself also externally, to falsity and deception of others" (R, 6:38). Kant highlights the thorny problem of ethical self-deception as at once psychological and political. The range of choices available in a given situation will also be affected by how a decision satisfies one's needs and expectations. Religious commitments are particularly instructive in this regard, because often they are intertwined with a person's sense of worth, with their deepest fears and longings, and with their conception of the very fabric of reality.

A different issue concerns the limits on how fallible conscience can be, which is related to excluding *diabolical evil*. The concept of radical evil does not necessarily refer to an extreme of evil deeds; it rather indicates the root (*radix*) of evil in our freedom. Kant reiterates that sensuous human nature contains "too little" to explain our capacity for evil. In other words, mechanistic and behaviorist personality models, according to which we simply respond to various stimuli, can grasp neither the complexity of human personalities nor the perfidy of our evil willing. Insofar as a determinist explanation "eliminates the incentives originating in freedom, it makes of the human being a purely animal being" (R, 6:35). On the other hand, an opposite extreme is also excluded: "an evil reason [*boshafte Vernunft*] as it were (an absolutely evil will) [*ein schlechthin böser Wille*], would on the contrary contain *too much*, because resistance to the law would itself be thereby elevated to incentive [*Triebfeder*]" (R, 6:35). The issue is not simply freedom to disobey the law, but rather an *evil law* legislated by practical reason; this would produce "a *diabolical* being [*einem teuflischen Wesen*]" (R, 6:35). Does Kant's denial of diabolical evil make his analysis inadequate for treating cases of unrestricted evil such as Nazism? In this regard, Richard Bernstein argues that the power of free choice *does* allow for diabolical evil. Bernstein agrees with Kant that to assert that "all human beings are innately devilish" would rule

---

what is hidden, where the human being knows how to distort even inner declarations before his own conscience" (MT, 8:270).

[20] *Gewissenruhe* is translated in the Cambridge Edition as "peace of mind." I am following Fenves in translating it more literally as "peace of conscience." See Peter Fenves, *Late Kant: Towards Another Law of the Earth* (New York: Routledge, 2003), p.86.

out the freedom of choice upon which morality is predicated.[21] Rather, through our cumulative choices we cultivate dispositions characterized by varying degrees of good or evil. He asks: "suppose we consider the case of someone who is not innately (in the strong sense of innate) diabolical but *becomes* diabolical, that is, who acts in a manner so that we infer that he has a disposition whereby his supreme maxim is to defy the moral law."[22] From this perspective, there is nothing to prevent a person or group from evolving in such a way that their supreme maxim comes to be directed toward evil: the willful dehumanization, dispossession, and extermination of others. Therefore, "it *must* be possible for an individual to become a devilish being."[23] Bernstein addresses the question of which incentives are most compelling (if not determining) in our moral choices. He quotes Kant that even "the most rational being of this world might still need certain incentives, coming to him from the objects of inclination, to determine his power of choice [*Willkür*]" (R, 6:26n.; I have cited the Cambridge translation of this passage). Bernstein also emphasizes the openness of choice, stating: "we *can* choose to be 'perverse', we *can* choose to be 'devilish', we *can* choose to defy what reason tells us we ought to do." Importantly, this point retains a sense of practical reason providing guidance in the form of an imperative. He simply insists that our power of choice is not bound by this guidance and that we can reject the promptings of reason: "Why not recognize that there can be incentives like the incentive to do evil for the sake of evil, or the incentive to defy the moral law, or the incentive to further the dominance of the 'master race' which cannot be assimilated to what Kant classifies 'natural inclinations'."[24] It is difficult to disagree with this assessment in light of even a cursory familiarity with history.

However, as we have seen, Kant clearly does *not* reduce human evil to natural inclinations, but roots it directly in our power to adopt evil maxims. Kant's emphasis is on evil as willed and hence "positive," that is, not simply the result of the "privation" of goodness caused by ignorance, as in many conventional theodicies.[25] In fact, it has been argued that Kant's introduction of "a *positive* evil that is the result of the will, rather than of will's self-abnegation" *does* provide the conceptual resources for understanding the responsibility accruing to even the most heinous crimes.

---

[21] Richard J. Bernstein, "Radical Evil: Kant at War with Himself," in María Pía Lara, ed., *Rethinking Evil: Contemporary Perspectives* (Berkeley: University of California Press, 2001), p.79.
[22] *Ibid.*, p.79.   [23] *Ibid.*, p.80.   [24] *Ibid.*, p.82.
[25] For Kant's summary of these views, see *Lectures on the Philosophical Doctrine of Religion*, 28:1078.

Therefore, "to contend that the Nazis 'knew' what they were doing was evil not only raises questions of moral responsibility, but also reformulates the very nature of evil itself, as something substantive rather than putative."[26] Kant's emphasis on actively choosing evil conveys the responsibility and guilt inherent to even the most extreme crimes. Yet, because the atrocities perpetrated by the Nazis, as the outstanding example of extreme evil, are immeasurably vile, we understandably seek to invoke the strongest possible condemnation. We do not wish to leave anything in reserve in our censure of anything even remotely like Nazism. Kant discounts the possibility of "malice," and thereby restricts the scope of his inquiry to what he terms "*perversity* of the heart" (R, 6:37); in excluding diabolical evil, this also rejects the ensuing claim of an *evil reason* manifested in an evil will (*Wille*). In fact, Bernstein agrees with Kant in emphasizing that *Willkür*, and not *Wille*, is the locus of human choice: "What becomes clear in the *Religion* is that *Wille* (in its more technical and narrow sense) does not act at all; it does not make decisions."[27] Hence moral agency occurs through our *Willkür*. The distinction allows Kant to attribute evil to freedom of choice, while preserving practical reason's moral law-giving. In principle, the moral law can be known, and can provide guidelines for judgment through the categorical imperative. Thus "it must be equally possible to *overcome* this evil, for it is found in the human being as acting freely" (R, 6:37). The distinction between "overcoming" and "extirpating" is crucial. We can never extirpate radical evil, which means that as human beings we can never reach ethical perfection. But this does not mean that we cannot overcome evil predilections through applying moral principles. Most importantly, even when *some* have given themselves over to evil individually and collectively, there remain others who can recognize and know this as evil, and who can work against it. Locating the capacity for good and evil in our *Willkür* has important political implications as well. As soon as we engage real-world dilemmas, the question of how our power of choice is informed and guided arises. This concerns the incentives predominant in our choosing, but also concerns the range of available knowledge. Our capacity to make choices concerning ethical dilemmas, often involving conflicts between competing goals and ends, must entail assessing available reasons and options. The very definition of *Willkür* as a power of free choice that is yet subject

---

[26] Andrew Hewitt, "The Bad Seed: 'Auschwitz' and the Physiology of Evil," in Joan Copjec, ed., *Radical Evil* (London: Verso, 1996), p.82.
[27] Bernstein, "Radical Evil," p.58.

to environmental influences shows that it is both noumenal and phenomenal. In this way, Kant's ethical thinking opens into the area of anthropology, including psychology, social existence, and politics, without being reduced thereto.

An issue that arises here, though not addressed by Kant at this stage of his argument, concerns the *evil state*. This connects with "despotically given coercive laws" (PP, 8:374), indicating the institutionalization of corrupt principles. On one level, we rightly think of the leaders and followers of the Nazis, from Hitler down, as having individually embraced the utmost degree of evil, especially in their systematic degradation and mass murder of fellow human beings. Individually, we unhesitatingly condemn them as evil beings.[28] However, it is additionally the case that for a period of a dozen years the Nazis and their ideology formed the governing power of a major European state, as well as its militarily occupied territories (sometimes less directly, as in the case of Vichy France).[29] From the moment a law was put forward on August 19, 1934, declaring Hitler as "Leader and Reich Chancellor," the line between corrupted wills and institutionalized state power became blurred.[30] It is instructive to understand this as the beginning of "the State of exception," in which the personal authority of the Leader supersedes judicially sanctioned laws.[31] Perhaps in a bid to legitimize their rule, the Nazis enacted a range of laws instituting their "worldview" and attendant policies. Kant throws some light on this perennial political problem in Part Two, section 11 of *Religion*, where he discusses the conflict between good and evil as involving an attempt by each to establish their hegemony *through law*. Through instituting parochial laws, authorities try to influence the minds

---

[28] Here the case of Adolf Eichmann bears some comment. As Hannah Arendt relates, during his post-war trial Eichmann attempted to portray himself as a "Kantian" who followed his "duty." Arendt rightly notes that "this was outrageous, on the face of it, and also incomprehensible, since Kant's moral philosophy is so closely bound up with man's faculty of judgment, which rules out blind obedience." After further questioning, Eichmann seemed to recognize that "from the moment he was charged with carrying out the Final Solution he had ceased to live according to Kantian principles, that he had known it." As Arendt points out, the maxim governing Eichmann's actions is better described in terms *antithetical* to the categorical imperative: "act in such a way that the Führer, if he knew your action, would approve it." Hannah Arendt, *Eichmann in Jerusalem: A Report on the Banality of Evil* (New York: The Viking Press, 1965), p.136.

[29] For an account of Vichy, see Julian Jackson, *France: The Dark Years, 1940–1944* (Oxford University Press, 2001). Jackson gives several examples of unjust laws instituted by Vichy, and not always at the direct behest of the Nazi occupiers (for Vichy's "Jewish Statute," for example, see pp.243–44).

[30] Richard J. Evans, *The Third Reich in Power: 1933–1939* (New York: The Penguin Press, 2005), p.42.

[31] Giorgio Agamben, *State of Exception* (University of Chicago Press, 2005).

and attitudes of a populace. Hence a core element in Nazi ideology was a comprehensive misappropriation of the very principle of law. Richard Evans summarizes: "the purpose of the law, in the eyes of the Nazis, was not to apply long-held principles of fairness and justice, but to root out enemies of the state and to express the true racial feeling of the people."[32] In a remarkably perverse endeavor, Nazism employed the instruments of state legislation to corrupt genuine principles of legality. As I have argued, the universality of law means that it applies equally to all. So-called Nazi "laws," however, divided human beings into various discrete sectors, so that "legislation" was designed to target specific groups – especially Jews. This is an extreme example of the possible corruption of what Kant terms positive laws enacted by particular states. It shows us how state power provides a means of propagating radically evil maxims among the general populace. This example also highlights the difference between actively choosing evil and mere "lawless freedom." The case of Nazism presents us not simply with the breakdown of judicial order, but with a far more insidious manipulation of positive law for evil ends.[33]

It is also crucial that corrupt parochial laws cannot be ethically binding. Arthur Ripstein stresses that examples often used to counter Kant's opposition to revolution, "most notably Nazi Germany," are in fact "conditions of barbarism in Kant's sense."[34] As he explains, "If the transition from the Weimar republic to Nazism is a transition from legality to barbarism, then what happened during the condition of barbarism, no matter how well organized, is just unilateral force, and not law."[35] Hence Nazi statutes do not really qualify as laws at all. Such barbaric political regimes and the laws they instate are rightfully resisted under a Kantian paradigm. We are enjoined to leave the state of barbarism and enter a rightful condition, and so resistance is legitimated under such conditions. Indeed,

---

[32] Evans, *The Third Reich in Power*, p.73. Evans provides examples of many of the "laws" following from this view of judicial authority. The increasing severity of these and their genocidal results are described in painful detail in Richard J. Evans, *The Third Reich at War* (New York: The Penguin Press, 2009), pp.217–59.

[33] While the example of evil laws instituted by an evil state is extremely important, it should not mislead us into conflating ethical-political concerns with this problem alone. The seemingly antithetical case of the *weak*, *minimalist*, or *negligent state* that does not properly oversee the activities of powerful non-state organizations such as corporations (e.g., to prohibit false advertising, to ensure safety standards in products, enforce environmental protection guidelines, etc.) is equally telling. *Both* types of case point to the necessity for the principle of publicity and for just laws.

[34] Arthur Ripstein, *Force and Freedom: Kant's Legal and Political Philosophy* (Cambridge, MA: Harvard University Press, 2009), p.341.

[35] *Ibid.*, p.349.

while *revolution* may be questionable on both ethical-political and pragmatic criteria (i.e., it may create a state of anarchy), under any conditions a continual *reform* of existing institutions and laws is central to Kant's ethical-political project.

INTERPRETING RELIGIOUS LANGUAGE

In accordance with his opposition to applying mechanistic paradigms to human beings, Kant criticizes deterministic explanations of evil choices and actions. It is in "representations of reason [*Vernunftvorstellungen*] alone" that we must locate the "determining ground of the free power of choice in general" (R, 6:40). Choices made in the present are not the inevitable consequence of past events. Whatever our "temporal circumstances and entanglements" may be, "through no cause in the world can [a human being] cease to be a free agent" (R, 6:41). Kant then addresses determinism based on inbuilt propensities. He invokes religious language, or what he calls the "mode of representation [*Vorstellungsart*] which the Scriptures use to depict the origin of evil, as having a beginning in human nature" (R, 6:41). This heralds a sustained engagement with the issue of representational forms expressing inner ethical states and assisting us in ameliorating them. Kant shows how doctrinal renderings can be assimilated to an autonomous ethical analysis: "Evil begins, according to the Scriptures, not from a fundamental propensity to it, for otherwise its beginning would not result from freedom, but from *sin* (by which it is understood the transgression of the moral law as *divine command*)" (R, 6:41–2, extrapolating on Genesis 2:16–17). The concept of sin expresses a freely chosen adoption of evil rather than determining influences. Kant notes that "the Scriptures express this incomprehensibility [of evil] in a historical narrative [*Geschichtserzählung*] … by projecting evil at the beginning of the world, not, however, within the human being, but in a spirit [*in einem Geiste*] of an originally more sublime destiny" (R, 6:43). In this mode of representation, elements of our own being that confront us as alien are represented in personified form.

Kant's model of ethical progress maintains a critical distinction between internal transformation and mere external conformity with socially sanctioned behavior. This distinction is characterized as a "*change of heart* [*eine Herzenänderung*]" in contrast with "a change of *mores* [*eine Änderung der Sitten*]" (R, 6:47). The figurative notion of *the heart* expresses a freely cultivated ethical orientation that is differentiated from passive adoption of conventions. There are several such terms that work in conjunction:

disposition or basic convictions (*Gesinnung*), the receptive mind (*Gemüt*), mode of thought (*Denkungsart*), and character (*Charakter*). Together they convey the actively fashioned ethical orientations cultivated through the course of our lives. While Kant recognizes that approximating an ethical disposition will be a gradual process, he also emphasizes the importance of an "ethical revolution" in our dispositions. Morality "cannot be effected through gradual *reform* but must rather be effected through a *revolution* in the disposition of the human being (a transition to the maxim of holiness of disposition). And so a 'new man' can come about only through a kind of rebirth, as it were a new creation (John, 3:5; compare with Genesis, 1:2) and a change of heart" (R, 6:47). The image of an inner revolution as a *rebirth* conveys a dramatic reorientation from an evil to a good will; it characterizes the clear intention to adopt supreme guiding principles based on moral laws. At the same time, the implementation of these ethical changes requires an incremental process. This second point forms the cornerstone of Kant's interpretation of religious doctrines and institutions as assisting ethical-political amelioration, because these affect our phenomenal characters. Kant therefore distinguishes "a revolution [that] is necessary in the mode of thought [*Denkungsart*]" from "a gradual reformation in the mode of sense [*Sinnesart*] (which places obstacles in the way of the former)" (R, 6:47). The double-edged perspective, paralleling that of noumenal and phenomenal character, shows that the inner revolution concerning our supreme maxim is but one component of ethical progress. We still require a gradual reform of our empirical *Willkür* in accordance with our supreme maxim; hence one "is a good human being only in incessant *laboring and becoming* [*kontinuierlichem Wirken und Werden*]." Only this autonomous ethical laboring can place us "upon the good (though narrow) path of constant *progress* [*Fortschreitens*] from bad to better" (R, 6:48). Moral labor is autonomy striving to realize itself under phenomenal conditions over the span of a lifetime, and is intrinsically connected with Kant's enduring focus on moral courage.

The image of God as knowing our hearts reconciles imperfection with constructive hope: "we can think [*denken können*] of infinite progression of the good toward conformity to the law as being judged [*beurteilt*] by him who scrutinizes the heart" (R, 6:67). This is a *way of thinking*, guiding us by an ideal of reason. Building on the differentiation between a change of heart and adaptation to convention, Kant reiterates that "a human being's moral education [*moralische Bildung*] must begin, not with an improvement of mores [*Sitten*], but with the transformation of his attitude of mind [*Denkungsart*] and the establishment of a character"

(R, 6:48).³⁶ A major theme, following from the gradual reform of both internal dispositions and external conditions, concerns education fostering ethical autonomy. This follows the lead of the second *Critique*, which as we saw concludes with a "doctrine of method" wherein "the lively presentation [*Darstellung*] of the moral disposition in examples [*Beispielen*]" is recommended in cultivating ethical autonomy (CPrR, 5:160). *Religion* similarly proposes that "this predisposition to the good is cultivated in no better way than by just adducing the *example* [*das Beispiel*] of good people (as regards their conformity to the law), and by allowing our apprentices in morality to judge the impurity of certain maxims on the basis of the incentives actually behind their actions" (R, 6:48). This proposes external guidance that fosters rather than suppresses autonomous reflection and judgment. Examples or models also provide test cases for assessing the relationship between maxims and actions, indicating something we can each reflect upon and actualize autonomously. Kant specifies "the right attunement [*die rechte Stimmung*] that ought to support the apprentice's feeling [or mental reception, *Gemüt*] for the moral good" (R, 6:48; translation modified). Hence we become attuned to the moral law by thinking and judging for ourselves, guided by examples that give tangible expression to moral principles.

An emphasis on active ethical cultivation appears elsewhere in Kant's late writings, where it is opposed to notions of direct intuitive knowledge. "On a recently prominent tone of superiority in philosophy" (1796), for example, attacks ethical and spiritual elitism. Kant writes that "an alleged philosophy is openly proclaimed to the public, in which one does not have to *work*, but need only hearken and attend to the oracle within, in

---

³⁶ In this way, Kant anticipates Hegel's emphasis on *Sittlichkeit*. In seeking to correct what he understands as the abstract quality of Kantian moral principles (*Moralität*), Hegel emphasizes that the social structures of any given society, i.e., *Sittlichkeit*, are vital to moral cultivation. See Paul Franco, *Hegel's Philosophy of Freedom* (New Haven: Yale University Press, 1999), pp.57, 282–83, 297–98. However, Kant also anticipates the *weakness* of ethics as an adaptation to socially prevalent mores. He critiques ethical mores based on honor and knowing one's "proper place," the privilege associated with social hierarchies, and the imperfections of positive laws. Elements of this principled critique also underpin *Religion*'s exposition of statutory forms of belief, and how they affect social and political attitudes. In the *Philosophy of Right*, Hegel portrays the state as an organism, and asserts that "this organism is the development of the Idea to its differences and their objective actuality." G. W. F. Hegel, *Philosophy of Right* (Oxford University Press, 1952), p.164. For Hegel the state in its given forms is not assessed *in relation* to formal regulative ideas; it *manifests* the order of ideas and is hence validated as such. In the same vein, Hegel's appropriation of religious discourse in a political context serves to legitimize rather than ameliorate: "the state is the divine will, in the sense that it is mind [*Geist*] present on earth, unfolding itself to be the actual shape and organization of a world" (p.166). In contrast with this mystifying stance, Kant's distinction between moral laws and positive laws is an essential component of the critical distinction between what *ought to be* and what *is*.

order to gain complete possession of all the wisdom to which philosophy aspires" (RPT, 8:390).[37] Kant questions related forms of passive spirituality such as theological voluntarism and reliance on received grace, reiterating criticism made in the first *Critique* and elsewhere. He stresses that "the concept of a will in the supreme being, as a reality inherent to him, is either an empty one, or (what is even worse), an anthropomorphic concept, which if – as is unavoidable – it is extended into the practical, corrupts all religion and transforms it into idolatry" (RPT, 8:400n.). In each case autonomous efforts at moral transformation are replaced by dependence on a hypothesized higher being. This analysis of passive religion questions notions of a *gift* purportedly coming to us in a passive way (which gained currency in postmodern religious thought following Jacques Derrida). Interestingly, in his commentary on Kant's essay included in Peter Fenves' edition, Derrida recognizes this problem: "The hierarchized opposition of *gift* to *work*, of intuition to concept, of genius's mode to scholar's mode is homologous to the opposition between *aristocracy* and *democracy*, eventually between *demagogic oligarchy* and *authentic rational democracy*."[38] These remarks emphatically link religious and political concerns, explicating the divergence between privileged knowledge and the open discussions constituting democracy. There is a complementarity between traditional mores promoting a passive stance toward political authorities, and the reliance of illuminati and other mystical enthusiasts on passively received inspiration.[39] Kant's stress on *work*, prosaic as this might seem in relation to gifts, grace, and illumination, is the correlate of our autonomy.

---

[37] For an alternative translation with accompanying essays, see Peter Fenves, ed., *Raising the Tone of Philosophy* (Baltimore: Johns Hopkins University Press, 1993), p.52. In this essay, Kant specifically refers to the philosophical endeavors of J. G. Schlosser; however, his critique of inspiration has a more general target as well, and it resonates with the arguments of *Religion* against all privileged claims to knowledge.

[38] Jacques Derrida, "On a Newly Arisen Apocalyptic Tone in Philosophy," in Fenves, ed., *Raising the Tone of Philosophy*, p.128; italics added.

[39] To be sure, despotic regimes are usually wary of secret societies which might provide a counterpoint to their total authority. Reinhart Koselleck, in discussing the Illuminati in Germany during the Enlightenment, notes how "the original compulsory secrecy … had yielded to a trend towards mystification, promoting faith in an omnipotent, secret, and indirect rule beyond the State." However, for Kant the key point connecting spiritual illumination and political paternalism is the cultivation of an attitude of general acquiescence in relation to authority; this is all the more powerful if the authority is shrouded in mystery. As Kosseleck remarks, "the secret became a control mechanism consistently wielded by the Order of the Illuminati, for example." Reinhart Kosseleck, *Critique and Crisis: Enlightenment and the Pathogenesis of Modern Society* (Cambridge, MA: MIT Press, 1988), p.78.

Ethical labors are not imposed by heteronomous authorities; nor can the responsibility for our ethical progress be taken over by others. Through ethical endeavor, we are actively becoming ourselves; i.e., we are learning to think and act in accordance with rational principles. Most importantly, the autonomy intrinsic to our "moral predisposition" reveals itself in resisting externally based compulsion, as appears in our capacity to resist tyranny.[40] Importantly, this includes not only tyranny imposed by force, but also the more subtle tyranny over minds, which is a major theme of *Religion*. Hence autonomy, associated with "the holiness that lies in the idea of duty," opposes norms based on external conditioning alone. Our resistance to heteronomy "must have an effect on the mind [*das Gemüt*] even to the point of exaltation, and must strengthen it for the sacrifices which respect for duty may perhaps impose upon it" (R, 6:50). As with all Kant's invocations of ideas and their religious representations, these references are regulative and motivational. *The Conflict of the Faculties* discusses these issues with regard to scriptural interpretation:

Scriptural texts which seem to enjoin a merely passive surrender to an external power that produces holiness in us must, then, be interpreted differently. It has to be made clear that *we ourselves must work* at developing that moral predisposition [*moralischen Anlage*], although this predisposition does point to a divine source that reason can never reach (in its theoretical search for causes). (CF, 7:43)

The inscrutability of our autonomy is not a pretext for inertia; to the contrary, it indicates a capacity only we can realize.

Kant outlines the psychological sources sustaining heteronomy by noting our resistance to moral self-discipline, and how we rationalize this abrogation. "Against this expectation of self-improvement, reason, which by nature finds moral labor vexing, now conjures up, under the pretext of natural impotence, all sorts of impure [*unlautere*, also meaning *dishonest*] religious ideas (among which belongs falsely imputing to God the principle of happiness [*Glückseligkeitsprinzip*] as the supreme condition of his commands)" (R, 6:51). These dishonest religious ideas are the doctrinal equivalents of the dialectical misuse of reason in metaphysics. However, they are empowered by popular traditions catering to emotional needs, and so akin to the "crude notions" circulating through cultural histories. These feed our desire for an anthropomorphized power also governed by happiness, that is, as one who can be flattered and from whom one might

---

[40] Kant refers to a passage from Juvenal celebrating freedom in resisting a tyrant's efforts, including the use of torture, to impel one to make false statements (R, 6:49n.).

thereby win special *favor*. In every religion, there are teachings that shift responsibility from human beings onto an objectified supra-human order. The distinguishing issue often concerns how we interpret the same doctrinal statement, either as supporting or as impeding ethical autonomy. Kant insists that "all religions [*alle Religionen*] … can be divided into *religion of rogation* [*der Gunstbewerbung*] (of mere cult) and *moral religion* [*die moralische*], i.e. the religion of *good life-conduct*" (R, 6:51). The archaic term "rogation," indicating religious forms of "solemn supplication," is an accurate if obscure translation of *Gunstbewerbung*, although it downplays the pejorative connotations. Most importantly, resonances of meaning within the text and within the wider Kantian corpus are obscured by this archaism. *Gunst* means "favor"; *Bewerbung* means "courting" and "wooing." Hence Greene and Hudson translate *Gunstbewerbung* as "endeavors to win favor," and Pluhar offers "the religion of the *pursuit of favor*."[41] Each of these expresses seeking something to one's advantage though entreaty to a greater power. Most significantly, towards the end of *Religion*, Kant also denounces what he calls a "groveling courting of favor [*kriechende Gunstbewerbung*]" (R, 6:185n.), and here the translation is more transparent. In each case, the ethical and political overtones of this concept are extremely important.

The term *Gunstbewerbung* appears twice within similar discussions in the *Critique of the Power of Judgment*, and is expressively rendered (in the Cambridge translation) as "currying favor." In this context, Kant is discussing "the idea of the **sublimity** of a religion and its object." Sublimity is experienced when we recognize in ourselves an "upright, God-pleasing disposition" also expressed as "a sublimity of disposition [*Erhabenheit der Gesinnung*] suitable to God's will" (CJ, 5:263). This sense of the sublime arising from inner moral worth is what differentiates religion from superstition associated with "fear and anxiety before the being of superior power, to whose will the terrified person sees himself as subjected without holding him in great esteem; from which of course nothing can arise but the attempt to curry favor and ingratiate oneself [*Gunstbewerbung und Einschmeichelung*], instead of a religion of the good conduct of life" (CJ, 5:264). These comments anticipate many of the distinctions central to *Religion*. Kant associates an autonomously cultivated reverence for the sublime with the religion of good life-conduct and with a God-pleasing

---

[41] Immanuel Kant, *Religion within the Limits of Reason Alone*, trans. Theodore M. Greene and Hoyt H. Hudson (New York: Harper & Row, 1960), p.47. Immanuel Kant, *Religion within the Bounds of Bare Reason*, trans. Werner Pluhar (Indianapolis: Hackett, 2009), p.59.

disposition. The moral disposition, reflecting the moral law, is the source of sublimity. To avoid projecting inner experience upon the world, Kant also reiterates that "sublimity is not contained in anything in nature, but only in our mind [*nur in unserm Gemüt*] (CJ, 5:264). By contrast, superstition founded on fear turns that which we cannot comprehend into a finite object and fosters a slavish cast of mind; *currying favor* is clearly associated with a base subservience to these religious forms of heteronomy. A few pages later, Kant contrasts sublimity with cultural productions that are "incapable of all respect for the dignity of humanity in our own person and the right of human beings." He mentions various novels, sentimental plays, and "shallow moral precepts" in this regard, and then proceeds to the fear-mongering characteristic of heteronomous religion:

> [E]ven a religious sermon that preaches a groveling, base currying of favor [*niedrige Gunstbewerbung*] and self-ingratiation, which abandons all confidence in our own capacity for resistance against evil, instead of the energetic determination to seek out the powers that still remain in us, despite all our frailty, for overcoming inclinations; the false humility that finds the only way to be pleasing to the supreme being in self-contempt, in whimpering, feigned remorse and a merely passive attitude of mind – none of these have anything to do with that which can be counted as the beauty, let alone the sublimity, of a mentality [*Gemütsart*]. (CJ, 5:273)

This opposes *two modalities of religion*: one representing genuine ethical cultivation, the other a groveling currying of favor that collapses into superstition.[42] These repetitions traversing two key texts indicate that the concept of *Gunstbewerbung* has a strategic significance in Kant's analysis of religious modalities. Indeed, variations of the term *Gunst* (favor) appear repeatedly throughout the latter portions of *Religion*, where they play an important role in questioning non-ethical practices.

Gunstbewerbung, designating cult-practice seeking favor, exemplifies the mutual reinforcement of self-love and subservience in dogmatic religion. Here one "flatters oneself" that "God can make him eternally happy (through the remission of his debts)," or that "God himself can make him a better human being without his having to contribute more than to ask for it." This draws upon the language of "What Is Enlightenment?" to indicate how succumbing to a condition of minority is sustained by heteronomous institutions and worldviews. Adding to the pejorative connotations

---

[42] It is also noteworthy that Kant reiterates these concerns in his *Lectures on Pedagogy*, where the issue specifically concerns the religious education of children. Kant emphasizes: "If religion is not combined with morality, then it becomes nothing more than currying favor [*so wird Religion blos zur Gunstbewerbung*]" (LP, 9:494).

of supplication, Kant attacks the associated view that improvement might occur through "mere wishing [*mit dem bloßen Wunsch*]" (R, 6:51). Again, immaturity is indicated, as well as a fantasy-laden approach to the exigencies of life. Most importantly, as I noted in discussing Kant's ethical writings, the person who chooses *not* to assess their maxims according to the categorical imperative seeks exemption from the universality of the moral law. In this vein, *favor*, which resonates with the privilege and special status of elites and notables of all kinds, is the antithesis of laws of justice applying to all. Kant rigorously distinguishes infantile wishing from constructive hope. The latter arises through having "made use of the original predisposition to the good [*Anlage zum guten*] in order to become a better human being" (R, 6:52). As with the postulates of practical reason, Kant recognizes the sustaining power of symbolic renderings of a purposive vision of human existence. The capacity for hope may be coupled with cultural representations of "cooperation from above" that can help sustain our courage in the face of adversity. However, we should focus on "*what a human being has to do himself* [*was er selbst zu tun habe*] in order to become worthy of this assistance" (R, 6:52). In emphasizing human initiative, Kant is *not* offering a confused notion of divine grace. He is simply not concerned with a literally understood reception of grace deriving from an anthropomorphically conceived God. Nor has he proposed a theological doctrine that grace is somehow dependent on human ethical striving (which, as some commentators have noted, does not conform to literal Christian notions of God's grace as freely given).[43] Kant is only concerned with autonomous ethical development. The *idea* of grace, as a correlate of the idea of God, is introduced as a widespread culturally

---

[43] Some of these views are discussed in C. Firestone and N. Jacobs, *In Defense of Kant's Religion* (Bloomington: Indiana University Press, 2008), pp.80–81. Noteworthy in this respect is the work of Gordon E. Michalson. In discussing the issue of grace, he initially emphasizes "that freedom reaches a limit when it attempts to correct its own fallenness" (*Fallen Freedom*, p.28). The inability of human freedom to rectify itself leads Michalson to suggest that Kant opens the door to divine intervention: "radical evil ... appears to confront humanity with a problem that it cannot solve through its own worldly autonomous powers, making this the key point where the tension between the this-worldly and the other-worldly enters in, in the form of a tension between autonomy and transcendent assistance" (p.4). Michalson reinforces this theological line of reasoning in stating that "our own sense of moral weakness is offset by the hope of a divine supplement to our imperfect efforts" (p.29). However, after exploring these questions, Michalson concludes that Kant's references to grace only have heuristic value, helping us move in a moral direction rather than making theological claims. He notes that "Kant is clearly less interested in the metaphysical question of whether or not God is actually 'acting' on my behalf than in the psychological question of the potential effect the *possibility* of such aid might have on my motivation" (p.95). This recognition that Kant is not concerned with literal theology becomes more emphatic in Michalson's later book, *Kant and the Problem of God* (Oxford: Blackwell, 1999).

formed symbol which can influence our ways of thinking and prioritizing. Kant is drawing out the potential ethical or contra-ethical significance of these inherited religious ideas.[44]

In this respect, Kant discusses parerga, i.e., secondary religious conceptions with no ethical significance. He lists these "*parerga* to religion within the boundaries of pure reason" as: (1) Of effects of grace (*Gnadenwirkungen*); (2) Miracles (*Wundern*); (3) Mysteries (*Geheimnissen*); and (4) Means of grace (*Gnadenmitteln*). These conjoin an undisciplined reason straying into supersensible speculation with a failure of ethical endeavor. Kant states the matter in a way that echoes his reference to impure or dishonest religious ideas: "Reason, conscious of its impotence to satisfy its moral needs, extends itself to extravagant ideas [*überschwenglichen Ideen*] which might make up for this lack, though it is not suited to this enlarged domain" (R, 6:52). These arguments assume the epistemology of the first *Critique*; the question of whether these religious notions actually correspond to supersensible reality is simply invalid. Kant's concerns are with the constructive or destructive effects of such historical belief systems upon the ethical dispositions of human beings, as cultural and political beings.

A reflective (*reflektierenden*) faith applies religious ideas in autonomous reflection. This practice is rigorously opposed to dogmatic faith; therefore Kant lists four crucial "disadvantages" resulting from dogmatic faith corresponding to the above-listed parerga:

(1) supposed inner experiences (effects of grace [*Gnadenwirkungen*]), enthusiasm [*Schwärmerei*]; (2) alleged outer experiences (miracles), superstition [*Aberglaube*];

---

[44] Kant mentions the possibility of "some supernatural cooperation" being needed to our "becoming good or better" (R, 6:44). However, this statement is followed by the oft-repeated insistence that "the human being must nonetheless make himself antecedently worthy of receiving it [i.e., supernatural cooperation]" (R, 6:44), and that "the command that we ought to become better human beings still resounds unabated in our souls" (R, 6:45). The focus on autonomous effort remains paramount, with a representation of grace acting as a symbolic means of motivational support. This is in keeping with Kant's discussions of Leibniz's "Realm of Grace" (A812/B840). Additionally, this remark about supernatural cooperation appears within a series of comments appropriating biblical language, described as "the mode of representation [*Vorstellungsart*] which the Scriptures use to depict the origin of evil." These include "the author of evil" who is "the Liar," the "fall into sin" and a good tree bringing forth "bad fruits" (R, 6:42–45). It is odd that many commentators have puzzled over Kant's turn to "the doctrine of grace," especially as they generally recognize that any appeal to heteronomous authority and supernatural intervention grossly violates the fundamental principles of the critical philosophy (as stated repeatedly in *Religion* itself). For the views of various commentators, see the summary in Firestone and Jacobs, *In Defense of Kant's Religion*, pp. 17, 25–28, 34, 44–45, 50ff., 66, 80–81, 93–95, etc. To varying degrees, these commentators assume that Kant is engaging in some form of literal theological speculation, despite his clear, consistent, and oft-repeated insistences to the contrary.

(3) presumed enlightenment of the understanding with respect to the supernatural (mysteries), illumination [*Illuminatismus*], the delusion of the initiates; (4) adventurous attempts at influencing the supernatural (means of grace [*Gnadenmittel*]), thaumaturgy [*Thaumaturgie*], sheer aberrations of a reason that has strayed beyond its limits, indeed for a supposed moral aim (one pleasing to God). (R, 6:53)

Each of these pseudo-religious preoccupations diverts us from the moral law. This multi-faceted critique addresses the interrelations among unfounded supernatural assertions, slavish courting of favor, and lack of ethical courage. Kant addresses the human attitudes that are affected by these culturally transmitted doctrines. This is why he repeatedly comments on effects of grace, means of grace, and other non-ethical efforts to obtain favor or advantage through cultic practices. He insists: "the summoning of the *effects of grace* belongs to the last class [thaumaturgy] and cannot be incorporated into the maxims of reason, if the latter keeps to its boundaries" (R, 6:53). These dogmatic attitudes lead us to believe that we "can only *come by* it [grace] by *doing nothing* [*durch Nichtstun*], and this contradicts itself. Hence we can admit an effect of grace as something incomprehensible but cannot incorporate it into our maxims *for either theoretical or practical use*" (R, 6:53). This is very important in that the practical application of religious ideas is specifically disassociated from supernatural claims.

In this regard, Kant draws on the Stoic approach to virtue advocating "courage and valor." He also notes of "the name virtue" that it is "a glorious one," but that people have often "boastfully misused and derided it (as of late the word 'Enlightenment')" (R, 6:57). The association of a courageous, adult approach to ethics and religion with the motto of Enlightenment is unmistakable, and it reappears later in *Religion*. Despite this Stoic underpinning, Kant draws mainly from the Christian tradition, drawing support for a courageous, rather than a slavish ethical disposition. Reflective faith as opposed to dogmatic faith, autonomy rather than heteronomy, provide the guidelines for understanding Christianity. Kant assesses the value of symbolic representations in rendering conflicts and corruptions in the depths of our inner beings. Concerning perverted dispositions as the true enemy of ethics, he notes that "we should not therefore be disconcerted if an apostle *represents* this invisible enemy – this corrupter of basic principles recognizable only through his effects upon us – as being outside us, indeed *as an evil spirit* [*als bösen Geist vorstellig macht*]" (R, 6:59). This representation "does not appear to be intended to extend our cognition beyond the world of the senses but only to make intuitive [*anschaulich zu machen*], *for practical use*, the concept of something to us unfathomable" (R, 6:59). Once again, there is no question of addressing supersensible knowledge claims concerning the origin of evil. Rather, Kant is concerned with the potential of these representations of radical evil to intuitively render ethical challenges. Whether "the tempter" (as represented by the apostle) is within or without, it is *our own guilt* which is the key issue (R, 6:60; also see Kant's note on the representational status of religious ideas). The focus is humanity's ethical struggles; intuitive renderings of these struggles are valuable only in assisting us in practical reflection.

Kant proceeds to a discussion of "the personified idea of the good principle." This builds on the *prototypon transcendentale* and the numerous references to archetypes (*Urbilder*) in the critical philosophy. In this case, the personified principle of "*Humanity* (rational being as pertaining to the world [*das vurnünftige Weltwesen*]) *in its full moral perfection*" is represented in the Christian notion of the Son of God (R, 6:60). Kant argues that "it is our duty to *elevate ourselves* to this ideal of moral perfection, i.e. to the prototype [or archetype] of moral disposition [*dem Urbilde der sittlichen Gesinnung*] in its entire purity, and for this the very idea, which is presented to us by reason for emulation, can give us force [*Kraft geben kann*]" (R, 6:61). Several important points arise here. The interrelated terms *Ideal* and *Urbild* convey image-concepts giving intuitively accessible form to abstract ideas of reason. As we have seen, examples of these include the ideal of God, the archetypes of the Stoic sage, the philosopher, and so forth. The term *Urbild* is applied to the figure of Jesus portrayed in Christian writings, clearly indicating that he is one of several prototypes representing ideas of reason. The *Lectures on Metaphysics* from 1790–91, immediately preceding the publication of *Religion*, anticipate this application of the concept of *Urbild* to the figure of Jesus:

> An archetype [*ein Urbild*] is actually an object of intuition, insofar as it is the ground of imitation. Thus Christ is the archetype of all morality [*So ist Christus das Urbild aller Moralität*]. But in order to regard something as an archetype, we must first have an idea according to which we can cognize the archetype … If we have no idea, then we can assume no archetype, even if it were to come from heaven. I must have an idea in order to seek the archetype concretely [*in concreto*]. (LM, 28:577)

In addition to applying the concept of archetype to Jesus, this passage emphasizes that an archetype can only be classed as such because it gives intuitive expression to an idea of reason (as also stated at R, 6:61 and G, 4:408–09). An archetype represents the maximum realization of an idea, in this case moral attainment.

Additionally, Kant emphasizes that Jesus should be understood as human rather than divine to be an effective ethical example (also see R, 6:63–64). Jesus personifies humanity as *vurnünftige Weltwesen*, a "rational worldly being." This indicates that the moral challenges represented in his life also concern our own ethical endeavors. It is *we* who must elevate ourselves to an approximation of this archetypal moral disposition, and it is reason, not a heteronomous source, that calls us to this ethical duty.[45] He refers to the "sufferings, up to the most ignominious death" that the representative of humanity endures, and remarks that "human beings cannot form for themselves any concept [*Begriff*] of the degree of strength of a force like that of a moral disposition except by representing [*vorstellt*] it surrounded by obstacles and yet – in the midst of the greatest possible temptations – victorious" (R, 6:61). He therefore advocates an enlightened religious faith representing autonomous ethical principles.[46] Practical faith does not rely on heteronomous authority; it requires that one become "conscious of such a moral disposition in himself" so as to "follow this prototype's example" if confronted with similar temptations and afflictions (R, 6:62). These comments build directly on earlier formulations of God as the transcendental ideal representing the omnilateral moral law. This is now augmented by the correlated image of a human being acting in accordance with the moral law, and who is in this sense "not an unworthy object of divine pleasure [*des göttlichen Wohlgefallens*]" (R, 6:62). These interpretations of religious representations build on the postulates of practical reason as strengthening our resolve, but with more graphic detail. Kant also refers to Jesus as a "model [*Vorbilde*] to us" (R, 6:62), and similarly notes how in biblical teaching it is "the ideal of the Son of God which is being placed before us as a model

---

[45] I am stressing these points partly in response to the efforts of Firestone and Jacobs to read a form of scholastic theology into Kant's discussions of the prototype (*Urbild*) as a Christian representation of the idea of a morally good person (*In Defense of Kant's Religion*, pp.156ff.). Their exposition ignores the frequent occurrence of the term *Urbild* in Kant's work to designate exemplars of formal principles. Moreover, they also ignore Kant's repeated statements that he is engaging *inherited representational forms* and not literally embracing dogmatic theological claims. Additionally, they attempt to interpret *Religion* in a manner that completely disregards the foundational ideas of the critical philosophy. For example, their reference to "gracious condescension on the prototype's part" (p.164) falls prey to the dogmatic anthropomorphism and baseless supersensible knowledge claims, not to mention passive reliance on supernatural assistance, that Kant spends most of *Religion* vehemently rejecting.

[46] A related passage distinguishes ethical from literal renditions of the crucifixion: "Only we must remember that (in this way of imagining [*in dieser Vorstellungsart*]) the suffering which the new human being must endure while dying to the *old* human being throughout his life is depicted [*vorgestellt*] in the representative of the human kind [*Repräsentanten der Menscheit*] as a death suffered once and for all" (R, 6:74).

[*zum Vorbilde*]" (R, 6:66). While *Urbild* indicates an original image, there is an anticipatory meaning attached to *Vorbild* that adds an active element to an image-concept. For example, in the *Lectures on Metaphysics*, Kant writes of "the faculty of anticipation [*Vermögen der Vorbildung*]" in which we "imagine something in advance" (LM, 28:235–36). Therefore, Jesus as *Vorbild* directs us toward a possible *future* condition in accordance with moral principles, to which we should aspire.

Kant should be taken at his word when he stresses that "only faith in the practical validity of the idea that lies in our reason has moral worth" (R, 6:63). There is no embrace of heteronomous religious systems in these arguments. Revealed religion is a representational means for working with our moral potentiality. The practical validity of religious representations is clarified by a modified version of *schematism*. While the first *Critique* uses schematism to explain mediation between categories and sense intuitions, the third *Critique* differentiates these schemata from *symbols* that generate representations of *ideas* in accordance with *mere analogy*. *Religion* further divides schematism into two types, and these parallel the differentiation between schematism and symbolism. Kant reminds us that it is helpful to personify ethical ideas to make them intuitively accessible, but stresses: "we do not thereby mean to say that this is how things are in themselves." Our propensity to render ideas in intuitive form must be distinguished from supersensible objects. Therefore, Kant refers to the Scriptures and their adaptation of "this manner of representation [*dieser Vorstellungsart*]" (R, 6:65n.). Given human limitations, some representation is not entirely optional for guiding moral practice: "We have here (as means of elucidation) a *schematism of analogy* [*Schematismus der Analogie*], with which we cannot dispense." This form of schematism means to "render a concept comprehensible through analogy with something of the senses" (R, 6:65n.). As socially formed and fallible beings, we require the pedagogical assistance of cultural representations to make principles and laws accessible. The *danger* in appropriating traditions concerns straying from an autonomous ethical focus into groundless theological speculation and reliance on heteronomous powers. While ethical principles can be represented in a schematism of analogy, "to transform it however, into a *schematism of object-determination* [*Schematismus der Objectsbestimmung*] (as a means of expanding our cognition) constitutes *anthropomorphism*, and from the moral point of view (in religion) this has most injurious consequences" (R, 6:65n.). The schematism of analogy draws from the world of sense to represent moral laws or a moral disposition.

Developing his inquiry into religious doctrines and images, Kant describes how an "intellectual [or intelligible, *intelligibele*] moral relation" is conveyed "in the form of a story [*Geschichte*] in which two principles, opposed to each other like heaven and hell and represented [*vorgestellt*] as two persons outside the human being … seek to establish their claims through law [*durchs Recht*], as it were before a supreme judge" (R, 6:78). This articulates a warping of lawfulness through the sophistical justification of evil intent. The battle on the level of law occurs within mind, heart, and disposition. However, in a figurative sketch mainly presented through biblical sources, Kant also explicates this ethical battle on the level of world history and institutions, indicating a transition to the ethical-political concerns that become increasingly prominent in the latter parts of the book. The allegorical evil being represents both our propensities toward radical evil, and the corrupt principles underpinning these tendencies. The principle of evil does not dominate through mere coercion, but seeks "to establish dominion over minds [*eine Herrschaft über die Gemüter*]" (R, 6:79). The ethical quality of our attitudes interlinks with the type of public institutions predominating in our lives. As narrated in Genesis, the evil one "succeeds in setting himself up as the supreme proprietor of all goods on earth." This is not prohibited by God as the supreme force of good, because the latter deals with humans "in accordance with the principle of their freedom, and whatever good or evil befalls them, it ought to be theirs to ascribe to themselves." In other words, while evil is aligned with dominance and heteronomy, God and good are aligned with autonomy. We cannot be forced or tricked into adopting ethical principles. Consequently, "a Realm of Evil [*ein Reich des Bösen*] was thus set up here on earth in defiance of the good principle" (R, 6:79).

In further reflecting on human history, "the Jewish theocracy" is cited as a remaining foothold for the *good* principle on earth. However, anticipating his harsher judgments of ancient Judaism, Kant assesses this theocratic government as based on the incentives of "reward and punishments" and as burdened with "a hierarchical constitution" (R, 6:79). Nevertheless, in Kant's account Hebrew sources transmit ethical-political principles, although he sees these as requiring augmentation from Greek sources. This conjunction prepares the ground for a "revolution" among the Jewish people, one that eventually occurs with the coming of "a person whose wisdom, even purer than that of the previous philosophers, was as though descended from heaven" (R, 6:80). Hence Kant highlights the person of Jesus as amalgamating the best of the Jewish and Greek cultural-religious worlds. The personified evil principle "provoked against him every persecution by which evil human beings could embitter him … without achieving anything in the least against him by this onslaught by unworthy people upon his steadfastness and honesty in teaching, and example [*Beispiel*] for the sake of the good" (R, 6:81). On a merely physical level "the good principle is the worsted party," because "he had to give up his life in combat" (R, 6:81). However, grasped on the level of principles, the result conveys a very different meaning:

> [S]ince the realm in which *principles* (be they good or evil) have power is not one of nature but of freedom, i.e. it is a realm in which one can control things only to the extent that one rules over minds [*über die Gemüter herrscht*] … so the master's very death (the last extreme of a human being's suffering) was the manifestation [*Darstellung*] of the good principle, that is, of humanity in its moral perfection, as example [*Beispiel*] for everyone to follow. (R, 6:82)

Although physically worsted, Jesus' nonviolent resistance to the force of evil remains ethically paramount. By displaying the integrity of good principles, Jesus' example achieves "the breaking up of its [the evil principle's] controlling power in holding against their will those who have so long been subject to it, now that another moral dominion [*eine andere moralische Herrschaft*] (since the human being must be subject to some dominion or other) has been revealed to them as freedom" (R, 6:83). In this way, the biblical narrative symbolizes and heralds a dominion of autonomy under moral laws with definite legal, political, and ethical connotations. The focus on historical and political issues is evident in the conflict of good and evil occurring simultaneously within the heart and in the polis. Kant reiterates that it is essential to "divest of its mystical cover this vivid [or popular] mode of representing things [*populäre Vorstellungsart*]." Much like Spinoza, Kant emphasizes that the biblical depiction is "apparently also the only one at the time suited *to the common people*" (R, 6:83). The formal principles of the moral law receive emotional power through religious narratives.

What are the specific ethical teachings Kant emphasizes in a hermeneutical engagement with religious representations? A capacity for critical reflection on our maxims and internalized mores is pivotal. However, as the arguments of *Religion* evolve, the ethical formulae of humans as ends in themselves and of the Realm of Ends increasingly take precedence. The problem of relating ethically to others cannot be grasped adequately without attending to the political frameworks and shared institutions within which our relations occur.

THE JURIDICO-CIVIL AND ETHICO-CIVIL SOCIETIES

Part Three of *Religion* concerns "The Victory of the Good Principle over the Evil Principle, and the Founding of a Realm of God on Earth [*eines Reichs Gottes auf Erden*]." With regard to "attacks of the evil principle," a person "can easily convince himself that they do not come his way from his own raw nature, so far as he exists in isolation, but rather from the human beings to whom he stands in relation or association" (R, 6:93). This comment does not overturn the prior explication of radical evil with its focus on freedom of choice, but rather links it to social-political levels of analysis. In discussing an individual whose "original predisposition" is good, Kant remarks: "envy, addiction to power, avarice, and the malignant inclinations associated with these, assail his nature, *as soon as he is among human beings*" (R, 6:93–94). Social-political interactions can have a corrupting impact on our ethical dispositions, so that internal and external ethical inquiries intermesh. The ethical task of addressing social-political conditions is clear:

> [T]he dominion of the good principle is not otherwise attainable, so far as human beings can work towards it, than through the setting up and the diffusion of a society in accordance with, and for the sake of, the laws of virtue – a society which reason makes it a task and duty of the entire human race to establish in its full scope. (R, 6:94)

The metaphysical battle of good predispositions and evil propensities within the human soul, symbolized as two warring powers, is acted out on the world stage. The exposition of moral fallibility coalesces into a political analysis of the conditions that either assist or hinder our free cultivation of good dispositions.

To address these issues, Kant introduces a critical distinction: "An association of human beings merely under the laws of virtue, ruled by this idea, can be called an *ethical* and, so far as these laws are public, an *ethico-civil* (in contrast to a *juridico-civil*) society, or an *ethical community*" (R, 6:94). This generally corresponds to the separation of *The Metaphysics of Morals* into the Doctrine of Virtue (*Tugendlehre*) and the Doctrine of Right (*Rechtslehre*). Kant defines *ethical* lawgiving as making duty to the law an incentive, while *juridical* lawgiving "does not include the incentive of duty in the law and so admits an incentive other than the idea of duty" (MM, 6:219). Both texts recognize the role of coercive laws in the harmonious functioning of societies. However, an ethical community "can exist in the midst of a political community and even be made up of all the members of the latter (indeed, without the foundation of a political

The juridico-civil and ethico-civil societies 249

community, it could never be brought into existence by human beings)" (R, 6:94). This is crucial: Kant does not disconnect moral community from existing institutions. Just as sub-communities can act as an ethical leaven in the larger public sphere (a model for his reconstruction of the visible church), reciprocally, the capacity to realize moral laws requires appropriate political conditions.[47] The ethical state is a composite regulative principle guiding our efforts to transform the public sphere toward greater autonomy and inclusivity: "the idea of such a state has an entirely well-grounded, objective reality in human reason (in the duty to join such a state), even though we cannot subjectively ever hope of the good will of human beings that these will work harmoniously toward this end" (R, 6:95). Kant invokes a variation of the Realm of Ends in rendering the "ethical community," in analogy with existing (juridico-civil) states, as "an *ethical state*, i.e., a *realm* of virtue [*ein Reich der Tugend*] (of the good principle)" (R, 6:95). Because the ethical-civil society represents shared laws of autonomy, it is distinguished from merely external forms of political society. Kant also contrasts each of these collective conditions with a *state of nature*; i.e., with a rendering of what we would be like without laws. Just as the "*juridical state of nature*" describes human beings without the constraints of external public laws, so the "*ethical state of nature* [*ethischen Naturzustande*]" describes our condition without laws of virtue. Kant explicitly critiques both juridical and ethical individualism in their extreme forms, insofar as these downplay shared laws applicable to all. In each case, "there is no effective *public* authority with power to determine legitimately, according to laws, what is in given cases the duty of each individual, and to bring about the universal execution [*Ausübung*] of those laws" (R, 6:95). We might live within a well-ordered political state, and yet remain in an ethical state of nature guided only by maxims of self-love: e.g., personal gain and pre-eminence whatever the cost to others.

Here Kant's focus on the political significance of inner attitudes becomes increasingly prominent. Political communities possessing external dominion "may indeed wish to have available a dominion over minds [*eine Herrschaft über die Gemüter*] as well." However, this would violate autonomous ethics: "for it would be a contradiction (*in adjecto*) for the

---

[47] Harry van der Linden argues that the juridico-civil society is the basis for the ethico-civil: "the ethical commonwealth can arise only within the legal state." *Kantian Ethics and Socialism* (Indianapolis: Hackett, 1988), p.158. More precisely: "legal progress and moral progress are best understood as feedback processes with regard to each other – that is, legal progress facilitates moral progress, which, in turn, stimulates further legal progress" (p.152).

political community to compel its citizens to enter into an ethical community, since the latter entails freedom from coercion in its very concept" (R, 6:95). This language replicates that of the personified evil principle seeking dominion over our minds. In fact, any use of coercion to forcibly condition the ethical mindset of a people is ultimately futile (R, 6:96). Kant is not saying that such efforts at indoctrination do not exist; in fact, he indicates the depth of the problem towards the end of Part Three. In discussing *servile faith*, he notes that the "spiritual power" of an externally enforced faith "can prohibit even thought, and actually hinder it as well." To this he adds: "true, to be free of this coercion one needs only to *will* [*man nur wollen darf*] … but it is precisely this willing on which a bar [*ein Reigel*] is being applied internally" (R, 6:133n.). Even the cultivation of free choice can be negatively affected by externally imposed authorities and laws. There are types of heteronomy that do not rely on physical force; they also condition our sense of identity, of what is right and wrong, possible and impossible.[48] This dreadful influence of corrupt cultural and political institutions shows that moral endeavor cannot be realized merely "through the striving of one individual person for his own moral perfection." It concerns the interactions of individuals in groups and polities, and so "requires rather a union of such persons into a whole toward that very end, [i.e.] toward a system of well-disposed [*wohlgesinnter*] human beings in which, and through the unity of which alone, the highest moral good can come to pass" (R, 6:97–98). Kant specifies the political nature of this endeavor as "a universal republic based on laws of virtue" (R, 6:98). Although such a republic cannot be completely instituted, he advocates practical ideas that guide intentionality and progressively modify political conditions over time.

Moreover, because transformation towards an ethico-civil condition is even more uncertain than developing a moral disposition, an encompassing reference point is invoked as a guideline. Kant proposes that "this duty [of the human race toward itself] will need the presupposition of another idea, namely, of a higher moral being through whose universal organization the forces of single individuals, insufficient on their own, are united for a common effect" (R, 6:98). Religious discourse can give public representation to universalizability and inclusivity, i.e., to the

---

[48] Spinoza also stresses that "obedience is not so much a matter of outward act as internal act of mind." He continues: "although command cannot be exercised over minds in the same way as over tongues, yet minds are to some degree under the control of the sovereign power, who has many means of inducing the great majority to believe, love, hate etc. whatever he wills." *Theological-Political Treatise*, trans. Samuel Shirley (Indianapolis: Hackett, 2001), p.186.

ethical-political *maximum*. As a model of justice, an ethical community is one in which "all individuals must be subjected to public legislation [*öffentlichen Gesetzgebung*], and all the laws binding them must be capable of being regarded as commands of a common lawgiver" (R, 6:98). However, just as the ethical community is differentiated from individual cultivation of a good disposition, so too is it distinguished from a strictly political community. With regard to the latter, Kant emphasizes the democratic-republican idea that "the mass of people joining in a union must itself be the lawgiver (of constitutional laws)." Just laws are those people would give themselves; they cannot be imposed heteronomously. Legislation therefore "proceeds from the principle *of limiting the freedom of each to the conditions under which it can coexist with the freedom of everyone else, in conformity with a universal law* [*einem allgemeinen Gesetze*], and the universal will [*der allgemeine Wille*] thus establishes an external legal constraint" (R, 6:98; cf. MM, 6:232). This universal will is essentially the will of the people, or Rousseau's *general will*, representing rights and autonomy for all under egalitarian laws.[49] Such a juridical-civil ideal remains, however, that of external political laws.

The transformation of our dispositions cannot be heteronomously enforced; it requires an autonomous grasp of moral laws. At the same time, our capacity to reflect on the institutions affecting moral dispositions requires a shared conceptual reference point that is yet pertinent to inner states (R, 6:98). Therefore, as a palpable symbol mediating between moral laws and their public manifestation in an ethical community, Kant again invokes the *transcendental ideal*:

[O]nly such a one can be thought of as the supreme lawgiver of an ethical community, with respect to whom all *true duties*, hence also the ethical, must be

---

[49] Rousseau defines the general will as the principle of association instituted in the social contract, "which defends and protects with all common forces the person and goods of each associate, and by means of which each one, while uniting with all, nevertheless obeys only himself and remains as free as before." The general will is the key idea reconciling liberty and collective association: "*Each of us places his person and all his power in common under the supreme direction of the general will; and as one we receive each member as an indivisible part of the whole*" (*The Social Contract*, Book I, Chapter VI, p.148). To be sure, Rousseau recognizes that "each individual can, as a man, have a private will contrary to or different from the general will that he has as a citizen. His private interest can speak to him in an entirely different manner than the common interest" (Chapter VII, p.150). The social contract does not obliterate the tensions between individual wills and the general will. Rousseau also anticipates Kant in proposing that the "passage from the state of nature to the civil state ... substitutes justice for instinct in his behavior and gives his actions a moral quality they previously lacked." Like Kant, Rousseau distinguishes freedom from unrestricted indulgence of individual desires; true freedom can be cultivated only within the social condition: "For to be driven by appetite alone is slavery, and obedience to the law one has prescribed for oneself is liberty" (Chapter VII, pp.150–51).

represented [*vorgestellt werden müssen*] as *at the same time* his commands; consequently he must also be one who knows the heart, in order to penetrate to the intimate parts of the dispositions of each and everyone. (R, 6:99; paraphrasing Acts 1:24, 15:8; Luke 16:5)

Kant is proposing the idea of God as surpassing the dichotomy between freedom and nature, between inner autonomy and outer representation. Public structures with shared principles are reconciled with the need to establish these in such a way that they are not *merely* coercive. Hence it is crucial that Kant differentiates his approach from any kind of *theocracy*. In the latter case, we would consider "a people of God in accordance with statutory laws, that is to say, such laws as do not involve morality of actions but only their legality" (R, 6:99). This point applies the distinction between moral and positive laws within the context of religious modalities. Merely external governance according to religious edicts is heteronomy under the guise of religious legitimation; in a theocracy "priests, as human beings who receive their orders directly from [God], would run an aristocratic *government*" (R, 6:100). Kant opposes the regulative idea of laws by and for all humanity, to the paternalistic rule of elites. Indeed, the idea of God becomes debased under theocratic systems: "the lawgiver, though God, is yet external, whereas we only have to do here with an institution, of which the lawgiving is purely internal, a republic under laws of virtue" (R, 6:100). God, as the ideal quintessence of the moral law, cannot legitimately be objectified, and therefore cannot abrogate our autonomy. This ideal supports an inclusive ethical-political vision conducive to individual autonomy under moral laws. Hence Kant establishes a virtual identity between the law of God and the moral law (R, 6:99n.).[50] He employs this moral principle as the ultimate criterion for distinguishing, not only good and evil positive laws, but also true and authentic from merely alleged divine laws. For example, any religious or political edict that promotes the violation of other people is simply false.

The same argument calls for organizations in "the form of a church" that assist us in realizing "the idea of a people of God" (R, 6:100). The notion of a church represents a configuration of people under ethical rather than merely juridical laws; it is another way of discussing an ethico-civil community. Therefore, Kant introduces the *"church invisible,"*

---

[50] In similar terms, Spinoza holds that the touchstone of religious truth is morality, and that "a man's beliefs should be regarded as pious or impious only insofar as he is thereby induced to obey the moral law" (*Theological-Political Treatise*, p.157). He adds that "Scripture itself tells us quite clearly over and over again what every man should do in order to serve God, declaring that the entire Law consists in this alone, to love one's neighbor" (p.159).

defined as "the mere idea [*eine bloße Idee*] of the union of all upright human beings under direct yet moral divine world-governance, serving as an archetype [*zum Urbilde*] of any such governance to be founded by human beings" (R, 6:101). This idea responds to the fallibility of individual conscience, the need for developing both ethico-civil and juridico-civil societies, and the strategic role of religious representations in contributing to ethical pedagogy. Like the *Urbild* of Jesus representing humanity well-pleasing to divine law, the invisible church is another archetype guiding our reform of existing institutions. As partially instantiated in religious institutions, this would then constitute "the *church visible* [which] is the actual union of human beings into a whole that accords with this idea" (R, 6:101). Specific instances of visible churches must be judged and modified according to ethical criteria expressed in the church invisible. The characteristics of this ideal church are (1) *universality*: whatever the variations of symbols and practices, the underlying moral principles are inviolable; (2) *purity*: the incentives must be moral; hence the church is "cleansed of the nonsense of superstition [*Aberglaubens*] and the madness of enthusiasm [*Schwärmerei*]"; (3) *relation* (i.e., organization among members) under the principle of freedom. This must be "neither a *hierarchy*" (which contradicts freedom and equality among members), "nor an *illuminatism*," which is "a kind of *democracy* through individual inspirations, which can vary greatly from one another, according to each mind." There cannot be arbitrary variations based on elitism or favoritism, as the reference to illuminatism conveys. Although the association of these subjective attitudes with democracy is debatable, here Kant is concerned with the dangers of private inspirations undisciplined by publicly accessible criteria. Finally, (4) its *modality* involves the unchangeableness of its constitution (which follows "secure principles *a priori*"). Moral faith should not be conditioned by "arbitrary creeds which … are fortuitous, exposed to contradiction, and changeable" (R, 6:102). Its constitution is based on regulative ideas of practical reason that generate criteria for assessing extant organizations.

THE REGULATIVE IDEA OF GOD VERSUS THEOCRATIC DESPOTISM

Part of Kant's project involves bringing institutions calling themselves churches into greater alignment with moral laws. He observes that "due to a peculiar weakness of human nature, pure faith can never be relied on as much as it deserves, that is, [enough] to found a Church on it alone"

(R, 6:103). This peculiar weakness is the tendency to conceive of being "well-pleasing to God" as requiring "some *service* [*Dienst*] or other which they must perform for God" (R, 6:103). *Service* characterizes particular cultic activities, such as ritual performances or prayer, which may become substitutes for moral endeavor. These activities, if harnessed to moral principles, can also have a supportive practical function. Yet they are problematic insofar as they dislodge or even oppose an ethical focus on others as ends in themselves. They also cultivate "passive obedience, however morally indifferent the actions might be in themselves" (R, 6:103). A related point had been made by Hume, who noted that "the greatest crimes have been found, in many instances, compatible with a superstitious piety and devotion."[51] These forms of service also have political implications, insofar as they conflate the ideal of God with worldly autocrats: "every great lord of this world has a special need of being *honored* by his subjects, and of being *praised* through signs of submissiveness; nor can he expect, without this, as much compliance with his orders from his subjects as he needs to rule over them effectively" (R, 6:103). This also echoes the *Theological-Political Treatise*, where Spinoza had observed that the majority of human beings "imagine God's power to be like the rule of some royal potentate."[52] Along similar lines, Hume also noted the propensity of various cultures to form their idea of the divinity on the model of a petty if very powerful human being, keen to receive adulation. He mentions the "votaries" who "will endeavour, by every art, to insinuate themselves into his favour; and supposing him to be pleased, like themselves, with praise and flattery, there is no eulogy or exaggeration, which will be spared in their address of him." To this Hume adds the important point, reiterated throughout the *Natural History*, that "in proportion as men's *fears or distresses* become more urgent, they still invent new strains of adulation."[53] These points supplement Kant's focus on the category error of encumbering the ideal of God with all-too-human features. Hume reminds us that these beliefs and practices respond not only to human ignorance but also to deep emotional needs. Moreover, as Spinoza illustrates, these needs can be

---

[51] Hume, *The Natural History of Religion*, p.182. A few pages earlier, Hume distinguishes between slavish observances and ethical religious practice, noting that "It is certain, that, in every religion, however sublime the verbal definition which it gives of its divinity, many of the votaries, perhaps the greatest number, will seek the divine favour, not by virtue and good morals, which alone can be acceptable to a perfect being, but either by frivolous observances, by intemperate zeal, by rapturous extasies, or by the belief of mysterious and absurd opinions" (p.179).
[52] Spinoza, *Theological-Political Treatise*, p.71.
[53] Hume, *The Natural History of Religion*, p.155; italics added.

manipulated by self-serving ecclesiastical and political authorities to cultivate irrational fear sustaining heteronomous power structures.[54] There is a form of *double-mirroring* evident here, constituting a vicious circle. The projected cosmic despot mirrors the behavioral patterns of worldly despots; in turn, religious doctrines become a political resource for instilling compliance to heteronomous authority among a given population. The well-being of the demos is generally not a consideration in the institution of despotic control.

Kant argues with reference to statutory laws based on the will of an anthropomorphized deity that "cognition of these laws is possible not through our own mere reason but only through revelation" (R, 6:104). Revelation is identical with cultural traditions claiming to reflect a suprahuman order; yet, insofar as these traditions do not convey universalizable moral laws, they reveal merely an ethically dubious parochialism. Building on this point, Kant notes that "even assuming divine statutory laws … even then pure *moral* legislation, through which God's will is originally engraved in our hearts, is not only the unavoidable condition of all true religion in general but also that which actually constitutes such religion and for which statutory religion can contain only the means of its promotion and propagation" (R, 6:104). If our concept of God is consistent, and if it reflects regulative principles of justice and truth, then the idea of God and the moral law are synonymous. Hence formal principles of universalizability can be coupled with the particular and contingent products of cultures, engendering concrete universals. This ethical religion helps us overcome authoritarian abuse of religious discourse, which is "an usurpation of higher authority, in order to impose a yoke upon the multitude by means of ecclesiastical statutes, under the pretense of divine authority" (R, 6:105). This comment illustrates how religious phenomena intersect the realms of ethical and the political.[55]

Because ethical practice requires "something that *the senses can hold on to* … some historical ecclesiastical faith or other, usually already at hand, must be used" (R, 6:109). This constructive appropriation of religions

---

[54] In Spinoza's words: "the supreme mystery of despotism, its prop and stay, is to keep men in a state of deception, and with the specious title of religion to cloak the fear by which they must be held in check, so that they will fight for their servitude as if for salvation" (*Theological-Political Treatise*, p.3).

[55] Kant's *Anthropology* discusses the role of religion in cultivating "internal constraint (the constraint of conscience)." He continues: "However, if morals do not precede religion in this discipline of the people, then religion makes itself lord over morals, and statutory religion becomes an instrument of state authority (politics) under *religious despots*; an evil that inevitably upsets and misguides character by governing it with *deception* (called statecraft)" (A, 7:333n.).

is only viable through a rigorous critical distinction between the literal claims of sectarian faiths and the ethical religion *expressed* in symbols and doctrines (R, 6:108). The drawbacks of dogmatism are manifested in "the so-called religious struggles, which have so often shaken the world and spattered it with blood [*mit Blut bespritz haben*], have never been anything but squabbles over ecclesiastical faiths" (R, 6:108). After noting how faiths have repeatedly vied with one another for cultural and political hegemony to the point of shedding blood, Kant addresses the doctrinal rigidity subtending such religious exclusivism.

> [Whenever] a church passes itself off as the only universal one [*für die einige allgemeine ausgibt*] (even though it is based on faith in a particular revelation which, since it is historical, can never be demanded of everyone), whoever does not acknowledge its (particular) ecclesiastical faith is called an *unbeliever* [*ein Ungläubiger*], and is wholeheartedly hated; whoever deviates from it only in part (in nonessentials) is called an *erring believer* [*ein Irrgläubiger*], and is at least shunned as a source of infection. (R, 6:108)

Hence the menace of *false universals* appears when belief systems impose themselves forcibly upon others (R, 6:109). Counteracting this heteronomy requires breaking the monopolization of scriptural interpretation by institutionally controlled authorities: "we require an interpretation [*eine Auslegung*] of the revelation we happen to have, i.e. a thoroughgoing understanding of it in a sense that harmonizes with the universal practical rules of a pure religion of reason" (R, 6:110). Cultural traditions cannot be ignored by those cultivating practical reason, since they remain influential for large groups of people. Traditions provide languages for articulating meaning, value, and purpose, and are deeply intertwined with social and political institutions. However, these cultural formations must be engaged by a strong ethical reading. Kant emphasizes that "this interpretation may often appear to us as forced [*gezwungen*], in view of the text (of the revelation), and be often forced in fact; yet if the text can at all bear it, it must be preferred to a literal [*buchstäblichen*] interpretation that either contains absolutely nothing for morality, or even works counter to its incentives" (R, 6:110). This point recognizes that religious writings are subject to multiple interpretations: ethical interpretation is one way to read these texts, but it takes priority over other approaches. Kant addresses "all types of faith – ancient and new, some written down in holy books" (R, 6:110–11), hence casting a wide net in approaching traditions. To be sure, any claim of an underlying moral teaching common to all religions is likely to raise suspicions if not outright scorn from contemporary scholars. Yet this is not a naïve *philosophia perennis*, especially one that suppresses cultural differences. Kant is claiming that all religions contain ethical principles that can ameliorate the evils of human interrelations. Insofar as they advocate love and respect for others, or principles of fairness and justice inclusive of all, then we have *some* common ethical ground to work with.

Kant refers to the religion of reason as "*authentic* and valid for the whole world." This is contrasted with "*scholarship* (which deals with the historical element of Scripture)" as "merely *doctrinal*" (R, 6:114). Scriptural scholarship is not disparaged; it is essential in explicating the teachings of traditions. However, with reference to Kant's concerns, authentic interpretation is driven by universalizable ethical principles that supersede mere scholarship (e.g., in the form of philology). *The Conflict of the Faculties* augments this distinction between *doctrinal* and *authentic* interpretation: "we must interpret the Scriptures *insofar as they have to do with religion*; otherwise our interpretations are either empty of practical content or even obstacles to the good. Only a moral interpretation, moreover, is really an authentic one – that is, one given by the God within us" (CF, 7:48). The God within us is explicitly linked with "concepts of *our* reason, insofar as they are pure moral concepts and hence infallible"; through this faculty "we can recognize the divinity of a teaching promulgated to us" (CF, 7:48). This again subverts a false dichotomy between reason and religion; true religion manifests rational principles.[56] If we link authentic interpretation to the imperative always to treat others as ends in themselves, then we have definite guidelines for approaching religious teachings.[57] Kant draws upon historical faiths as means for cultivating the realm of ends (R, 6:115 and 121). Further emphasizing the religious nature of the moral law, he introduces the expression "*saving faith [seligmachenden Glauben]*"

---

[56] Spinoza writes of how "God's eternal Word and covenant and true religion are divinely inscribed in men's hearts – that is, in men's minds." He also contrasts this true religion with "superstition," and applies this latter term to dogmatism and literalism: "instead of God's Word they are beginning to worship likenesses and images, that is, paper and ink" (*Theological-Political Treatise*, pp.145–46). For the dogmatists, "it should be no crime to denigrate the mind, the true handwriting of God's word, declaring it to be corrupt, blind, and lost, whereas it is considered to be a heinous crime to entertain such thoughts of the letter, a mere shadow of God's word" (p.167).

[57] In the *Lectures on the Philosophical Doctrine of Religion* Kant also states the priority of ethical religion over revelation. "Revelation is divided into the *outer* and the *inner*. An *outer* revelation can be of *two kinds*: either through works, or through words. *Inner* divine revelation is God's revelation to us through our own reason; this latter must *precede all other* revelation and serve for the estimation of outer revelation. It has to be the touchstone by which I recognize *whether an outer revelation is really from God*, and it must furnish me with proper concepts of him" (LPR, 28:1117). Inner revelations are also discussed at R, 6:122; both texts prioritize ethical over statutory modes of religiosity.

to describe the cultivation of a good disposition that might make "every individual receptive to (worthy of) eternal happiness" (R, 6:115). There are two essential points concerning saving faith. The first is that "despite the diversity of ecclesiastical faiths, it can yet be met in any in which, tending to its goal of pure religious faith, it is practical" (R, 6:115). Clearly, it is not specific doctrinal contents that constitute saving faith, but rather fostering morality. A key criterion of this practical faith is that it emphasizes "our own work, and not, once again, a foreign influence [*ein fremder Einfluß*] to which we remain passive" (R, 6:118). Kant notes that "ecclesiastical faith" may hold "faith in vicarious satisfaction" as a duty, making good life-conduct secondary to this; for "the pure faith of religion," however, "the reverse holds true." That is, "a *good life-conduct* is (as supreme condition of grace) unconditional *duty*, whereas the satisfaction from on high is merely a *matter of grace* [*eine bloße Gnadensache*]." Hence the idea or postulate of grace can support us in living a good life. Yet ecclesiastical faith, focusing on passive reception of grace, "is accused (often not unjustly) of ritual superstition [*den gottesdienstlichen Aberglauben*; note the association with divine service], which knows how to reconcile a criminal life-conduct with religion" (R, 6:118–19). Once again, the danger of literal conceptions of grace is that these may degenerate into mere superstition unleavened by ethical principles.

Nevertheless, Kant does not simply oppose superstition to "naturalistic unbelief." He returns to the image of the Son of God as a guide for ethical practice, rather than as indicating supernatural interventions. "The living faith in the prototype [*das Urbild*] of a humanity well-pleasing to God (the Son of God) refers, *in itself*, to a moral idea of reason, insofar as the latter serves for us not only as guideline [*zur Richtschnur*] but as incentive [*zur Triebfeder*] as well" (R, 6:119). The archetype of the ethical human being only becomes recognizable as such by manifesting the moral law in the course of a human life. In other words, Jesus expresses "the prototype lying in our reason [*unserer Vernunft liegende Urbild*] which we put in [*unterlegen*, attribute to] him (since, from what can be gathered from his example, the God-man is found to conform to the prototype), and such a faith is all the same as the principle of a good life-conduct" (R, 6:119). The representation of higher assistance does not replace autonomous ethical endeavors, but rather provides practical guidance by means of a publicly accessible symbol. Hence, understood as two modes of representing the moral law, the religious and the rational do not conflict (R, 6:119). Moral religion symbolically explicates practical principles. However, there is an antinomy between moral religion and literal dogmatic religion (R, 6:120). Exclusive dogmas standing in opposition to each other are irreconcilable with the universalizability of moral principles. As Kant specifies, all historical religions are in principle classifiable under both modalities: "History testifies that all forms of religion have been ruled by this conflict between the two principles of faith; for all religions have had their expiations [*Expiationen*], however they have constructed them. On the other hand, the moral predisposition in every person [*die moralische Anlage in jedem Menschen*] has not failed, for its part, to make its demands heard" (R, 6:120; translation modified).[58] Despite occasional lapses in consistency, Kant is not simply opposing moral religion in the form of Christianity to other non-moral religions. All human beings have moral predispositions, and every tradition is an admixture of principles with more dubious, culturally contingent features. Moreover, the way we interpret traditions affects our ability to reform them. Hence, "the basis for the transition to the new order of things must lie in the principle of the pure religion of reason, as a revelation (though not an empirical one) permanently taking place within all human beings." This principle, which is synonymous with the moral law, forms the guide for mature religious reflection (R, 6:122).

Kant links the religion of reason with "a true enlightenment," described as "an order of law originating in moral freedom." This idea of reason is "impossible to display [*Darstellung*]," but it serves as a "practical regulative principle" taking on reality through human actions. There is an affinity between the modification of ecclesiastical forms and "the political idea of the right of the state, insofar as this right ought at the same time to be brought into line with international law which is universal and *endowed with power*" (R, 6:123n.). Equally important is the associated critique of imperialism in both political and religious institutions. Just as a particular state will "strive, when things go its way, to subjugate all others to itself and achieve a universal monarchy [*eine Universalmonarchie zu errichten strebe*] … So too each and every church entertains the proud pretension of becoming a universal one" (R, 6:123n.). Clearly, the kind of universalizability Kant advocates in religion and political life has nothing to do with the ascendency of one parochial cultural unit over others. He distinguishes between universalizability compatible with diverse social-political forms, and a false universal that imposes itself unilaterally. The

---

[58] Kant also writes of "the moral predisposition in us" as "at the same time the interpreter of all religion" (R, 6:121).

expression "universal monarchy" to describe these imperialist endeavors is apposite.[59]

In a related vein, Kant turns to ancient Judaism to develop his critique of *theocracy* as a form of religious heteronomy. "The fact that the constitution of this state was based on a *theocracy* (visibly, an aristocracy of priests or leaders who boasted of instructions directly imparted to them from God), and that God's name was honored in it (though only as a secular regent with absolutely no rights over, or claims upon, conscience), did not make that constitution religious" (R, 6:125). The specific categorization of ancient Judaism as a theocracy goes back to Josephus, the Jewish historian of the first century CE. As Eric Nelson has documented, this designation of the biblical state of Israel as theocratic had a significant influence on early modern theorists such as Cunaeus, Grotius, and Hobbes, where it was largely free of pejorative connotations.[60] Nelson also notes that in the case of Spinoza, by contrast, the attribution of theocracy to ancient Judaism was used in a "deflationary" manner. Concerning Spinoza's analysis, Nelson observes: "Its intention is to remove the aura of authority that accompanies the Biblical text, in the service of an avowedly secular politics."[61] Spinoza was almost certainly a direct influence on Kant in this respect: both question voluntaristic portrayals of God as a monarch in order to undermine the religious authority behind all forms of despotism.[62] Spinoza argues that "all the prophets who laid down laws in God's name ... did not perceive God's decrees adequately, as eternal truths."[63] With specific reference to the revelation received by Moses, Spinoza notes

---

[59] It was a common fear among the European powers of the early modern period that one or another of them would seek to establish such domination. In discussing the negotiations of the Westphalian Congress that began in 1644 and which finally brought the Thirty Years War to a close in 1648, for example, Peter H. Wilson notes how "the rival delegations were quick to accuse each other of using religion as a pretext for seeking universal, hegemonic monarchy." *The Thirty Years War: Europe's Tragedy* (Cambridge, MA: Harvard University Press, 2009), p.676.

[60] See Eric Nelson, *The Hebrew Republic* (Cambridge, MA: Harvard University Press, 2010). Nelson cites Josephus' *Against Apion* on the issue of ancient Judaism as a theocracy (see especially pp.89ff.).

[61] *Ibid.*, p.134.

[62] Cohen held that "Kant obtained from Spinoza his knowledge and judgment of Judaism." Hermann Cohen, *Religion of Reason: Out of the Sources of Judaism* (Cincinnati, OH: Hebrew Union College Press, 1993), p.331.

[63] Spinoza, *Theological-Political Treatise*, p. 53. This notion of eternal truths is explicated in the *Ethics*, for example at Part II, Prop.43, Scholium: "the human mind, in so far as it perceives things truly, is part of the infinite intellect of God (Cor.Pr.11, 11), and thus it is as inevitable that the clear and distinct ideas of the mind are true as that God's are true." Spinoza, *The Ethics*, trans. Samuel Shirley (Indianapolis: Hackett, 1992), p.92. This model of reason differs from Kant's critical model in key respects; yet both Spinoza and Kant contrast reason with culturally conditioned theological principles.

that he "perceived a way by which the people of Israel could be united in a particular territory to form a political union or state, and also a way by which that people could be constrained to obedience." However, rendering God as a monarch is a projection of anthropomorphic characteristics:

> Therefore he [Moses] perceived all these things not as eternal truths [of reason], but as instructions and precepts, and he ordained them as laws of God. Hence it came about that he imagined God as a ruler, lawgiver, king, merciful, just and so forth; whereas these are all merely attributes of human nature, and not at all applicable to the divine nature.[64]

As Nelson notes, Spinoza is not attributing literal validity to biblical notions of theocracy; anthropomorphic portrayals of God are an erroneous if politically effective way of rendering laws in a publicly accessible form. Spinoza describes specific characteristics of this theocratic model in a way that anticipates Kant's remarks. He proposes that "it was God alone … who held sovereignty over the Hebrews … Hence this form of government could be called a theocracy, its citizens being bound only by such a law as was revealed by God."[65] Spinoza further notes that one of the most problematic aspects of such a theocracy is that it places undue power and authority in the hands of the priests, insofar as they become the supreme interpreters of the word of God.[66]

Kant's general concerns follow upon Spinoza's, in that each differentiates principles and laws generated by reason (understood in their varying ways) from cultural renderings of divine law. It is essential to differentiate the transcendental ideal, representing the maximum inclusiveness of regulative principles, from the theological-political heteronomy manifest in all forms of theocracy. However, more problematic is the argument that the ethical laws of Judaism take the form of merely external legislation: "although the Ten Commandments would have ethical validity for reason even if they had not been publicly given, yet in that legislation they are given with no claim at all on the *moral disposition* in following them (whereas Christianity later placed the chief work in this) but were rather directed simply and solely to external observance" (R, 6:126). Kant distinguishes between theocracy as heteronomous, and an understanding of the idea of God as reflecting internal moral dispositions

---

[64] Spinoza, *Theological-Political Treatise*, p. 53. Compare *Ethics*, Part II, Prop. 3, Scholium: "nobody will rightly apprehend what I am trying to say unless he takes great care not to confuse God's power with a king's human power or right" (p.65).
[65] Spinoza, *Theological-Political Treatise*, p.189.
[66] Ibid., pp.190ff.

compatible with autonomy. These distinctions occur throughout his analyses of historical faiths, including all forms of Christianity. However, as blanket categorizations of Judaism, rather than as a critical distinction applicable to all traditions, these views are mistaken. The problem lies in attributing the external observance alone to Judaism, while the characterization of an inter-dependence of external observation and internal transformation is reserved for an idealized Christianity.[67] The pejorative treatment of Jewish doctrines indicated in some of these comments has incited at least one commentator to accuse Kant of anti-Semitism.[68] On a personal and biographical level, there is compelling evidence that Kant most certainly was *not* an anti-Semite.[69] This is not to say, however, that his work is not culturally conditioned in ways that sometimes distort

---

[67] Cohen noted that "the inner affinities between Kant's philosophy and Judaism are evident in the substantive similarity between the ethics of the Kantian system and the basic ideas of Judaism, though Kant himself neither intended nor was even aware of any such accord." Hermann Cohen, "Affinities between the Philosophy of Kant and Judaism," in Eva Jospe, ed. and trans., *Reason and Hope: Selections from the Jewish Writings of Hermann Cohen* (Cincinnati, OH: Hebrew Union College Press, 1993), p.77. Specifically, Cohen observes that "what is really characteristic of Kant's view of God, however, is his concept of a non-personal, truly spiritual dimension: the sublimation of God into the Idea. And this is nothing less that the core-meaning of the Jewish God-idea too" (p.82).

[68] See Michael Mack, *German Idealism and the Jew* (University of Chicago Press, 2003). Unfortunately, this discussion of Kant's thought is riddled with numerous errors concerning the most basic points of epistemology and ethics. For example, Mack uses a caricatured rendition of Kant as an unreconstructed metaphysical dualist to establish an anti-Semitic paradigm in his work (with Judaism supposedly correlated with a disparaged materialism). Along with the discussion of Judaism in *Religion*, Mack bases his views on two comments in the *Lectures on Ethics* that are indeed reprehensible. However, Kant's *Lectures on Ethics* derive from unofficial student transcripts. The transcript where the questionable references to Jews occur is that of J. G. Herder which, as the editor of the English edition cautions, "*is not altogether reliable.*" See J. B. Schneewind, "Introduction," in Kant, *Lectures on Ethics*, ed. Peter Heath and J. B. Schneewind, trans. Peter Heath (Cambridge University Press, 1997), p.xiv. The disparaging comments indicated are as follows: "Every coward is a liar; Jews, for example, not only in business, but also in common life" (LE, 27:61). Reference is later made to "the Jews, for example, who are permitted by the Talmud to practice deceit" (LE, 27:75). It is important that nothing like these passages appears in the more reliable transcriptions of Collins, Mrongovius, or Vigilantius.

[69] For relevant biographical information concerning Kant's cordial relations with Jewish students and colleagues, see Manfred Kuehn, *Kant: A Biography* (Cambridge University Press, 2001), especially pp.161–62, 333. This issue is also addressed by Susan Meld Shell in *Kant and the Limits of Autonomy* (Cambridge, MA: Harvard University Press, 2009). The documents Shell's close relations to students such as Marcus Herz and contemporaries such as Moses Mendelssohn (pp.307ff.). Moreover, she notes the more positive attitude toward Judaism evident in the third *Critique*: "the *Critique of Judgment* seems to lift Judaism, at least in its 'ancient', radically iconoclastic form, above Christianity as historically practiced" (p.313). However, Shell argues that the repressive regime of Frederick William II in the early 1790s created conditions under which Kant thought it strategically important to highlight the Christian tradition as a possible vehicle of Enlightenment, as indicated in *Religion*. This constructive approach to Christianity had as its negative correlate a downplaying of the links between Judaism and "moral religion" (pp.313ff.).

its treatment of Judaism and other traditions. Kant's work aspires to an inclusive vision that still informs efforts to overcome parochialism and injustice of all kinds. While he sometimes perpetuates stereotypes of Jews and others, this is not anti-Semitism. It simply tells us that Kant, like all of us, was subject to limitations of vision arising from biographical and cultural influences. I am not arguing that Kant is wrong to undertake critical analyses of religious traditions guided by moral principles. As we have seen, he criticizes them all, especially Christianity. My point is that his one-sided treatment of Judaism largely reflects the biases of Christian Europe in the eighteenth century.

THE MORAL LAW MADE PUBLIC

As Kant delves more deeply into the Christian tradition, Jesus is presented as a religious teacher emphasizing inner ethical transformation over cultish behavior. "The teacher of the Gospel" declared "that servile faith [*den Fronglauben*] (in days of divine service, in professions and practices) is inherently null; that moral faith, which alone makes human beings holy 'as my father in heaven is holy' [paraphrasing Matthew 5:48] and proves its genuineness by good life-conduct, is on the contrary the only one which sanctifies" (R, 6:128). Although this appropriates Christian discourse as the preferred vehicle for presenting the moral law, it deliteralizes theological concepts by focusing on good life-conduct in accordance with moral laws, as opposed to servile faith. The teacher of the gospel through his teaching, suffering, and "meritorious death," gave to us "an example [*Beispiel*] conforming to the prototype [*dem Urbilde*] of a humanity well-pleasing to God" (R, 6:128–29). As with all uses of the term *Urbild* in the critical philosophy, this represents an ideal to which we can conform to a greater or lesser degree through autonomous efforts.

If a tradition prioritizes dogmatic belief over ethical precepts, then its effects in the world will be correspondingly marred. Kant argues that purely external observance lends itself to despotism and domination, and illustrates this with historical details by rapidly summarizing

> how mystical enthusiasm [*mystische Schwärmereien*] in the life of hermits and monks and the exaltation of the holiness of the celibate state rendered a great number of individuals useless to the world; how alleged miracles accompanying all this weighed down the people with the heavy chains of a blind superstition [*blinden Aberglauben*], how, with the imposition of a hierarchy [*Hierarchie*] upon free human beings, the terrible voice of orthodoxy [*die schreckliche Stimme der Rechtgläubigkeit*] rose from the self-appointed canonical expositors of scripture,

and this voice split the Christian world into bitter parties in matters of faith. (R, 6:130)

Here the links between dogmatic understandings of Scripture and despotic forms of social ordering are especially clear. Kant additionally notes how spiritual despotism exercised the "threat of excommunication," how it incited the populace "to foreign wars (the Crusades) which would depopulate another portion of the world." Finally, likely with reference to the Thirty Years War, he remarks on how dogmatism led to "bloodthirsty hatred against their otherwise minded confreres in one and the same so-called universal Christianity" (R, 6:131). These criticisms are if anything far more damaging than those leveled against the Jewish tradition. Moreover, they are not simply a litany of regrettable imperfections, but are thematically connected by an analysis of the conflicts engendered by narrow dogmatic authority. He therefore notes "the root of this strife … in the fundamental principle of an ecclesiastical faith which rules despotically" (R, 6:131). The conflict of religious interpretations is a confrontation between two types of principle, which once again can be summarized as heteronomy versus autonomy.

In light of the chequered history of the Christian faith, Kant echoes his "Enlightenment" essay in proclaiming that "the present" is the pre-eminent age of religion, because of "the seed of a true religious faith now being sown in Christianity." This offers hope of "a continuous approximation to that church, ever uniting all human beings, which constitutes the visible representation [*die sichtbare Vorstellung*] (the schema) of an invisible Realm of God on earth" (R, 6:131–32). Most importantly, one of the prerequisites of cultivating ethical religion is that "reason has wrested itself free from the burden of a faith constantly exposed to the arbitrariness of its interpreters [*der Willkür der Ausleger*]" (R, 6:132). The question of interpretation is intertwined with rethinking our maxims and practice; are these predicated on universalizable, or merely contingent and arbitrary principles suiting individual needs and predilections? Kant's treatment of religious symbolism is extremely focused in this section of the text, where the terms "representation" (*Vorstellung*), "presentation" or "manifestation" (*Darstellung*), and "symbolic" (*symbolische*) occur repeatedly. Overall, he insists that Christian doctrines concerning the meaning of history "take on their proper symbolic meaning [*symbolische Bedeutung*] before reason" (R, 6:136). In the same vein, "the Realm of Heaven can be interpreted as a *symbolic representation* [*symbolische Vorstellung auslegen*] aimed merely at stimulating greater hope and courage and effort in achieving it" (R,

6:134). This ideal realm acts as a symbol with a regulative function, orienting us toward developing an ethical commonwealth. He also stresses that "a Realm of God is here represented [*vorgestellt*] not according to a particular covenant," which means "not a messianic Realm but according to a *moral* one" (R, 6:136n.). Although a critique of both Jewish and Christian Messianism is indicated here, the point is to downplay merely external statutory laws, through a symbolic rendering of the realm of ends embodying inclusive ideals.[70] Kant does not impose an enlightened vision upon religious traditions, but rather discerns and elicits it within various religions (R, 6:140).

The religion of reason exemplifies the highest good; hence "this religion possesses the great prerequisite of the true church, namely the qualification for universality, inasmuch as by universality we mean validity for every human being (*universitas vel omnitudo distributiva* [universality or distributive totality])" (R, 6:157). The visible church is a means whereby just egalitarian principles applicable to all are propagated (R, 6:158). Therefore, under the heading of Christianity as a "natural religion," Kant discusses Jesus as a teacher of *autonomous moral laws*, rather than coercive statutory beliefs. Jesus is "not indeed the *founder* [*Stifter*] of the *religion* which, free from every dogma, is inscribed in the heart of all human beings (for there is nothing arbitrary [*willkürlichem*] in the origin of this religion)" (R, 6:159). This focus on internal ethics, contrasted with rote activities that merely put on a display of piety, is explicated through a series of biblical passages. For example, Jesus' teachings emphasize "not the observance of external civil or statutory ecclesiastical duties but only the pure moral disposition of the heart can make a human being well-pleasing to God" (R, 6:159; citing Matthew 5:20–48). Likewise, the inner disposition is stressed in the teaching that "to hate in one's heart is tantamount to killing" (R, 6:159; citing Matthew 5:22). However, it is also crucial that this focus on dispositions is not dissociated from activities in the world: "an injustice brought upon a neighbor can be made good only through satisfaction rendered to the neighbor himself, not through acts of divine service" (R, 6:159). The continuity between Kant's ethics and his interpretation of religion is quite precise. Ultimately, the cultivation

---

[70] Kant refers to both Jews and Christians who "wanted to make a political and not a moral concept of this messiah" (R, 6:137n.). This comment indicates a moral interpretation of Messianism, although this is not pursued. In the early twentieth century, Hermann Cohen developed this line of analysis, noting in a Kantian manner that "*Messianism*, however, means the dominion of the good on earth" (*Religion of Reason*, p.21).

of moral dispositions that sustain concern for other human beings is the governing principle of Christianity as a moral religion.

These principles of moral religion are often explicated by contrasting them with the non-ethical parochial practices impeding its cultivation. Kant therefore excoriates "the crafty hope [*hinterlistige Hoffnung*] of those who, through invocation and praise of the supreme lawgiver in the person of his envoy, would make up for their lack of deeds and ingratiate themselves into his favor [*und sich Gunst zu erschmeicheln meinen*]" (R, 6:160, citing Matthew 7:21[71]). As we have seen, the predilection to *seek favor* concerns a demand for unfair treatment, wherein one seeks to override moral laws by gaining an arbitrary exemption. This brief presentation of Christianity as a natural religion culminates in an explication of the core moral principles rendered in Scripture: "Love everyone as yourself, i.e. promote his welfare from an unmediated good will, one not derived from selfish incentives" (R, 6:161). Following this comment, Kant contrasts the rule of "self-interest – the God of this world," with "beneficence toward the needy motivated simply by duty (Matthew, 25:35–40)" (R, 6:161–62). This terse comment encapsulates the realism of Kant's view of actual human beings and institutions, i.e., as generally motivated by selfishness and self-love. It contrasts this existing state of affairs with the possibility of acting from moral laws.

In popular religious forms, moral elements are often disguised or completely displaced by non-ethical practices. Like Spinoza, Kant indicates that this is partly because the teachings are presented in a form of exposition "which accommodated itself to the prejudices of the times" (R, 6:163).[72] Religions present ethical teachings in representational formats shaped by historical influences and designed to be accessible to the general public. In response to the ensuing problems of narrow dogmatism and parochialism, Kant reiterates the danger of phenomenal representations being grasped literally. Describing "the true *service* of the church under

---

[71] "Not every one who says to me, 'Lord, Lord', shall enter into the kingdom of heaven, but he who does the will of my Father who is in heaven" (Matthew 7:21). Importantly, this follows the well-known passage at Matthew 7:19–20, "Every tree that does not bear good fruit is cut down and thrown into the fire. Thus you will know them by their fruits." *The New Oxford Annotated Bible*, Revised Standard Version (New York: Oxford University Press, 1977).

[72] *The Conflict of the Faculties* discusses statutory teachings as "different forms in which the divine will is represented sensibly [*Formen der sinnlichen Vorstellungsart*] so as to give it influence on our minds [*Einfluß auf die Gemüter*]" (CF, 7:36). Kant notes that "the Scriptures contain more than what is in itself required for eternal life; part of their content is a matter of historical belief, and while this can indeed be useful to religious faith as its mere sensible vehicle (for certain people and certain eras), it is not an essential part of religious faith" (CF, 7:37). For Spinoza on this issue, see *Theological-Political Treatise*, p.17.

the dominion of the good principle," he sharply differentiates this from mere statutory observation: "but that service in which revealed faith is to come ahead of religion is a *counterfeit service* [*Afterdienst*] through which the moral order is totally reversed, and what is mere means is unconditionally commanded (as an end)" (R, 6:165). These analyses invoke radical evil, in which the order of maxims is *inverted*; for example, self-love takes precedence over a concern for others. Counterfeit service is described as "*slavish service.*" Heralding his inquiry into priestcraft, Kant discusses those who "wish to be regarded as the exclusive chosen interpreters of a holy Scripture," noting that "they transform service of the church (*ministerium*) into a *domination* [*eine Beherrschung*] of its members (*imperium*)" (R, 6:165). Heteronomy appears not only in authoritarian structures and in the self-glorification of high officials, but also in the monopolization of interpretive authority. The related problem of religious delusion illustrates the interconnections between *psychological* and *institutional* forms of domination. Religious delusion is the elevation of statutory observances to ultimate value without reference to ethical ends (R, 6:168). It is at one and the same time a category error and an ethical failure. Traditional representations can assist ethical practice only insofar as we do not fall into the delusion of mistaking the conditioned sign for the (ethical) thing itself.

Along similar lines, in an earlier writing Kant differentiates between "a *symbolic* anthropomorphism, which in fact concerns only language and not the object itself," and "*dogmatic* anthropomorphism" that oversteps the boundaries of reason (PR, 4:357). We now see that when anthropomorphic representations become dogmatic, i.e., when they are construed as designating supersensible objects, they adversely affect ethical practice. Discussing the idea of a divine will representing the objective order of moral laws, Kant insists that anthropomorphism "is highly dangerous with respect to our practical relation to his will and to our very morality; for, since *we are making a God for ourselves*, we create him in the way we believe that we can most easily win him over to our advantage, and ourselves be dispensed from the arduous and uninterrupted effort of affecting the innermost part of our moral disposition" (R, 6:169). Anthropomorphism is not just the projection of human characteristics upon the divine being. It is a way to familiarize representations of the divine within a manageable form so as to influence and manipulate the law for personal ends. Ironically, in constraining our conceptions of God within familiar representations, we also curtail our own freedom. Such religious practices are directed toward the end of "pleasing God" rendered as a grand potentate; they present human beings "as his obedient, and because obedient, well-pleasing subjects [*Untertanen*, indicating 'vassals']" (R, 6:169). These demonstrations of obedience might involve sacrifices of various kinds, but "festivals too, or even public games, as among the Greeks and Romans, have often had to serve, and still serve, to make the Divinity favorable [*günstig*] to a people, or also to individuals, in keeping with their delusion" (R, 6:169). The concept of favor here bridges the psychological focus on delusion with the ethical and political issue of injustice. Kant reserves his most stringent criticisms for some of the cultic practices appearing in the history of Christianity, writing of how "sacrifices (penances, castigations, pilgrimages, etc.) have always been regarded as more powerful, more likely to work on the favor of heaven [*die Gunst des Himmels*] … The more useless such self-inflicted torments are, the less aimed at the universal moral improvement of the human being, the holier they seem to be" (R, 6:169). This analysis conjoins the pointless expenditure of effort, lack of ethical reflection, and an instrumental approach to winning special favor.[73] The political consequences of these delusory practices are twofold. On the one hand, they sustain an attitude of unquestioning obedience favorable to despotic regimes. They are also well designed to maintain the status quo within a particular social-political configuration. Rote observance does not threaten the corruptions and injustices in a given society, but rather diverts people's focus away from them.

Once one departs from a focus on ethical practice, "there are no bounds left for the counterfeit service of God (superstition)"; that is, virtually any practice can be rationalized or sanctioned. Moreover, with regard to such service "there is no essential difference among the ways of serving him as it were mechanically [*mechanisch*] which would give one way an advantage over another. In worth (or rather worthlessness) *they are all the same*"

---

[73] Kant likewise describes a person who misguidedly believes that "this divine service might win for him the favor of heaven [*die Gunst des Himmels*] prior to any expenditure of his own powers toward a good life-conduct, hence quite gratuitously" (R, 6:172). Hume notes that virtues in the form of "public spirit, filial duty, temperance, or integrity" are not generally granted "religious merit," and that "in all this a superstitious man finds nothing, which he has properly performed for the sake of his deity." In other words, common ethical practice is simply unable to fulfill the needs of those under the spell of superstition. However, "if he fast a day, or give himself a sound whipping; this has a direct reference, in his opinion, to the service of God. No other motive could engage him to such austerities. By these distinguished marks of devotion, he has now acquired the divine favour; and may expect, in recompense, protection and safety in this world, and eternal happiness in the next" (*Natural History of Religion*, p.181).

(R, 6:172).[74] This reference to mechanical practice echoes critiques of the rote use of reason and accompanying debasement of human autonomy. Kant evenly applies an overarching critical principle: all rote or mechanical practices are seen as basically worthless, insofar as they fail to cultivate increased ethical awareness, and as *ruinous*, insofar as they work against ethical amelioration. Both enthusiasm and superstition are addressed here. For example, believing that "we can distinguish the effects of grace [*Wirkungen der Gnade*] from those of nature (virtue), or even to produce these effects in us, is *enthusiasm*" (R, 6:174). In this context, *nature* concerns our own moral efforts to cultivate virtue under phenomenal conditions. Similarly, "the delusion [*Wahn*] that through acts of religious cult we can achieve anything in the way of justification before God is religious *superstition*, just as the delusion of wanting to bring this about by striving for a supposed contact with God is religious *enthusiasm*" (R, 6:174). This follows Hume's explication of reliance on supernatural assistance as superstition, with a correlated discussion of enthusiasm as an upsurge of emotion misconceived as contact with a divine source. Enthusiastic claims to favored knowledge of the divine are specious because "this feeling of the immediate presence of the highest being, and the distinguishing it from any other, even from the moral feeling, would constitute the receptivity of an intuition for which there is no sense in human nature" (R, 6:175). While these arguments are deflationary, they also awaken us to the possibility of a genuine religious orientation informed by the moral law. Kant therefore concludes this section by reiterating that the only antidote to religious delusion is a focus on "bringing about the religion of good life-conduct as its true goal" (R, 6:175).

PRIESTCRAFT AND COUNTERFEIT SERVICE

The later sections of the text augment Kant's concerns with institutional barriers to cultivating an ethical orientation. Here the problem of *priestcraft* (*Pfaffentum*) indicates authoritarian patterns of belief and the institutional control thereof. Kant points out that priestcraft "takes on the sense

---

[74] Following this comment Kant gives a few examples: "pilgrimage to the sanctuaries in Loretto or Palestine," and "by means of a *prayer-wheel*, like the Tibetan," indicating the multi-religious nature of his references to statutory forms of service (R, 6:173). Kant does not privilege one historical practice over others; nor does he spare any of them from censure: "They all deserve equal respect, so far as their forms are attempts by poor mortals to give sensible representation to the Kingdom of God on earth, but equal blame as well, when (in a visible church) they mistake the form of representation [*die Form der Darstellung*] of this idea for the thing itself" (R, 6:176n.).

of reproach only through the related concept of the spiritual despotism [*geistlichen Despotismus*] found in all ecclesiastical forms, however unpretentious and popular they declare themselves" (R, 6:176n.). The interrelated themes of servility and despotism are central, and they are attacked from a variety of angles.[75] In this context, Kant notes the moral element that might be associated with an anthropomorphic higher power: "if they think of him as a moral being, then their own reason will easily persuade them that the condition of earning his pleasure [*sein Wohlgefallen zu erwerben*] must be their morally good life-conduct" (R, 6:176; translation modified). However, many religions go beyond mere moral service. They instill belief that God wishes to be served "in a manner which we cannot recognize through mere reason, namely through actions in which, on their own, we cannot indeed detect anything moral but which we arbitrarily take upon ourselves nonetheless, either because commanded by him, or else in order to attest our submissiveness [*Unterwürfigkeit*] to him" (R, 6:177). In this way, submissiveness becomes instituted as a virtue apart from any ethical elements. This submissiveness is the direct correlate of a personified divine power imagined as prone to willfulness and arbitrary decisions favoring some over others.

Non-moral expressions of submission are merely tools for "the fulfillment of [the religious person's] wishes [*seiner Wünsche*]" (R, 6:177). The link between seeking to please a humanly construed authority and satisfying our wishes is most significant: both demeanors point to a lack of maturity and moral autonomy. Kant proposes that anyone who acts in this way is "under the delusion [*in dem Wahn*] of possessing an art of achieving supernatural effect through entirely natural means." These endeavors to manipulate higher powers are associated with "*sorcery* [*Zaubern*]," although Kant explains that he prefers "to substitute the otherwise familiar word *fetishism* [*Fetischmachens*]" (R, 6:177). Both "sorcery" and "fetishism" are used contemptuously by adherents of so-called higher religions as a way to disparage practitioners of animistic or polytheistic religions. However, for Kant any attempt to invoke the favor of a higher power is a form of fetishism; it matters little what the power is called or what rote activities are utilized. "Whoever gives precedence to observance of statutory laws, requiring a revelation as necessary to religion … transforms the

---

[75] In *Conflict of the Faculties* Kant links priestcraft with political domination, expressing concern about how, without the "judgment of the relevant faculties [of a public university] with regard to orthodoxy" there is a danger that "priestcraft [*ein Pfaffentum*] would spring up – that is, the working men of ecclesiastical faith would assume control [*eine Herrschaft*] and rule the people according to their own purposes" (CF, 7:60).

service of God into mere fetishism [*bloßes Fetischmachen*]; he engages in a counterfeit service [*einen Afterdienst*], which sets back all the work leading to true religion" (R, 6:179). Once again, Kant challenges the stereotype of a stark contrast between enlightenment and religious belief by emphasizing an enlightened religiosity commensurate with the moral law. In this vein, he observes that "it is in this distinction [between an ethical disposition and fetishism] that true *enlightenment* consists; through it does the service of God for the first time become a free and hence moral service" [*Dienst*] (R, 6:179; translation modified). Here he also invokes the crucial distinction between heteronomy and freedom under universal laws to convey the quality of genuine moral service. "If, however, the human being departs from it [moral service], the yoke of a (statutory) law will be imposed on him instead of the freedom of the children of God" (R, 6:179). This point duplicates the observation in "What Is Enlightenment?" where Kant cautions those who do not pursue enlightenment that "it becomes so easy for others to set themselves up as their guardians" (E, 8:35; cf. OT, 8:145).

The crucial distinction between autonomous laws and authoritarianism prepares the ground for a critique of priestcraft as an amalgamation of fetish-service and despotism. "Priestcraft is therefore the constitution of a church to the extent that a *fetish-service* is the rule; and this always obtains wherever statutory commands, rules of faith and observances, rather than principles of morality, make up the groundwork and the essence of the church" (R, 6:179). This emphasizes the underlying principle of an ecclesiastical tradition, a procedure that parallels the explication of the underlying maxim governing our ethical or non-ethical choices. The key criterion is that

> if that principle imposes humble submission [*die gehorsame Unterwerfung*] to a constitution as compulsory service and not the free homage due to the moral law *as supreme* [*zu oberste*], then, however few the imposed observances … it is enough for a fetish-faith through which the masses are ruled and *robbed of their moral freedom* through obedience to a church (not to religion). (R, 6:180; translation modified)

Mechanical practices based on heteronomy rob a populace of moral freedom, and hence of *true religion*. Moreover, whenever an authoritarian constitution governs a community, the specific organization matters little. It "can be monarchical or aristocratic or democratic: this is merely a matter of organization; its constitution still is and remains under any of these forms despotic [*despotisch*]" (R, 6:180). Also crucial is whether an elite clergy (*ein Klerus*), "believes that it can actually dispense with reason, and ultimately with scriptural scholarship itself." Rejecting reason is tantamount to dispensing with open, public discussion, and hence with freedom, equality, and truth. The elite become "the single authoritative guardian and interpreter [*Bewahrer und Ausleger*] of the will of the invisible lawgiver." This language again combines political analysis with issues of interpretive tyranny. The guardians "need not convince but *only give orders*," thereby abrogating human autonomy as well as the principle of publicity. Their strategy is to exert "influence over minds [*Einfluß auf die Gemüter*], and also, in addition, through pretense of the benefit which the state could allegedly derive from the unconditional obedience to which a spiritual discipline has habituated the very *thinking* of the people [*eine geistige Disziplin selbst das Denken des Volkes*]" (R, 6:180). With these remarks, the interdependency of spiritual and political despotism becomes exceptionally transparent. The image of the evil principle as *prince of this world* seeking power over minds is echoed in the practices of despotism in ecclesiastical traditions working to deform our ethical freedom from within (compare R, 6:79 and 187). Through spiritual disciplining, a populace is conditioned to be more amenable to political manipulation. Kant draws out the dire implications of this despotic ecclesiastical practice: "Thus the habit of hypocrisy undermines, unnoticed, the integrity and loyalty of subjects; sharpens them in the simulation of service [*Scheindienst*] also in civil duties, and, like all wrongly accepted principles, brings about exactly the opposite of what was intended" (R, 6:180). The simulation of religious service, or illusory service, obscures our grasp of genuine moral principles; this makes us ethically muddled and subject to corrupting ideological manipulation.

There are two antithetical religious representations of human beings: either as capable, with guidance, of progressing toward a realm of ends, or as vassals and minors requiring external control. I noted previously that Kant integrates the Stoic notion of ethical courage into his interpretation of authentic religious morality. He draws from religious discourse to explicate ethical courage sustaining us in the face of inevitable obstacles and setbacks. By contrast, heteronomous representations have the effect of "transforming godliness [*Gottseligkeit*] into a fawning slavish subjection to the commands of despotic might" (R, 6:183; translation modified). This type of pious individuals "never place any reliance in themselves but constantly look about them in constant anxiety for a supernatural assistance, and even think that in this self-contempt (which is not humility) they possess a means of obtaining favor [*ein Gunst*]. The outward expression of this (in pietism or false piety) is indeed a sign of a slavish cast of mind [*ein knechtische Gemütsart*]" (R, 6:184n.). Hence a slavish mindset is not only ethically passive, but cunningly manipulates heteronomously construed powers to obtain special favor. The combination of overt self-abasement with sly self-promotion is markedly differentiated from the *humility* of genuinely engaging our intellectual and ethical limitations. Kant returns to the theme of how a "groveling courting of favor [*kriechende Gunstbewerbung*]" characterizes a "false devotion" which is also a "compulsory service" combining "superstition" with "the enthusiastic delusion [*den schwärmerischen Wahn*] of allegedly supersensible (heavenly) feelings" (R, 6:185n.; translation modified). These arguments assail religious practices in which subservience becomes merely a way to gain special advantages.

To his previous concerns with self-deception and peace of conscience, Kant now adds "casuistry, as a kind of dialectic of conscience" (R, 6:186). Since for Kant dialectic signifies the sophistical misuse of argument, this point reinforces the theme that working with the faculty of conscience requires caution and discernment. It is instructive that Kant introduces a negative principle of critical reflection to offset ethical self-deception: "it is a moral principle [*Grundsatz*], requiring no proof, that *we ought to venture nothing where there is danger that we might be wrong*" (R, 6:185). The principle is negative because it does not enjoin a specific maxim or course of action, but provides a means of reflecting on moral error, whereby injury to others might occur. In this way the danger of harming others parallels the strategic function of radical evil in ethical reflection; it works against ethical complacency and dogmatism. To illustrate this point, Kant turns to a suggestive example from the history of Christianity that is at once theological and political (and here he also returns to the themes of false universals and hegemony discussed at R, 6:108–09). "Take, for instance, an inquisitor [*einen Ketzerrichter*] who clings fast to the exclusiveness [*der Alleinigkeit*] of his statutory faith even to the point, if need be, of martyrdom, and who has to pass judgment upon a so-called heretic [*sogenannten Ketzer*] (otherwise a good citizen) charged with unbelief" (R, 6:186). Kant's depiction of the positions of victimizer and victim is significant: the inquisitor's faith is an *exclusive* one, precisely the antithesis of the inclusive universality of the moral law. The so-called heretic is portrayed as a good citizen, whose only crime is non-conformity to an intolerant ideological system. In response to this scenario, Kant applies the negative principle of conscience to illustrate that the wrong inherent in taking another's life is far more certain than putative theological truths.

He was indeed presumably firm in the belief that a supernaturally revealed divine will ... permitted him, if not even made a duty for him, to extirpate supposed unbelief [*Unglauben*] together with the unbelievers [*den Ungläubigen*]. But was he really as strongly convinced of such a revealed doctrine, and also of its meaning, as is required for daring to destroy a human being on its basis? *That to take a human being's life because of his religious faith is wrong is certain*, unless (to allow the most extreme possibility) a divine will, made known to the inquisitor in some extraordinary way, has decreed otherwise. But that God has ever manifested this *awful will* is a matter of historical documentation and never apodictically certain. (R, 6:186–87; italics added)

As with many key passages in the text, this one contains numerous insights. First, the argument conjoins the negative principle of fallibility with the uncertain nature of historically transmitted doctrines and their possible interpretations. It contrasts an exclusive form of religious demeanor with self-reflection in accordance with universalizable principles. Additionally, the argument validates a plurality of religious traditions and orientations. While Kant readily engages in critical analyses of all traditions in an endeavor to discern non-parochial ethical principles within them, he also upholds the freedom of religious belief and practice in its multifarious forms (so long as these do not violate moral laws).

The example of the Inquisition establishes rules for assessing all forms of domination and oppression, both physical and psychological. Statutory teachings ascribed to revelation (merely a matter of "historical documentation") should be rejected unequivocally if they oppose human rights. Since all historical faith is subject to error, "consequently, it is unconscientious to act upon it, granted the possibility that what it requires or permits is perhaps wrong, i.e., at the risk of violating a human duty in itself certain" (R, 6:187). Culturally conditioned traditions expressed in context-dependent symbolic media cannot be granted unquestioned authority. The critical role of conscience is therefore intertwined with an ethical hermeneutics of religion. The inviolability of others, as ends in themselves rather than means to an end (e.g., sustaining the hegemony of a particular belief system), remains the ultimate guideline and criterion. To the question concerning whether it can be legitimate to impose an article of faith, Kant responds unequivocally: this "would be compelling the people to profess as true, at least inwardly ... something which they do not know with certainty to be such." Freedom of thought and belief, including the right to publicly question dominant belief systems, would be abrogated by any imposition of heteronomous faith. Therefore, religious authorities who impose their beliefs on others "must answer for all the abuse arising from such servile faith" (R, 6:187). This analysis turns the tables on those who attempt to justify authoritarianism; they have given themselves over to radical evil in suppressing the rights and freedoms of others.

The interconnections among religious, political, and mental subjugation appear plainly in a note appended to these passages. Echoing his principled support for the French Revolution, Kant maintains that he is "not comfortable" with rationalizations concerning how "a certain people (intent on establishing civil freedom) is not ripe for freedom," or how "the bondmen of a landed proprietor are not yet ripe for freedom." He correlates these paternalistic views with the religious principle that "people are in general not yet ripe for freedom of belief" (R, 6:188n.). Kant argues sharply against these specious justifications of inequality and oppression, which he describes as "three bonds" on the levels of "state, household, and church." In response to these forms of imposed bondage, he proposes that "we do not ripen to freedom otherwise than through our *own* attempts (and we must be free to be allowed to make them)." This ethical and political model is predicated on principles we can grasp freely and apply through autonomous judgment. There is no warrant for authoritarian systems imposing servitude. Any attempt to keep people away from civil and religious freedom "is an intrusion into the prerogatives of the Divinity itself, which created human beings for freedom" (R, 6:188n.). This is clearly not an isolated remark; it draws from a consistent vision running through Kant's critical writings. The critique of heteronomy in religion and politics is sustained by a *religious vision of autonomy.*

This vision generates a ringing denunciation of all efforts to diminish the scope and significance of religion to passive reliance on heteronomous powers. An antithesis is framed in terms of the priority of either *virtue* (indicating our autonomous cultivation of moral dispositions) or *grace* (indicating reliance on alleged supernatural forces). Not only is grace outside the scope of possible knowledge, but the practical value of this religious idea is equally questionable: "even to accept it as an idea for a purely practical intent is very risky and hard to reconcile with reason; for what is to be accredited to us as morally good conduct must take place not through foreign influences but only through the use of our own powers" (R, 6:191). Kant does not refute claims that supernatural assistance might occur; it is no more possible to disprove than to prove such claims. His main concern is that our ethical focus not be misdirected by literally construed ideas of divine assistance. The issue of passivity versus activity in ethical and religious endeavor is associated with questions of which *means* we utilize in cultivating moral improvement, how we understand their function, and therefore what our supreme maxims will be. Kant specifies that "the concept of a so-called *means of grace* [*eines so-genannten Gnadenmittels*] [which], though self-contradictory ... serves here as a means of self-deception [*zum Mittel einer Selbsttäuschung*], which is as common as it is detrimental to true religion" (R, 6:192). Adding a touch of irony to his exposition, Kant observes that what was intended as a means of attaining favor instead becomes a means of self-deception. Nevertheless, our focus on inner ethical dispositions, which are invisible, can be *abetted* by representational forms giving visible intuitive shape to ethical ideas and practices. "Yet, for the human being the invisible needs to be represented [*repräsentiert*] through something visible (sensible), indeed what is more, it must be accompanied by the visible for the sake of practice [*des Praktischen*] and, though intellectual, made as it were an object of intuition (according to a certain analogy)" (R, 6:192). The entire hermeneutical strategy of working with the existing cultural resources of religion to further autonomous ethical practice is contained in this passage.

In this same vein, Kant discusses how various formal religious practices can become attached to genuine ethical duties. As with historical traditions generally, the value of these formalities is in making principles more readily applicable: "these formalities have from antiquity been found to be good sensible intermediaries that serve as schemata for duties, thus awakening and sustaining our attention to the true service of God" (R, 6:193). By expressing universalizable ethical principles for members of a community, these practices help bring them into realization in the public sphere. Four of these "observances of duty," with attached formalities serving a schematic function, are: (1) "establishing *this good firmly within us*, and repeatedly to awaken in our heart the disposition for it," which is linked with the formal practice of "private prayer"; (2) "*propagating it externally* through public assembly," linked with the practice of attending services or "church-going"; (3) "*transmitting* it to posterity through the reception of new members," which in Christianity relates to the practice of "baptism"; (4) "*maintaining this fellowship* through repeated public formalities which stabilize the union of its members into an ethical body," linked with the practice of "communion" (R, 6:193). In this way, the hermeneutical procedures applied to religious ideas and scriptural narratives are also directed to formal practices and institutions. The relationship of principles to collective formalities parallels that of principles and imagination. As noted in chapter 3, the imagination is subject to enthusiasm (*Schwärmerei*) without guidance by regulative principles of the understanding (PR, 4:317). In the same way, the hermeneutics of religious representations involves the risk of the cultural media overwhelming the ethical core. Kant describes "an indispensable means [*unterworfenes Mittel*] yet at the same time one subject to the danger of misconstruction [*die Gefahr der Mißdeutung*]." Such misinterpretation takes the symbolic media, valuable only for "representing [*vorstellig*] to ourselves our duty in the service of God," and makes this a focal point obscuring ethical ends. When this occurs, then "through a delusion [*Wahn*] which creeps upon us, it is easily taken for the service of God itself and is also commonly given this name" (R, 6:192; translation modified). The mere means becomes an end in itself, and the preoccupation with means of grace is an instance of this religious delusion. Any focus on "God's superabundant grace [*überschwengliche Gnade*]" is "a grace dreamed up in slothful trust, or itself perhaps an instance of hypocritical trust" (R, 6:193).

Kant specifies "three kinds of delusory faith in overstepping the boundaries of our reason with respect to the supernatural (which according to the laws of reason is neither an object of theoretical or practical use)" (R, 6:194). The first, "faith in *miracles*," contravenes the laws of possible experience. This focus on miracles also indicates "moral unbelief" (R, 6:63 and 6:84), so this type of religious preoccupation is antithetical to both theoretical and practical reason. The second, "faith in *mysteries*," requires that we accept "as necessary to what is morally best for us, that of which we ourselves can form no concept through reason." In this way, rather than sharpening our application of practical reason, religious mysteries undermine our capacity for ethical judgment. Finally, the third is "faith in *means of grace* [*Gnadenmittel*]." This last is described as "the delusion that through the use of purely natural means [e.g., ceremonial practices, fasting, invocations] we can bring about an effect which is a mystery to us, namely the influence of God upon our morality" (R, 6:194).

Having assessed miracles and mysteries in previous sections, Kant now explicates means of grace in relation to the themes of praying, churchgoing, initiation, and propagation of a church-community. While each of these might further moral cultivation, they can also become substitute practices. "*Praying*, conceived as an *inner ritual* service of God and hence as a means of grace, is a superstitious delusion (a fetish-making)" (R, 6:194). The inner nature of prayer does not prevent it from lapsing into a means of grace serving heteronomous purposes. In a note, Kant also focuses on the interrelated themes of prayer as an effort to gain favor (*Gunst*), and as literally construed (*buchstäblichen*; this latter point is repeated three times, though this is obscured in the Cambridge Edition by being translated twice as "verbal") (R, 6:195–96n.). By contrast with these preoccupations with the letter of doctrine (literalism), the "spirit of prayer [*der Geist des Gebets*]" manifests as "a sincere wish to please God in all our doings and nondoings, i.e., the disposition, accompanying all our actions, to pursue these as though they occurred in the service of God" (R, 6:195). Hence an ethical disposition, manifested in relations with others, constitutes the true end toward which prayer should be directed. This wish to please God ethically may be clothed in words and formulas ("*in Worte und Formeln einzukleiden*"), even inwardly, but this sheathing "can, at best, only carry with it the value of a means for the continual stimulation of that disposition in us" (R, 6:195–96). Preoccupations with literal meaning and externally directed performances can lead to "a courtly service [*Hofdienst*] in which the expressions of humiliation and glorification are, as a rule, all the less morally felt the more verbose they are" (R, 6:198). There is a direct political import of this critique beyond the *ancien régime* language Kant employs: spiritual heteronomy cultivates an attitude of slavishness and hypocrisy that influences all our relations.

The same interpretive procedure, contrasting rote, literal practice with ethical spirit, is followed with regard to the three other types of formality. Church-going is described as "a sensuous display [*sinnliche Darstellung*] to the community of believers ... obligating them *collectively*, as citizens of a divine state which is to be represented [*vorgestellt*] here on earth" (R, 6:198–99). The communal activity of church-going invokes the realm of ends. However, this constructive function occurs only if "this church does not contain formalities that might lead to idolatry." The concern here, stated in a slightly different form, is similar to Kant's criticisms of prioritizing mere symbolic means before ethical ends, as in counterfeit faith. He insists that "such sensuous portrayal [*sinnliche Darstellung*] of God is contrary to the command of reason: 'Thou shalt not make unto thee any graven image, etc.'" (R, 6:199; the same biblical passage is cited at greater length in CJ, 5:274). Clearly, the problem cannot be the mere employment of representational devices; Kant has stressed how these can be pedagogically useful if not strictly necessary for cultivating ethical dispositions. Rather, it is the usurpation of moral principles by statutory practices that is at issue. Earlier, Kant had explained that idolatry is the result of accepting "revelation alone," without recourse to moral concepts (R, 6:169n.), and described prioritizing an objectified God *before* virtue as idolatry (R, 6:185). This understanding of idolatry is consistent with accepting representations as important to the cultivation of ethical religion, so long as the latter remains prioritized. Initiation into a church-community "is a solemnity rich in meaning which imposes grave obligations." However, if a ceremony such as baptism is understood as exercising supernatural transformation without encouraging ethical practice, it becomes a delusory mechanical practice; therefore, this initiatory practice is "not a *means of grace*" (R, 6:199). Finally, Kant addresses "the oft-repeated solemn ritual of *renewal, continuation*, and *propagation of this church-community* under the laws of *equality (communion)*" (R, 6:199). Communion can refocus one on universal principles of justice; this type of ritual "has in it something great which expands people's narrow, selfish and intolerant cast of mind [*Denkungsart*], especially in religious matters, to the idea of a cosmopolitan *moral community*" (R, 6:199–200). In other words, religious rituals of community should help us transcend the parameters of self-love and parochial identifications and ideologies. We should be opened to the wider vistas of the community of humanity as such, under moral laws.

While it would be pleasant to conclude on this inspiring note, Kant does not fail to warn us of the drawbacks attached to this fourth type of religious formality. He describes the view that "special graces [*besondere Gnaden*]" are attached to the ritual of communion as "a delusion of religion which cannot but work counter to religion" (R, 6:200). This delusion is multi-faceted. First, it is both epistemologically dubious and morally harmful. Additionally, infusing ritual activity with the status of a means of grace lends itself to manipulation by authorities seeking to control a populace. Kant offers the following summation: "*Priestcraft* [*Pfaffentum*] would thus be, in general, the dominion which the clergy has usurped over minds [*über die Gemüter*] by pretending to have exclusive possession of the means of grace" (R, 6:200). This point strongly re-emphasizes that priestcraft is not just an error in judgment, as in taking a mere means as an end in itself. It is a form of domination operating internally and externally. If grace is something that can, as it were, be bought and sold, then there will always be those who strive to profit by claims to control the product.

Because genuine morality requires an element of renunciation on both psychological and material levels, the religious practitioner might prefer to take the juvenile position of a supplicant in relation to an objectified higher power who can grant wishes. In this respect, Kant notes that rather than focusing on God's attributes of *holiness*, based on the ideal of the realized moral law, and *justice*, based on laws of equality, one may prefer to single out *mercy* as signaling preferential treatment. "Hence the human being would rather be a favorite [*ein Favorit sein*], for much is then forgiven him" (R, 6:200). What is most crucial is the antithesis between moral religion, requiring self-knowledge guided by universalizable principles, and a religion of currying favor, which caters to baser motivations and self-love.[76] The interrelated themes of mechanical means and seeking undeserved favor combine in an assessment of religious images of special intermediaries who can assist us in obtaining benefits. If we cannot possibly imagine ourselves as favorites because "duty has been too grossly offended against," then it may satisfy us to be informed that "everything is again made good through the intercession of some one else who is favored [*Begünstigen*] in the highest degree" (R, 6:200). In the next paragraph, Kant similarly critiques what he calls "the delusion of this supposed favorite of heaven [*Himmelgünstlings*]." The same line of thinking, focusing on currying favor for personal benefit, has been theologically extended to include hypostasized spiritual beings with favored status, which in Christianity would include dogmatic supernaturalist portrayals of Jesus. These intermediaries extend the anthropomorphic projections characterizing theological voluntarism; they can be called upon to assist us in obtaining undeserved rewards. Along the same lines, Kant assails religious concepts of an elite "who, in their opinion, have been exceptionally favored [*Begünstigten*] (the elect)" (R, 6:201). In each of these ways of favoring some over others, or gaining favor at the expense of others, autonomous egalitarian principles have been subverted. A fixed hierarchical way of thinking, combined with emphasis on the arbitrary willfulness and supernatural interventions of the divine sovereign and his intermediaries, is simply inimical to egalitarian moral laws. Kant's argument strikes deeply at many traditional attitudes and practices: ethical indolence, religious literalism, subjugation to heteronomous forces, and *ancien régime*-style courting of an absolute authority or its intermediaries to gain undeserved privilege or favor. He does not spare Christian theology in this regard. We altogether lose sight of moral principles and responsibilities concerning the wider ends of leading good lives and instituting just societies, whenever we subscribe to heteronomous models of directly or indirectly manipulating higher powers for personal gain.

Heteronomous religion draws from baser elements in human relations and reassigns these to the idea of a cosmic sovereign. Concerning the person who seeks favor through imploring a favored intermediary, Kant

---

[76] *The Metaphysics of Morals* also explores links between favor and unequal treatment. Kant discusses a person with surplus wealth expending some of their resources through "practicing beneficence." He remarks that "having the resources to practice such beneficence as depends on the goods of fortune is, for the most part, a result of certain human beings being favored [*Begünstigung*] through the injustice of the government, which introduces an inequality of wealth that makes others need their beneficence" (MM, 6:454). The link between "being favored" by authorities and injustice is significant, and it highlights the ethical-political problems in religious doctrines that encourage self-serving attitudes of seeking favor rather than applying universalizable laws.

remarks that "he usually transfers his conception of a human being (his faults included) over to the Divinity." Heteronomous models of God prioritize grace or mercy over virtue and justice, emphasizing arbitrariness that can be courted for private benefit. Expanding this line of analysis, Kant observes how one seeking privileged treatment from human rulers will focus on their "benevolent grace" rather than "legislative rigor" or "scrupulous justice." To be sure, Kant does not rule out an element of benevolent judgment or mercy in human lawmakers, where this is appropriate (R, 6:200); his model of ethical-political laws is not rigid but principled. However, in political life the individual motivated by self-interest will "try to get the better of one of these properties, the fallible wisdom of the human will, to bring the other into compliance." The same tactic of separating mercy or grace from justice is used in heteronomous forms of religion. In relating to a deity modeled after a fallible human sovereign, "so too does the human being hope to achieve the same thing with God by appealing exclusively to his *grace*" (R, 6:200). In a final constellation of these pivotal themes, the appeal to grace is explicitly linked with the person who "busies himself with every formality." This busy activity involves taking "solemn rituals" that should serve for "enlivening truly practical dispositions as though they were means of grace" (R, 6:201). This encapsulates the heart of Kant's analyses of religion: a solemn ritual can very well serve to "enliven" our practical dispositions, and in this respect assists ethical cultivation; however, taken as ends in themselves such rituals are simply diversionary. Focusing on means of grace is connected with "ineffective wishes" (*tatlosen Wünsche*, literally "deedless wishes"). Once again, the evocation of immature minority is evident; rather than act, one prefers to imagine that a higher power relieves one of responsibility. Such a person "leaves it all up to the all-gracious Providence to make a better human being of him, while he busies himself with piety (which is a passive respect for the divine law)" (R, 6:201). Religion sustains this condition of ethical and political minority whenever grace and piety are prioritized over freely chosen virtue. This is especially dangerous, not only psychologically but politically, because we become trained to disregard our responsibilities toward social justice.

The key is not simply to dismiss historical religions as retrograde, but rather to interpret them in accordance with progressive moral laws fostering autonomy, equality, and justice. Hence Kant advocates "virtue, combined with piety." Likewise, even notions of grace can serve as practical postulates insofar as they further rather than *undermine* ethical practice. The final passage of the text concludes that "the right way to advance is not from grace to virtue but rather *from virtue to grace*" (R, 6:202; italics added). Here the recurring theme of how our principles are *ordered* forms the summation of Kant's arguments, and again the problem of radical evil resurfaces. Whenever I seek special favor I make self-love my supreme governing maxim at the expense of laws of virtue, and at the expense of others. This is the ultimate criterion for critically engaging all forms of religion. Are they in the service of virtue articulated through the formulae of the categorical imperative, directed toward the betterment of all? Or do they set one person against another by sustaining heteronomous structures of authority that diminish ethical reflection and practice in favor of punishments, rewards, and privileges?

The interplay between religious and political orientations sketched here is one that remains profound and illuminating. It shows how religious worldviews are influenced and shaped by temporal models of political authority, as well as how such religious worldviews can reinforce political heteronomy. Kant stands with those who have worked to break this cycle of domination wherever it exists. He draws from religious discourse a variety of representations of ethical principles that resist being co-opted for self-serving and parochial ends. As concrete universals, they give expression to the moral law, inclusive of all persons.

Bibliography

WORKS BY IMMANUEL KANT

These works are cited within the text by volume number and page following the German Academy edition. The pagination corresponding to these editions is given in the margins of the English translations published by Cambridge University Press. The *Critique of Pure Reason* is cited according to the first edition (A) or second edition (B) pagination.

German references are to:

Kant's gesammelte Schriften, Akademie Textausgabe. Berlin: Walter de Gruyter, 1900–.

Other editions consulted:

Immanuel Kant. *Religion innerhalb der Grenzen der bloßen Vernunft*, ed. Karl Vorländer. Hamburg: Felix Meiner Verlag, 1990.

English translations, unless otherwise noted, are from:

Guyer, Paul, and Allen W. Wood (gen. co-eds.). *The Cambridge Edition of the Works of Immanuel Kant in English Translation*, 16 vols. Cambridge University Press, 1992-.

Individual works listed according to volume of the German Academy edition and original date of publication in square brackets, followed by bibliographical data for the English translation. The abbreviations used are given in bold at the end of the citation.

[Vol. 2, 1763] *The Only Possible Argument in Support of a Demonstration of the Existence of God*, in *Theoretical Philosophy 1755–1770*. **OPA**.

[Vol. 3, 1787 (**B**); vol. 4, 1781 (**A**)] *Critique of Pure Reason*, trans. and ed. Paul Guyer and Allen W. Wood. Cambridge University Press, 1997.

[Vol. 4, 1783] *Prolegomena to Any Future Metaphysics*, trans. Gary Hatfield, in *Theoretical Philosophy after 1781*. **PR**.

[Vol. 4, 1785] *Groundwork of the Metaphysics of Morals*, trans. and ed. Mary J. Gregor, in *Practical Philosophy*. **GR**.

[Vol. 5, 1788] *Critique of Practical Reason*, trans. and ed. Mary J. Gregor, in *Practical Philosophy*. **CPrR**.

[Vol. 5, 1790] *Critique of the Power of Judgment*, ed. Paul Guyer, trans. Paul Guyer and Eric Matthews. Cambridge University Press, 2000. **CJ**.

[Vol. 6, 1793] *Religion within the Boundaries of Mere Reason*, trans. George di Giovanni, in *Religion and Rational Theology*. **R**.
[Vol. 6, 1797] *The Metaphysics of Morals*, trans. and ed. Mary J. Gregor, in *Practical Philosophy*. **MM**.
[Vol. 7, 1798] *The Conflict of the Faculties*, trans. Mary J. Gregor and Robert Anchor, in *Religion and Rational Theology*. **CF**.
[Vol. 7, 1798] *Anthropology from a Pragmatic Point of View*, trans. Robert B. Louden, in *Anthropology, History, and Education*. **A**.
[Vol. 8, 1784] "An Answer to the Question: What Is Enlightenment?," trans. and ed. Mary J. Gregor, in *Practical Philosophy*. **E**.
[Vol. 8, 1784] "Idea for a Universal History with a Cosmopolitan Aim," trans. Allen W. Wood, in *Anthropology, History, and Education*. **IH**.
[Vol. 8, 1786] "What does it mean to orient oneself in thinking?," trans. Allen W. Wood, in *Religion and Rational Theology*. **OT**.
[Vol. 8, 1786] "Conjectural Beginning of Human History," trans. Allen W. Wood, in *Anthropology, History, and Education*. **CB**.
[Vol. 8, 1791] "On the miscarriage of all philosophical trials in theodicy," trans. George di Giovanni, in *Religion and Rational Theology*. **MT**.
[Vol. 8, 1793] "On the common saying: That may be correct in theory, but it is of no use in practice," trans. Mary J. Gregor, in *Practical Philosophy*. **TP**.
[Vol. 8, 1795] "Toward Perpetual Peace," trans. Mary J. Gregor, in *Practical Philosophy*. **PP**.
[Vol. 8, 1796] "On a recently prominent tone of superiority in philosophy," trans. Peter Heath, in *Theoretical Philosophy after 1781*. **RPT**.
[Vol. 9, 1800] *Lectures on Logic*, trans. and ed. J. Michael Young. Cambridge University Press, 1992. **L**.
[Vol. 9, 1803] *Lectures on Pedagogy*, trans. Robert B. Loudon, in *Anthropology, History, and Education*. **LP**.
[Vols. 21–22; c. 1796–1804, first published 1936–38] *Opus Postumum*, ed. Eckart Förster, trans. Eckart Förster and Michael Rosen. Cambridge University Press, 1993. **OP**.
[Vol. 27] *Lectures on Ethics*, ed. Peter Heath and J. B. Schneewind, trans. Peter Heath. Cambridge University Press, 1997. **LE**.
[Vol. 28, 1817] *Lectures on the Philosophical Doctrine of Religion*, trans. Allen W. Wood, in *Religion and Rational Theology*. **LPR**.
[Vols. 28–29] *Lectures on Metaphysics*, trans. and ed. Karl Ameriks and Steve Naragon. Cambridge University Press, 1997. **LM**.

Collections in the Cambridge Edition:

Anthropology, History, and Education, ed. Günter Zöller and Robert B. Louden, trans. Mary J. Gregor, Paul Guyer, Robert. B. Louden, Holly Wilson, Allen W. Wood, Günter Zöller, and Arnulf Zweig. Cambridge University Press, 2007.
Notes and Fragments, ed. Paul Guyer, trans. Curtis Bowman, Paul Guyer, and Frederick Rauscher. Cambridge University Press, 2005.
Practical Philosophy, trans. and ed. Mary J. Gregor. Cambridge University Press, 1996.

Religion and Rational Theology, trans. and ed. Allen Wood and George di Giovanni. Cambridge University Press, 1998.
Theoretical Philosophy 1755–1770, trans. and ed. David Walford and Ralf Meerbote. Cambridge University Press, 1992.
Theoretical Philosophy after 1781, ed. Henry Allison and Peter Heath. Cambridge University Press, 2002.

Other translations of Kant's works consulted:

Immanuel Kant, *Religion within the Limits of Reason Alone*, trans. Theodore M. Greene and Hoyt H. Hudson. New York: Harper & Row, 1960.
   Religion within the Bounds of Bare Reason, trans. Werner S. Pluhar. Indianapolis: Hackett, 2009.

OTHER WORKS CITED

Adorno, Theodor. *Kant's Critique of Pure Reason*, trans. Rodney Livingstone. Stanford University Press, 2001.
Agamben, Giorgio. *State of Exception*, trans. Kevin Attell. University of Chicago Press, 2005.
Allison, Henry E. *Kant's Transcendental Idealism*. New Haven: Yale University Press, 1983.
   Kant's Theory of Freedom. Cambridge University Press, 1990.
   "Reflections on the Banality of (Radical) Evil," in Lara, ed., *Rethinking Evil*.
Ameriks, Karl, ed., *The Cambridge Companion to German Idealism*. Cambridge University Press, 2000.
Andress, David. *The Terror: Civil War in the French Revolution*. London: Little, Brown, 2005.
Arendt, Hannah. *Eichmann in Jerusalem: A Report on the Banality of Evil*. New York: The Viking Press, 1965.
Aristotle. *The Complete Works of Aristotle*, 2 vols., ed. Jonathan Barnes. Princeton University Press, 1984.
Beck, Lewis White. *A Commentary on Kant's Critique of Practical Reason*. University of Chicago Press, 1960.
Beiser, Frederick C. *German Idealism: The Struggle against Subjectivism 1781–1801*. Cambridge, MA: Harvard University Press, 2002.
Bernstein, Richard J. "Radical Evil: Kant at War with Himself," in Lara, ed., *Rethinking Evil*.
Blanning, Tim. *The Pursuit of Glory: Europe 1648–1815*. London: Penguin Books, 2007.
Bronner, Stephen Eric. *Reclaiming the Enlightenment: Toward a Politics of Radical Engagement*. New York: Columbia University Press, 2004.
Byrne, Peter. *Kant on God*. Farnham, UK: Ashgate, 2007.
Cassirer, Ernst. *Kant's Life and Thought* (1918), trans. James Haden. New Haven: Yale University Press, 1981.
   The Philosophy of Symbolic Forms, vol. 1, *Language* (1923), trans. Ralph Manheim. New Haven: Yale University Press, 1955.
Caygill, Howard. *A Kant Dictionary*. Oxford: Blackwell, 1995.

Cheah, Pheng. *Spectral Nationality: Passages of Freedom from Kant to Postcolonial Literatures of Liberation*. New York: Columbia University Press, 2003.
Cohen, Hermann. "Affinities between the Philosophy of Kant and Judaism" (1910), in Eva Jospe, ed. and trans., *Reason and Hope: Selections from the Jewish Writings of Hermann Cohen*. Cincinnati, OH: Hebrew Union College Press, 1993.
Religion of Reason: Out of the Sources of Judaism (1919), trans. Simon Kaplan. Atlanta: Scholars Press, 1995.
Collins, Arthur. *Possible Experience*. Berkeley: University of California Press, 1999.
Copjec, Joan, ed. *Radical Evil*. London: Verso, 1996.
Derrida, Jacques. "On a Newly Arisen Apocalyptic Tone in Philosophy," in Fenves, ed., *Raising the Tone of Philosophy*.
di Giovanni, George. *Freedom and Religion in Kant and His Immediate Successors: The Vocation of Humankind, 1774–1800*. Cambridge University Press, 2005.
Doyle, William. *The Oxford History of the French Revolution*. Oxford University Press, 2002.
Dupré, Louis. *The Enlightenment and the Intellectual Foundations of Modern Culture*. New Haven: Yale University Press, 2004.
Englund, Stephen. *Napoleon: A Political Life*. Cambridge, MA: Harvard University Press, 2004.
Evans, Richard J. *The Coming of the Third Reich*. New York: The Penguin Press, 2004.
The Third Reich in Power: 1933–1939. New York: The Penguin Press, 2005.
The Third Reich at War. New York: The Penguin Press, 2009.
Fenves, Peter. *Late Kant: Towards Another Law of the Earth*. New York: Routledge, 2003.
Fenves, Peter, ed. *Raising the Tone of Philosophy: Late Essays by Immanuel Kant, Transformative Critique by Jacques Derrida*. Baltimore: Johns Hopkins University Press, 1993.
Ferry, Luc. *Political Philosophy 1: Rights – The New Quarrel between the Ancients and the Moderns*, trans. Franklin Philip. University of Chicago Press, 1990.
Firestone, Chris L., and Nathan Jacobs. *In Defense of Kant's Religion*. Bloomington: Indiana University Press, 2008.
Flikschuh, Katrin. *Kant and Modern Political Philosophy*. Cambridge University Press, 2000.
Foucault, Michel. *Discipline and Punish: The Birth of the Prison*, trans. Alan Sheridan. New York: Vintage Books, 1979.
Franco, Paul. *Hegel's Philosophy of Freedom*. New Haven: Yale University Press, 1999.
Freud, Sigmund. "Thoughts for the Times on War and Death" (1915), in James Strachey, ed. and trans., *The Standard Edition of the Complete Psychological Works of Sigmund Freud*, vol. XIV. London: The Hogarth Press, 1957.

Friedman, Michael. "Philosophy of Natural Science," in Guyer, ed., *The Cambridge Companion to Kant and Modern Philosophy*.
Furet, François. *Revolutionary France: 1770–1880*. Oxford: Blackwell, 1988.
Gadamer, Hans-Georg. *Truth and Method*, 2nd rev. edn., trans. Joel Weinsheimer and Donald G. Marshall. New York: Crossroad, 1992.
Garton Ash, Timothy. "Velvet Revolution: The Prospects," *New York Review of Books*, 56, 19, December 3, 2009.
Gaskin, J. C. A. "Hume on Religion," in Norton, ed., *The Cambridge Companion to Hume*.
Glover, Jonathan. *Humanity: A Moral History of the Twentieth Century*. London: Pimlico, 2001.
Goetschel, Willi. *Constituting Critique: Kant's Writing as Political Praxis*. Durham, NC: Duke University Press, 1994.
Green, Garrett. "Modern Culture Comes of Age: Hamann versus Kant on the Root Metaphor of Enlightenment," in Schmidt, ed., *What Is Enlightenment?*
Green, Ronald M. *Religion and Moral Reason: A New Method for Comparative Study*. Oxford University Press, 1988.
Guyer, Paul. *Kant and the Claims of Knowledge*. Cambridge University Press, 1987.
  "Transcendental Deduction of the Categories," in Guyer, ed., *The Cambridge Companion to Kant*.
  Kant on Freedom, Law, and Happiness. Cambridge University Press, 2000.
  Kant. London: Routledge, 2006.
Guyer, Paul, ed. *The Cambridge Companion to Kant*. Cambridge University Press, 1992.
  The Cambridge Companion to Kant and Modern Philosophy. Cambridge University Press, 2006.
Haakonssen, Knud. "The Structure of Hume's Political Theory," in Norton, ed., *The Cambridge Companion to Hume*.
Halbertal, Moshe, and Avishai Margalit. *Idolatry*, trans. Naomi Goldblum. Cambridge, MA: Harvard University Press, 1992.
Hegel, G. W. F. *Philosophy of Right* (1821), trans. T. M. Knox. Oxford University Press, 1952.
Herman, Barbara. *Moral Literacy*. Cambridge, MA: Harvard University Press, 2007.
Hewitt, Andrew. "The Bad Seed: 'Auschwitz' and the Physiology of Evil," in Copjec, ed., *Radical Evil*.
Höffe, Otfried. *Kant's Cosmopolitan Theory of Law and Peace*, trans. Alexandra Newton. Cambridge University Press, 2006.
Hume, David. *A Treatise of Human Nature* (1739–40), ed. L. A. Selby-Bigge. Oxford University Press, 1965.
  "Of Superstition and Enthusiasm" (1741), in *Essays: Moral, Political, and Literary*, ed. Eugene F. Miller. Indianapolis: Liberty Classics, 1987.

The Natural History of Religion (1757), in *Dialogues and Natural History of Religion*.

Dialogues Concerning Natural Religion (1778), in *Dialogues and Natural History of Religion*, ed. J. C. A. Gaskin. Oxford University Press, 1993.

Israel, Jonathan. *Radical Enlightenment: Philosophy and the Making of Modernity, 1650–1750*. Oxford University Press, 2001.

Enlightenment Contested: Philosophy, Modernity, and the Emancipation of Man 1670–1752. Oxford University Press, 2006.

Jackson, Julian. *France: The Dark Years, 1940–1944*. Oxford University Press, 2001.

Korsgaard, Christine M. *Creating the Kingdom of Ends*. Cambridge University Press, 1996.

Kosseleck, Reinhart. *Critique and Crisis: Enlightenment and the Pathogenesis of Modern Society* (1959). Cambridge, MA: MIT Press, 1988.

Kriegel, Blandine. *The State and the Rule of Law*, trans. Marc A. LePain and Jeffrey C. Cohen. Princeton University Press, 1995.

Kuehn, Manfred. *Kant: A Biography*. Cambridge University Press, 2001.

Lara, María Pía, ed. *Rethinking Evil: Contemporary Perspectives*. Berkeley: University of California Press, 2001.

Lefort, Claude. *Democracy and Political Theory*, trans. David Macey. Minneapolis: University of Minnesota Press, 1988.

Lilla, Mark. *The Stillborn God: Religion, Politics and the Modern West*. New York: Knopf, 2007.

Locke, John. *An Essay Concerning Human Understanding* (1690), ed. Peter H. Nidditch. Oxford University Press, 1975.

Longuenesse, Béatrice. *Kant and the Capacity to Judge*, trans. Charles T. Wolfe. Princeton University Press, 1998.

Kant on the Human Standpoint. Cambridge University Press, 2005.

"Kant on *a priori* Concepts," in Guyer, ed., *The Cambridge Companion to Kant and Modern Philosophy*.

Louden, Robert B. *Kant's Impure Ethics: From Rational Beings to Human Beings*. Oxford University Press, 2000.

Mack, Michael. *German Idealism and the Jew*. University of Chicago Press, 2003.

Mansel, Philip. *Paris between Empires: Monarchy and Revolution 1814–1852*. London: Phoenix Press, 2001.

Marx, Karl. "On the Jewish Question," in Robert C. Tucker, ed., *The Marx–Engels Reader*. New York: W. W. Norton, 1972.

Mayer, Arno J. *The Furies: Violence and Terror in the French and Russian Revolutions*. Princeton University Press, 2000.

Michalson, Gordon E., Jr. *Fallen Freedom: Kant on Radical Evil and Moral Regeneration*. Cambridge University Press, 1990.

Kant and the Problem of God. Oxford: Blackwell, 1999.

Muthu, Sankar. *Enlightenment against Empire*. Princeton University Press, 2003.

Nancy, Jean-Luc. *The Ground of the Image*, trans. Jeff Fort. New York: Fordham University Press, 2005.
Neiman, Susan. *Evil in Modern Thought*. Princeton University Press, 2002.
Nelson, Eric. *The Hebrew Republic*. Cambridge, MA: Harvard University Press, 2010.
Norton, David Fate, ed. *The Cambridge Companion to Hume*. Cambridge University Press, 1993.
O'Neill, Onora. *Constructions of Reason: Explorations of Kant's Practical Philosophy*. Cambridge University Press, 1989.
  "Vindicating Reason," in Guyer, ed., *The Cambridge Companion to Kant*.
  Towards Justice and Virtue: A Constructive Account of Practical Reasoning. Cambridge University Press, 1996.
  Bounds of Justice. Cambridge University Press, 2000.
Pinkard, Terry. *German Philosophy 1760–1860: The Legacy of Idealism*. Cambridge University Press, 2002.
Plato. *Complete Works*, ed. John M. Cooper. Indianapolis: Hackett, 1997.
Rawls, John. *Lectures on the History of Moral Philosophy*, ed. Barbara Herman. Cambridge, MA: Harvard University Press, 2000.
Riley, Patrick. *Will and Political Legitimacy: A Critical Exposition of Social Contract Theory in Hobbes, Locke, Rousseau, Kant, and Hegel*. Cambridge, MA: Harvard University Press, 1982.
Ripstein, Arthur. *Force and Freedom: Kant's Legal and Political Philosophy*. Cambridge, MA: Harvard University Press, 2009.
Rosanvallon, Pierre. *Democracy Past and Future*, trans. Samuel Moyn. New York: Columbia University Press, 2006.
Rousseau, Jean-Jacques. *The Social Contract* (1762), in *The Basic Political Writings*, trans. Donald A. Cress. Indianapolis: Hackett, 1987.
Schmidt, James, ed. *What Is Enlightenment? Eighteenth-Century Answers and Twentieth-Century Questions*. Berkeley: University of California Press, 1996.
Schmitt, Carl. *Political Theology* (1922), trans. George Schwab. University of Chicago Press, 1985.
  The Concept of the Political (1932), trans. George Schwab. University of Chicago Press, 1996.
Schneewind, J. B. *The Invention of Autonomy: A History of Modern Moral Philosophy*. Cambridge University Press, 1998.
  "Introduction," in Immanuel Kant, *Lectures on Ethics*, ed. Peter Heath and J. B. Schneewind, trans. Peter Heath. Cambridge University Press, 1997.
Sen, Amartya. *The Idea of Justice*. Cambridge, MA: Harvard University Press, 2009.
Shell, Susan Meld. *The Rights of Reason: A Study of Kant's Philosophy and Politics*. University of Toronto Press, 1980.
  Kant and the Limits of Autonomy. Cambridge, MA: Harvard University Press, 2009.

Silber, John R. "The Ethical Significance of Kant's *Religion*," in Immanuel Kant, *Religion within the Limits of Reason Alone*, trans. Theodore M. Greene and Hoyt H. Hudson. New York: Harper & Row, 1960.

Spinoza, Baruch. *The Ethics* (1677), trans. Samuel Shirley. Indianapolis: Hackett, 1992.

Theological-Political Treatise (1670), trans. Samuel Shirley. Indianapolis: Hackett, 2001.

Strong, Tracy B. "Foreword," in Schmitt, *Political Theology*.

Sullivan, Roger J. *Immanuel Kant's Moral Theory*. Cambridge University Press, 1989.

Taylor, Charles. *Modern Social Imaginaries*. Durham, NC: Duke University Press, 2004.

A Secular Age. Cambridge, MA: Harvard University Press, 2007.

Todorov, Tzvetan. *Imperfect Garden: The Legacy of Humanism*. Princeton University Press, 2002.

van der Linden, Harry. *Kantian Ethics and Socialism*. Indianapolis: Hackett, 1988.

Velkley, Richard L. *Freedom and the End of Reason: On the Moral Foundation of Kant's Critical Philosophy*. University of Chicago Press, 1989.

Wilentz, Sean. *The Rise of American Democracy: Jefferson to Lincoln*. New York: W. W. Norton, 2005.

Wilson, Peter H. *The Thirty Years War: Europe's Tragedy*. Cambridge, MA: Harvard University Press, 2009.

Winkler, Heinrich August. *Germany: The Long Road West*, vol. 1, *1789–1933*, trans. Alexander J. Sager. Oxford University Press, 2006.

Wood, Allen W. *Kant's Moral Religion*. Ithaca, NY: Cornell University Press, 1970.

Kant's Rational Theology. Ithaca, NY: Cornell University Press, 1978.

"General Introduction," in Immanuel Kant, *Religion and Rational Theology*, trans. and ed. Allen Wood and George di Giovanni. Cambridge University Press, 1998.

Kant's Ethical Thought. Cambridge University Press, 1999.

Kant. Oxford: Blackwell, 2005.

Kantian Ethics. Cambridge University Press, 2008.

"Kant's Practical Philosophy," in Ameriks, ed., *The Cambridge Companion to German Idealism*.

"Rational Theology, Moral Faith, and Religion," in Guyer, ed., *The Cambridge Companion to Kant*.

"The Supreme Principle of Morality," in Guyer, ed., *The Cambridge Companion to Kant and Modern Philosophy*.

Yovel, Yirmiahu. *Kant and the Philosophy of History*. Princeton University Press, 1980.

Index

Allison, H., 74, 76, 79, 87, 90, 95, 97, 98, 223
analogies of experience, 97, 98
ancien régime, 13, 26, 27, 30, 169, 278, 280
anthropology, 164, 166, 201, 231
archetype *see* (image, original)
Aristotle, 84, 85, 89, 112, 169, 170, 198
autonomy, 1, 4, 10, 12, 13, 18, 24, 26, 44, 110, 133–40, 142, 161, 162–63, 188, 195, 204–16, 218, 223, 236, 241, 242, 246, 253, 262, 264, 269; and law, 54, 112, 202; and reason, 58, 140, 206, 272; epistemological, 2, 12, 13, 75, 100; ethical, 16–17, 58, 66, 116, 165, 170–72, 184–87, 216, 233, 234, 235, 238, 244, 247, 252, 258, 270; political, 8, 11, 12, 36, 43, 46, 47, 49, 51, 190, 275, 281

Beiser, F., 70, 78, 80, 105
Bible, the, 37, 43, 169, 214, 222, 246, 247, 260, 265; *see also* scripture

Cassirer, E., 92, 204
categorical imperative, 9, 10, 11, 14, 15, 16, 17, 18, 62, 119, 137, 162, 164, 171, 179, 183–200, 201, 203, 205, 220, 230, 231, 240, 282; formula of universality, 184–87; formula of humanity, 188–90, 247, 257; formula of autonomy, 190; formula of the realm of ends 191–92, 247; *see also* realm of ends
categories of the understanding, 72, 74, 77, 79, 83, 89–93, 94, 95, 96, 98, 100–01, 102, 104, 106, 107, 109, 120, 121, 122, 129, 141, 166; transcendental deduction of, 89–92, 105
character, 136–39, 162, 222, 226, 234
Cheah, Pheng, 7, 8, 11, 45, 50
Christianity, 3–11, 18, 19, 57, 64, 118, 211, 212–13, 214, 220, 240, 242, 259, 261–66, 268, 273, 276, 280
churches, 3, 4, 27, 55, 65, 249, 252–53, 259, 265, 267, 271, 278
Cohen, H., 260, 262, 265
conscience, 53, 227–28, 255, 260, 273

courage, 49, 53, 54, 234, 242, 264, 272
Critique of Practical Reason, 14, 130, 131, 139, 165–218, 222, 235
Critique of Pure Reason, 1, 2, 10, 11, 12, 13, 17, 25, 33, 34–39, 52, 54, 69–105, 108–60, 162, 165, 166, 174, 177, 179, 202, 204–06, 213–14, 220, 241
Critique of the Power of Judgment, 1, 13, 22, 60–61, 62, 88, 94, 139, 143, 154, 156, 157–58, 184, 187, 199, 209, 211, 216, 220, 238–39

delusion, 39, 110, 126, 143, 242, 267, 268, 269, 270, 277, 279, 280
democracy, 29–31, 45, 191, 236, 251, 253; *see also* republican political model
Descartes, R. (and Cartesianism), 53–68, 70, 78, 79, 80, 100, 119, 121, 149, 150–51
despotism, 36, 40, 43, 57, 64, 69, 170, 236, 253, 255, 260, 264, 268, 270, 272; *see also* domination; heteronomy
dialectic, 84–85, 103, 108–60, 273
disposition (*Gesinnung*), 66, 138, 139, 177, 179, 183, 193, 199, 205, 207, 218, 222, 224, 234, 235, 238, 242, 244, 246, 251, 278; ethical disposition, 176–77, 194–95, 200, 206, 208, 209, 213, 215, 216, 217, 228, 235, 239, 241, 243, 245, 248, 250, 258, 261, 265, 267, 271, 275, 278, 281
divine right, 27, 41, 168
dogmatism, 13, 36, 37, 43, 69, 124–28, 133, 161, 256, 259, 263, 264, 266, 267
domination, 13, 16, 26, 29, 49, 56, 173, 187, 225, 237, 246, 247, 249–50, 260, 267, 270, 274, 279, 282; *see also* despotism; heteronomy
duty, 176–78, 180, 182, 231, 237, 258, 266, 274

empiricism, 13, 34, 70, 71, 74, 79, 93, 99, 106, 109, 124–28, 134, 159
enlightenment, 19–20, 25, 28, 32, 33, 38, 39, 48–62, 92, 165, 174, 217, 220, 224, 242, 244, 259, 264, 271

291

enthusiasm (*Schwärmerei*), 13, 38, 39–43, 54, 63, 88–89, 92, 101, 111, 125, 143, 144, 206, 236, 253, 263, 269, 273, 276
epistemology, 32, 34, 35, 36, 38, 44, 47, 56, 69, 84, 121, 149, 168, 241, 279
ethics, 6, 9, 11, 58, 69, 106, 111, 116, 121, 132, 135, 137, 139, 162–218, 239, 265; applied ethics, 15, 18, 81, 116, 163–64, 166, 174, 183, 186, 215, 216, 242
ethical-political program, 13, 26, 34, 44, 51, 56, 111, 114, 117, 190, 192, 203, 246; defined, 9–10; ethical-political laws, 119, 167; ethical-political model, 12, 15, 17, 62, 66, 215, 252, 281; ethical-political principles, 31, 246; ethical-political progress, 12, 58, 153, 182; *see also* political, the
evil (radical), 18, 105–06, 139, 158, 176, 179–81, 212, 213, 221–33, 246, 267, 273, 275, 282; diabolical evil, 228–30
experience, 69, 71, 72, 74, 75, 76, 77–78, 80, 81, 82, 83, 85, 86, 88, 91, 93, 99, 102, 105, 106, 108, 109, 111, 114, 121, 122, 123, 124, 126, 132, 134, 140, 147, 150, 151, 162, 176, 201, 206, 215, 217, 221, 277

favor(*Gunst*), favoritism, 8–11, 15, 115, 167, 170, 185, 194, 196, 208, 227, 238, 242, 253, 254, 266, 268, 270, 272, 276, 279, 282; currying favor (*Gunstbewerbung*), 238–40, 273, 277
freedom *see* (autonomy); negative freedom, 172
French Revolution, 13, 42–43, 62–68, 168, 198, 275
Freud, S., 178, 218
Furet, F., 27, 29, 62, 63, 64, 65

Glover, J., 19, 223
God, 2, 13, 14, 16, 18, 27, 100, 102, 118, 144, 168, 172, 174, 237, 240, 243, 246, 260, 261, 274, 277, 281; arguments for, 140, 147–60; idea of, 139, 144, 145, 149, 173, 199, 204–16, 218, 219, 220, 234, 243–62; *see also* ideal, transcendental; realm of God
grace, idea of, 214, 240–42, 258, 275, 279, 281; effects of grace, 241, 269; means of grace, 241, 242, 276, 277–78, 279, 281
Groundwork of the Metaphysics of Morals, 14, 162–218, 222
Guyer, P., 70, 71, 72, 75, 78, 90, 95, 100, 118, 119, 130, 191, 208

happiness, 112, 113, 166–67, 202–03, 207, 211, 212, 237, 256–57, 264, 274, 276
Hegel, G.W.F., 68, 83, 235
hermeneutics, 22, 160, 174, 175, 220, 238, 244, 247, 256
heteronomy, 36, 162, 170, 172, 183, 209, 246; ethical heteronomy, 4, 16–17, 168–70, 184, 186, 201, 215, 217, 218, 237; heteronomous concepts/thought, 2, 12, 14, 15, 37, 60, 91–92, 100, 153, 161, 173, 250, 272, 280; heteronomy and religion, 11, 18, 153, 197, 206, 219, 239, 241, 242, 256, 261, 264, 267, 271, 275; political heteronomy, 26, 35, 51, 57, 58, 112, 135, 173, 190, 255, 275, 282; *see also* despotism; domination; theology
highest good, 202, 203, 204, 205, 207–08, 210, 212, 214, 250
history, Kant's views of, 67, 68, 114, 165, 221
Hobbes, T., 47, 67, 113, 170, 219, 260
Hume, D., 33–34, 36, 40–42, 43, 50–55, 78, 126, 157, 158–59, 160, 177, 227, 254, 268, 269

idealism, 70, 71, 74, 78, 100, 117, 122, 135
ideals, 7–8, 9, 15, 18, 110, 112, 114, 115, 116, 165, 176, 180, 193, 202, 203, 205, 211, 212, 214, 220, 234, 243, 253, 263, 279; defined, 141, 142–43; transcendental ideal, 120, 140–47, 174, 199, 243, 244, 251, 261
ideas, 10, 11, 98, 106, 107, 109, 111, 113, 116–20, 123, 132, 133, 134, 141, 142–43, 149, 159, 162, 197, 202, 210, 243; innate, 74, 171; political significance of, 7, 9, 32, 53, 62, 66, 114, 136, 139, 195; practical ideas, 109, 110, 113, 116–17, 136, 140, 197, 243
ideology, 4, 32, 42, 43, 54, 57, 92, 111, 126, 170, 188, 223, 231, 273
illusion, 70, 71, 74, 84, 85, 92, 98, 106, 108, 109, 114, 115, 119, 122, 125, 140, 143, 150, 151, 161
image (*Bild*), 88, 95–96, 117, 142, 143, 165, 212, 220, 246, 257; anticipatory image (*Vorbild*), 244–45; original image (*Urbild*), 110, 115–16, 117, 141, 142–43, 144, 145, 146, 181, 199, 203, 205, 212, 213–14, 243–45, 253, 258, 263
imagination, 86–89, 95–96, 108, 142, 143–44, 154, 220, 276
imperialism, 50–55, 259
incentives, 148, 172, 173, 179, 205, 229, 256, 258
inclinations, 164, 176, 177, 180, 181, 183, 193, 200, 217, 222, 223, 225, 229, 239
institutions, 4, 8, 16, 17, 18, 19, 30, 33, 45, 49, 51, 59, 64, 71, 114, 115, 167, 172, 175, 182, 190, 192, 198, 200, 231, 239, 246, 247, 249, 251, 253, 256, 266, 267, 276
interest, 201–02, 205, 208–09, 215, 217
intolerance (religious), 27, 255, 256, 273–75, 279
Israel, J., 32–33, 48, 153

Jesus, 243–45, 246–47, 253, 258, 263–66, 280
Judaism, 246, 260, 262, 264
judgment, 45, 60, 82; autonomous judgment, 32, 35, 46, 52, 62, 82, 83, 111, 113, 115, 142, 160, 168, 171, 174, 175, 190, 196, 217, 221, 235, 275; capacity to judge, 86, 87, 93–94, 127, 198,

218, 227; empirical judgment, 83, 90, 96, 98; ethical judgment, 15, 31, 116, 142, 164, 165–68, 175, 189, 192, 200, 221, 277
justice, 3, 8, 11, 16, 27, 46, 58, 62, 117, 175, 192, 196, 203, 225, 232, 251, 255, 257, 279, 281

law, 9, 12, 18, 30, 34, 35, 43, 46, 54, 55, 56, 62, 73, 114, 231, 261; autonomous law, 54, 58, 59, 62, 67, 112, 113, 114, 117, 138, 180, 186, 190, 196, 219, 249, 251, 265, 271; laws of nature, 71, 99, 126, 133, 134, 135, 136, 137, 163, 172, 185, 202; moral law, 98, 115, 119, 121, 131, 139, 149, 163, 165, 167, 171, 173, 174, 176, 180, 181–82, 183, 190, 192, 195, 197, 198, 199, 201, 202, 213, 215, 226, 234, 239, 242, 244, 247, 248, 251, 252, 253, 255, 257, 258, 259, 263, 266, 271, 273, 274, 279, 280, 281, 282; rule of law, 28, 47, 63, 66, 113, 174, 190, 232, 248, 249, 251; unjust laws, 25, 28, 29, 56, 57, 114, 170, 231–32, 246, 280
Lefort, C., 5, 8
Leibniz, G. W., 19, 70, 73, 82, 104–06, 110, 119, 151, 202, 241
Locke, J., 40, 42, 43, 78
Longuenesse, B., 81, 82–83, 90, 94, 97, 98, 145, 147, 183, 185

metaphysics, 33, 36–39, 44, 46, 47, 54, 59, 69, 71, 74, 82, 84, 85, 91, 92, 93, 99, 100, 101, 104–06, 108, 109, 110, 117–24, 131, 145, 172
monarchy, 27, 41, 63, 65, 168, 259, 260
Muthu, S., 25, 31, 48, 50

Nazism, 221, 223, 227–28
noumenal, 74, 102–04, 121, 135–40, 172, 207, 227, 231, 234

O'Neill, O., 34, 36, 37, 38, 45, 52, 82, 175, 185

parochialism (and parochial values), 3–11, 164, 167, 168, 171, 173, 182, 184, 198, 200, 201, 225, 231–32, 255, 259, 263, 266, 274, 279
phenomenal, 101–04, 135–40, 172, 207, 227, 231, 234
Plato (and Platonism), 50, 110–12, 115, 142, 146, 169, 171
political, the, 3–4, 5, 7–8, 9, 19, 36, 45, 49, 52, 53, 66, 114, 248, 249, 255; *see also* ethical-political program
postulates of empirical thinking in general, 97, 98–100, 114, 129, 204
postulates of practical reason, 16, 118, 123, 129, 130–31, 179, 204–16, 218, 240, 244, 281
power of choice (*Willkür*), 134–35, 136, 137, 176, 181, 183, 200, 201, 222, 223, 226, 227, 229, 230, 234, 248; *see also* will

predispositions (*Anlage*), 66, 69, 83, 85, 96, 165; to the good, 224–27, 237, 240, 248, 257–59
priests/priestcraft, 41, 221, 252, 260, 261, 267, 269–72, 279
principles, 7, 31, 37, 71, 136, 241, 261; constitutive principles, 97, 98, 129, 131, 157, 204, 206, 215; dynamical principles, 97, 129, 204; epistemological principles, 10, 69, 82, 93, 98, 108, 109, 115, 257; ethical principles, 6, 7, 8–11, 12, 15, 16, 18, 155, 165, 171, 175, 176, 177, 195, 212, 217, 219, 230, 235, 242, 244, 246, 247, 253, 257, 258, 259, 263, 265, 271, 272, 273, 274, 282; mathematical principles, 97, 129, 204; political principles, 13, 29, 31, 45, 49, 50, 62, 64, 167, 188; regulative principles, 2, 14, 15, 16, 34, 57, 96, 97, 98, 99, 107, 115, 116, 119, 124, 125, 128–33, 137, 139, 142, 143, 146, 148, 152, 157, 160, 181, 183, 184, 185, 189, 203, 204, 206, 210, 215, 216, 235, 249, 253, 255, 259, 261, 265, 276; *see also* publicity
privilege, 26–29, 30, 31, 54, 66, 170, 182, 183, 185, 240, 280, 281, 282; *see also* favor
propensity, 179, 213, 217, 227, 248
prototype *see* (image, original)
publicity (principle of), 2, 6, 13, 18, 26, 36, 44, 46, 52–54, 56, 57, 59, 73, 113, 127, 232, 272

realm of ends, 8, 9, 15, 63, 113, 187, 191–92, 196–97, 198, 199, 200, 202, 203, 205, 210, 211, 215, 249, 257, 272, 278; *see also* categorical imperative
realm of God, 212, 214, 248, 264, 265, 269
reason, 44–45, 54, 62, 96, 108, 116, 148, 257, 264, 270, 272; and communication, 52, 53, 59; judicial model of, 45, 46, 91, 92; mechanical/instrumental use of, 51–52, 58, 94, 156, 174, 175, 178, 189; metaphysical misuse of, 98, 102, 104–06, 118, 119, 123, 126, 148, 149, 151, 155, 156, 162, 237, 241; practical reason, 104, 111, 124, 126, 127, 131, 137, 162, 168, 171, 176, 195, 201, 209, 213, 218, 229, 244, 258, 277
reform, 24, 66, 167, 198, 233
religion, 3–4, 5, 6, 10, 11, 16, 21, 34, 44, 55, 57, 65, 71, 101, 104, 107, 124, 132, 168, 172, 199, 217; authoritarian religion, 51, 53, 239, 241, 255, 256, 259, 269, 274, 275, 278, 281; historical religion, 92, 107, 119, 140, 218, 219, 255, 258, 281; moral religion, 43, 176–77, 205, 206, 238–40, 255, 256, 257–59, 265, 271, 278, 279
Religion within the Boundaries of Mere Reason, 19, 21, 22, 23, 28, 43, 54, 55, 134, 139, 155–56, 160, 179, 206, 210, 214, 218, 219–82
representation (*Vorstellung*), 72, 80, 86, 87, 89, 98, 105, 122, 157, 195, 216, 222, 245, 258,

264–65, 272, 278; representation of the "I", 76–79, 87, 95, 121
representational forms, 10, 11, 14, 16, 18, 57, 73, 88, 89, 115, 124, 133, 145, 165, 173, 199, 200, 203, 211–15, 218; religious representational forms, 220, 233, 237, 241, 242–43, 244, 246, 247, 250, 266, 267, 269, 276
republican political model, 29–30, 42, 65, 191, 251; *see also* democracy
revelation, 40, 43, 160, 255, 256, 257–59, 260, 270, 274, 278
rights, 3, 12, 24, 25, 27, 29, 30, 62, 63, 64, 66, 67, 167, 169, 174, 188, 190, 224, 274
Rousseau, J.-J., 12, 24–26, 32, 33, 41, 51, 62, 64, 169, 224, 225–26, 251

science, 2, 71, 133, 134, 136
schematism, 89, 95, 98, 104, 138, 139, 154, 166, 245–46, 276
Schmitt, C., 5, 197–98, 199
scripture, 3, 18, 43, 233, 237, 241, 252, 257, 264, 266; *see also* Bible
self-deception, 15, 79, 138, 178, 180, 200, 227, 228, 276
self-love, 166–67, 178, 179, 180, 185, 200, 224–26, 239, 249, 266, 279, 280, 282
Sen, Amartya, 20, 192
service, 254, 258, 263, 265, 266, 268, 269, 271, 276, 277, 278; counterfeit service, 267, 268, 271, 272, 278
sin, 233; original sin, 222
skepticism, 34, 36, 37, 38, 46, 74, 126, 127, 133, 153
social contract, 16, 30, 112, 113, 251
soul, the, 77, 79, 102, 118, 120–23, 124, 177, 204–16
sovereignty, 196–200, 211, 261; absolutist model of, 27, 67, 197–98, 280
Spinoza, B., 39–40, 43, 220, 247, 250, 252, 254–55, 257, 260–61, 266

state of nature, 46–47, 52, 66, 67, 113, 190, 226, 249
Stoicism, 142, 145, 207, 212, 213, 242, 243, 272
superstition, 13, 41, 43, 54, 60, 144, 215, 238, 239, 241, 253, 254, 258, 263, 268, 269, 273, 277
symbols, 10, 18, 92, 107, 139, 142, 198, 200, 220, 221, 240, 241, 242, 245, 251, 256, 258, 264–65, 274, 278

Taylor, C., 26, 27, 169
theocracy, 246, 252, 253, 260–61
theology, 1, 2, 3, 7, 11, 12, 13, 18, 33, 38, 39, 44, 99, 103, 104, 106, 107, 108, 117–24, 132, 144; anthropomorphism in, 147, 153, 154, 155–56, 173, 199, 215, 236, 244, 245, 261, 267–69, 270, 280; heteronomous theology, 22, 47, 54, 71, 85, 92, 93, 146–47, 172, 173, 211, 213, 215, 221, 245, 261, 274, 280; theological voluntarism, 134, 153, 173, 174, 197, 199–200, 211, 236, 260, 270, 280
thing in itself, 72, 73, 75, 101, 103, 135
traditions, 3, 8, 10, 12, 16, 19, 47, 56, 111, 171, 200, 218, 220, 237, 239, 256, 259, 262, 263, 274, 276
truth, 1, 8, 11, 16, 26, 35, 46, 51, 52, 55, 56, 58, 62, 70, 73, 80, 81, 83–84, 113, 114, 115, 117, 128, 255, 260, 272, 274

universality, 112, 133, 145, 155, 164, 174, 183, 187, 188, 196, 198, 203, 232, 251, 256, 259, 265, 273, 279

will (*Wille*), 134, 136, 139, 180, 181, 183, 190, 194, 195, 207, 223, 227, 230; *see also* power of choice
Wood, A., 31, 91, 103, 149, 166, 171, 174–75, 184, 185, 186, 188, 191, 208